Fantasy-Production

**SEXUAL ECONOMIES AND OTHER PHILIPPINE
CONSEQUENCES FOR THE NEW WORLD ORDER**

Hong Kong University Press thanks Xu Bing for writing the Press's name in his Square Word Calligraphy for the covers of its books. For further information see p. iv.

Fantasy-Production

SEXUAL ECONOMIES AND OTHER PHILIPPINE
CONSEQUENCES FOR THE NEW WORLD ORDER

Neferti Xina M. Tadiar

香港大學出版社
HONG KONG UNIVERSITY PRESS

Hong Kong University Press
14/F Hing Wai Centre
7 Tin Wan Praya Road
Aberdeen
Hong Kong

www.hkupress.org
(secure on-line ordering)

This edition published by Hong Kong University Press is not available
in: Brunei, Cambodia, India, Indonesia, Laos, Malaysia, Myanmar,
the Philippines, Singapore, Thailand and Vietnam.

British Library Cataloguing-in-Publication Data
A catalogue record for this book is available from the British Library.

Printed and bound by Liang Yu Printing Factory Ltd., Hong Kong, China

Hong Kong University Press is honoured that Xu Bing, whose
art explores the complex themes of language across cultures,
has written the Press's name in his Square Word Calligraphy.
This signals our commitment to cross-cultural thinking and
the distinctive nature of our English-language books published
in China.

"At first glance, Square Word Calligraphy appears to be nothing
more unusual than Chinese characters, but in fact it is a new
way of rendering English words in the format of a square so they
resemble Chinese characters. Chinese viewers expect to be able
to read Square Word Calligraphy but cannot. Western viewers,
however are surprised to find they can read it. Delight erupts
when meaning is unexpectedly revealed."

— Britta Erickson, *The Art of Xu Bing*

Contents

Acknowledgements

It took me a long time and many different life paths to write this book. In that time and on those paths, I have been taught, inspired, encouraged and helped by a great number of people. I would like to acknowledge here those individuals to whom I am especially grateful.

Arif Dirlik jumpstarted my academic publishing career more than ten years ago when he included my first article, 'Sexual Economies in the Asia Pacific Community', in his collection, *What is in a Rim? Critical Perspectives on the Pacific Region Idea* (Westview Press, 1993). I am deeply grateful to Arif for that initial interest and for his continuing faith in my work. To him I owe not only the publication of my first essay but also the publication of this book. It is only fitting that that first published article now forms the basis of this book as well as its first chapter. I am also very grateful to those who provided original occasions for writing earlier versions of the other chapters of this book: Naomi Schor, whose early passing away is deeply regretted, for 'Manila's New Metropolitan Form' (originally published in *differences: a journal of feminist cultural studies* 5, 3 [1993], reprinted in *Discrepant Histories: Translocal Essays on Filipino Cultures*, ed. Vicente L. Rafael [Temple, 1995] and now Chapter 2); Vince Rafael and Itty Abraham, for 'Domestic Bodies of the Philippines' (originally published in *Sojourn: Journal of Southeast Asia* 12, 2 [1997] now Chapter 3); Jojo Abinales, for 'History as Psychology' (originally published in *Pilipinas: Journal of the Philippine Studies Group of the Association for Asian Studies*, no. 32 [1999], now Chapter 4); and Roland Tolentino, for 'The Noranian

Imaginary' (originally published in his *Geopolitics of the Visible: Philippine Film Cultures* [Ateneo University Press, 2000] and substantially reworked and extended as '*Himala* "Miracle": The Heretical Power of Nora Aunor's Star Power,' originally published in *Signs: A Journal of Women and Culture* 27, 3 [2002], and now Chapter 6). I cannot say enough how important the interest expressed in a simple invitation can be to the possibility and shape of the articulation of one's ideas in the world. I want to thank Vince Rafael, in particular, for his enthusiastic interest and unwavering trust in my work even in moments of my own self-doubt and uncertainty. His support of my academic career has been inestimable, and I am very grateful to him for the respect and friendship that he has extended to me over the years.

Carol Hau and Lisa Rofel encouraged and practically lobbied me to put this book out. I am grateful to them for their warm insistence and intellectual faith and friendship. To Edel Garcellano, vigilant critic, loyal friend, and political interlocutor, and to Nick Atienza, inspiring teacher, colleague and dear friend, I am greatly indebted for their humour, biting wit and lucid insight into Philippine culture and politics as well as their own life examples of political commitment and poetic imagination.

A long while ago, in Minneapolis, Rey Chow, John Mowitt, Nancy Armstrong and John Frow encouraged my intellectual eclecticism, and Ricardo Roque, Silvia Lopez, Oscar Pereira, Karen Franz, Ferdinand Limos, Edwin Cubelo, Grace Montepiedra, and Joey (Joy) Pascual allowed me to experience a conviviality of foreigners that became integral to my own intellectual pursuits. In Durham, Jonathan Beller, Cesare Casarino, Eleanor Kaufman, Sara Danius, Stefan Jonsson, Saree Makdisi, Sabine Engel, Arun Agrawal, Dan Pillay, Michael Hardt, Mark Simpson, and Rebecca Karl provided intense philosophical engagement, political camaraderie and gastronomic community. Fredric Jameson, Ken Surin, Toril Moi, Naomi Schor, Arif Dirlik, Ariel Dorfman and V. Y. Mudimbe were inspiring and challenging teachers. My time at Duke with all of them and in the intellectual atmosphere they helped to create had a profound influence on my work, which I am still reckoning with. To all of them, I also owe the book that follows this one.

I thank my colleagues, Donna Haraway, Jim Clifford, Angela Davis, Teresa de Lauretis, Gary Lease and Barbara Epstein, for their admirable support of intellectual idiosyncrasy, political passion and maverick scholarship, and for their enjoyable collegiality. Together with my students, who have challenged me in so many unexpected ways, they have made the Department of History of Consciousness a place of impassioned and creative practice. Chris Connery extended the dynamic milieu of the Center for Cultural Studies beyond the University to include Santa Cruz at large. I thank him for his warm comradeship, which has been an important and sustaining part of this homebase. Sheila Peuse is HistCon's and my guardian angel in the bureaucratic universe. Alice Kelly always helped, not least with cheer. Cheryl Van de Veer provided invaluable assistance in copyediting the manuscript and filling in missing references. Kalon Tariman found the photographs and permissions to publish them. Johanna Isaacson did a fabulous, painstaking job on the index. Three anonymous readers provided very helpful comments and suggestions, which I have tried to heed. Mina Kumar offered much appreciated editorial enthusiasm and speed in the early stages. Phoebe Chan kept things moving along and responded to all my anxious inquiries with equanimity and efficiency.

Research for this book was supported by several faculty research funds granted by the University of California, Santa Cruz. I finally sat down and put this book together while on a research fellowship at the Center for Southeast Asian Studies at Kyoto University. I thank my colleagues at the Center for the much needed time and especially Carol Hau, Jojo Abinales, and Donna Amoroso for the much valued and much enjoyed company. Filipina women and Filipina feminists have shaped my political education in ways that are impossible to do justice to by means of the individual citations in this book. Their movements have become so much a part of my own thought and aspirations. I hope some of that is evident here.

Needless to say, any and all shortcomings of this work are the consequence of my own limits.

Finally, I wish to thank my dear life-source of a family, Fred, Florence, Aisha, Carlo, Thea, Alfredo and Gino Tadiar, from whom I learned what it means to dream and how. My profound love and gratitude goes to Jon and Luna, together with whom I dream and hope every single day.

Introduction:
Dreams

In the face of the apparently insurmountable challenges of social reality, that in a previous stage drove figures like Romaine Rolland and Antonio Gramsci to speak about the skepticism of intelligence, to which they opposed the optimism of willpower, let us also oppose to it the confidence in imagination, that essentially poetic device.
— Roberto Retamar

The project then is to claim for us, the once-colonized, our freedom of imagination.
— Partha Chatterjee

Of what consequence are Philippine dreams? Shortly after the deposing of the Philippine dictator Ferdinand Marcos and his family in 1986, a home videotape of a carousing party held on their yacht made the rounds of the same televisions around the world that had just aired the four-day carnival of their fall. 'We are the World,' sang the Marcoses with the gusto and full rhapsodic feeling worthy of this glorious chart-topping World Aid anthem. That video, along with endlessly replayed footage of and jokes about Imelda Marcos's enormous shoe collection, encapsulated for the international audience the ridiculously pompous yet tawdry dreams of the rulers of this third world nation. In this picture of the Marcoses drunk with power, pursuing their delusions of grandeur, the Philippines appears to be a country dominated by misplaced dreams. It is a place of ironic contrasts and tragic contradictions, where politics is a star-studded spectacle set amid the gritty third world realities of hunger and squalor. A third world place in first world drag.

Of course, the generic image of this place full of ironic juxtapositions is apprehended from a place presumed to be free of such unconscious irony (All the better to appreciate yours, my dear!). To be ironic (a deliberate act) is after all quite different from being in an ironic condition (an unwitting state). The view of the ironies of third world existence comes with a long history of delighting in the contradictions that colonials/traditional peoples represent when they bear the trappings of an alien modernity. In images such as the ubiquitous Masferré photograph of the g-string clad Ifugao man holding a camera, or the generic photojournalist snapshot of a *hijab*-wearing Muslim woman talking on the cellular phone, part of the delight undoubtedly stems from the inner knowledge on the part of the viewer that that alien modernity in the hands of the ever non-modern is really theirs. Or at least it is one they are already fully familiar with.[1]

Contrary to what one might expect, this is not a view held exclusively by past and present colonizers. It is also partially shared by present and wait-listed postcolonials, resident and non-resident, in the new home or the old. They too appreciate the irony of seeing street children in Manila wearing t-shirts with Ivy League university names or first world logos whose references and connotations these urchins cannot possibly understand. They too can appreciate the irony of 'more Filipinos singing perfect renditions of American songs (often from the American past) than there are Americans doing so … [in spite of] the fact that the rest of their lives is not in complete synchrony with the referential world that first gave birth to these songs.'[2] Having read *Time* travel writer Pico Iyer's account of this outlandish Philippine predilection for mimicking American popular music, Arjun Appadurai can thus describe the Philippines in this ironic fashion: as 'a nation of make-believe Americans, who tolerated for so long a leading lady who played the piano while the slums of Manila expanded and decayed'.[3] *Evita* meets *Les Miserables*.

To be sure, Appadurai's point in bringing up the case of Filipinos singing American songs would appear to be completely opposite to that of airing the video of the Marcoses singing 'We are the World'. The running images of the Marcoses' cultural repertoire and collections (besides the shoes, there were the tacky lesser art works by Western 'masters') are meant to hammer in the egregiousness of the Marcoses' fantasy world, the pernicious implications of their derivative desires for and imitative performances of Western glamour and enlightenment.[4] Appadurai's point, in contrast, is to argue that beyond the one-sided story of global 'Americanization', within which Filipino 'mimicry' could only be a sign of domination, there is the much more complex story of global cultural flows and exchanges, within which such imitative renditions can also be seen as a form agency, perhaps even resistance. Both illustrative uses of the Philippines, however, deploy third world dreams for the ironic critique of power. For the mainstream international media, the ironies of ruling third world dreams serve a critique of despotic power (irony reveals deception). For Appadurai, the ironies of subordinate third world dreams serve a critique of the masses' supposed lack of power and, correspondingly, a critique of Western hegemonic power (irony reveals agency). In both cases, however, while showcasing the blurred boundaries between Western and third world dreams, irony as critique creates an interpretative boundary between dreamers and analysts, between those who dream and those who unpack the meanings and consequences of their dreamings. I will say more about the political pitfalls of irony towards the end of this book. Here I have no intention of offering a 'reality' contrary to the above representations. In foregrounding their rather generic form, I merely want to open up another purview, one that recognizes that these representations are forms of dreaming too. More importantly, I want to suggest that this division of effort wedged by irony attests to something other than a reinvention of the division between ideology and critical consciousness. The efforts to represent the ironies of others' dreams attest to the new importance of dreams and imagination in today's world.

Indeed, this is the larger point of Appadurai's Philippine example. As he writes, 'The world we live in today is characterized by a new role for the imagination in social life.'[5] Imagination has become socialized, entered the everyday life of ordinary people. No longer confined either to the sacrosanct realms of art, myth and ritual or to the reactive realm of ideology or to the space of individual desire (the last two for which Appadurai reserves the term *fantasy*), imagination has become a central force in the creation of new social projects. As he writes:

> No longer mere fantasy (opium for the masses whose real work is elsewhere), no longer simple escape (from a world defined principally by more concrete purposes and structures), no longer elite pastime (thus not relevant to the lives of ordinary people), and no longer mere contemplation (irrelevant for new forms of desire and subjectivity), the imagination has become an organized field of social practices, a form of work (in the sense of both labor and culturally organized practice), and a form of negotiation between sites of agency (individuals) and globally defined fields of possibility ... The imagination is now central to all forms of agency, is itself a social fact, and is the key component of the new global order.[6]

While I quite agree with this concept of imagination as a form of work and as a form of negotiation of agency, that is, as *culturally organized social practice*, I am less persuaded by the modernist account of imagination's abrupt historical emergence as a new social force.[7]

My own inclination is to understand the social force of imagination as having a longer history.[8] If imagination has come to the attention of social analysts as a new social fact, it is because it has for a long while now been at work in what would appear to be more material practices of economic production and state power. We have only to look at the history of the capitalization of people's dreams in the cinema (as a precursor of the Internet) to see that social imagination has been part of production for quite some time now.[9] We also need to look no farther than the makings of modern nations to recognize that imagination has also long been part of the organization of communities and their subjection to the powers of the state. My point is that imagination, as culturally organized social practice, is an intrinsic, constitutive part of political economy. Capitalism and state rule, and not only nationalism, are suffused with imagination. Unless we think that political and economic structures are the sole invention of those in power, it makes important sense to see the social force of imagination at work in these 'structural realities' before its expression in recent, more visible 'culturalist' forms such as ethnic nationalism and the active construction of new diasporic identities through electronic media.

I say all this because if imagination has only now entered the everyday social life of people, in particular, of third world peoples, then they — we — have only been collectively dreaming the dreams of others, trapped in their imagination of us and our worlds. Or perhaps we have not been dreaming at all and, instead, have lived in the rote mythographies of our given social identities. It would seem even that our imaginations were confined by the boundaries of our political territory. And now that globalization has arrived, and (some) people have immediate access to other lived imaginaries through new telecommunicational technologies and increased labour migration, we are all of a sudden imagining for ourselves, creatively dreaming beyond our nation-bound imaginations (if not re-inventing them) and exerting that dreaming on the world in ways that we had never done before. I do not doubt that there have been shifts in the organization of the world, and that these shifts are at once expressed and brought about by new forms of social imagination. But to my mind the 'newness' of imagination is to be found in its relative autonomization from other realms of social life rather than its socialization. If anything, social imagination has become increasingly appropriatively privatized, codified as a cultural database, invested in and fought over as patentable because expropriateable property. Whence the 'new' — that is, changed — importance and agency of dreams.[10]

The tawdry dreams of the Marcoses to be equivalent with world power ('We are the World') as well as the dreams of 'ordinary' Filipinos singing American songs, apparently nostalgic for a world they never lost,[11] are deeply implicated in the dreamwork of the capitalist inter-state world-system. Such dreams are symbolic enactments of practices of imagination that effectively operate in and as the political and economic organization of the Philippine nation-state. If we understand imagination as a form of work, we must see that it is work that is incorporated into a system of production of universal value.[12] In this aspect, that is, in its role in a global system of production, the material imagination constituting the Philippine nation can be seen as a form of labour. Inasmuch as the Philippines is, as a supplier of global labour, a constitutive part of the world-system, its material dreams are the consequences of — as well as bear consequences for — that international order of political and economic dreamwork, which I call fantasy-production. 'Fantasy-production' denotes the imaginary of a regime of accumulation and representation of universal value, under the sway of which capitalist nations organize themselves individually and collectively in the 'system' of the Free World. While it would seem paradoxical to use the word 'system' to describe an order of 'freedom', I do so not in order to substitute one totalizing fantasy of selective freedom with another totalizing fantasy of absolute constraint but rather to suggest the level at which the scattered and seemingly arbitrary or anarchic actions of different nation-states achieve some measure of coordination and logical coherence to constitute a working international order (or, a form of governmentality). I use 'system' to highlight the effective horizon or field of possibilities within which the social imaginations of whole nations are generated, nurtured and confined. The dreams of Filipinos, rulers and ruled, cannot be understood apart from the global material imaginary, this dominant field of reality, on which they play out. To cast these dreams as the expressions of autonomous, self-contained Filipino subjects (whether they aspire to or resist world power) is to ignore the global order of dreamwork in which the international media system, the source of many of our interpretative representations of the world, plays a constitutive and paradigmatic role.[13]

When I speak of dreams, I use the term loosely to indicate that our actions are also wishes, the expression of which is constrained by the unconscious or, more accurately, imaginary structures and logics of organization of our material realities. In my usage, fantasies are the hegemonic forms of expression of our desiring-actions. Dreams are the concrete work of imagination while fantasies are the abstract forms into which this work becomes subsumed within the world-system of production. Fantasies are, on this view, alienated means of production, while the desiring-actions in dreams are living labour. As Marx explains the relation, 'the means of production appear *éminemment* as the effective form of *capital* confronting living labour. And they now manifest themselves moreover as the rule of past, dead labour over the living.'[14] Inasmuch as this process of subsumption is never fully successful, that is to say to the extent that our dreams are never fully captured by fantasy-production but are also shaped by other logics whose calling they heed, dreams will always exceed fantasies. However, to the extent that dreams fuel and further the logics of the dominant global order, they perform the work of fantasies.

This book is about the practices of fantasy-production on the part of the Philippine nation and the contributions of this particular postcolonial national formation to global systemic transformations leading to the establishment of the New World Order, the international division of labour and organization of multinational capitalist production that emerges at the end of the Cold War. In this book I propose to view the political and economic strategies of the Philippine nation-state as part of the dream-work of an international order of production founded upon the conjoined, if sometimes contradictory, logics of nationalism and multinational capitalism. Fantasy-production names this international order of desiring-actions on the part of nations, an order in which gender, sexuality and race are constitutive principles of organization as well as practical effects.

Fantasy-production practices create a common imaginary geography and history — that of the Free World — as the ground of their operation. In the multinational era of the New World Order, this common ground is the scene of the International (community) and its privileged acting figure is the territorial nation-state. In the transnational era of globalization, that common ground has become the place of the Global (network) and its privileged acting figure, deterritorialized capital-flows.

Even if the new, deterritorialized global order appears to be a de-subjectivized one (with 'economies' now replacing 'nations'), it nevertheless depends on and mobilizes the subjectifying operations of signification fundamental to the older, territorial world order. As I will show, what are now widely-accepted conditions of a radically transformed global order are reconfigurations of dominant strategies of the nation-state, which is accommodating to changes that it has itself been instrumental in bringing about.[15] This is in itself not new. In the so-called postcolonial world, the nation has long been the agent and product of inter- as well as trans-national affairs (whether conceived as imperialist or not). This book's focus on the Philippines enables us to see what the transformative processes of globalization, such as 'denationalization' and deterritorialization, might look like on the side of the imaginary of a postcolonial nation and what they might entail in terms of the resources of that nation. It also allows us to understand the ways in which the nationally-inflected actions of a 'minor' country such as the Philippines contribute to an order that apparently transcends and takes precedence over it. It allows us to seriously consider the achievement of global capitalism from the perspective of the work of imagination on the side of a third world nation and its seemingly nation-bound people.

When Partha Chatterjee argues that we, the once- (and yet-) colonized, must claim 'our freedom of imagination', he is not arguing only for the present and the future but also and primarily for the past.[16] From the perspective of transnationalism, nations are precisely things of the past. To inquire into the imaginations of postcolonial nations in the moment before the establishment of the New World Order, the moment of inauguration of globalization, is to probe into the immediate and still living pasts of this hegemonic global present in order to find the forgotten creative labour of other dreams. More, it is to free this forgotten creative labour in our own presents so that we may imagine the world differently.

METHODS OF DREAM INTERPRETATION

In order to probe the imaginary dimensions of the political and economic relations and practices of the Philippine nation-state, and in particular the organizing significance of the logics of gender, race and sexuality in these material relations, I have taken critical resource in a number of theoretical discourses. As the above discussion demonstrates, I draw much of my understanding of the 'work' and 'labour' of imagination and dreams from Marxist accounts of the subsumption and alienation of labour under the capitalist mode of production. However, in this endeavour I have also run up against the obstinate refusal of more orthodox Marxisms to factor in the categories of gender, race and sexuality in their conceptualizations of capitalist social relations and, consequently, the limits posed by their political imaginations of social change.[17] It is for this reason that while I rely heavily on the analytical framework of Marxism to make my critique of the capitalist forms structuring Philippine dreams, I have also drawn on other theories, which attend more closely to the imaginary dimensions of social life and political struggle.

I make use, for example, of some conceptual instruments of psychoanalytic theory in order to render the subjective dynamics enacted on the arena of international exchanges. The concept of 'fantasy' that I employ here derives from Slavoj Žižek who merges the two theoretical discourses of Marxism and psychoanalysis to arrive at an understanding of ideology as 'an (unconscious) fantasy structuring our social reality itself'.[18] Fantasy is a field of symbolically structured meaning (the unconscious) that shapes and regulates our desires, our modes of acting 'in reality'. In its historical, concrete expression it is an imaginary framework that subsists within actual material practice. The 'illusion' is thus not on the side of ideas, consciousness and belief, that is, on the side of 'knowing', but rather, as Žižek would say, on the side of 'doing'.[19] This concept of ideological fantasy allows us to view the 'work of imagination' in the seemingly objective practices and structures of political economy that determine as well as comprise much of the social life and modern history of nations. Fantasy is thus not 'thought divorced from projects and actions'.[20] Rather, 'it is belief which is radically exterior, embodied in the practical, effective procedure of people'.[21]

My own reliance on the concept of fantasy and other concepts drawn from psychoanalysis is not, however an application of psychoanalytic theory to the field of international relations. As many scholars have argued, psychoanalysis emerged out of the same historical conditions that gave rise to imperialism. Or put more forcefully, psychoanalysis is as much a product and instrument of this history of imperialism as it is a theory of its subjects. This has not led me to dismiss its analytical power any more than I would dismiss the analytical power of Marxist social theory. Rather, it leads me to recognize the worldly role that such theories (or at least their 'applications') play in the practical shaping of social forms.[22] Or, seen differently, this acknowledgement of psychoanalysis's historicity allows me to understand its objects and logics (i.e., desiring subjects and the dynamics of libidinal forces) not only as resulting from historically contingent and finite social formations. These objects and logics are also to be seen as discursive product-effects of the coding practices of psychoanalysis, which can now be deployed as technologies to shape, even engineer, not only the social formations out of which they emerge but other social formations as well.

Understanding the socio-historical 'origins' of both psychoanalysis and Marxism allows me to view their analytical operations as also historical, social technologies operating in the world. Or, as I put it in Chapter 2, it means viewing metropolitan theoretical regimes as forces of production and instruments of stratification that peripheral social formations such as the Philippines have historically been subjected to. Unlike Žižek then, I do not see the logic of subjectification, which he argues underlies the constitution of particular historical fantasies and identifications, as obtaining transhistorically.[23] Instead, I see that this onto-logic obtains within and is delimited by the historical time of modern imperialism. Now, when this history begins and when it ends is by no means an undisputed matter. My own view is that, in global temporal terms, this history begins in the late nineteenth-century with the decline in power of the previous world empires of Spain and Portugal and the rigidly hierarchical form of territorial colonial rule that they were exemplary realizations of. This beginning is also signaled by the rise of the US empire, which excelled in the new form of colonial rule, characterized by the central role of capital in the social and political organization of its colonial possessions. While a major geopolitical shift occurred after the Second World War and the emergence of the Cold War, the history of modern imperialism can be said to have continued throughout the twentieth century and to only now approach some closure (at least on the geopolitical scale of the international order).[24]

What I call fantasy-production is a mode of production and signification whose history approximates this history of imperialism that I have sketched. Elsewhere, I discuss the beginnings of this 'oedipalization' of nations in the late nineteenth century, by which I mean the process of symbolic constitution of nations as modern subjects with the imperialist rivalry of Western powers.[25] In this dreamwork of imperialism one can see the early makings of the 'sexual economies' of the postcolonial, free world system. I would however argue that the logic of subjectification and order of desiring-actions, which I analyze here, begins to formally 'govern' the organization and practice of individual nation-states with the decolonization of Asia and Africa after the Second World War. Economically, the mode of production and signification of the Free World fantasy appears as the regulatory ideal and strategy of 'development' propagated and pursued by the World Bank and the International Monetary Fund (both institutions established in 1944). Politically, it appears as the structure and ideal of an international juridical order represented and implemented by the United Nations.

Recognizing the historicity of fantasy-production in its worldly compass goes hand in hand with recognizing the same for its constitutive subjective dynamics. Feminist, anti-racist, multiculturalist and postcolonial social theories have been crucial in this regard, all challenging the universal and ontological pretensions of dominant cultures and their role in maintaining oppressive social orders. I rely on much of this work — the work for example of Gayatri Spivak, Maria Mies, Angela Davis, Teresa de Lauretis and Donna Haraway — to critique the cultural logics of subjectivity and social relations that obtain in national and international political and economic structures. These social theories have greatly contributed to our understanding of the dominant workings of gender, race and sexuality in the structuring of social relations, not only on the level of individuals but also on the level of large social collectivities such as nations.

My own interpretation of the role of gender, race and sexuality as organizing principles of political and economic practice within and among nation-states depends on an understanding of capitalist production and state power as, among other things, systems of signification.[26] Gender, race and sexuality are categories for signifying, by way of organizing, social relations of power and production. While they would appear to be only secondary effects of meaning of practical, material relations, in this book, I view the logics of gender, race and sexuality as intrinsic to those practical, material relations. Systems of production entail and act as particular modes of representation and codes of signification, which in turn serve as media of dreams and desires.[27] As Arturo Escobar similarly argues about the system of capitalist production emerging out of Europe, 'the Western economy must be seen as an institution composed of systems of production, power, and signification. The three systems, which coalesced at the end of the eighteenth century, are inextricably linked to the development of capitalism and modernity. They should be seen as cultural forms through which human beings are made into producing subjects. The economy is not only, or even principally, a material entity. It is above all a cultural production, a way of producing human subjects and social orders of a certain kind.'[28] *Fantasy-production* views the forms and dynamics of subjectivity produced and operating through contemporary international politics and economics as emerging precisely out of dominant cultures of imperialism. Besides the 'orientalism in economics' that persists in the world project of 'development', logics of patriarchy, sexism, homophobia and racism deeply inform and are generated by the practices of accumulation and power of postcolonial nation-states acceding to the tacit rules of the world system.[29]

In her discussion of the prevailing dichotomy 'between the "realpolitical" non-West and the "imaginative" West,' Rey Chow argues: 'since the West owns not only the components but also the codes of fantasy, the non-West is deprived not only of the control of industrial and commercial productions, but of imaginary productions as well.'[30] Like Chow, I too foreground the subjective dramas of the 'non-West' — here, the Philippines — in an attempt to 'tip the balance' of this assymetrical relation. I would only want to emphasize that while the West owns the codes of fantasy, the non-West is no less an active and willing participant in the hegemonic modes of imaginary production that are predicated on these codes. In their 'realpolitical' actions, postcolonial nation-states of the non-West demonstrate that they have acquired a certain fluency in these codes of fantasy of the West, making full use of them in the pursuit of their elites' desires but at the expense of the 'freedom of imagination' of the majority of their peoples. My point is not to deny the fact that the non-West has many dreams of its own. It is, rather, to decry the fact that, as Ngugi wa Thiong'o puts it, 'A post-colonial state often crushes those dreams and turns people's lives into nightmares.'[31]

To offer a glimpse of the early work of Philippine fantasy-production, let me turn to the example of Carlos P. Romulo, the most prominent Philippine statesman involved in the world project of the United Nations. Romulo made his first appearance on the world stage as aide-de-camp to US General Douglas MacArthur, in the dramatic fulfillment of MacArthur's 'I shall return' promise to liberate the Philippines from Japanese occupation on the shores of Leyte in 1944. In his first speech to the US Congress in 1944, Romulo, now Resident Commissioner of the Philippines to the United States paid 'tribute to that unknown soldier and those like him who had carried the first principles of Americanism into the Philippines'.[32] Romulo presumed to speak for the entire nation and its dreams when he spoke:

> Mr Speaker, twenty-eight years ago today, upon this floor, America gave its first pledge of freedom to the people of the Philippines.
>
> On that day the Congress of the United States approved the Jones Act, promising independence to the subject Philippines in a covenant that is without parallel in the world's history.
>
> It is not my purpose to review the Filipinos' fight against America during the early days of American occupation, nor stress the fact that it took the United States three and a half years of actual fighting to subdue the Philippines. We were not conquered in the final analysis, by guns, but by the practical demonstration in the Philippines of America's concept of democracy. American teachers brought us new methods of education. Public health, road building, government training — such things were given us. Gradually our feeling toward America changed from resentment and suspicion to confidence and loyalty.
>
> That loyalty was sealed by the passage of the Jones Act ...
>
> The Jones Act was our victory. You let us win it upon this floor. It was a pledge made, and America has kept that pledge ...
>
> We Filipinos, too, kept the pledge. You gave us the Jones Act. We gave you Bataan. For, Bataan and Corregidor were dividends paid back out of our loyalty and our faith in America ...
>
> On that bloodstained Philippine peninsula Americans and Filipinos must meet over a common grave where lie the bodies of their sons ...
>
> We will meet, my fellow Americans, over that common grave. Out of that grave, a dream.
>
> Others have died for that dream of world recognition of the ordinary civilities and the divine rights of man.[33]

Romulo went on to enumerate those who have died for this universal dream expressively fulfilled by the example of American democracy:

Jesus, Abraham Lincoln, the first Filipino President under the US Commonwealth, Manuel Quezon, and 'a boy named José, from Manila, and another boy named Joe, from Missouri' who died for this same dream on the peninsula of Bataan. This speech was one of the first of many that Romulo would give to rally US support for Philippine 'independence' and 'democracy'.

In this speech one can glean many of the characteristic conceits of the dominant fantasy of US-Philippine relations in play by 1944: the mutual covenant consisting of bilateral exchanges of American 'freedom' for Philippine 'territory', the upholding of 'America's concept of democracy' as a universal good, the Philippines' fraternal loyalty to and faith in the US as reciprocity for the 'gift' of independence, and the essential identity of Filipino and American dreams. In Romulo's narrative, moreover, we see the dominant interpretation of the messy and violent history of US-Philippine relations. In this fantasy, the good conquest of the Philippines by American democracy leads to the mutual recognition of and struggle for shared ideals expressed in the two countries uniting forces against the Japanese during the Pacific war. Anti-colonial Filipino struggles culminate in the passage of the Jones Act, the realization of which would coincide with the fulfillment of a historical destiny. Romulo's narrative fantasy is not only a revision of a more troublesome Philippine history of violent colonial oppression and revolutionary Filipino desires in the pacific terms of American understanding ('for only Americans could comprehend the democratic dreams of our Filipino leaders').[34] It is also a willful prophecy, the guiding logic of Romulo's future practical accomplishments and actions in the sphere of world politics. 'Out of that grave, a dream.'

By the end of the Second World War, the Philippines was indeed already materially 'pledged' to the US. Despite the provision for Philippine independence in 1946 outlined in the 1934 Tydings-McDuffie Law, for which anti-imperialist, protectionist and racist forces in the US had lobbied, the Philippines still figured in the US's postwar vision of a new international order. Two concerns were at the forefront of this vision: economic prosperity and political security. In the Philippines, those two concerns were addressed through the passage of several mutual treaties: the Bell Trade Act, the Military Bases Agreement and the Military Assistance Pact. The issues of free trade and security, moreover, were very closely tied. They were the continuing proof of Philippine 'loyalty and faith in America', collateral for the granting of 'freedom'.

The passage of the Bell Trade Act in 1946 guaranteed the continuation of the 'free trade' agreements of the Commonwealth period, which had provided for the unlimited, tariff-free Philippine importation of US manufactured goods and for the limited, exclusive export of Philippine agricultural products (sugar, tobacco, coconut oil, hemp) to the US. The Bell Trade Act legislated the continuation of these asymmetrical exchange relations beyond Philippine independence. Such 'free trade' had already served to enrich and entrench a native ruling class eager to collaborate with the former colonizer as well as US corporations invested in local industries and thus had served to destroy local, subsistence economies in favor of the cash crops of the agricultural export economy.[35] The Bell Trade Act also granted American investors and corporations the same economic privileges and rights as Filipino citizens to own and exploit Philippine natural resources by means of a coerced amendment to the 1935 Philippine constitution, called the Parity Amendment.[36] This amendment as well as the provision tying the Philippine Peso to the US Dollar were 'designed to make American capital feel at home in the Philippines'.[37] Besides these economic dividends, there were also territorial dividends to be paid to America for so-called Philippine independence and the shared dream of democracy. The Military Bases Agreement (1947) and the Military Assistance Pact (1947) provided for, respectively, the establishment of US military bases on Philippine territory for 99 years and US military aid and logistical, technical and intelligence assistance to the Philippine military. Thus were the post-war bilateral 'special relations' between the US and the Philippines established and the 'mutual covenant' realized. These relations became the basis for long-standing fraternal collaborations between Filipino elite rulers and US economic and political forces, collaborations that have robbed and continue to rob Filipinos of true freedom over their historical fate.

Throughout these developments, Romulo played the role of mediator between the Philippines and the US, in all his diplomatic actions helping to realize the common destiny of the two countries that he espoused. Not only was Romulo a signatory of the United Nations

Charter (1945), he also served as President of the General Assembly (1949–50), as Philippine Ambassador to the United States (1952–1962), and as Secretary of Foreign Affairs under arguably the two most egregiously corrupt administrations in the history of the Philippine Republic, that of Elpidio Quirino (1948–1953) and Ferdinand Marcos (1966–1986). In these different capacities, Romulo negotiated agreement after agreement, settlement after settlement between the Philippines and the US, securing the guarantees of mutually-benefiting ties between the two governments: from war reparations to rent for the military bases, from a trade agreement that expanded 'parity rights' to encompass all Philippine industries (The Revised Bell Trade Act, 1954) to a treaty that continues to ensure joint US-Philippine military operations, from chronic US financial loans and aid, which underwrote rampant rent-seeking in the Philippine government, to a regional military security pact (SEATO, 1954), which supported the Cold War aims of the US.[38] By serving as the middleman of these bilateral transactions, Romulo was not only fulfilling the fantasy of US-Philippine relations that he had so affectingly spoke about in his speech to the US congress. In mediating regional and world political-military cooperation (besides being instrumental in the passage of SEATO, Romulo was twice President of the UN Security Council in 1957 and 1980), he was also helping to lay down the geopolitical foundations for the present-day fantasy of the Asia Pacific community (See Chapter 1).

In his Pulitzer Prize-winning autobiographical works, Romulo writes of 'the immortal seed of heroes' that runs through his Filipino veins, 'the mark of [his] manhood, the symbol of [his] dignity as a human being'. He writes of the fraternal bonds between Filipinos and Americans and the deep primordial satisfaction of American sportsmanship and fair play that became a part of his practice of diplomacy. And he writes of his own personal struggle to be treated with respect and dignity as the micro-instance of the struggle of his country to be treated 'as a full-fledged nation' on the world stage. The particular masculinist character that Romulo offers in these narratives as representative of the nation demonstrates precisely the gendered subjective dynamics of international relations that he, in his capacity as Philippine statesman, helped to play out. That is to say, while this masculinist posturing would seem to be merely a matter of individual disposition, it is in fact the subjective effect and regulative ideal of the system of political and economic relations characterizing post-Second World War Philippines. Politically, the Philippines was now a formally independent, sovereign nation, and a founding member of the fraternity of free nations represented by the United Nations. Economically, it was an underdeveloped neo-colony seeking competitive advantages in an inter-capitalist state system dominated by the political-militarist and economic world power, the US. The Philippine nation-state was in other words now a minor player in the Free World, which meant maneuvering within an international field of normative political and economic actions that hold particular dominant gendered assumptions and implications. It is against this field that we must view Romulo's expressed symbolic and subjective ideals of Philippine nationhood.

Put simply, the symbolic and subjective ideals performed by Romulo are instruments for the mobilization of the material institutions — foreign loans, financial and military aid, state power, a supranational juridical order and international trade agreements — that such ideals were important codes for organizing. In this respect, Romulo's nationalism was a mode of imagination that actively maintained and indeed helped to internationalize the codes of fantasy of the Free World. I am not saying that this state nationalism did not pose difficulties and resistances to US interests, for any review of the history of the post-Second World War period will show the uneven, acrimonious and violent processes through which state power was consolidated and bilateral 'agreements' were achieved.[39] However, it is precisely by working with the codes of the Free World ('parity', 'free trade', national and regional 'security', and later, economic 'protection' and 'controls'), that is, by trading in the symbolic and material currency of an emergent international community of exchange, that the Philippine nation-state contributes to the effective hold and crushing effect of such fantasy-scenarios on the rest of the nation's dreams.

To illustrate: the Philippines' formal political status as a free and sovereign nation and economic status as an independent national economy were the bargaining means by which conditions for bolstering competitive local powers and capital were secured. In exchange for 'freely' offering Philippine territory and military forces to the project of the Cold War (for example, heeding Romulo's advice, President Quirino sent 5,000 Philippine troops to contribute to US forces in the Korean war), the Philippine state consistently received not only political and military backing but also large financial remunerations that became the basis of long-standing rent-seeking clientelist relations between the Philippines and the US and between the Philippine state and local elites. In exchange for 'parity' rights and other privileges accorded US businesses, local elites secured their monopolies of agricultural export industries, through which peasant workers came to be increasingly exploited. When unrestricted free trade combined with massive deficit spending brought about a serious foreign exchange crisis, nationalism became once more the means of instituting a system of import and exchange controls (1949–1961). These controls, however, only served to bolster luxury goods manufacturing industries and to increase sites of graft and corruption. The limits to industrial growth set by a dependence on subsidized imported capital goods and raw materials as well as the unabated corruption of state-connected businesses caused another balance-of-payments crisis that was answered with US and IMF-sponsored policies of renewed free trade and decontrol and the devaluation of the peso (1962–1972).[40] In turn, deepening social crises and labour unrest fueled growing militant activist and revolutionary movements, which led to US support for the dictatorial regime of Ferdinand Marcos (1972–1986).

While this brief outline makes quick summary of what were very complex and convoluted historical developments, I merely want to point out that throughout these changes in national policy, the ideals of 'sovereignty', 'security' and 'development' were not simply bandied about but rather put to real work by representatives of the Filipino polity. That is to say, the Philippine state's deployment and manipulation of the codes of international fantasy has fundamentally enabled the systemic exploitation and oppression of the great majority of Filipino lives. One might argue that the codes themselves have no agency and that it is the capitalist world-system and the rapacious dreams of its ruling elites that have wrought the nightmare lives countless Filipinos have lived and continue to live. My own view, however, is that such codes of fantasy are crucial components of the world-system and the rapacious and tawdry dreams of its third world despots like the

Marcoses. They are not the indifferent means of autonomous motive agencies. They also exercise a captivating material power over our practical imaginations. Thus at this moment when I write, as the marauding US state pressures the United Nations to take pre-emptive military action against Iraq, the Deputy Speaker of the Philippine Congress, Raul Gonzalez, cites UN Security Council provisions of international military cooperation to direct the role of the Philippine nation-state in the impending war. As Gonzalez said in behalf of the Philippine state, 'This country does not want war and prays for peace, but if war is inevitable and the UN supports it, we must abide by its treaty obligations.'[41] The alienation of the very codes of international fantasy embodied in the UN that the Philippines itself had helped to found and extend is what allows these treaty obligations to delimit the possibilities of Philippine action to such disastrous ends. Moreover, as the rest of this book will show, to the extent that the organizing codes (as alienated social agencies) are themselves informed by logics of gender, race and sexuality, their practical invocation and mobilization will bear particular consequences for the social groups they implicate. On this view, the masculinist and fraternal ideals held by Romulo as he participated in laying down the geopolitical foundations for the present-day fantasy of the Asia Pacific are important in accounting for the inordinate burden that Filipino women have had to bear for their nation's role in the world.

This book thus takes as its central concern the gendering, racializing and sexualizing significance and consequence of the practical deployment of the codes of the Free World fantasy in Philippine politics and economics in the contemporary period. In order to offer an understanding of the dynamics of Philippine fantasy-production, I look at a broad range of phenomena characterizing the contemporary national formation of the Philippines, including the prostitution economy, the mass migration overseas of domestic workers, urban restructuring and the popular revolt deposing the Marcos dictatorship, as well as representational works of art, poetry, historical narrative and film, which try to intervene in these social conditions. I analyze how the normative scenarios and practical and ideal categories of fantasy-production (e.g. 'development' and 'growth', economic 'interests' and political 'security', 'dependence' and 'sovereignty', etc.) significantly shape the subjective and social meanings and effects of these very different kinds of activities and, further, how they delimit the possibilities of historical transformative agency within the forms of dreaming they allow. In this way, I delineate the contours of the dominant national imaginary impelling and regulating the transformation of the Philippine economy from a prostitution industry to a domestic labour export industry, as well as the transformation of the Philippine state from an authoritarian, crony capitalist state to a putatively liberal-economic, elite-democratic one.

While it would appear that this fantasy-production I refer to is a unitary system governed by a single, evolutionary logic of progression (precisely what I claim it is not but rather how the world is represented to be and enjoined to behave), I intend neither to diminish nor to ignore all the mishaps, internal conflicts, failed as well as successful resistances, differentiations, singularities and sheer chaos and contingency that fill and animate the very movements out of which such a fantasy-history is erected. Much of this book is devoted precisely to the debris of fantasy-production, by which I mean the inassimilable remainders of its operation, and to their potential for steering history away from its present victors. In the first section, for example, my examination of the crisis management role of the nation-state discloses some of the social powers beyond its control (the powers that it in fact is at pains to control). Nevertheless, I feel it is equally important, precisely in the very affirmation of these missed potentials, to delineate the points of their capture. To dwell a little while on the horizon of their vanishing helps us remember what we must wrestle with and for whom (a whom, I should add, that is not fully there beforehand, that is inseparable from the struggle for its liberative realization).

There is more to this reiterative act than political commemoration. Re-staging the unitary and evolutionary terms of fantasy-production helps to delineate the unsurpassed limits of present imaginaries, many of them now under the sway of what Anna Tsing calls 'globalist fantasies'.[42] Fantasy-production practices depend on a transcendent field of meaningful action, which they are the very process of materializing. This field, conceived in an earlier moment through the notion of 'the international community' and re-conceived in the present moment through the notion of 'global networks', is founded first in the physical, substantial presence of the earth, and then in the seemingly immaterial (increasingly 'wireless') but nevertheless still substantial presence of global communication systems. Generated by the very same practices that make it the invisible or rather vanishing ground of their operation, this field consists of a universal, space-time coordinate system (a secularist spatio-temporal order) that continues to go virtually unchallenged as the locating system for all real, practical, political and/ or economic action, not to mention the basis of any world, or at least worldly, history.[43] It is this abstract system for synchronizing and charting planetary-time with global geopolitical space — a vanishing field for the operations of the global market as well as international politics — that enables fantasy-production practices to be business as usual.

'Today', particularly for the emerging global middle class, the fantasy of the free world has become as transparent or unremarkable as the languages of its production, organization and dissemination. By transparent I mean the categories and operations of the free world have lost their visibility as ideals and projects. To too many they have become nothing more than the vehicles and rules of global traffic — sheer means — for what would appear to be unquestionably vital and desirable exchanges. In this book, I highlight the ways in which categories such as the nation, the state, bodies and flows serve as figurative media of world-production. These figures are more than conceptual tools. They are social technologies created out of the very practices they are used to describe.[44] Just as feminized 'bodies' and the integrity attributed to them are produced out of the 'penetration' of the national economy (as itself a consolidated territorial entity) by foreign capital investments, so is the national 'state' produced out of the practices of 'negotiation' with its local and international counterparts.[45] Similarly, the fluidity later attributed to such bodies (in migrant 'flows' and 'brain drain' movements as well as 'floating populations' in 'seas of development') can be viewed as the effect of subsequent political and economic strategies of 'channelling' adopted to supercede state strategies of 'containment'.

Although it would seem, judging from the predominant language of globalist fantasy-production, that juridical subject-forms are now outmoded forms, this book shows that such conceits of so-called 'older' (or, 'advanced') societies, which are said to be surpassed by new, post-industrial forms of organization, are still very much present. They are redeployed in national contexts such as the Philippines as instrumental bids to transnational inclusion (sometimes inadequately understood as third world adoptions of the structures of Western modernity), as when the government or business community present themselves as 'partners' to Western nations in the project of world development.[46] And they are redeployed in the global context as partial, flexible means of negotiating power and accumulating capital.[47] Like the nation-state, 'bodies' and 'subjects' have not so much disappeared as much as lost their prior, foundational guarantees. This 'freeing up' of older categories allows some 'others' to claim what might have been once unequivocally denied them (subjectivity), thereby requiring greater and greater violence to make the remaining, as well new, 'others' perform what is still an essential material conceit (bodies) for the operation of power. My discussion of the post-industrial corporeal racialization of Filipina domestic workers, in Chapter 3, speaks directly to this point.

This book argues that the fantasies of a postcolonial nation like the Philippines are at once symptomatic of and productive of an international system of desiring-actions among nations. It does not argue that these fantasies are *merely* symptomatic. However, it does make the case for the continuing power of the imaginary of the international capitalist system to shape and set limits to the possible imaginings of the contemporary postcolonial nation-state and its peoples. Unless we seriously interrogate the extent to which even counter-hegemonic movements participate in a dreaming that will ultimately not be ours, we cannot really understand or harness the cultural resources for other kinds of dreaming that we have at our disposal.

At the same time, *Fantasy-Production* views dreaming-actions of dominant political agencies such as the state as the product of a continuing struggle with contending forces from below. All the social texts I discuss show the power of people's desires to impel actions on the part of the state and state apparatuses. Indeed, much of the book is devoted to viewing the contradictory demands that these dominant agencies have to accommodate precisely in order to pursue their interests. That these contradictions show themselves in pathologized forms of 'gender trouble' — as in the 'bulimic' behaviour of the post-authoritarian metropolitan government, which I discuss in Chapter 2 — is precisely the consequence of the normative gender and sexuality logics on which the fantasy-practices of the Philippine nation-state are predicated.

This book offers then not only a critique of fantasy-production but also a pursuit of alternative imaginaries and the unorthodox possibilities for historical change that they might bear. While I begin with an ideological critique of fantasy-production and the rules of its history, I also begin to move towards another kind of cultural analysis and history, one that is not fully caught in the experience of necessity or expediency but rather takes the risk of faith in possibility. To this end, I attempt to theorize and demonstrate the importance of following dreaming practices that tangentially escape the logic of desiring subjects, for the writing and making of other histories.

Like the notion of marginality, tangentiality refers to what is essential to the governmental power of prevailing orders but falls from its valorizing purview. Unlike marginality, however, tangentiality does not designate positions, places or identities, whose prior and continuing exclusion from fields of power is the instrument and effect of the logic of domination. It does not designate, in other words, the product-objects of a productive repression. It refers rather, to forces and movements that are harnessed to comprise the substantive content of universal structures (such as 'the nation'), but, at every point on the boundaries of which, tend elsewhere, at once exceeding and falling short of their universal function.[48] What I refer to as tangential, then, are the collective dream forces and movements that are harnessed for the construction of hegemonic subjects and their counter-hegemonic opposition, and yet escape the universal and universalizing forms of both.

To give an example from the book, against the hegemonic 'strong man' regime of the dictator Ferdinand Marcos (1972–1986), which engineered the 'prostitution' economy of the nation and the 'feminization' of Philippine labour, rose the counter-hegemonic 'feminine' popular uprising symbolically led by Corazon Aquino (see Chapter 5). However, between these two antagonistic representative subjects of the nation, whose dramatic confrontation in the televised event of the 1986 'EDSA revolution' made national and international 'history', we can see, in the phenomenal mass following of the film actress, Nora Aunor, an emerging social movement, coursing through but tangential to both. To my thinking, the subjective inventions of Nora's mass following, which consisted almost exclusively of lower-class women, helped set the stage for the people's performance of power, which deposed the Marcos regime. These life-inventions of disenfranchised women provided primary resources for the reorganization of labour under the subsequent government of Aquino, which oversaw the nationalization of the domestic labour export industry. As I will argue in the last chapter, it is the capture of the heretical, 'feminine' power of this tangential social movement figured by the persona of Nora Aunor that fuels and shapes the foundation of a new national as well as global political economic order via the production of a new sociality — domestic labour.

The emergence of this tangential social movement (as Foucault reminds us, emergence 'always occurs in the interstice') is not, however, a spontaneous and pure self-presencing of 'the people'.[49] It is the by-product of the constitutive contradictions of fantasy-production claiming the privileged place of its dreaming, in this case, the revolting community represented by Aquino taking the place of the state. Tangential movements are, in this way, the unruly product (and unrecognized mediator) of dialectical struggle.[50] However, they are also what fall away from 'history' as it has dialectically come to be.[51]

'Following' such movements is more than the democratic restoration of diversity and heterogeneity to the world. Both furthering and diverging from secularist, critical realist histories that see this restoration as their end, I propose heretical visions in pursuit of impeded histories as well as histories yet to be made. Such visionary pursuits are not impelled by utopian hope. Rather, they are the liberating, creative acts of an impossible yet mundane faith. If cultural criticism is to participate in the sway of history in directions tangential to the dominant aims of fantasy-production, it must heed the wayward dream-acts of living social movements, such as Filipinas dreaming new tastes, trying out new lives. *Fantasy-Production* thus ends by exploring the potential of such dream-acts to serve as the practical and theoretical means of a liberative rephrasing of history.

PART I

Fantasy-Production

·

Bodily Resources and Libidinal Dynamics of National Crisis and Development

T here is a story that I first heard in the Philippines a long while back.[1] It goes something like this: Do you know the origins of the American national anthem? Well, when José Rizal (the Philippine national hero) went to the United States, he wanted to watch that all-American game, baseball. But when he got to the stadium there were no more seats left. The only place to watch the game from was at the top of the flagpole. So he took it. Seeing how high up he was, the Americans stood up and sang out to him, 'José, can you see?'

From this facetious account of origins can be gleaned some of the operative features of the dominant fantasies of the postcolonial Philippine nation. In this particular postcolonial fantasy we see a reworking of the subjective predications of the neo-colonial relations between the Philippines and the US. In radically misconstruing the hegemonic account of the origins of US nationalism, the joke surreptitiously invokes a counter-narrative that in many ways correctly places the Philippines at the origins of modern 'America'. Offhand, one can read the joke's absurd substitution of Rizal for the US flag and its location of the origin of the US national anthem in a perversion of colonial history (formally expressed in the 'American' mispronunciation of José) as a mockery of 'American' patriotism and its originary power. The ridiculous picture of Rizal, 'The First Filipino', balancing on top the flagpole like a monkey, as early US colonizers thought Filipinos to be, can also be seen as a mockery of Rizal whose legitimacy as the national hero has been put to question in the last few decades in part because of allegations that he was propped up to serve US interests.[2] The joke hence functions as a disguised defiance of 'America's' authority over the determination of Philippine national identity. Parodying the US's histrionic concern for its 'little brown brother', whose 'littleness' has always meant inexperience, weakness and inferiority and, to that extent, has always served as a legitimation for US rule, it overturns the imaginary conditions of US neo-colonial power. But the mockery of Rizal is also a mockery of 'the Filipino' and the character of *his* 'special relation' to 'America'.[3]

Indeed, what is crucial about this joke is its portrayal of the imaginary reality of US-Philippine relations. The scene is terribly familiar: 'the Filipino' hoping and trying to find his/her place in the heart of 'America', and finally finding recognition in a most ignoble fashion. But it is not only self-depreciation that is demonstrated in this joke. Equally critical is the transfer of that national self-depreciation unto the US, for the latent truth of this representation is that the Philippines functions as an unacknowledged nodal point of 'American' national identity. The mockery of the Filipino aspiration to be incorporated into the scene of 'American' desire becomes a manifestation (one might say, a manifesto) of the way in which the Philippines serves 'the American Dream', both as a productive colony and an absent presence in the US imaginary. Of the US fantasy, Lauren Berlant writes:

> It would be all too easy to ridicule the Dream, and to dismiss it as the motivating false consciousness of national/ capitalist culture. But the fantasy of the American Dream is an important one to learn from. A popular form of political optimism, it fuses private fortune with that of the nation: it promises that if you invest your energies in work and family-making, the nation will secure the broader social and economic conditions in which your labor can gain value and your life can be lived with dignity.[4]

The Philippines has served this US fantasy to the extent that its labour, its natural and social resources, its territory and its symbolic presence, together with those of other US colonies and territories, have served to guarantee precisely those social and economic conditions promised by 'America'. The political, economic and ideological value produced by the Philippines and other US colonial possessions for the US nation throughout the twentieth-century is inestimable. Despite the ideological assertion that it was more trouble than it was worth, we have only to mention a few of its services to get a sense of the Philippines's importance to US interests: a source of agricultural products (sugar, hemp, coconut, log, minerals); a market for US goods; a source of cheap imported agricultural labour (for agricultural industries in California and Hawaii); a territory for the largest US military bases outside of the North American continent (a launching pad for US intervention in Korea, Vietnam, the Gulf War; a stronghold of Cold War 'security'); a site of overseas investment of industrial and finance capital, as well as a site of expenditure of military surplus capital and technology (a site of constant counter-insurgent military activity); and a dumping ground of excess goods and toxic waste. It has also served the US by bearing the burden of its erasure as a constitutive condition and contradiction of US values and freedoms.[5] The joke thus restores to full visibility a presence perceived as an absence or 'lack'.

The fantastic reversal performed by the joke (it is not we who want you but, rather, you who want us) is in fact the truth of the fantasy of US-Philippine relations, a demonstration of the ideological dreamwork, which upholds actual US-Philippine relations. Filipinos want to partake of 'the American Dream', when in fact they are already a constitutive part of that dream. As I will discuss at length in Chapter 1, that dream, which constitutively shapes US ideological, political and economic 'greatness' as a national superpower, begins in the late nineteenth century as the dream of empire, and then transforms by mid-twentieth century into the dream of the (First) Free (Enterprise) World (against the socialist challenge of the Second World). It is a dream that has deep historical underpinnings and broad regional reach. Thus, in the Taiwan context, Kuan-hsing Chen writes, 'After the Second World War, the material power of the US made it the central object of identification, and later dis-identification, as the neocolonial master of the region. American systems of representation and modes of living infiltrated the space of the national-popular imaginary, and redirected its flows of psychic desire and cultural energy. This chain of movements still traverses the social body.'[6]

Reversing the direction of influence, the joke is not therefore on 'us' (the *petit* US) but on the US, whose identity as a bona fide nation (indeed, as the highest instance of democratic and sovereign nationhood — a superpower) is shown to depend on the figure and strivings of the absurd nation. That claim is the tendentious dimension of the joke. Of course the national absurdity that is the Philippines, as the historical mascot of the Free World in Asia, is precisely the constitutive, contradictory consequence of the workings of US imperialist desire — in a word, its symptom. Perpetually striving and failing to realize the ideals of freedom, equality, sovereignty and progress defined by and as the US, the Philippines is the embodiment of the blocked fulfillment of these ideals within the prevailing, global fantasy. In this way the Philippines has served as an intractable object of US (as well as Philippine) desire — the object of countless projects of aid, development, modernization and structural readjustment, all of which have resulted in the unabated crisis that is the Philippine economy and government, and the unimpeded growth of US-multinational capital and political power.

The fantasy-scenario of the joke above is thus a symbolic expression and effected framework of 'real' political and economic relations between the Philippines and the US in the neo-colonial moment (1946–1972). Fantasy is not, as in the Althusserian sense, the imaginary representation of real material practices but, rather, the symbolic-material practices that organize what we take to be 'reality'. It is already this 'reality', in other words, that is profoundly imaginary, by which I mean, suffused with subjectifying meanings and effects of dominant orders of signification. As the purported ground of international affairs, political and economic structures and relations assume form and force in thoroughly subjective and subjectifying ways. Hence to speak, for example, of national desires is not to speak metaphorically of what are essentially political and economic interests of a nation. It is to grasp the subjective predicates and subjectifying effects of the actual practices that produce those interests (political power and economic wealth) attributable to individual nations, or their dominant, representative agencies. Put differently, it is to grasp the ways in which nations are invoked and behooved to act as unitary, individual subjects on the world-scene. 'Fantasy-production' is an attempt to think of these imaginary dimensions of political economy, that is, of structures of production and power on national as well as international scales. It names a socio-symbolic logic or dreamwork obtaining in the organization of the international community and the scene of its exchanges (the affairs of the world market and international relations).

Most political and economic scholarly works on the Philippines have no time for dreams or fantasies. If they do have time for dreams and fantasies, they are cast as the illusory possessions of individual men who have shaped the destiny of their nation with their desires. As for the means with which those men purportedly shape their nation's destiny, the political and economic 'systems' they manipulate to feed those dreams, those are simply the hardware of modern nationhood and development. Culture, as software, is brought in only to account for the failure of that hardware to produce in the Philippines the same structures of representational democracy and rational economic growth that it produced in advanced, metropolitan nation-states. This book argues, however, that cultural imagination, dreams and fantasies subsist and operate precisely in such political and economic hardware. As Arturo Escobar's cogent and comprehensive critique of the discourse and practice of 'development' shows, in rational techniques and strategies of national planning, in international programs promoting economic growth and sustainable subsistence production and in the institutional practices of the World Bank and the International Monetary fund, are the workings of a dream.[7] That dream, which Escobar traces to the triumphant post-Second World War US's willful vision that 'the American dream of peace and abundance be extended to all the peoples of the planet', was predicated on the invention of a problem (Third World poverty) for which a whole array of practices, apparatuses, institutions arose as necessary solutions.[8] This imaginary or dreamwork of 'development' produces not only an object for its desiring-actions (the Third World or the underdeveloped world) but also a subject of these actions (the First World or the developed world). *Fantasy-Production* focuses on this subjective dimension of the practical affairs of 'development' in the context of the Philippines and in particular on the role of race, gender and sexuality in the organization of those affairs. By recognizing not merely the discursive constructedness of the political and economic relations established as worldly realities, but also the *desiring* or libidinal character of these relations, we are able to better understand the constitutive significance of race, gender and sexuality in the practical making of the Philippines's contemporary worldly realities.

The dream of 'development' has an easily discernible historical precedent in the imperialist fantasies of a previous age. In these earlier fantasies, the role of gender and sexuality in the structuring of relations is evident. As Anne McClintock describes them: 'In these fantasies, the world is feminized and spatially spread for male exploration, then reassembled and deployed in the interests of massive imperial power.'[9] Needless to say, the hetero-masculine imperial power is also a white (that is, unmarked) national subject in constitutive symbolic identification with Progress, which takes the place of God as the new universal mandate.[10] Today's world inherits these subjective relations and their principles of constitution in the geopolitical imagination that governs international relations. That is to say, the principles of race, gender and sexuality that constituted and were effected by imperialistic relations continue to operate in the material organization of the Free World. They do so through the practical pursuit of such universal ideals as 'development', 'national sovereignty', 'security', 'the international community' and 'global civil society', which comprise some of the subjectifying categories and conceits of the international dreamwork that I am calling fantasy-production. Although anti-colonial and other liberatory social movements brought and continue to bring new and tremendous forces and practices of desire into the world, these are constantly – even if never fully – subsumed by forms of fantasy, which shift to accommodate and recodify the radical potential of such movements in conservative ideals.

Caught within this international dreamwork, how then do postcolonial nations dream of themselves? While the critique of imperialist and developmentalist fantasies may elucidate the dreams of metropolitan powers, alone it says little about the dreams of the countries that figure as their objects. On the other hand, too often the response to such critiques has been to affirm Third World and postcolonial resistance at the cost of diminishing the violence of their subjection to and active participation in such fantasies. It is also, I believe, too easy to separate out the elites and the masses or the state and the people and then to blame the first for complicity with the dreams of power and to free the latter of responsibility for the consequences of those dreams. I do not see myself as fully escaping these tendencies. I do however attempt to direct my analytical focus away from pre-constituted social actors and onto the practices of fantasy-production that give rise to the social relations through which such social actors are constituted. That is to say, I try to view particular social subjects (the state, the national elite, the people) and their characteristic agency as also the effects (and not simply the sources or causes) of dominant dreaming practices.

From this view, which recognizes a dominant field of practices, a 'common material imaginary', shared by first world and third world nations alike, we can attend to the *kinds* of dreaming engaged in by both that effectively produces prevailing social and economic conditions on a world scale. My own interest is in the particular ways that the Philippine nation participates in the dreamwork of the Free World.

As an order of signification and production, the Free World fantasy consists of certain scenarios, categories and moves that delimit even as they spur practical forms of action on the part of designated actors. (It is in this regard neither a single narrative nor a unified logic of unfolding, whether evolutionary or otherwise.) Nationhood, sovereignty, development, modernity, democracy and progress are just such practical-ideal notions guiding official state projects as well as popular struggles against them. These practical-ideal notions carry with them particular assumptions of subjectivity as well as subjectifying consequences that have become dominant to the extent that the hegemonic cultures they emerge out of determine the main contents of fantasy-production. It is not at all surprising then to find the processes of their enactment imbued with expressions of desire and lack, love and disaffection, pride and shame and dignity and debasement. National dilemmas are subjective predicaments. Observe the way in which the problem of the US bases and the 'debt crisis' of the late 1980s are posed by then Senator Joseph Estrada as he addresses 'the heart of our national predicament — the lack of national sovereignty':

> Mr President, the current debate over US military bases in the Philippines clearly revolves around two things: money or freedom? ... We are once more being tempted by this occasion to renounce our national identity in order to lessen, in whatever way, the severe depression of our national economy ...
>
> We don't think of the future. In our actions one can trace the pitiful happiness of a slave — who permits and hopes that another human will carry him. It's alien to the dream of a slave that he should use his own powers ...
>
> We confront numerous possibilities, but it's a reflection of our weak self-determination as a government that we cannot show any evidence of our well-considered preparation for a life without military bases. This is perhaps the reason why the Americans are not worried about current negotiations, nor do they show the slightest anxiety (sic). They see the Aquino government as bluffing. I'm afraid if we don't change our perspective and posture

toward these bases, it will be a foregone conclusion that we will not get anything from these talks — neither money nor freedom …

The crisis that afflicts us is also the chance to discover our native powers. In our power lies our authentic nationhood. In our hands lies our freedom. In unity lies the honor of the country.

Let us not exchange our national honor for the silver of the foreigners.

Money or freedom — this is the choice that confronts a country that can see itself behaving like a bond-slave, a country whose freedom (our national honor) is exchanged for the silver dollars of its US master. The language of this appeal, whereby the nation's sovereignty is compromised as a consequence of its selling of itself (in other appeals, of its people), articulates and is shaped by the subjective categories and social forms that organize the real, political and economic context in which such an appeal is made. In other words, the explicit invocation of slavery and the implicit suggestion of prostitution in Estrada's speech are part and parcel of the fantasy-practices that produce those metaphorical allusions as actual, historical conditions obtaining in the Philippines. These conditions are exemplified by the state-sponsored prostitution industry that both dominated and paradigmatically structured the Philippine economy during the Marcos dictatorship. Fantasy-practices are, however, also the symbolic means of materially transforming such conditions. Money or freedom — this subjective 'choice' is re-enacted over and over again in the quotidian as well as world-historical struggles of Filipinos. Indeed, Estrada's speech came in the wake of the 1986 'People Power' revolt against the Marcos dictatorship, the symbolic phrasings and affective energy of which undoubtedly helped to shape Estrada's anti-US bases appeal just as the subjective performance of 'the people' in that revolt also paved the way for the mass appeal of his presidency. That first revolt took on many of the gendered and sexualized meanings of Philippine fantasy-production and staged them in a polar antagonism between the 'feminine' figure of Corazon Aquino and the 'strongman' figure of Ferdinand Marcos.

In the most recent 'People Power' uprising, now touted as the sequel to the first (i.e., 'People Power 2'), this scenario is replayed but in a new configuration. Now, no longer freedom-fighting Senator but rather corruption-ridden President, Estrada became (for the politicized middle class which emerged out of 'People Power 1') the despised embodiment of tainted money that needed to be renounced for the redemption of Filipino 'honour'. And in a graffiti drawing, which circulated widely on e-mail as part of the popular protest, his avid supporter, Senator Tessie Aquino-Oreta, became depicted as the 'money-hungry/dick-sucking whore' who mirrored the decadence and immorality of the Estrada state. Needless to say, the gender and sexuality entailments of this fantasy-scenario have grave consequences for the social groups they implicate, such as women. One of the concerns of this book is to foreground these conditions of violence shaped by the organizing tropes of Philippine fantasy-production.

This first section describes the dominant fantasy-scenarios structuring prevailing political and economic conditions of Philippine social life in the post-Third World era. Very importantly, it focuses on the gendered and sexualized meanings and effects of the actions on the part of peoples and states over which such scenarios exercise significant, determining power. In Chapter 1, 'Sexual Economies', I look at how prostitution becomes the organizing trope and actual state-sponsored industry of the Philippine economy during the period of Ferdinand Marcos's authoritarian regime. As I demonstrate at length in this chapter, this is not only a matter of nationalism taking on gendered and sexualized meanings.[11] The gendered lineaments and sexualized contents of this mode of production also constitute its practical dynamics. I argue that the international organization of capital and labour, which takes hold at this particular moment, depends on a heteronormative logic of gender and sexuality for the configuration of national political relations and strategies of economic structuring.[12]

In Chapter 2, 'Metropolitan Dreams', I show how the same contradictory dynamics of gender and sexuality that shape Philippine political economy are at work in the restructuring of the built environment of the national capital, Metro Manila, and can be read in the strategies of the state governing this metropolitan transformation. I argue that the flyovers, or overpasses, constructed in the early 1990s are new metropolitan forms designed to address the crisis of the aftermath of the Marcos regime which emerged with the deposing of that regime by popular revolt in 1986. These materially concrete structures are technologies of metropolitan desire that help to produce, simultaneously, the transnationalizing national subject; the bodies to be regulated in the name and as the property of that subject; and the new 'democratic' state replacing the Marcos dictatorship as the negotiating agent of this transaction. I also discuss the subsequent transformation of this new metropolitan form and its realization of a new national subject: 'civil society'.

In Chapter 3, 'Domestic Bodies', these transformations are viewed in relation to the deterritorialization of the nation enacted by the mass exodus of Filipina domestic workers. We can detect the early stirrings of 'civil society' in the reconstitution of the nation vis-à-vis the tragic figuration of this overseas domestic body as modern day slaves. Slavery reappears in the Free World as a refurbished technology of social relations supporting new, post-industrial forms of expropriation of surplus value. I try to show the historical proximity of slavery to the dominant form of femininity supporting state-sponsored prostitution in order to account for the particular kinds of labour relations racially engendered by the export of Philippine domestic labour during the subsequent period. I also suggest that the processes of gendered racialization that obtain in these new domestic labour conditions serve as the violent means by which a nascent global, postcolonial middle class tries to attain the unmarked, universal 'humanity' historically denied them. While the expansion of this export industry induces a crisis in the nation as a consequence of its bodily dispossession (and the dispossession of its territorial power), it also bolsters a new economic nationalism that helps to reconfigure the role of the Philippine state in the global economy.

1

Sexual Economies

This chapter is comprised of two interventions at two different historical moments, each marked by a pivotal US-led 'world' war.[1] The first intervention was made in the context of the 1991 Gulf War and its fantasy of a New (Free) World Order composed of peaceful, prosperous regional communities of 'free' nations. The second intervention issues out of the context of the current 'global war on terrorism' and its fantasy of a global civilization of good states and peoples winning the universal crusade against a marauding transhistorical *and* regressive barbarism. These two moments serve as a measure of the changes in the prevailing national and international fantasies within which the Philippines configures and coordinates its desires.

1991: With the celebrated emergence of the Asia-Pacific community, the Philippines is confronted with the tensions of its historical identity and the political and economic crisis that is its persistent reality. As a region, the Asia-Pacific community designates a political and economic constituency represented primarily by the United States, Japan, Canada, Australia and New Zealand, a group known as the OECD (Organization for Economic Cooperation and Development) Five, and secondarily by newly industrialized countries (NICs) such as South Korea, Taiwan and Singapore. Such a representation and the excitement for regional prosperity that it generates, however, elide the contradictory third world status of the rest of the Asia-Pacific — developing countries like the Southeast Asian nations that threaten to disrupt the congenial unity that the dream of 'community' conjures. Once a dominantly geographical area comprised of dispersed political territories, the Asia-Pacific community is increasingly sold to the idea of constituting a purely economic network among its member nations. Indeed, the dream of 'community' is steadily being realized as a transnational corporation with the power to regulate and determine national as well as individual lives. For the fantasy of the Asia-Pacific community is one that takes form and force within a particular global purview, namely, the First World fantasy of the Free World or the international community, which shapes international relations through the political and economic practices of individual nations. It is, in other words, the shared ground upon which the actions and identities of its participants are predicated — it is a field of orientation, an imaginary determining the categories and operations with which individuals as well as nation-states act out their histories. Among these categories is sexuality — in this fantasy, the economies and political relations of nations are libidinally configured, that is, they are grasped and effected in normative terms of sexuality. This global and regional fantasy is not, however, metaphorical but real insofar as it grasps a system of political and economic practices already at work among these nations.[2]

Individuals as well as governments act not only *as if* a unified global community did exist, but also *as if* nations were individual citizens who compose this community and who, like individuals, behave in particular (sexual) ways and act with particular desires.[3] That international community *in effect* works in the way it is imagined, but only because it is realized as this totality through the displacement of its constitutive contradictions unto third world bodies. That is, capitalism is impelled by desire (visibly demonstrated by the endless processes of accumulation and consumption) — desire, in other words, for surplus wealth/pleasure, produced by and producing a fantasy of political-libidinal economies that regulate individual and national lives. The Asia-Pacific community is predicated on this fantasy of a global (Free World market) economy. Indeed, as a regional reproduction of an ideal international community, it reproduces the same sexual economies and relations at work in global capitalism, intensifying them to the greater profit of its main promoters, and to the greater loss of the populations whose labour must pay for it. It is the logic of these libidinal processes that I would like to trace in this rendering of the fantasy of the Asia-Pacific community.

PACIFIC DESIRES

Invoking the Asia-Pacific as a leader and symbol of an emergent international order, therefore, obscures the intensification of globalized capitalism to which this community is dedicated. It is, in effect, to invoke international cooperation without the competition and violence necessary to this global organization. I argue that the Asia-Pacific, as a dream and an actuality, functions as a locus of containment of the threat the region poses to the dominant powers who benefit from its promotion. With the Vietnam War and other anti-imperialist revolutionary struggles being waged in Southeast Asia, (as well as in Africa, the Middle East and Latin America), from the late 1960s to the mid-1970s, the Asia-Pacific region emerged as a threat to the global power of the United States, that is, to its political authority as well as economic superiority. The end of the Cold War and the burgeoning economy of Japan and the NICs only increased this economic and political threat and the necessity of its containment. Hence, the intensified efforts to push for the realization of the Asia-Pacific community, a dream dedicated to the greater dream of global capitalism.

Thus Japan's Prime Minister Nakasone could wholeheartedly claim: 'In the Pacific we are witnessing the birth of a new kind of capitalism. Here the vigour and competitiveness of Western — particularly American — capitalism has been enriched by the Asian cultural heritage.' Furthermore, 'Asian free enterprise has shown itself capable of fostering a competitive dynamism of its own. The distinguishing mark of the Pacific Basin countries has been their commitment to free enterprise economics.'[4] More than fifty years ago, Japan was advocating the founding of a very different Asian empire, a desire that all but ended in the Second World War. But forty years earlier, the United States had already set its sights on the very same region, which was to whet its appetite for global power: 'the Pacific is the ocean of the commerce of the future. Most future wars will be conflicts for commerce. The power that rules the Pacific, therefore, is the power that rules the world. And, with the Philippines, that power is and will forever be the American Republic.'[5] This desire to be a Pacific power has brought about these two wars: the 'war of pacification', which the United States used to refer to the Philippine-American war at the turn of the century, and the Pacific war, which it used to refer to the war between itself and Japan during the mid-century. One might well argue, however, that this war over the Pacific continues to be waged today but in a very different way. Global conflict is no longer envisioned in the fantasy of East-West relations (i.e., relations of the Orient and the Occident, and, later, of the two power blocs, the US and the USSR), nor is it predominantly envisioned in the fantasy of the First and Third Worlds, or of North and South. These global unities have ceased to function in the same way in a decidedly post-Cold War, post-Gulf War era. Japan and the US are no longer up in arms over the Pacific or even over 'the last land left in all the oceans', the Philippines; instead, they are now in cooperation. This new mode of relation realized through incorporation is libidinal/economic in character, and thus can be truthfully described as a marriage of interests.

THE PACIFIC MARRIAGE

It has been claimed that the idea of a Pacific community is 'a baby whose putative parents are Japanese and American and whose midwife is Australian'.[6] This marriage between Japan and the US, however, masks as well as reveals the particular global desires and tensions still at play in the Free World. War has been consummated in a sexual relationship that stabilizes the tenuous unity of the international community. In this arrangement, sexual union is war through economic incorporation. Indeed, what this marriage evinces is an unequal and potentially antagonistic relation at the heart of the economic union, whether this union refers to the Asia-Pacific or to the larger international community. What it further reveals is the desire for incorporation into these global unions. Hence the Japanese initiative in proposing the formation of the Pacific community during the late 1960s, confirming what Nakasone could later admit as 'Japan's need to become an "*international* nation"; that is to say, a nation that must bear a heavy share of international responsibilities in keeping with its international position.' The desire for incorporation might thus be seen as a desire for citizenship in the international community, a citizenship that entails more than an allegiance to the ideals of internationality, which entails also a buying into the preconditions of the Free World. But Japan has only lately begun to see itself as attaining this citizenship, which other nations such as the United States have long since held — thus recognizing that there are nation-citizens with more rights and responsibilities than others, that is, with more power than others. If there is such a thing as an international state, clearly, the US is seen to hold some kind of presidential power — hence the uneasiness of the marriage. For in desiring inclusion, Japan shows itself to be lacking in political power, in spite of its economic wealth (a condition secured with her disarmament as a consequence of her losing to the US in the Second World War). The Asia-Pacific community is, in this light, a way for Japan to marry into power and the US to domesticate her desires for power. For in the transformation of this international community into a multinational corporation, the preoccupation with the balance of power becomes the participation in the bargain for power — that is, power becomes a matter of negotiating economic shares and political management or control.

I say *her*, because in this heteronormative sexual scenario, Japan is the wife and the US her husband. The antagonism that the fantasies of East-West, First World-Third World, and North-South relations have historically addressed (as frameworks of global contradictions) has been transmuted into libidinal cooperation, that is, into the fantasy of masculine-feminine relations. Deterritorialized, these global polarities are now predominantly enacted according to a prevailing mode of heterosexual relations. But the allies and partners that territories and possessions of a past age have been transformed into are not categories that pertain to particular nations at all times. As it is well known in the Philippines with reference to the US, 'there are no permanent friendships, only permanent interests'. More than this wavering interest, the positions in partnerships, that is, of masculine and feminine, are continually in flux, and dependent on who are in relation. In other words, masculine and feminine are defined against each other and function according to the specific historical relation at work. Hence, in its relation to the US, Japan may occupy a feminine position, but in relation to the Philippines, it may occupy a masculine position. Since nations maintain simultaneous and crossing international relations, masculine and feminine should be seen not as essential features of even specific relations, but rather as diacritical marks of certain political practices and economic modes of operation within and between nations that are libidinal in character, such as investment of capital and extraction of interest.

The logic of this socio-libidinal economy at work among nations can be demonstrated in the 'special relations' of the Philippines and the United States. The fantasy of this particular relationship is paradigmatic not only because of the intimate history shared by these two nations and the particular sexual form it has taken, but also because of the tremendous difference between them in terms of national wealth and global power. In effect, they encapsulate two extreme positions within the Asia-Pacific community and thereby make more glaring the antagonisms it must contain. Furthermore, the Philippines' role in relation to the US and Japan evidences the costs entailed by the offspring of the latter's marriage of interests, that is, by the realization of the Asia-Pacific community.

THE PHILIPPINE-AMERICAN ROMANCE

The Philippines is second only to Bangladesh as the country with the worst growth rate in Asia.[7] She owes this position to a large extent to her enormous debt to and dependence on the US, the World Bank, and the International Monetary Fund, a relation that is 'secured' through various policies and treaties, not least significant of which is the US military bases agreement. This 'involvement' of the US in the Philippines is as a territory to be invested in (whether in capital or in arms) in the name of national and regional *security*. While 'security' has long been touted as being an issue of military defense of political sovereignty, the end of the Cold War and the move to steer clear of 'politics' in the promotion of the Asia-Pacific community have brought out the full implications of its economic and financial significance. As an economic arrangement, 'security' also has its romantic overtones, inasmuch as it means the cementing of a relationship or the insuring of its stability. But the question to be asked of the international arrangements being made in the Asia-Pacific is: who is 'getting off' on this? Who is 'getting fucked' and by whom?

In the case of Japan, clearly some leverage, that is, some bargaining power, is gained in her marriage of interests with the US. In the case of the Philippines, that 'security' is at least questionable. For the 'special relationship' of the Philippines and the US is no marriage, and the Philippines is no wife; she is, rather, America's mistress. Feminized in this relationship of debt and dependence, the Philippines produces the surplus pleasure (wealth) that the US extracts from its bodily (manual) labour. It is indeed her inexhaustible labour and her abundant natural resources that draws the US to her, that is used to 'attract' the latter's interest and investments. Philippine security therefore comes to mean the political stability necessary to attract foreign investors, the source of its capital. An advertisement the Philippine Government took out in the *New York Times* (28 July 1974) demonstrates the sexual marketing of the country's domestic attractions:

> We've put our house in order … There are attractive investment packages for you if you want to explore, develop and process mineral resources … Easy entry for expatriate staff … Doesn't that sound like an offer you can't refuse? We like multinationals. Manila's natural charms as a regional business center have been enhanced by a special incentive package … your expatriate-managers will enjoy Asia's lowest living costs among the most outgoing people in the Pacific … Accountants come for $67, executive secretaries for $148. Move your Asian headquarters to Manila and make your cost accountants happy … The country is lovely. And loaded. Beneath the tropical landscapes of our 7,000 islands lies a wealth of natural resources …[8]

The 'prostitution' or feminized commodification of the Philippines, which is attendant to such rhetoric, is made possible by and perpetuates a logic in which certain divisions of labour and patterns of sexual relations converge and collabourate in the driving of the national economy. Those who are at the wheel of the nation are its representatives, and the behavior they exhibit bespeaks the character of the nation. Thus does the Philippine-American relationship appear as a romance-fantasy that has each government courting and manipulating the other for his or her security and happiness:

> Philippine presidents, out of tradition but more of necessity, have always had a love-hate relationship with the Great White Father in Washington. Cory Aquino is no exception. Right now, she is displaying the classic behavior of a spurned lover, one who not too long ago was playing beautiful music with no less than George Bush himself.
>
> What explains this cyclical and all too predictable behavior of virtually everybody who has ever lived in Malacañang? First, there is the realpolitik aspect. Nobody gets to be president of this country without, more or less, the imprimatur of whoever happens to call the shots in the White House. Second, Washington tends to keep a tight leash on Philippine presidents, especially on the matter of keeping American bases in this part of the world. Third, America's love is never constant, never enduring; Filipino presidents come and go, but American interest in this country is eternal. Or so it seems.[9]

The article from which this extract was taken goes on, relating the 'tragic pattern of presidential love-hate for America' in which the various presidents experienced 'the sweet love of American support, followed by an acrimonious parting of ways', sharing 'the common fate of being at the mercy, if not in the physical custody of America'. This custody that makes Filipinos a kept people, however, is actively pursued by those who in their desire to share in the rights and privileges of the international community buy into this economic arrangement (free enterprise, free love) — this open relationship which economically means the letting down of protectionist barriers and 'liberalization' of imports, that is, easy entry and exit.

This 'special relationship' is the manifestation and consequence of an imperialistic dream that at the turn of the century was steeped in sacred tones. As Sen. Beveridge exclaimed:

> We will not repudiate our duty in the archipelago. We will not abandon our opportunity in the Orient. We will not renounce our part in the mission of our race, trustee under God, of the civilization of the world ... of all our race He has marked the American people

as his chosen nation to finally lead in the regeneration of the world. This is the divine mission of America, and it holds for us all the profit, all the glory, all the happiness possible to man. We are trustees of the world's progress, guardians of its righteous peace. The judgement of the Master is upon us: 'Ye have been faithful over a few things; I will make you rule over many things.'[10]

The religious rhetoric of US colonization has become today the libidinal action of American capitalism. And the goal of economic and political conversion then zealously expressed, also by Sen. Beveridge, was:

American soil is producing more than Americans can consume ... The trade of the world must and shall be ours. American law, American order, American civilization and the American flag will plant themselves on shores hitherto bloody and benighted but by the agencies of God henceforth to be made beautiful and bright.[11]

This process of evangelization has become explicitly the process of seduction. But while the form has changed, the dream yet seeks the same coveted object, the Philippines — a body resistant to its desire and to its ideals of democracy and freedom, i.e., free enterprise. The Philippines needs to be converted and seduced because it is a contradiction to these ideals to the extent that it is residually feudal or pre-capitalist and threatening to become communist or anti-capitalist. As a colony it therefore had to be 'emancipated' and granted independence, converted to that American order, which has become today a global order, in order to contain the potentially eruptive antagonism that could develop from the contradiction it poses (by serving as a locus for its displacement), a contradiction that is nevertheless necessary for the motoring of capitalism. What one might glean from this history of decolonization is the same logic at work in the granting of autonomy to the Asia-Pacific region. Now constituted as a self-governing unit, it could thereby be more efficiently engaged in the global economy.

The coveting of former colonies, however, did not cease with 'liberation'. These recalcitrant bodies, now members of an independent region, must continually be lured into feeding the desires of power. As Luz del Mundo observed:

> The Western powers are now reaping the effects of their ignoring 'nationalist' aspirations of Arab countries and their greedy grabbing of spheres of influence on Arab oil resources in the past several decades, thus triggering retaliatory moves from OPEC. Now they turn their attention to the Asia-pacific region. ASEAN is now at a stage where it has more countries from Europe, the Middle East and Latin America interested in entering into partnership with ASEAN. Japan sees this and wants to preempt the ASEAN as its own preserve; a prize and plum to be won permanently by persuading its other OECD partners, particularly the US and Australia, that through the creation of a Pacific community, Japan will be certain to remain an ally of the West ...[12]

Part and parcel of this 'prize and plum to be won' that is the ASEAN is the Philippines. Thus, the Philippines plays a curious role in the marriage of Japan and 'the West' — 'won' back from Japan in World War II by the US, it must now be shared as the price of alliance and as insurance of Japanese fidelity. For this price is paid by neither the US nor Japan, that is, neither 'the Great White Father' nor his recent spouse — but by the Philippines, mistress-infant to one, stepdaughter-servant to the other, the body that keeps the two in relative harmony by acting as a membrane for the coursing of their desires, and as a locus for the playing out of their antagonism. Such is a typical international triangle: an incestuous *ménage à trois* as well as a perverted Oedipal affair.

A MODEL ASIAN-PACIFIC FAMILY

As Aida Fulleros Santos and Lynn F. Lee show in their analysis of the Philippine Aid Plan (PAP), a current project of the US and Japan, the marriage of the two powers is convenient but uneasy. There are obvious tensions in this 'triangular relationship between institutions in the US, Japan and the Philippines': 'Japan has not agreed entirely that aid to the Philippines be conditioned by the US perception of their common regional interests, and that Japan be "guided" by the US while giving the bulk of ODA [Official Development Assistance] funds ... Japan sees its strategic interests as similar to the US but does not have exactly the same view on the best ways of furthering these mutually shared interests. For the US, the PAP concretizes a political strategy for the US and Japan to work together to further their mutual interests in the Asia-Pacific region and globally … PAP shows the US strategy — US political direction and Japanese funding.'[13] In spite of the tensions, however, the US-Japan cooperative effort is bound to make the Philippines pay, for aside from giving the two more leverage with the Philippine government in defining and determining 'regional security', it also increases the Philippine foreign debt. 'In the long term, foreign investment that may flow on from PAP will contribute to the net outflow of money from the Philippines.'[14] Indeed, what the PAP scheme shows is that such marriage of powers only augments their individual exploitation of the country of their desires.

In her relationship to the US, the Philippines is an exploitable body, an industry hooked up to the US desiring machine through a system of flows of labor and capital in the guise of free exchange (export-oriented, capital and import dependent) but functioning in the mode of dialysis, which gives one the strength and life depleted from the other. As such, the Philippines is the prostitute of 'America' who caters to the latter's demands (ostensibly demands of global production and consumption), in other words, a hospitality industry, a hostess to 'American' desires, a hooker.[15] As the greatest of her foreign investors, that is, the most powerful of her multinational clients, the US establishes free trade zones on the body/land of the Philippines over which it exercises a considerable degree of monopoly (the way it derives its pleasures) by obtaining free entry and exit rights (investment of capital and repatriation of profits). This mode of relations between the Philippines and America operates according to a fantasy of heteronormative relations between masculine and feminine ideals that has become dominant in economically advanced nations — a sexual masquerade in which the Philippines serves the US as a feminine ideal, servicing its power the way the Philippine prostitutes service US military men, symbols of US national (masculine) strength. The fantasy is shared, of course. Hence 'America' in turn becomes the Philippines' masculine ideal, determining the shape of the desire expressed by this 'bar waitress' who might speak for the Philippines as well: 'Sure I would like to marry an American! I want to help my family. If I marry a Filipino, it will be the same; but if I marry an American, maybe it will be better.'[16] The sex worker's desire to marry into a better life (i.e., foreign, 'American'), however, is not forthcoming, as it has been pre-empted by other partners of the US

New investment flows in the Philippines are dominated by Japanese as well as Taiwanese capital. 'For both Japan and Taiwan, the motives for investment are primarily the need to recycle trade surpluses and the exploitation of advantages offered by the Philippines, e.g., a cheap labour force, natural resources, trade preferences vis-à-vis the developed countries, as well as a location for polluting industries.'[17] In other words, the interest Japan and Taiwan take in the Philippines is not very different in form from the interest the US takes in her, for the attractions the Philippines holds are all the same for these capital-bearing nations. In this scenario, speaking of interest and involvement is the same as speaking of investment, and to speak of any of these things is to use the language of politics and economics as well as the language of love and sexual enjoyment. Thus with the increase of Japanese loans and grants to the Philippines, Japan joins in the feminization of the latter: 'As Japan chalks up more trade surpluses, Japanese penetration of the country's economy will, no doubt, increase.'[18] Japan is adopting the Free World fantasy of the advanced nations of the West not only in order to enter the international community but also 'to step out of the shadow of the US'[19] and exercise equal if not greater power in a new global order. She is therefore yet determined by the threat of an emasculation similar to that which she participates in effecting on developing nations such as the Philippines. Thus the protectionist measures she adopts in the form of high tariffs on processed or semi-processed products is in effect a successful defense against being penetrated, i.e., 'getting fucked'.[20] Who is penetrating whom — in translated terms, which countries export capital, technology and finished products to which countries — hence becomes a gauge by which to measure economic strength. It is no surprise then that even those in developing nations who want to get in on the action that the Asia-Pacific community promises point out the necessity of correcting the uneven trade among member nations — demonstrated, for example, by the fact that 'tropical products from the Pacific Developing Countries (PDCs) suffered from low import penetration into the American, Japanese, Canadian and Australian markets'[21] — a problem whose proposed solution lies merely in an equalization of flows through political reform ('national goodwill') rather than in a transformation of the mode of relations among these nations. Furthermore, development is always seen in terms of inside and outside, feminine and masculine, domestic and international. Hence the possibility of critiquing the economic growth registered by the Philippines in recent years in the following way: 'one finds that most of the permanent or "structural" features of the growth have originated from the outside. These have come in the form of loans, official assistance, and the expansion in world markets ... the impetus has come mainly from without.'[22]

Thus subjected to extensive and intensive penetration of its economy by powers such as the US, Japan and the rest of the OECD Five as well as the NICs, the Philippines finds itself hyperfeminized in its relations. It is not an accident that the American expression 'to fuck someone over' means to exploit or abuse someone, and 'to be fucked up' means to be abused in a perverted way. Nor is it surprising that the homophobic cast of the notion of perversion operating here carries over to international affairs.[23] The way in which this dominant fantasy of sexual relations has developed as an essential condition of advanced capitalism might be traced through the history of imperialism up to the present. Indeed, one could show that the hyperfeminization of certain countries signifies their condensation of the contradictory symptoms of patriarchy, modern heterosexism, colonialism and imperialism. Thus the hyperfeminization of the Philippines is a historically new phenomenon, which is not to say that this process of objectification did not exist earlier, for it might be argued that the production of the prostitute as a feminine ideal has long been a cultural corollary to commodity fetishism in the age of capitalism, and that it is on these grounds that feminization can be seen to signify the process of management through investment (such was the new mode of control of the colonies in the age of imperialism). But what is new is the way in which prostitution has become a dominant mode of production of neo-colonial nations in late capitalism — that is, neo-colonial nations are now like prostitutes to be invested in for the extraction of surplus pleasure (wealth)[24] — and the extent to which this feminizing process has intensified on a global scale since the mid-1970s. Indeed it is the intensification of global capitalism that has led to the visible manifestation of its internal contradictions in the catastrophe of developing nations — the sexual fantasy is henceforth literally realized on the bodies of women. That is to say, this hyperfeminization is not merely metaphorical but translates into the concrete exploitation and abuse of actual women.

SEXUAL LABOUR AND COMMERCE

In the case of the Philippines this phenomenon is most clearly seen in the feminization of exploited labour. 'The export-oriented, debt-propelled strategy has given rise to the global commodification of Third World women in the form of female labour export, exploitation of their cheap labour power and their utilization through sexual trade, whether it be in the legitimate "tourism" or hospitality and mail-order bride business or in prostitution which has phenomenally spread.'[25] Indeed, what the case of the Philippines and other Southeast Asian nations demonstrates is the veritable feminization of the Third World of Asia (rather than simply the Third World, which was once synonymous with Asia). In these countries the sexuality of commerce thus necessarily means the commerce of feminine sexuality, that is, the selling and trading of women forced or induced into the prostitution industry not only within these countries but internationally as well.

In the Philippines, there are between 300,000–500,000 prostitutes[26] working not only in the areas surrounding the US bases servicing American military men on leave but also in Japanese-owned hotels catering to Japanese business men on vacation. The 'boom of the sex industry' is only the necessary consequence of the 'development' of a larger hospitality industry, that is, one that hosts the capital and arms of touring men[27] and multinationals. In fact, the establishment of the Ministry of Tourism in 1973 was a key achievement of the Marcos State in its revitalized efforts to transform the nation into a lucrative business beginning with the declaration of Martial Law: 'Before 1973 the Philippines was not much of a tourist spot. The combination of street crime and well-organized demonstrations against American imperialism and the Vietnam War created a less-than-friendly environment for a fun seeker. When President Ferdinand Marcos declared martial law on

21 September 1972, a lot of that changed. Criminals were rounded up and the political opposition jailed. In 1973 the Ministry of Tourism was established with former Marcos press agent Jose Aspiras in charge, and the number of visitors rapidly increased from less than 150,000 in 1971 to more than a million in 1980.'[28] With the military imposition of stability in an otherwise crisis-ridden country, the number of hotels and tourists, multinationals and investors increased rapidly. Martial law was not, however, merely the whim of a dictator in pursuit of power (although that was undoubtedly at work as well), but part of the engineering of a new economic order necessary to meet the intensified demands of global capitalism. Marcos' indebtedness to the World Bank and the IMF, for which the Filipino people are still paying dearly, is only the logical consequence of the latter's instrumental role in this cooperative prostitution of the country through 'authoritarian modernization':[29]

> [T]he Bank set in motion in the Philippines a development program with two key objectives: 'pacification' and 'liberalization'. The pacification component consisted of rural and urban development programs aimed at defusing rural and urban unrest. Liberalization referred to the drastic restructuring of Philippine industry and external trade strategy to open up the country more completely to the flow of US capital and commodities. To implement this strategy of 'technocratic modernization', the Bank encouraged the formation of an authoritarian government and carefully cultivated a technocratic elite.[30]

Having mostly been educated in the US, this elite was heavily influenced by the Keynesian revolution in economics during the 1950s and the principles of technocracy, which were 'fine-tuned' during the 1960s. Thus the technocrats who replaced the industrial elite in the 1970s could be said to share 'a strong sense of fraternity with their World Bank and IMF counterparts'.[31] As one columnist wrote in 1981, 'Now we're completely under the thumbs of the IMF because our principal planners are IMF boys.'[32]

This situation hardly changed when Corazon Aquino came into power in 1986 — the fraternal identification with these governing bodies of international finance transcended national changes. Hence

Aquino's finance minister, Jaime Ongpin, could sincerely claim, 'I don't blame the IMF for what they did. If I were in their shoes, I would have been tougher.'[33] Such are the outstanding young men of the nation whose consolidation with the government and fraternal bonding with international economists, financiers and other managers of nations was the single-handed, multi-armed achievement of Martial Law. Part of the legacy of Martial Law is the desire for authoritarian (masculine) rule evidenced in the repeatedly expressed desire on the part of many Filipinos for a 'strong leader' (in complaints, for example, that Aquino was not 'man enough' for the position), a desire stoked not only by the absence of Marcos and fuelled by the tradition of patronage politics, but now especially by the ostensible success of authoritarian regimes in NICs.

With Marcos and his boys and cronies manning the nation, modernization and militarism went hand in hand in restructuring the economy, now characterized by import liberalization, privatization, foreign capital-dependent and export-oriented industry. Free Trade Zones and tourist belts were essential components of the government's 'incentive packages' to attract capital to the Philippines, and thus similar in constitution. Both relied on a predominantly female and wholly feminized labour force. Both employed a 'get laid or get laid off' policy. In the case of the tourist industry, labour and raw material were the same: women. It is not an accident that 'Sin-city', Manila, the 'sex-capital of the world',[34] was touted and fashioned by Imelda Marcos as 'the City of Man'. The 'beautification' projects meant to raise Manila to the level of a modern metropolis in order to compete for international attention and capital (see chapter 2) only evidences the veritable state 'prostitution' of the Philippines. This means not only the selling of women but the feminization and parceling out of the land: in Ermita, the red-light district in Manila, different zones of bars and clubs are owned and primarily patronized by different nationalities, so that one could identify, for example, an Australian strip or a German one, and so forth — a free trade zone which makes Manila into a multinational brothel.[35] Thus one could in all truth declare, 'The government is not only selling women to foreigners, but also the sovereignty of the nation itself'.[36]

IMPERIAL SONS, NATIONAL PIMPS

The rise of a 'strong-man' regime was a World Bank-endorsed response to the growing and intensifying crises felt in the nation as a result of the political and economic system installed by US colonization being pushed to its limits by the acceleration of global capital. Other developing countries underwent similar post-war crises and responded with similar 'strong-man' regimes.[37] The nationalist tenor of these Third World dictatorships only manifests that, defined in the age of imperialism, nation-statehood is figured and operates in certain masculine terms. The Philippines' own early experience with nascent nationalism in the late nineteenth century evidences this form of masculinization, a masculinization that found its symptomatic expression in the militarism of inter-imperial rivalry. Given these conditions and the infantilization of the colonies that predominated in an earlier age, early anti-imperialistic nationalism could only be articulated as a son's demand for independence and sovereignty:

> ... the nation is gendered and domesticated within the circle of sacrifice and the idealization of loss that binds the child-patriot to this motherland. By doing so, the patriot not only expresses his love but also reverses the relationship of dependency between mother and child. He posits his future authority over her, imagining himself and others like him as potential patrons, 'bequeathing' to the *patria* the legacy of freedom. In this way, the motherland inherits from her sons an 'immense fortune' — a surplus of symbolic wealth with which to nurture future sons. Offspring and lover, the patriot is now also father to the nation. It is thus wholly without irony that Filipinos have regarded Rizal as the 'father' of Philippine nationalism and that one of his biographers has referred to him as the 'first Filipino'.[38]

The infantilization of the Philippines continues to be felt. Former Senator (and now, former President) Estrada expressed it when he spoke against the presence of the US bases: 'our current relations with the US is not untarnished. It's not the relation of two friends, but the relation between the master and a ward who is forcibly being suppressed to remain a child.'[39] The representation of this relation is the result of the general mode of exchange between the Philippines and the US; it is a discourse built up also from an exchange of representations that is most evident in the media. The New York Times, for example, recently wrote:

> Even among Filipinos who want the United States military to stay, it is commonly said that this is a nation that has never been allowed to progress beyond adolescence, beyond an immature need to hide behind someone or something else for protection.
>
> ... many Filipinos admit that too often they seek out godfathers rather than take responsibility for their own actions.
>
> Led by several fierce, hard-headed nationalists, who say with a touch of pride that they are willing to buck popular opinion, the Philippine Senate seems poised to try to end the country's dependence on what is being portrayed as the biggest godfather of them all, the American military ...[40]

The patronizing recognition of that 'touch of pride' is then explained (and thus legitimated) by a Filipino political analyst whose understanding of the significance of rejecting the bases affirms his identification with this infantilized image: 'It will be therapeutic, a national primal scream that may mature us.' In all such attempts to articulate the problems of the Philippine national identity, the motherland seems, however, to have disappeared; the maternal has vanished, leaving only traces of a feminine body transposed over the national territory.

Thus are the national resources configured for exploitation — as raw material for processing or export. With the government's model of development necessarily bolstering 'domestic industrialization' and other economic activities considered 'productive', meaning 'infrastructure and other capital investments that have long-term impact on the economy', women-dominated activities have to suffer. 'There is no budget support for women's subsistence and income substitution/generation economic activities, the budget makes their work, and contribution to the local and to the national economy, effectively invisible.'[41] In effect, their productive capacity is erased and their increasingly bodily labour must henceforth function as raw material for the national industries. Small scale industries and firms, subsistence agricultural production, education, the 'underground economy', all of whose labour force is predominantly comprised of women, these are activities that must be sacrificed in the name of development. The destruction of domestic income-generating activities results in the effective dispossession of the female and feminized labour force, thus making it more accessible for exploitation and circulation as commodified products. At the same time that the feminized labour force is deterritorialized — forced to seek employment abroad, pushed out of the country by the sheer absence of means of living, pulled into advanced countries by the spaces of demand for cheap and tractable labour — it is also further grounded in the female body.

With the erasure even of the reproductive function of the nation, all its resources are extricated from any organic life or vital community of their own, processed and packaged, and made ready for circulation and unimpeded exploitation. Thus is labour produced for the export-oriented policy of authoritarian modernization. In the export-processing zone, there is not much distance between human labour and raw material. Furthermore, the replacement of manual strength by machines eliminates unskilled males from the newly-tailored definition of human labour, since within a modern, patriarchally divided society, unskilled females are the preferred operators of those unfulfilled functions of the machines requiring physical dexterity, patience, tractability and long periods of immobility, all learned in the domestic sphere. As one manager explained, 'We hire girls because they have less energy, are more disciplined and are easier to control.'[42] Supervisors and managers, on the other hand, are male, thus reinforcing the configuration of industrial, technologically advanced countries where the necessary intangible services and skills, education and information technology for such positions are produced, as masculine. This gender division of symbolic capital and bodily labour into, respectively, masculine and feminine, thus results in a floating population of unemployed, unskilled men.[43] It also enables the 'sons of the nation', i.e., the technocratic and political elite at the wheel of the nation, to cooperate fraternally with international capital in the stimulation and regulation of trade flows, thereby at once becoming supervisors and pimps of the nation.

In the actual export of women coerced into the 'entertainment industry', there is no more difference between raw material and labour, for the prostitute applies her labour power to her own body in the production of herself as a commodity.⁴⁴ A testament to the ever-increasing efficiency of multinational capital, prostitutes are at once the raw material, labour and machines of new national industries in advanced countries such as Japan: 'Filipino women in Japan are grist to Japan's 10-trillon-yen-a-year sex mills. The boom in the sex industry in Japan is an indication of the economic prosperity enjoyed by that country.'⁴⁵ One might add that it is this economic prosperity without military prowess that has made Japan the leader among national sex industries. Sex takes on a crucial role in the domestic staging of political and economic fantasies of nations.

Global conditions have taken another shift. With the increase of hostilities in the Philippines, not only in the sense of antagonism to Japanese sex tours and to the presence of the American bases, but also in the sense of military and insurgent fighting, the climate has become largely unfavorable or at least precarious for foreign investments of any kind. Hence the necessity of drawing labour and raw material into the developed countries which now employ the strategy of import liberalization. The increase of hostilities within the Philippines is also symptomatic of the World Bank-determined economic strategies for development reaching their effective limits. The depletion of natural resources and destruction of the productive capacity of outmoded economic forms, especially those that have been female-dominated, have forced the transformation of an already feminized labour force into the semi-processed products that await final processing for the realization of surplus value. In this sense, and as I will discuss further in chapter 3, women are the last abundant resource of the nation — they are like the surplus products they themselves sell for subsistence, now sold themselves by their own feminized nation. Free-floating, they are 'excess liquidity' that is 'mopped up' in 'stream-lining operations' at the injunction of 'international capital'⁴⁶, their mobility now regulated by their sex (more accurately, their sexual function, which is, their penetrability⁴⁷) and their passport. Sexuality and nationality thus become deterritorialized indicators of vulnerability to exploitation, as well as instruments of such exploitation.

EXPORT ORIENTAL LABOUR

The fate of Filipino women exported to other countries as domestics and prostitutes demonstrates the logic that subjects their own feminized nation to the same treatment. The cruel scenario that becomes typified from the accumulation of recounted individual experiences presents itself as the same operations that have cohered through the process of history into a system of exploitation of the Third World. Yayori Matsui, a Japanese journalist, reports that in 1988 there were 7,000–8,000 Filipinas who were working as domestic helpers in Singapore and 30,000 working in Hong Kong.[48] She also reports that nearly 100,000 Asian migrant women working as 'entertainers in the booming sex industry' enter Japan each year, 90% of whom come from the Philippines, Thailand and Taiwan, and 80% of that total coming from the Philippines.[49] 'Usually they are picked up by recruiters in their own countries and sent to Japan with a promise or contract stating that they will work as waitresses, models or ordinary hostesses (not engaging in prostitution). However, in reality, they are sold out by the recruiters to promoters in Japan … The women are then sold again, by the Japanese promoters, to clubs or other sex business owners, at double the price. Sometimes they are simply rented at a monthly charge of US$1,600 to US$6,400. In order to cover such expenses, the owners force the women into prostitution, taking advantage of their vulnerability, the prime cause of which is their illegal visa status. Without the protection visa status affords, there is no limit to the abuse and exploitation that these women may have to face.' The sexual relations that marked the Philippines' political and economic links with the US have become literally realized in the case of Japan — military prowess and domination has in Japan become masculine prowess and domination, international politics acted out by male sexual violation, military arms translated into raping penises. As one reporter described:

> I visited the tiny theater where Maria was working. On the stage of the smoke-filled room, just big enough for 40 people, she stood naked. Then an announcement was heard: 'We have something special tonight, a direct import from the Philippines! Come and get it, quick!' An office worker type climbed up to the stage, and dropped his pants. I saw Maria raped again and again, in full view of the audience.[50]

But the international economy of forced prostitution is not simply a symptom of Japan's repressed political fantasies — it is in fact a constitutive part of the current mode of relations between Japan and the third world populations[51] from which she derives her economic prosperity. The series of transactions between recruiters and promoters and sex business owners are analogous to the series of transactions between national and multinational bodies regulating trade flows of capital, goods and labour. With intangible services, information and technology dominated by multinational production, nations such as the Philippines and other Southeast Asian countries are reduced to providing physical labour, which makes the national government no more than a recruiting agency for the sale of its feminized labour to markets in more advanced economies. Indeed, it is the government that does the 'mopping up of excess liquidity' for smooth transfers and expedient profits. To the extent that it functions as a multinational corporation, the Asian-Pacific community acts as the promoting agency which secures the uninterrupted flows between the recruiters and the business owners by functioning as a regional membrane managing individual national interests. Finally, multinational companies and industries function like the sex business owners — the employers of feminized labour from various developing countries.

With appalling frequency, women have been found to have been kept in physical, psychological and financial bondage. Locked in cells, their passports and air tickets confiscated, and desperate to earn money for their families as well as for themselves (in some cases, if only to buy a ticket home and, perhaps in all cases, to earn a pass to freedom), they are in no easy position to resist the brutally enforced sex work for which they were imported. In fact, those who do resist are physically and sexually abused — raped, beaten and starved, often to the point of critical or fatal injury. The irony of this situation is that their bodies abroad are worth more than their skills and education at home. Produced as physical commodities, they cease to be treated as humans. To their consumer-clients, they are indeed what they are advertised (on t-shirts around the US bases) to be: 'little brown fucking machines powered by rice'. More than a hundred years ago, Gustave Flaubert observed that 'the oriental woman is no more than a machine: she makes no distinction between one man and another man'.[52] The equivalence of the oriental woman and a sexual machine was already functioning then in congruence with the relations of imperial nations and their colonies. It only took a global shift in those relations in the age of neo-colonialism to equate the two terms with the entire economy of the colony, now an 'independent' developing nation. But it is precisely because of the historical development of these colonies from political appendages to economic dependents that developing nations, particularly their labour, now operate as sexual machines for their developed 'masters' (the word used to designate the club owners).

Like the women who are rented out to clients, transnationally developing nations operate through the subcontracting of their properties, whether buildings, facilities, land or labour, to client companies. In the words of Industry Minister Ongpin: 'We are paying special attention to ... international subcontracting, where we provide facilities for large multinationals to come in and do the more labour-intensive aspects of their operations in this country.'[53] What this provision of facilities entails, however, is a specialization which destroys the nation's productive capacities and reduces it to a field of operations, a place 'to come in and do ...' — very much the way these women are reduced to a sexual function. Short-term investments and limited time horizons are merely economic equivalents of the 'short-times' clients enjoy with their prostitutes, a practice that belies the promise of permanent friendships and financial security. This is a lesson the United States continually teaches because it has epitomized the practice in the actions of its servicemen. As one bar waitress asserted: 'While they are here, they love you very much. Then they return to the States and you are forgotten. They take no more notice of you. They might support you for one year, but they tire of that and see someone new in the States.'[54] The difference between this relation, however, and that of transnational corporations and their feminized labour is, in the latter there is neither pretense nor hope of love. The relations have been streamlined into efficient versions of what they always were: strictly economic transactions. Corporations are not personified in the same way nations are, hence their operations manifest more blatantly the mode of relations they are founded upon.

While transnational corporations seem to transcend the ideologies and boundaries of nations, their existence and prosperity nevertheless do depend upon them. The possibility, for example, of extracting and enslaving labour rests on the nation-state and its institutions. Passports and visas become both a means of protection and a means of exploitation. National differences also become a means of disempowerment. Immigrant women in Japan are imprisoned in the confines of their national languages and cultures. At the same time, however, national unities also function as a means of empowerment. Thai women in Japan appear, in some accounts, to be more oppressed than Filipino women because the Thai community is smaller than the Filipino community, and therefore they have less access to organized efforts to address their problems.[55] Nevertheless, nationalities are used as instruments of exploitation. The fact that Filipino women are imported in Japan to replace the Japanese (and to some extent Okinawan) sex workers who used to service US soldiers in Okinawa demonstrates that certain national ideologies of discrimination and 'difference' are at work here.[56]

It is curious that while the Japanese have historically been referred to as 'Orientals' by Westerners, it is other Asians, specifically people from developing nations within Asia, who are referred to by the Japanese as 'Orientals'. Statements in the Japanese press like 'Asian women are favorite goods with "Oriental Charm" and an exoticism for Western and Japanese men' and 'Japan's sex industry has need of Asian women, especially Filipinas'[57] shows the extent to which Japan has come to distinguish herself from Asia. A feeling of racial superiority is not new to Japan, nor is a culture of patriarchy. What is new is the merging of these discourses of race, sex, and capital in multinational industries and in the production of a new species of inferior beings:

> There is a general feeling among the Japanese that they are superior to other races, but especially to the peoples of the Southeast Asian region. A Japanese priest confessed in a meeting with Filipino priests that Japanese Catholics looked down on Filipinos in Japan, who as a rule are Catholics, as 'the kind of people who would do anything for money'.
>
> 'Most Japanese are allergic to Filipinos who scare them as bearers of some infectious disease,' said the Japanese priest.[58]

Indeed what in the prevailing fantasy defines prostitutes and Orientals in their inferiority is financial parasitism, moral depravity, sexual proclivity and communicable disease. And since the political weakness and economic dependence of nations marks them as inferior, it is not difficult to see how the equivalence between developing nations, Orientals and prostitutes can be made. Japan herself has not been immune to this hierarchic configuration of nations. Thus at another time, 'in order to convince the West that it was really in earnest and civilized enough to be treated as an equal, Japan had to fight and win a war'.[59] One might, in the vein of this fantasy, explain the heavily documented Japanese bestial treatment of imported prostitutes in part by the historical emasculation of Japan. For equality in the international community requires proof of a certain kind of masculinity and the debasement of a certain kind of femininity or, better, feminization. However, one must also bear in mind the possibility that for Japanese women the imported prostitutes are not merely 'feminine' and not really women, but altogether a different species. As Matsui interprets Japanese gender relations: 'Men buying prostitutes is never socially condemned, nor is women's acceptance of it condemned — women often say: "If my husband goes to a 'professional' woman, it's not a problem, but if he is attracted to an ordinary woman, I get hurt and jealous." Such a double standard of women is still deep-rooted among the Japanese and they consider the prostitute as a special kind of woman, and fail to treat them as human beings and to accord them their human rights.'[60] While the 'double standard' might arguably be attributable to Japan's patriarchal structure, feudal history and tradition of 'prostitution', it must also be seen as the result of a new configuration of any such historical social systems within an advanced capitalist economy. The elevation of women's status in Japan in areas not 'traditionally' open to them necessitates the displacement of the contradictory conditions of capital, which they too have historically borne, on other peoples. At the same time, women in Japan can find their place in society by either joining the white-collar workforce, the masculine sphere, or remaining in the home as housewives and mothers, the feminine sphere; in other words, in the global orientation of this economy there are two dominant paths that are open for those who have the means of staying human whether one is male or female: to act productive or to be reproductive, to act masculine or to be feminine. Within the scenarios of fantasy-production, anything outside of this dichotomy thus becomes relegated to the less than human, reduced to the 'professional' animal or thing.

FAMILIAL & PEDOPHILIC EXPLOITATION

So far I have been speaking of the feminization of developing labour. But as the Philippines' relations with the United States and Japan (as paradigms of power) show, in this context, feminization also necessarily means dehumanization, and emasculation necessarily means debasement. Within a Japanese-style management system in which the company takes on a feudal familial structure, those who are not seen as productive sons or reproductive daughters are food for machines. Feminized objects can have no human role in this system. Increasingly multinational corporations, and the nations whose filial loyalties they command, are adopting this family mode of organization (even as it has come into crisis in Japan) — hence the call for 'families of nations'. Soon the international community will be dominated by 'first families' (also called regional blocs) of the world. The Asia-Pacific Economic Community is one such bid to becoming a first (world) family-corporation, one that will rival the other family-corporation building up in Europe. But within this family are collectives of labour, which embody all the historical contradictions of international capital, which therefore cannot 'mature' in order to compete with or equal the nations that have established themselves as their parents. At the same time they are rendered incapable of producing or reproducing their own means of subsistence. In this way, they are supposed as being like children or things. This is the condition of the Philippines within the Asia-Pacific family — subject to a socio-libidinal economy that deploys deterritorialized relations of power through sex and money.

Ward, child, mistress, commodity — the Philippines is a historical condensation of these different relations tending towards equivalence, an equivalence that does not rest easy but which must continually be secured through systematic violence. But the tendency towards equivalence is evident in the mass production of a new commodity, the child-prostitute. The phenomenal scale of forced prostitution of children in Southeast Asian nations is yet another testament to the subordination, infantilization and feminization at work in the production of labour-material necessary to maintain the level of prosperity attained by advanced economies such as Japan and the NICs. Lured by promises of prosperity and familial security and coerced by the dire circumstances of their lives if not by their own desperate and equally desiring parents, children are turning into the raw material of an intensified prostitution industry. In Japan as well as in an expanding roster of other client-countries (not least of all within Philippine urban centers, where children are 'imported' from the countryside) the average age of imported prostitutes is decreasing rapidly due to several related factors: the increasing fierceness of competition in the sex industry, the increasing organized resistance of women, and the increasing risk of AIDS.[61] Hence the great demand for young, tractable, virgin boys and girls.

What this phenomenal explosion of forced child prostitution demonstrates is the constant need for capital to produce new commodities and the desire to consume them. The debt-servicing policy of developing nations is using up all traditional and non-traditional (such as feminized labour) resources and is now exploiting new non-traditional products: children. Hence in 1990 the United Nations Children's Emergency Fund (UNICEF) could truthfully report that 'the heaviest burden of the debt crisis is falling on the growing minds and bodies of children in the developing world'.[62] UNICEF's concern, however, only reveals itself as a concern for capital. As a deputy executive of UNICEF put it: 'Human capital is a far more important factor in economic growth than physical capital. Investment in a human capital in the form of nutrition, basic education, and health cannot be postponed … The underemphasized tragedy of the disinvestments in human capital in the 1980s is that the results will be carried forward in stunted bodies and deficient educations well into the twenty-first century.'[63] In other words, children are another resource for multinational capital to invest in. But as the child-prostitution industry attests, children need not be long-term investments — they are marketable now. If the price of production of a prostitute is minimal, the cost to produce a child-prostitute is even less. Such is the cold logic of the Free World.

Within the Free World, therefore, pedophilic exploitation is only an intensified mode of the relations already prevailing between multinational corporations and their developing labour. With these international pedophilic tendencies in mind it is difficult to see how any familial harmony can be achieved within the Asia-Pacific community. For the regional security it promises means the exploitation, disempowerment and enforced dependency of feminized and infantilized collectives — the poor Southeast Asian relations of the OECD Five and the NICs. The call for privatization in the current movement towards global incorporation is therefore a call for the privatization of the antagonisms and crises of nations. It is, in effect, a privatization of the violence endemic to global capital. With the effacement of nations in the creation and incorporation of new global families, emerges a deterritorialized Third World — a new 'race' of infantilized, feminized and commodified peoples distributed over the world, motoring globalized production (See chapter 3). It is, therefore, no longer a matter of nations acting like people but, rather, of people embodying their nations. The libidinal character of national economies makes it easier for the crises of nations to become at once deterritorialized and grounded in the bodies of people. Those who occupy the mobile, masculine ranks of global management are free to move and accumulate profit like capital but those who remain in the sluggish, feminized terrain of labour must bodily bear the burden of their nations.

Such is the prospect of the labouring populations of developing nations such as the Philippines. It is indeed a dim prospect. And yet the existence of other such collectives leaves space for hope, for other desires to emerge within this already over-determined region. Whence the efforts to redefine the community, to seek alliances with the collectives that share the burden of capital's contradictions. Instead of the desire for 'security', which condemns the labouring populations of nations like the Philippines to an increasingly oppressive existence, alternative voices are calling for solidarity with other Third World collectives — solidarity based not on a shared region or a common investment in the Free World, but a solidarity based on common struggles of alternative imagination and visions of a cooperative political strength yet to be founded. As one such voice expressed:

There is an international network in Asia and the Pacific of advocacy for a wide range of social, economic, and political issues heretofore unimagined, much less articulated: denuclearization, demilitarization or disarmament, rights of indigenous or ethnic peoples to their ancestral domain, human rights as guaranteed by international covenants to individuals and groups, development with consultation and consent, environmental protection (which daily grows into a universal concern of critical proportions), and increasingly, women's and children's rights and welfare.

It is incumbent upon the governments of ASEAN and the Pacific community of island states to seriously consider the possibility of a continuing dialogue with these advocates, whose rallying cry has been 'regional solidarity' based on common causes and shared problems, instead of the more unstable and potentially more volatile ideal of 'regional security' which has traditionally drawn strength from the realpolitik of confrontation, containment and the balance of power.[64]

This is the challenge that the concept of the Asia-Pacific poses — not as an economic network of dominant classes, but as an emergent political constituency composed of peoples desiring an alternative community. Instead of a non-aligned movement which only secures the citizenship of these countries in the Free World, labouring populations within the Asia-Pacific (and not their representative governments) must engage in a movement of alliances not for aggression but for the assertion of shared desires for self-determination and for the strength to forge an alternative international community that does not buy into another fantasy of the Free World. In other words, we must struggle against the practices that reproduce the political-libidinal relations of our present lives and engage in alternative modes of production in order to realize a more just form of community. But we can only begin working for this if in our actions we are already dreaming other worlds in other ways.

2002: Since its emergence in the dominant field of fantasy-production, the Asia Pacific has figured in countless dreams. In just over a decade, that it was ever a new invention — able to generate giddy visions of strange and exciting futures, to call forth unexpected alliances and applications, and to cast worldly possibilities in a new light — seems entirely lost to its present-day users, having attained the status of a mundane material fact no more remarkable than the highway overpass or the cellular phone.[65] As I will argue in the next chapter, however, infrastructures and technologies such as highway overpasses and cellular phones are themselves the means and products of new modalities of fantasy-production. To the extent that it has become a real entity and location — that is, insofar as there is a *there* there — the Asia Pacific now serves as a pathway, and not merely an object, of new and changed desires.

WORLD DREAM ORDERS

Many desiring-actions on the part of governments, corporate and finance capitalists, social movements and peoples have made and continue to make the Asia Pacific into a real place. In 1992, after almost a hundred years of anti-imperialist struggles, the US finally withdrew its military bases in the Philippines, the precipitous result of the combined pressure of popular and radical nationalist movements and of growing neo-liberal trends among the local elite. This greatly symbolic historical event was quickly followed by the aggressive building and consolidation of intra-regional political, economic and cultural networks through APEC (Asia Pacific Economic Cooperation), ASEAN (Association of Southeast Asian Nations), Asian Star Cable TV, and other power- and capital-intensive dream organs of national and multinational elites. With projects such as AFTA (Asian Free Trade Agreement), which was ratified by ASEAN in 1992, and the astonishingly rapid growth rates exhibited by the 'tiger' economies, excitement over unprecedented regional prosperity and cooperation in the New World Order overrode the Cold War concern for regional 'security'.

While these projects have largely represented the conflicting interests of the new regional ruling classes, advocating for example alternately protectionist and liberalizing agendas for individual nations as well as for the region as a whole, other intra-regional networks and social movements have also risen to oppose and challenge the dominant dream-forces of the globalizing Free World fantasy. In 1996, for example, the People's Conference Against Imperialist Globalization (PCAIG) was organized to take place in Metro Manila in opposition to the Fourth APEC leaders Summit scheduled a day earlier.[66] The 18 heads of state comprising APEC agreed upon the common objective to 'enhance the competitive environment in the Asia-Pacific region' through the implementation of national competition policies. In contrast, the 123 delegates from 30 countries and 53 Philippine delegates attending the People's Conference resolved to reject APEC and it's program for increased trade liberalization, financial deregulation, privatization of national industries and market-driven economies and confirmed their commitment to mass-based movements committed to people's interests.[67] Although often largely divergent and even opposed in vision and practice, the dream-actions of state organs such as APEC and those of non- or anti-state organs such as NGOs, activist organizations and people's organizations all contribute to the very material realization of the Asia Pacific as a *region*, within which and over which significant social struggles nevertheless continue to be fought.

That the Asia Pacific region has become a social and material fact — a real place — does not mean then that it is an uncontested reality nor that it is any less imaginary than it was upon the moment of its invention. Epeli Hau'ofa has, among others, sought to underscore the contingency and mutability of the dominant land-based imaginings that support the historical diminishment and subordination of Pacific peoples.[68] He contrasts the discourses of economic development, whose 'smallness view' he traces to the nineteenth-century imperialist reduction of the boundless world of Oceania into contained territories and islands of the Pacific, with the actual life practices of ordinary people traversing across the artificial territorial boundaries of neocolonialism. Far beneath the desiring-order of bureaucrats, politicians and economic planners that sustains neo-colonial relationships of dependency between Oceania and the advanced capitalist economies of Australia, New Zealand and the US, 'there exists that other order, of ordinary people who are busily and independently redefining their world in accordance with their perceptions of their own interests, and of where the future lies for their children and their children's children'.[69]

Hau'ofa's vision has been considered utopic and romantic by some, and yet it is part of a broader material re-imagining of the region, a re-imagining that was already at work in the multinational dream of an Asia Pacific community and continues to operate in the transnational dream of global capitalism. Not surprisingly, his argument that the expansion of the world economy in the post-World War II era helped to liberate ordinary people from the legacy of colonial confinements finds consonance with the new fantasy of globalization as the liberated flows of capital, goods and people surpassing the geo-political, economic and socio-cultural limits of the nation. Inasmuch as they contest the older territorial fantasy of the Free World, within which the regional dream of the Asia Pacific takes form, such oceanic desires on the part of ordinary people also become the new forces of dreamwork commandeered for capitalism.[70] In giving full expression and support to these oceanic desires, Hau'ofa's vision thus participates in realizing the transformation of the geo-imaginary of fantasy-production from a world of nation-states to a world beyond nation-states.

Even this relatively new 'ground' of fantasy-production is, however, in the course of being revised. The renewed presence of some 1,600 US troops in the Philippines under the mantle of the global war on terrorism launched by the de facto US military-police regime attests to the way that the region is once again actively being re-dreamt into a new geopolitical configuration.[71] In 1999, after much lobbying on the part of Washington since the rejection of the new bases treaty in 1991, the Philippines signed the Visiting Forces Agreement (VFA) with the United States. The VFA, which allows the US continued 'access rights' to the Philippines under the provision of 'training exercises', has been used by both governments to legitimate this current US military base in the Southern Philippines. From this base, a geopolitical line of potential offense is drawn along an axis of 'evil' nations purportedly harboring weapons of mass destruction. The axis from East to West Asia, specifically from North Korea to Iraq, cuts right through the harmonious whole of the New World Order, and its regional incarnation in the Asia Pacific community. It also connects two previously separated imaginative geographies, Asia and the Middle East, in a veritable re-integration of the two Orients into a single 'theater of operations' for a re-testosteronized Western civilization embarking on its widely-known and awaited destined clash with the Islamic world. This fateful line drawn between the first and second fronts in the US war on terrorism (respectively, Afghanistan and the Philippines) thus also reconfigures the global fantasy of a borderless region that quickly followed on the heels of the New World Order. Against the neo-liberal global fantasy of a world without borders that has held sway over the major regional economies throughout the last decade of the twentieth century, the emerging global political dispensation led by the US security state is dreaming new territorial world boundaries into being.[72]

In the New World Order, the fantasy of families of nations, which was realized through regional economic blocs such as the EEU (European Economic Union), NAFTA (North American Free Trade Agreement) and APEC, aimed to supersede the fantasy of East-West relations of the Cold War era and to subsume the North-South antagonisms of the post-Cold War era. Despite the initial euphoria and material successes of its realization, this has not been an easy fantasy to sustain. The 1990s saw both the spectacular rise of East Asian and Southeast Asian economies (South Korea, Taiwan, and Singapore, as well as Thailand, Indonesia, Malaysia and the Philippines), in what was dubbed the Asian miracle, and the sudden meltdown of the same economies in the Asian financial crisis of 1997. In less than ten years, the fantasy of world harmony that surged with the fall of the last symbolic remnant of the Cold War, the Berlin Wall, found itself mirrored in the shards of the broken promises of the 'Asia Pacific Age of Fortunes'. Such rapid miraculous rises and catastrophic crises, including the skyrocketing New Economy exemplified by Silicon Valley (and its recent free fall), overtaking the regulatory control of national and international governments; the challenges to existing state powers by expanding transnational networks of activists and terrorists, exemplified by the anti-WTO and anti-globalization movements and the bombings of the Oklahoma City building and the World Trade Center; and in general the intensified antagonistic confrontations between contenders for global power and radical people's movements — in a word, the explosive proliferation and amplification of social struggles on a global scale since the 1991 Gulf War have led many to characterize the world of the succeeding decade as a New World Disorder.

In the recent juridical acts passed and the military actions taken by the US military-police state, yet another globalist fantasy is in the making, set to introduce a pernicious clarity and predictability into the putative reigning chaos of the world of globalization. After a longer period of assault, first by people's struggles everywhere, and second by the finance capitalist appropriation of the real gains made by such social struggles through economic liberalization and deregulation, the military-political sector of the global ruling class is currently seeking re-enfranchisement.[73] From the perspective of this faction of the global ruling class, which perceived itself to be losing power and wealth to new players in the new global economy, September 11 was the climactic result and encapsulation of the New World Disorder. The 'war without borders' is meant to fix this catastrophe. What is effectively the imposition of global martial law with the proclamation of a permanent state of emergency is an attempt on the part of this global faction to re-align nation-states across both East-West and North-South axes along an imperial axis. The 'global war on terror', in other words serves as a measure to organize 'free, democratic' nations into an international political-military tributary system of 'strong' (in the third world, 'warlord') states, a system modeled on the tyrannical postcolonial regimes long sponsored by the United States government and its military-industrial and multinational corporate patrons. Partly intended to disrupt the regional economic networks that continue to threaten US hegemony with ever-greater marginalization, this tributary system of crony states, led by none other than the US Superstate, would be supported by a reinvigorated resource-based extractive economy grafted onto the high technology industries of finance capital.[74] Welcome to the post-September 11 World Reorder.

My point in providing this extended summary and broad sketch of the major geopolitical shifts of the last ten years is to consider the changes in the gendered and libidinal dynamics of the global and regional dreaming that the Philippines and its representatives participate in.

Of the sexual economies that I mapped out earlier, what has changed and what remains the same? It would appear that in the era of globalization that quickly followed the New World Order the nation-state — the fundamental component of fantasy-production — has become shakier than ever. The intense debates held in scholarly as well as realpolitik circles about the role of the nation in a globalized world only shows, however, that the denaturalization of this world-historical unit of representation and production demands ever more active constructions of new fantasy-scenarios, which involve nations as well as other emergent global actors such as diasporic social formations and transnational networks. Subjectivity and its constitutive aspects — race, gender and sexuality — continue to exercise great determinative force, I would argue, in these practical constructions and reconstructions of national, multinational and global agency.

We need only look at the vengeful, desperate and murderous expressions of militarist state masculinity everywhere trying to seize and hold on to 'resources' (oil, territory, people) that are everywhere moving beyond their control to recognize the libidinal dynamics of the apparently objective political and economic vicissitudes I have just described. As Rosalind Petchesky has written of the post-September 11 retaliatory cocking of the US 'permanent war machine', 'global capitalist masculinism is alive and well but concealed in its Eurocentric, racist guise of "rescuing" downtrodden, voiceless Afghan women from the misogynist regime it helped bring to power'.[75] The US beefs up its security state in cowboy rhetoric and rules, ready to do battle with the ever-troublesome 'neopatriarchal states' of the Middle East, which with plenty of arms encouragement during the Cold War have developed a master criminal figure of its own, bold enough for the global supercop to take as its 'dark doppelgänger'.[76] Needless to say, all the players in these scenarios are figures of men at war.

In the meantime, within the Asia Pacific, the marriage of interests that once characterized US-Japan relations has changed, as has the Philippine-American romance. When the Japanese Prime Minister Koizumi rushed to Washington soon after the attacks on the World Trade Center to offer his nation's solidarity and help through the Self Defense Force, he was pressed with the question of Japan's bad debts. 'Japan has been the sick man of global capitalism for over a decade, since the bursting of its eighties' bubble, but the situation is now deteriorating fast. The malaise has spread from the banking and finance sectors to infect the whole system, draining life from a once confident and powerful economy.'[77] It would appear that despite its efforts to buddy up with Western Europe, notably in its financial backing of the Gulf War (the original post-Cold War masculinist 'rescue' mission, triggered by the 'rape' of Kuwait by Iraq),[78] Japan's subsequent economic deflation and decade-long recession has made it somewhat of a diseased pariah in the international fraternity. In spite of this, it is clear that Japan has maintained its membership in the ranks of masculine nations, as evidenced by its sick man status (sick but nevertheless still a man). Today, however, all nation-states are masculine, even if, as the case of the Philippines shows, the more peripheral among them continue to experience a certain amount of 'gender trouble' (more on this in the succeeding chapters).[79]

In the recent signing of an anti-terrorism treaty between the US and the now ten members of the ASEAN, Malaysian Foreign Minister Syed Hamid Albar commented: 'This is not a case of Big Brother United States imposing on ASEAN. This is something that both ASEAN and the United States want.'[80] Although Albar's comment recalls the infantilizing fantasies of neocolonialism expressed in the phrase 'little brown brothers' first used by William Howard Taft to refer to Filipinos at the turn of the century (while also alluding to Orwell's portrayal of totalitarianism), it's overt refusal of these fantasies also reveals a changed situation for Southeast Asian nations. Equal, democratic partnership is the new conceit. ASEAN nations are models of the rational, free, self-interested political-economic man, seeking mergers rather than marriages.[81] And while 'security' is once again on the agenda, it is much less the desired outcome of national romances than the cooperative activity that guarantees participants their state shares of liberty, equality and fraternity. No wonder then that at this latest Asian regional security meeting, US Secretary of State Colin Powell's rendition of the 'South Pacific' romantic theme song, 'Some Enchanted Evening', with lyrics bent to foreign relations, was not seen as a symbolic recapitulation of his military-diplomatic mission — i.e., to woo Southeast Asian nation-states into a new security arrangement with the US. The serenade was simply 'a good break' in the chummy negotiations for 'mutual commitments'.[82]

The presumption of masculine profiles by third world Asian nation-states is not, of course, a sudden development nor is it by any means a reversal of the feminization I described and instantiated earlier. The fraternal identification of third world national-political elites with their first world counterparts has long been posited by the structure of imperialism. Of course, under imperialism, the rivalry and fraternity of nation states were confined to imperial powers. Only with the decline of Euro-American hegemony signaled by the rise of the Asia Pacific as a new center of gravity for global capitalism do the hitherto emasculated East Asian nation states emerge as masculine contenders for global power.[83] And as East Asian nation states grew globally 'competitive', rising Southeast Asian nations quickly followed (gendered and sexual) suit. This is, as I've emphasized, not a matter of mere ideological troping (unless we recognize, as Donna Haraway reminds us, 'the tropic quality of all material-semiotic processes').[84] The transformation of the heteronormative sexual scenarios of bilateral Asia Pacific relations marks a reorganization of international political and economic practices along more multilateral, homosocial lines.

Before Japan became the sick man of global capitalism, the Philippines was already widely known as the sick man of Asia. The Ramos administration (1992–1998) was supposed to have changed that with 'Philippines 2000', its bid for the country to join the roster of NICs by the millennium through strategies of liberalization of foreign investments and the deregulation and privatization of national industries. As Ramos announced near the end of his term, 'the sick man of Asia has gotten out of the hospital'.[85] Then, the Philippines was being touted as a 'cub' in a den of 'tiger' economies. The gender of this figuration was unstated but unquestionable. 'Tiger' stood not only for aggressive industrial growth but neo-patriarchal states, neo-Confucian social orders and monopoly businesses run on family 'Asian values'. Those economies, as exemplified by the case of South Korea, depended on the destruction of women-dominated subsistence production and the displacement of feminized labour-intensive, light manufacturing industries either in free trade/export-processing zones or offshore sites (cheaper Southeast Asian countries, such as the Philippines). They also crucially depended on, as particularly embodied by Singapore, a 'strong' authoritarian state 'manning' the nation. The Philippines' thus far failed attempts to replicate these conditions — in no small measure a consequence of indefatigable organized women's and people's movements and dynamic, socially inventive, cultural-economic struggles of everyday life — constitute the continuing crisis it presents to the region as a whole.

With the dream of regional economic integration steadily realized, global 'competitiveness' has come to apply less to individual nations than to the region as a whole. In this respect, the 'cub' and 'sick man' figures serve as practical spurs for shaping up the crisis-ridden, underdeveloped Philippines for the greater good of the team. What the new regional teamwork means is reorganization of international political relations among individual nation-states towards greater cooperation through mutual security agreements and, especially in the case of the junior partners of Southeast Asia, an 'opening up' of integral national economies to multilateral, intra-regional trade and deregulated global finance capital.[86] In this context, bilateral relations supporting the heteronormative sexual scenarios, which I outlined earlier, seem to recede from view, though they have hardly disappeared. While national sovereignty continues to be a rallying point of social movements, as in the nationalism versus globalization debates, it makes little sense now, with the transnationalist dissolution of national boundaries, to speak of the 'penetration' of national economies by foreign investments as a gauge of economic weakness or feminization.[87] Once the object of government seduction schemes (recall the New York Times ad taken out by the Philippine government in 1974), foreign investment has lost its charms. It has become transformed into a mere rational necessity in the homosocial network of states trafficking in feminized labour flows.

So what then of prostitution as the dominant mode of production of neocolonial nations? As I argue in the next chapter, the national sex industry has been deregulated and privatized in a way that purges the dissolute feminized national body from the new transnational men's club in which the maturing, recuperating post-authoritarian Philippine state seeks permanent membership. And yet, to the extent that the libidinal dynamics and meanings of nationalism and capitalism remain principally unchanged, the permeability and porousness of the nation cannot but produce some gender trouble for the transnationalizing, fraternalizing state. Despite the masculine imperatives of its global participation (implied in the fraternal rivalry of 'competitiveness'), the Philippine state nevertheless depends on its feminized national bodies as its productive force and naturalized resource. Instead of overseeing a 'hospitality' industry that is territorially based, the Philippine state has had to remake itself into a flexible agency (no longer aspiring for 'sovereignty') that manages flows of people and capital exceeding its territorial control. And yet, in spite, or rather because, of the deterritorialization of the domestic through the export of national labour, domestic and international continue to be coded respectively as feminine and masculine in an attempt to regulate the contradictory forces of globalization affecting nation-state power.

It is against this slightly altered but not altogether changed historical context and mode of production in the wake of the material realization of the Asia Pacific dream, that we can understand the shift in the claims of women's movements from a nationalist emphasis on the 'prostitution' of the nation and its women to a transnationalist emphasis on the 'displacement, commodification and modern-day slavery of women' brought about 'imperialist globalization'.[88]

In the next two chapters, I discuss at length the struggles of the state in relation to the uncontrollable excess of the nation, embodied in the 'floating population' of the metropolis and the deterritorialized domestic bodies of overseas Filipino labour, that have led to its reformation. That struggle is no better physically enacted than in the state's decades-long effort to restructure its urban capital, the culmination of which is the founding of a new metropolitan form.

2

Metropolitan Dreams

MANILA'S NEW METROPOLITAN FORM

I have always experienced Metro Manila as a generally flat city. Ostensibly because of flooding problems, it has no underground transport system, nor do the majority of its houses have basements. With the exception of commercial office buildings, hotels and condominiums, most of its structures are no more than a few stories high. Moreover, there is no single public monument from where a view of the entire metropolis can be seen. As such, most people have no access to an aerial perspective. I, like most residents, maneuver around the city without a mental aerial map (without, even, a sense of North, South, East and West); instead, I get around with images of seriality, that is, routes that I can trace by imagining the flow of adjoining objects on particular pathways.[1] This is the kind of fluency one develops in a congested, view-constricted space like Manila. One might call it imaginary urban tunnelling, except that all the tunnels are aboveground. And when one moves through this saturated space, submerged in the inundation of people and matter, it is like swimming underwater in a shallow metropolitan sea.

A new metropolitan form

Since the toppling of the Marcos dictatorship and the much-touted restoration of democracy by the Aquino administration, which replaced the Marcos regime in 1986, a new metropolitan form that is altering the face of the metropolis and the experience of its spaces has emerged: 'flyovers'. (Fig. 2.1) The construction of flyovers, that is, overpasses at major interchanges, is the response of the Department of Public Works and Highways (DPWH) to the massive congestion of traffic caused by an ever-increasing population (estimated to be around 10 million). It is, in other words, a state as well as corporate[2] measure to cope with the vehicular and human flooding of the city, naturalized like the water floods the city periodically experiences as an 'overspill of growth'. The significance of flyovers, which are a new form of the built environment, extends beyond the decongestion of traffic (which, in fact, also has significant social effects). As Neil Smith writes, 'the production of space also implies the production of meaning, concepts and consciousness of space which are inseparably linked to its physical production'.[3] Congruently, one immediately observes that this new metropolitan form radically alters the cityscape, providing moving, expansive aerial perspectives not hitherto available to the greater urban population, thereby altering the space experienced by commuters and pedestrians alike. Apart from producing height and depth in a relatively flat space

Figure 2.1 Flyover construction: A new metropolitan form. Photograph from the *Philippine Daily Inquirer.*

(relative, that is, to modern industrialized cities), the flyovers displace mechanisms of orientation that rely on contiguity and concrete detail and demand a more abstract system of finding directions, such as that employed by motorists on US freeways. To inquire into the effects of this new metropolitan form *on* subjectivity is, however, to imply that the relation between physical production and the production of meaning is one of cause and effect. Even with the invocation of human practice as the mediator between material production and consciousness, the theoretical division of phenomena into these spheres curtails an analysis of the multiple ways in which this urban form inserts itself into metropolitan lives.

Anthony D. King argues that 'physical and spatial urban form actually constitute as well as represent much of social and cultural existence: society is to a very large extent constituted through the buildings and spaces that it creates'.[4] Flyovers constitute a particular social order, but not merely as physical structures affecting collective human consciousness and actions. Nor do they merely represent, they *are* a system of representation: a medium. In other words, this metropolitan form is a mode of material as well as symbolic production. It is a mode of regulation and control but also a medium of desire that helps to produce the effect *of* subjectivity. Hence it is the site of political conflict and struggle, where different systems of value and practice intersect. It is not therefore isolable from either the discourses that proliferate around it, or from the practices in which it participates and the conditions in which it is engaged. In fact, I argue that this form of built environment is only an *attempt* on the part of the state in conjunction with private investors to institute a form of social order. Collective movements, in this case, in the form of the vehicular and human flooding creating traffic, are also attempts to shape a society that can accommodate them. Users of the streets act as a form of pressure, forces which structure the social and urban space, indirectly through the state responses they provoke, but also directly through their presence and activity. Flyovers are a metropolitan form intended to accommodate some of these pressures.

Standstill traffic is perhaps one of the most talked-about (at least among the middle and upper classes), most widely experienced of urban problems in Metro Manila. It is hence not surprising that flyovers, as the solution to it, should also generate as much discussion as the vehicles they are trying to mobilize. The discourse, in other words, is as responsible for the urban construction as is the traffic itself. One might say it is itself a form of traffic. Indeed, this 'public work' is the product of numerous social demands, the loudest of which have been calls for solutions to 'the traffic problem'. As one columnist of the Manila Chronicle still complains even after all the flyovers have been built:

> Manila's streets are scenes of anarchy in more ways than one. Sidewalks seem to be running out of fashion. Rather, they are transformed into commercial or residential purposes which take priority over the needs of pedestrians. This is proven by the car repair shops, stores, eateries, playgrounds, garbage dumps and shanties that sidewalks are used for themselves [sic] without a second thought. Naturally pedestrians end up walking on the streets or roads, competing with vehicles. With the unsurprisingly large number of private vehicles in the city due to the lack of efficient public transportation and the equally large number of public transport vehicles, it is obvious that there are not enough streets to contain both with ease, plus pedestrians. Add to the conventional vehicular traffic the unconventional types that also are part of the traffic such as tricycles, wooden pushcarts of scavengers, delivery persons or vendors, animal-drawn transport, plus bicycles and motorcycles and the recipe for chaos is almost complete. What gives it the finishing touch is the absolute absence of discipline or adherence to rules of communal interest, traffic rationality, safety and thoughtfulness.[5]

The traffic problem as this writer sees it lies in two things: excess and lack — among other things, excess of people and vehicles, lack of discipline and law enforcement. The terms of this account, excess and lack, are the points at which other discourses that exert force on metropolitan organization converge. In this discourse, the urban excess is constituted mainly by pedestrians pushed off their proper place, the sidewalk, by illegitimate activities, 'unconventional' vehicles and motorists who would have taken public transportation if not for its inefficiency. Excess hence refers to the by-products of maldevelopment and mismanagement, to what is designated as informal production, that is, people who engage in activities recognized as non-productive, unregulated and, hence, illegitimate according to the standards of the national economy. It is to this surplus population, which engages in 'unconventional' forms of livelihood, and its own by-products that the chaos of the streets is attributed. Anarchy, chaos and the lack of 'traffic rationality' are here inextricably related as forces that have brought about the new structuring of street space by means of flyovers.

The massive migration of people from the provinces to the metropolis is not, as many accounts would have it, simply due to the growth of the national economy, nor is it due to the natural attraction that the big city holds for the countryside. It is, rather, an eruption of the contradictions of the nation's, and correspondingly, Manila's development.[6] 'Manila's development has been sustained by the economic surplus extracted from its hinterland.'[7] The surplus population found in the city is the human form of this economic surplus, that is, the labour from which profit is extracted and accumulated as capital (the capital that comes to the nation's capital). The pools of unregulated labour flowing into Manila's streets and corroding the urban structure might hence be viewed as this disgorged rural labour come to find and claim its capital. But rural migrants are also fleeing from the ravages of development — the migration is at the same time an exodus. Apart from the intolerable levels of exploitation they have suffered in the countryside, especially in agricultural industries controlled by feudal capitalists, they have also suffered the ravages of counter-insurgency campaigns meant to quell people's armed resistance against national development, that is, against the economic organization supporting the ruling classes. Much of the urban poor therefore can be rightly viewed as refugees. Their 'refuge' is the streets of Manila, paths strewn with waste — refuse like themselves — which many of them live off. In other words, the human flood engulfing Manila is a wave of capitalism's contradictions demanding accommodation.

It is not then merely the power of capital that has brought about this state of the metropolis. It is also resistance and antagonism. As Aprodicio Laquian, one of Marcos's Presidential Action Officer on Housing and Urban Development, shows, centralized urban plans for Manila have been blocked in the past as well by popular movements and collective entrenchment. The implementation, for example, of the

'Major Thoroughfares Plan for Metropolitan Manila' prepared by the National Urban Planning Commission in 1945 was partially prevented by the financial expenditure demanded by the Hukbalahap rebellion which was taking place in the countryside against US colonialism and US-sponsored national rule. Additionally, the plan's implementation was obstructed by the 'unplanned development' brought about by the migration of people fleeing this war in the rural areas. And the master plan for the city prepared by the National Planning Commission in 1954 had to be confined to the suburban areas surrounding Manila because of the de facto development and congestion of the city itself.[8] Laquian, however, concludes that the lack of planning and control that has resulted in the city's main problems, 'transportation, peace and order, housing and floods', is due to fragmented local governments and particularist politics. A 'single metropolitan authority' that will override the latter is therefore his proposed solution to Filipino excesses.[9]

That solution was realized with the imposition of martial law. Supported by the World Bank and its developmentalist plans for the Philippines, President Marcos integrated the four cities and thirteen municipalities that comprised the Greater Manila Area, and created the Metro Manila Commission, a 'supralocal metropolitan government' headed by the First Lady Imelda Marcos, on 7 November 1975.[10] 'Metro Manila was thus ruled by the principle of concentration and unification of powers in a single body and, as a result of the composition of that body, in actual fact a single person.'[11] In its bid to join the international community of advanced nations, the Marcos regime launched a program of economic development that was export-oriented and foreign capital dependent. To attract foreign investments, it built five-star hotels, an international convention center, a cultural center, specialized medical centers, and numerous other 'beautification projects', all under the supervision of the MMC. 'Since Martial law, the efforts of the First Lady have been focused on making Manila a center for the "jet set" and the "beautiful people."'[12] This meant the eradication of unsightly structures such as slums. Consequently, every international visit or event held in Manila resulted in the eviction of squatters or the relocation of their shanties from the site of the event or the routes to be taken by Imelda's guests. Hence, although the city was Imelda's personal domestic showcase, it was 'beautified' for the eyes and pleasure of foreigners and to attract the flow of foreign capital. In her vision, Manila was to be 'the city of Man', the practical definition of which excluded the urban poor.[13]

The urban poor, however, help to sustain the very same economy in behalf of which they are marginalized. Scavengers, for example, are cheap, casual labour working for the large waste recycling industry — 'they work for the organization but are not part of it.[14] It is on this informal economy that multinational corporations increasingly depend to keep labour costs low and to underwrite the reproduction of its consumers. As informal workers the urban poor embody the contradictions integral to the ruling classes' political and economic power. They are at once marginalized and essential. Without martial law to contain or repress them, these contradictions are relatively freer to surface. Hence, the 'crises' (the same problems Laquian perceived before martial law, but now intensified) that seem to have erupted during the Aquino administration, in its desire to restore democracy and encourage private enterprise, that is, to restore free market capitalism, are in fact merely the greater continuing crisis that is Philippine development manifesting its full-blown symptoms.

The current crisis, as it realizes itself in all the problems that Manila is experiencing as a 'dying city', might be viewed as a necessary crisis for the renewed expansion of global capital, or the crisis that has necessitated a makeover of capital's infrastructure for greater and more efficient accumulation. It is, on this view, still part of the global crisis of the 1980s that has brought about the transformation of the dominant mode of global production into flexible production. In other words, the desires that fueled the Marcos's beautification projects and urban streamlining for development are the same desires fueling government political and infrastructural projects today. The continuity of the state's function can be gleaned from the highly-publicized role Manila's then newly-elected Mayor Alfredo S. Lim took upon himself in 1993. Lim's scum-cleaning (anti-prostitution, anti-pornography, anti-graft, anti-crime) campaigns, which propelled this retired, bemedalled policeman into politics, might be seen as continuous with Marcos's slum-clearing projects to the extent that their respective metropolitan gentrification drives stem from desires determined by an identification with global capital.[15]

Capital, however, requires different strategies for the containment of its contradictory and antagonistic elements. During martial law and under the centralized power of the metropolitan government, these strategies entailed military control, direct domination and bodily repression and territorial confinement — such as erecting walls to hide slums, relocating squatters, and imprisoning and torturing members of urban resistance movements (including squatter organizations). After 1986, with the new administration's renewed vows to democracy and its decentralization of metropolitan government, stratification strategies became more a matter of channeling flows in the way that the flyovers channel traffic, lifting the middle and upper classes who drive private cars out of the congestion created by the 'urban excess'. Indeed, Imelda's desire to remove these 'eyesores' is achieved with flyovers to the extent that the height and distance they provide render Manila an aerial sight — a space deprived of detail and content and reduced to abstract textures from which one can extract a particular kind of aesthetic pleasure. From this suspended pathway the city looks greener because the foliage of walled-in neighborhoods become visible, and the roofs of shanties look like variegated pieces of mosaic or a collage, especially because movement blurs marks of decay and makes details of the corroding urban landscape and its trash disappear into a 'postmodern' spectacle of the heterogeneity and fragmentation of its pronounced uneven development.[16] Of course, this transcendent perspective is not legitimately available to the lower classes who, as pedestrians and public transportation commuters, are routed through crowded ground-level streets.

Smith asserts that 'what (capital) achieves in fact is the production of space in its own image'.[17] Flyovers, on this view, produce space in the image of transnational capital. Michael Sorkin writes of one transnational capitalist, the CEO of Citicorp, as being 'a true Baron Haussmann for the electronic age, plowing the boulevards of capital through the pliant matrix of the global economy'.[18] The new boulevards of capital, which transcend space and time with 800 telephone numbers, credit cards, modems and faxes, are, so to speak, electronic flyovers. The figure of speech is not merely a happy coincidence. As the previous chapter demonstrated for national-sexual relations, figures are symbolic instruments and effects of practical organization. Flyovers attempt to realize the transnational conceptual space occupied by what Sorkin calls the new city (the postindustrial city which he compares to television), by allowing the subjective experience of 'the dissipation of all stable relations to local physical and cultural geography, the loosening of ties to any specific space'.[19] In this sense, they aspire to achieve the shape of non-cities, i.e., 'ultra-urban' places that end up by transcending the definition of 'city' or 'nation'.[20] A flyover is, as Lim described Makati, a business and commercial district in Metro Manila, 'a place that has no history and no memories for the race of Filipinos'.[21] As such, it can serve as the site of transnational identification. Just as one might identify with and through a city or nation, one might identify with that which transcends geographical places, i.e., the international community. The international community is precisely the point of symbolic identification that defines the parameters (the field of action) of Philippine fantasy-production.

But flyovers realize the transnational conceptual space of this community not only by serving as a site of symbolic identification, but also by concretizing the socio-economic network of the national bourgeoisie, that is, of the classes with access and links to the transnational economy. They are not representations of this transnational economy — they are its means of production. Flyovers connect major shopping areas, foreign-invested malls, commercial and business centers, and exclusive residential neighborhoods, channelling consumption to corporate-owned spaces and goods, and integrating its managerial class. In its differentiation of urban space — enabling middle and upper classes better, more efficient means of commuting as well as raising them out of their urban immersion in the contradictory conditions of their economic upliftment — the flyover restructuration is a part of the process of reproducing uneven development, 'the systematic geographical expression of the contradictions inherent in the very constitution and structure of capital'.[22] In other words, flyovers physically realize the new division of labour in which First World-Third World or core-periphery relations are being produced within rather than among nations.[23] On this view, it is the network, rather than any downtown center, which constitutes the core space of the national economy (Fig. 2.2).

Figure 2.2 EDSA-Ortigas Flyover: Network as 'center'. Photograph from the *Philippine Daily Inquirer*.

Traffic and the economy

As media and circulatory pathways become increasingly important to the production of global capital, so do they become increasingly important to its articulation. Hence, the same language is used to describe economic investments and traffic movement: flows, bottlenecks, channelling and regulation are all terms deployed in the discourses of economy as well as traffic. As one columnist makes explicit: 'Traffic is a metaphor for the economy. Can a society that cannot control its streets be expected to manage its monetary system?'[24] But the relationship between the two is more than metaphorical, for in fact, both partake of the same logic. 'Traffic management is practice for economic management. If we can't succeed in regulating the flow of vehicles and pedestrians, can we expect to do better with savings and investments?'[25] In other words, both traffic and the economy are governed by a system of values and practices predicated upon the regulation of 'flows'.

The economic strategy of liberalized regulation or deregulation of industries and capital flows advocated by businessmen as well as international investors and banks (such as the International Monetary Fund) is deployed in the management of traffic by the replacement of traffic lights and traffic police at interchanges by flyovers. Flyovers in fact demonstrate well the new strategies of management that accord with the transnational mode of production: *the paths themselves become the means of regulation and decentralized control.* Thus the economic trend towards privatization is merely the internalization of mechanisms of control — an ascribing to private initiative in a self-regulating system of production and circulation: the global economy. If the flyovers are like freeways, they are free only in the sense of the free market. Flows are liberalized ultimately to the benefit of capital expansion. This is the meaning of democraticization: the process by which state control is replaced by the delimiting and channelling of desire.[26]

The system of representation constituted by the discursive articulation of the flyovers is also an economy of desire, for which the traffic system and the national economy are privileged figures. But the traffic field as well as the economic field are not prefabricated, self-regulating systems — they are sites of political contestation and struggle. In other words, roads and streets are sites of intersubjective as well as intercollective encounters and relations that produce conflicting articulations of space. Congestion and chaos are two complex results of contradictory articulations of space, for example, which the state attempts to override by building flyovers. It is in this sense that traffic is constituted by various social movements;[27] it is in a very literal sense in which collective action can be understood — in terms of pedestrians, cars, passenger jeepneys, street hawkers and vendors, etc. The particular movements of the 'urban excess' are articulatory practices that participate in the production of urban space. It is not therefore the lack of attributes of power such as planning, will, discipline, strict law enforcement, political firmness and inner strength on the part of the state of its 'citizenry' or adherents, that has brought about the chaos and decay which has become the monument of the city.[28] Rather, it is the crisis of conflicting desires and social practices, caused by the intensification of the constitutive contradictions of capital.

Such contradictions are visible within the state itself to the extent that the national and local, metropolitan governments, now no longer united as they were during martial law, pursue ostensibly conflicting paths of development — while the national government leans towards deregulation and privatization (building flyovers, 'depoliticizing' power rates), metropolitan governments tend towards totalitarian control and centralized policies (shutting down businesses, censoring sexual entertainment). However, overriding these different state strategies is an impelling desire for upward mobility.

Desires for unhampered flows

The state understands traffic as it understands the economy — as a system of practices upon whose efficiency the nation's development depends. As one headline evidences — 'Smoother Quezon City Traffic Flow Seen' — the building of flyovers is predicated upon a desire for greater efficiency, smoother flows, etc. The desire for these qualities is consonant with the desire for development and modernization. Hence it is a desire with a more general significance. 'There are several specific institutions, particular areas of endeavour, which in microcosm tell a cautionary tale of how and why things don't work in this country. Traffic is one of them.'[29] Like almost everyone writing for the newspapers, this writer calls for management and control — that is, for the attributes of power whose lack in the state is constantly bemoaned by the middle and upper classes. The ultimate consequences of the latter's frustration with the 'problems' of Manila can be gleaned from an only half-ironic article entitled, 'Fascist Tack to Traffic':

> Our plan for traffic is intimately tied into our scheme for managing the metropolis … The central problem, as we see it, is a lack of proper enforcement, which may even be a blessing, considering the stupidity of some of the traffic regulations and the inadequacy of the infrastructure. The roots of this problem are that Manila is a largely laissez-faire state. Entry into the city is completely unregulated, and the population is growing at a rate that has long since outstripped the availability of resources.
>
> Some of the measures we have outlined may seem to be overly

authoritarian, even fascist [the writer recommends, among other things, the handcuffing of jaywalkers to center island railings, the erection of chain barriers to trap traffic violators and the deployment of a military-like Patrol and Pursuit squadron]. We believe that such regulations need to be stringent as a reaction to the current chaotic conditions. Manila drivers — and pedestrians — need to be shown that we are serious about imposing order in the streets.[30]

As a state response to this hegemonic call (the 'we' voice of this article) for channelling, regulation and order, flyovers achieve in traffic what is attempted for the rest of the city with the various campaigns or 'drives' of local autonomous city governments.[31] On the occasion of Manila's 422nd anniversary, Mayor Lim promises his constituency, 'We shall clear up the streets and unclog the thoroughfares to allow the city to breathe again — and let the lifeblood of its commerce flow freely once more to give life to our city.'[32] What Lim articulates, for which he has become immensely popular among the middle and upper classes, is a desire for what Sigfried Giedion views as 'the fundamental law of the parkway — that there must be unobstructed freedom of movement, a flow of traffic maintained evenly at all points without interruption or interference.'[33] The 'meaning' of highways identified by Giedion is in fact what flyovers in Manila manage to convey: 'the liberation from unexpected light signals and cross traffic, and the freedom of uninterrupted forward motion.'[34] In other words, the desire for this unhampered flow and speed (as well as the progress they imply), which produces and is produced by the flyovers, is the same desire that Lim acts on.[35]

Flyover dreams

The desire articulated by this new metropolitan form, however, doesn't emanate from a subject outside of that articulation; rather, the articulation itself helps to produce the effect of subjectivity, that is, the desiring subject. Driving on one of these freeways produces the experience of being a free, mobile unit (what Giedion calls 'the space-time feeling of our period'[36]) — a self that can transcend the human mass, that is, the corporeal excess and chaos which constitutes Manila's 'laissez-faire' state. In other words, this liberalized flow or 'drive' allows one who is afforded the privilege of overseeing the city to occupy a self removed from facial confrontations with its social contradictions, which are heightened in congested moments (creating eye-gridlocks with the 'eyesores' Imelda tried to eliminate such as beggars, street children, scavengers, street hawkers and the urban poor in general, not to mention street and labour activists protesting on the streets). Since martial law, there have in fact been many state 'drives' to rid the metropolis of squatters, scavengers and waste, and to clear the streets of vendors, tricycles, jeepneys and provincial buses, which obstruct the movement of the metropolis's citizenry — 'drives' to clear pathways for the city's privileged subjects to move freely. Flyovers fulfill this task, providing a relatively exclusive, suspended network which allows the ghettoed, privileged metropolitan subjects to 'breathe' — granting them, in the language of capital, (upward) 'mobility'.

Indeed, the effect of subjectivity that flyovers help to produce is that of a mobile cell ('the lifeblood of commerce') in free-flowing circulation — an *I* occupied by a free-floating consciousness. Manila's hegemonic consciousness is constituted by the organization of these discrete, mobile selves, by that suspended network which images the conceptual space of transnational capital. It becomes clear that the collective *I* employed by metropolitan residents speaks as this consciousness that views the metropolis as a space to be made their own: 'We want spaces that we can live and grow in, spaces responsive to our needs and our lifestyles. Safe, secure, comfortable and ultimately, beautiful to us who will inhabit it.'[37] Such is the desire of metropolitan subjects on 'the road to that dream house in Lim's dream city',[38] a desire to inhabit which is consistent with being cells, discrete entities that occupy space. This desire to inhabit is predicated upon the modern Western house, with its characteristics of verticality, concentration and centrality, qualities that also shape the individual self. Gaston Bachelard observes that 'the house is one of the greatest powers of integration for the thoughts, memories and dreams of mankind'.[39] The metropolitan subject who finds his or her desires congruent with Lim's, is captivated by this power of the house. The mankind whose dreams he or she buys into, however, is the same mankind for whose development and progress the dreams and desires of countless others continue to be sacrificed.

It is in the image of the Western house, its rationally designed and partitioned spaces, and its 'valorization of a center of concentrated solitude,' that Metro Manila is once again being envisioned. Except that the valorized center has become multiple and mobile, demanding a new kind of metropolis house. In this blueprint, flyovers perform the function of corridors leading to and from the exclusive, walled-in neighborhoods where the upper strata are ensconced. One might view this new metropolitan form as a network house, a decentralized spatial system resembling an archipelago whose islands are interconnected by bridges. I say islands because subdivisions where the paradigms of the Western house with its solid, monolithic structures, geometrically-defined and partitioned spaces as well as its attention to housing content have most completely applied, are surrounded by a sea of 'unplanned development'. In these areas inundated by poverty and its haphazard production of space there is no other way to go but up and that is what flyovers do — they secure these centers or spaces of concentration by building elevated horizontal links among them. Such is the architectural structure that enables the new metropolitan selves to circulate as and dwell in discrete cores of being.[40]

In 'The Housing of Gender', Mark Wigley observes that the role of the architect as defined in classical architectural theory ('a privileged figure for cultural life') 'is, after all, no more than the principle of economy. The propriety of place derives from the elimination of all excess.'[41] Indeed, both state projects — the flyovers and Lim's 'clean up drives' — are predicated on this principle of economy; that is, they are part of the process of subjecting the metropolis to an economic regime intended to streamline its spaces. Lim's over-all project might therefore be viewed as 'cleaning house'. In fact, during the last local elections, Lim touted a broom as part of his campaign image. That the image associated with him used to be a gun (he used to be depicted as Clint Eastwood and John Wayne) only underscores the continuity between his purification drive (not to mention his 'Clean and Green Campaign') and Imelda's beautification projects — both are dedicated to the task of sweeping away urban refuse. For the dream house of the metropolis, or the house that the metropolis through its subjects is dreaming into being, depends on the elimination of the urban excess from its spaces.

State bulimia

The job of eliminating this excess is carried out by the state through its various campaigns to clean up the city. This excess is a corporeal excess from which metropolitan subjects must be removed as a condition of possibility of their discrete, mobile selves. It is this detachment from the fleshly (the bodily masses) that Manila's desire requires and that the flyovers' reduction of concrete places to fixed, abstract names reinforces. In fact, Lim's determination to 'clear up' the streets is merely another expression of his consuming 'drive' 'to rub out Manila's image as the flesh center of Asia.'[42] This tourism-sponsored identity of Manila is created by the flesh trade, that is, the thriving prostitution industry which, as I showed in Chapter 1, first received an enormous boost from the Marcos regime in the latter's scheme to attract foreign investment and interest through 'tourism'. Lim's 'clean-up drive' has hence been comprised mainly of raids in the red-light district, Ermita, and the shutting-down of clubs, bars and other 'entertainment' establishments in the same area. But the flesh and the desires they arouse, which this purification process attempts to eradicate, includes the graft and corruption pervading the bureaucracy and police as well, for their motivating 'base instincts' are merely another form of the corporeal excess. Such is the refuse of the government's streamlining efforts.

But this regime, which the state subjects the city to, might be characterized as bulimic. That is, the various 'drives' of the government are carried out in spurts, followed by binges of laxity, indulgence and negligence. This inconsistency is what is constantly decried as the 'lack of strict enforcement' and 'lack of will' on the part of the state. Sally Ann Ness, an American ethnographer who spent some time in the Philippines doing fieldwork, observed this 'sporadic nature by which rules were tightened and relaxed in a seemingly endless fashion.'[43] While Ness naturalizes this characteristic as part of the cultural rhythm that pervades other aspects of society, the law-abiding classes consider it a deplorable cultural habit of weakness that is a legacy of our colonial past. But the bulimic character of the state's purgings is not unrelated to the stomach purgings of women afflicted with what is taken as a pathologized complex. This bulimic behavior is an effect of the contradiction between ideal images and illegitimate desires both of which are promulgated by dominant ideological apparatuses. The pathologization of this contradictory behavior solidifies it as a psychological and cultural condition, which attracts numerous efforts and institutional programs to cure or address it, such as the public clamouring for consistency of the state's 'drives', that is, the strengthening of its will.

However, in the case of the national 'disorder', the state's lack or weakness of self-discipline and will (which is viewed as a trait of its emasculation), is produced by a conflict between ideal national images and illegitimate capitalist desires. This conflict can be gleaned from Lim's purifying regime. Lim's anti-prostitution drive is, for example, in actuality merely a purging of the entertainment establishment's contents, that is, female prostitutes, stripteasers and 'hospitality girls'. The option of converting the bars and clubs into 'legitimate' businesses that he offers to the owners (who are almost all exclusively foreigners) is, however, hardly considered an option. As one club owner complains: 'people come here because of the beautiful girls. You remove them and nobody will come anymore.'[44] True enough, the foreign-capital dependent economy depends on these women as well as an almost exclusively female labour force in other industries to attract foreign investments (the somebodies who need to come). The desire for these flows of foreign investments are in fact what has led to the 'prostitution' of the country and the image of Manila as a 'flesh centre' that Lim wants to rub out.

The ambivalent relation between Manila's excess, composed of its informal labour, and the state, which attempts to control or eliminate it, is clarified by George Yúdice's comparison of the informal economy to irrationality. As Yúdice argues, '"Irrationality" is born of the guiding (market) "rationality" of modernity.'[45] Just as irrationality is produced as well as contained by rationality, so is the 'irrational' urban excess produced as well as contained by the 'rational' regime of the state. Thus, on the one hand, this excess must be disavowed or contained to preserve the country's moral value; on the other, it must be released and exploited to increase the country's surplus value.

Configurations of the metropolitan body

The bulimic behavior of the state might be seen as a conflict of identification that results in a conflicted relation to the urban excess it is trying to eliminate; or put another way, the bulimia of the state makes manifest its conflicted relation to the metropolitan body. If by body is meant 'the concrete, material, animate organization of flesh, organs, nerves, muscles, and skeletal structure which are given a unity, cohesiveness, and organization only through their psychical and social inscription as the surface and raw material of an integrated and cohesive totality,'[46] then the metropolitan body might be understood as the totality of corporeal labour inscribed by modes of production and symbolization such as that articulated by the flyovers. On this view, Manila's metropolitan body can be understood as the immense pool of surplus cheap labour — the sea — surrounding the archipelago edifice system of the upper strata. The liquidity attributed to the informal sector is not merely a figure of speech — it refers both to the liquidity of its petty cash and the liquidity of its spatial practices, which corrode the solid infrastructures (such as the fences pedestrians wear away in their insistence on jaywalking). Indeed, part of the liquidity of the urban excess lies in the nature of its labour. As Smith asserts: 'The particularity of labour implies the particularity of its spatial attributes.'[47] Much of this labour has been characterized as 'homework' in that it consists of work that is either an extension of conventional domestic work or 'women's work' or it is work carried out at home. Also the street becomes the site of both work and residence. In all cases, this informal work might be viewed as a perversion or transgression of modern divisions of public and private spaces and activities, as well as the Western notion of home, which is predicated upon this division. It is hence not surprising that the urban excess creates living spaces whose boundaries are mobile and porous, or that their movements ignore the private as well as public boundaries erected by others. In fact, the 'prostitution' of informal workers whose casual services are procured on a contractual basis demands the periodic dissolution of the boundaries of their selves, bodies and homes in exchange for subsistence.

The realization of the urban excess in terms of the informal sector's liquidity and the female sexuality in which it traffics allows a sex-gender reading of the state's conflict of identification. Wigley notes that in the dominant cultural logic of Western architecture 'women lack the internal self-control credited to men as the very mark of their masculinity. Their self-control is no more than the maintenance of secure boundaries. These internal boundaries, or rather boundaries that define the interior of the person, the identity of the self, cannot be maintained by a woman because her fluid sexuality endlessly overflows and disrupts them.'[48] Western perceptions of colonial bodies, including Filipinos, has historically affixed this debased fluid, feminine sexuality onto the latter, and have thereby served to erect masculine ideals embodied in the nation-state. The nation-state becomes the instrument with which the ruling classes produce and contain the feminine sexuality that it has displaced onto its labour. The excessive and fluid sexuality attributed to women as well as to colonial bodies is housed and contained in a feminized national body that hence becomes the jurisdiction of a masculine nation-state (for an early example of the project to house the historical subject of the nation, see Chapter 4). The house, which is ostensibly produced by the need to control this feminine sexuality but is also the means by which that sexuality is produced, is the paradigm of the nation as well as the metropolis.

Lim's regime to achieve his dream city, the metropolis as house, is indeed an effort to eliminate this threatening fluid sexuality to the extent that the objects of his purging are women and feminized labour. As Wigley shows: 'The building itself is subjected to the economic regime it enforces. Just as the house is a mechanism for the domestication of women, it is itself understood as a domesticated woman.'[49] Imaged as just such a house Metro Manila is thereby produced as a domesticated female body, and the metropolitan state, as the controlling and self-controlled masculine order to which it is submitted. These gendered identities, however, are secured only at the level of the nation. For at the level of the international community, that is, in the eyes of global capital, the Philippines is feminized global labour, and that includes the state. The ambiguity and ambivalence of Manila's gendered identity hence stems from its vacillation between identifying with global capital and identifying with global labour.

Lim's proposed plan 'to give life to' Manila, to let it breathe again, and to 'let (its) lifeblood ... flow freely,' manifests the construction of the city as an organic body. But the configuration of this metropolitan body is also contradictory and ambivalent depending on its point of identification — the point from which it sees itself or from which it is seen. For while capital demands an 'open-economy'[50] — meaning a feminine, permissive and porous metropolitan body,[51] a national identity based on masculine ideals of power and selfhood demands a centrally-controlled, self-protective economy — meaning a contained and disciplined metropolitan body. In other words, the metropolitan state is hailed to *be* this body at the same time that it is hailed to *possess* (and control) this body, to be a pliant, porous feminine people, or a strong-willed, self-disciplined masculine nation-state (See the next chapter). Such is the gender trouble of the state, one that is completely predicated upon the heteronormative political-libidinal dynamics of capitalism and nationhood, that is, on the 'rules' of fantasy-production.[52]

The state's conflict of identification and its consequently ambivalent attitude towards its metropolitan body is part of the reason that the urban excess is neither eliminated nor contained but rather, discharged — displaced from the spaces and structures of the upper strata and permitted everywhere else, flooding the rest of the metropolitan area.[53] The state's ambivalence towards the urban excess demands a new mode of regulation other than that which relies on 'older' centralized strategies of containment and eradication such as those used by Marcos. In the 'prostitution' of the metropolitan body, the Marcos regime's pimping strategy was territorial, involving the parceling out of natural resources (including property rights, which resulted in these foreign-owned prostitution establishments) to centralized monopolies. Lim's strategy is more a matter of deterritorialization in that it drives prostitutes to work informally, that is, unregulated by syndicates of pimps and clubs. Lim's efforts actually encourage the decentralization of prostitution and its related 'graft' activities, such as drug dealing. By deregulating the trafficking of commodified female sexuality (tendered by prostitutes) and other illegitimate substances, such efforts also see to its perpetuation in liquid form. This is not unlike the function of flyovers in relation to the urban excess. For flyovers mediate between the formal and informal economies and between the state and the urban excess, accommodating their respective 'rational' and 'irrational' modes. Thus, Lim's authoritarian drives are coextensive with the mode of production of flyovers; they each retain the excesses of Manila by displacing them into the neglected tarn of the metropolis.

Endurance and fluidity

The demands for deregulation and free flows made by the new mode of production articulated by flyovers show that a certain kind of fluidity is congruent with modernization and development. It is hence important to distinguish between the organizing and organized mobility of capital and the ostensibly unorganized liquidity of labour. As infrastructural supports of this new mode of production, flyovers negotiate between these two kinds of flows, accommodating both by channelling them through different spaces. What in effect flyovers make manifest are the metropolis's conditions of fluidity, which they are predicated upon and produced by. The image of Manila as it is realized by the performance of the flyovers is as a sea of fluids separating into channeled flows of mobile particles and a stagnating lake of liquid excess. In other words, in the configuration of the metropolis as an archipelago, a body of fluidity dotted with congealed, scattered centers, there are no spaces of interiority for the repression of contradictory desires — Manila has no unconscious. Flyovers bring out the upper strata into *relief*, detaching them from the lower strata but not masking the latter, securing domination through bypasses and overpasses rather than through enclosure and censorship. The stratification of metropolitan space is, in other words, not a matter of masking, containment and repression, but rather, of accommodating and channelling flows — not a matter of centrality and rationally ordered spaces, but of decentralized cores and winding pathways. What in fact this new mode of production reveals in its emergence to accommodate the metropolis's 'rationality' and 'irrationality' (whose polarization in the psyche Bachelard imaged as the polarization of the attic and cellar in the house), is their fluid and symbiotic coexistence. Metropolitan stratification can hence be seen as, rather than merely a matter of inside and outside, also a matter of velocities of solid and liquid elements.

These conditions call into question the deployment of modern, Western theories and epistemologies of urban space, subjectivity and sexuality to understand metropolitan formations like Metro Manila. As Wigley recognizes: 'Sexuality in the age of psychoanalysis is the sexuality of the interior. Each of the new regimes of classification — perversion, fetishism, homosexuality, voyeurism, etc. — presuppose the institution of some kind of "closet" that masks them, a supplementary realm of withdrawal.'[54] It is not that such theoretical regimes are inapplicable to Philippine conditions. That is, it is not a matter of dismissing these theories of space and subjectivity as irrelevant or immaterial to some radically different formation, but rather a matter of viewing them as historical forces (modes of production) among a multiplicity of forces impinging on and impelling the conditions of Philippine social formations. One must recognize that there are other regimes besides the sexual-economic regimes of capital that the metropolitan body is subjected to, among them are the regimes of First World theories. Indeed, I have tried to show that the epistemologies of modern, Western formations — the 'metaphysics of being' implied by paradigms of the house and the body — are instruments that are used in the attempts to stratify Metro Manila through the desires of and for development.

Flyovers, themselves, introduce a verticality and depth to the city that is endemic to these epistemologies. Hence while this new metropolitan form might be seen to displace and delimit modern paradigms and structures of containment as well as the constructions of sexuality and subjectivity that they help to make, it also deploys them. In fact, part of the innovation of flyovers lies in the way they insert themselves in this heterogeneous metropolitan body to become the coordinating mechanism of its various modes of production. In other words, as a new metropolitan machine regulating Manila's metropolitan life in behalf of capital, the flyover network requires, produces and exploits these conditions of fluidity.

The fluency and fluidity that characterize the social as well as spatial practices of the urban excess, however, cannot be reduced to being properties ultimately functional for capital. In other words, such qualities are not merely a residual mode of production that participates in the reproduction of uneven development. The mobility and porousness of boundaries of self and body that might be observed among larger sectors of the population, for example, would have historical determinants that include but are by no means limited to the exigencies of colonialism and capitalism. For Ness, who observed fluency and fluidity in so many other aspects of Philippine cultural life, they belong in the realm of the pre-economic: 'Sources from which activity tended to develop and into which activity dissolved still appeared to be fluent, not solid, mobile, not stable … Fluency of all kinds, as opposed to strength or single-minded determination, for example, was tacitly recognized as of primary importance for coping with the environment in a variety of ways.'[55] Although this account tends to be culturally essentializing, as does much other ethnographic writing, it does bring out a crucial dimension of this fluidity, which is its significance for 'coping with the environment.' If one recognizes that this environment consists of fundamentally oppressive socio-economic and sexuality-gender structures, one will also recognize 'coping' as a matter of resistance to such structures. Moreover, 'coping' is a persistence in, or better, insistence on practices that are on some level disharmonious to capitalist development and subjectification (even though on another level they might be 'accommodated' by the state); it is also simply life-enabling, both collectively and individually. In other words, this fluency and fluidity are forms of social and individual subsistence as well as resistance.

Take for example the unregulated movements of jeepneys (passenger vehicles originally made from surplus US military jeeps after the second world war). Their unruliness stems from the 'informality' of their functioning, which often serves the interests of its users. Jeepneys are unruly not only because their drivers want to make as many trips as possible and because this is a way for them to act on and express a certain antagonism towards the 'private classes', but also because they stop anywhere along their route where passengers indicate. There are many functional and structural characteristics of the jeepney that render it more collective-oriented, and that is part of the reason that it has been valorized as well as aestheticized as the Filipino cultural symbol *par excellence*. This essentializing practice exemplifies the proclivity of the national bourgeoisie for isolating objects with very concrete significance in daily lives and imbuing them with the capacity to embody cultural identity. In *Perfumed Nightmare*, however, Filipino filmmaker Kidlat Tahimik, presents the jeepney not as a reified national icon but as a living artifact realizing the desire to forge a life out of the ravages of oppression and domination. As his main character declares: 'We have turned the vehicles of war into vehicles of life.' In short, the fluidity that characterizes jeepneys as well as the urban excess of which they are a part, are not an 'authentic' cultural trait, rather, they are a mark of the desire to live.

This desire might be seen to extend over the metropolis in general. As a colonial body for nearly 500 years, Metro Manila is also a testimony to its own 'coping' with the exigencies of global capital. Its chaos, its horizontality, its porous surfaces and its fluidity as well as the forms of subjectivity such conditions enable are expressions of the desire of its population to survive — evidence that it is not a 'dying city' but, rather, an enduring one.

ROADS TO 'CIVIL SOCIETY'

Getting there

Manila used to be the place my parents would go to for a few days at a time while my siblings and I stayed at home in San Fernando, 270 kilometers to the north of it. I did not feel then that we lived outside of Manila. To me, Manila was an elsewhere, not a centre. It was elsewhere to the town I grew up in, which had and was its own centre. As in other towns, the plaza was the town's center, with the Catholic Church, the municipal hall and the market neatly arranged around it. The street where I lived was an elongated, rounded back of asphalt surfacing out of the dirt, which led to or away from the town plaza, depending on where you were going. The mountains were on the east, the sea on the west.

In the beginning (for our stories had beginnings), we lived on the side closer to the mountains. Right behind our house was the backside of a hill where mischievous, magical dwarves were said to dwell. From the top of it you could see the whole cove as well as the buildings of the US airbase and the Voice of America arrayed on the green peninsula. On this hill sat the Provincial Capitol, the Provincial Jail and a friendship Chinese Pagoda. Most intriguing for me, was what we children used to call the Japanese hole — a perfectly round tunnel entrance into the hill where guerillas hid from the Japanese during the Second World War. My siblings, neighboring cousins and I would sometimes scale this hill, to sit in the Pagoda and take in the view of the town and the sea, and thrill to run by the Japanese hole as we clambered down again. From the stories we heard of the war, we imagined that there were Japanese stragglers who still had not heard that the war was over. And I imagined that my grandfather, whom the Japanese had taken away to be shot but whose body was never found, was also a straggler, hidden somewhere in some lost thicket of time.

Later on we moved to the side of the sea. Behind our house the railroad tracks that began in Manila ended. San Fernando was the northernmost destination of this line. The trains still ran then, at least for a short while. Late at night, we could hear the sounds of their chugging and their long whistles against the roll of the ocean on the shore where the fishermen would in the early morning disembark with their fresh catch for the market. Those sounds formed the background of my dreams. Sometimes we children would ride the train a few towns down south, towards Manila, only to be met by a car that would take us back home. With great excitement, we rode the train along the coast through occasional fields of tobacco and untilled land, bypassing the centers of towns. Always the sea on our right, the hills on our left, closer to one and then to the other, undulating between, moving at a steady, rhythmic pace. One, two, three towns and the ride was over.

Manila was cars and lights. It was the neon Coke sign that greeted us at the end of the highway, the horizontal order of trees lining Quezon Boulevard and the gleaming white Quezon Memorial looming directly ahead. Manila to me was the strangely smooth, sweet water, which came out of my urban cousins' faucets. Knowing it to be 'treated', I could taste a modern cleanness in it that corresponded to the sleek, concrete expanse of Unimart, the supermarket in Greenhills, which was to be for me an abiding image of American modernity in Manila. Clearly, this was not the authentic, historical Manila of my parents' youth: Escolta, Quiapo, Oregon, Santa Ana, with their small, winding streets, bustling with the activities of people *spilling out of small shops and houses, and the stop and start of jeepneys and tricycles. This modern cleanness was, rather, the Manila of my urban cousins' new upward mobility.*

Manila was to me series upon series connecting apparently disconnected things. It was also a sophisticated fluency of movement through these series — fundamental channels of urban life such as streets and bus lines, water pipes and shopping aisles, not to mention inner circles and social avenues. When my family moved to Manila, I felt like a straggler. There were many laters in my stories of San Fernando, just as there were many living pasts in my daily life there, but they could not be realized once San Fernando had become, from the vantage point of Manila, only a beginning. Even when I had lived in Manila for a long, long time, it seemed I was always only ever getting there.

Dreaming states

If the state has dreams, it is only because the state has first been dreamt. By whom? Who dreams the state? And what is the character of this dreaming?

The bulimic response of the state to Manila's urban excess appears to be the product of two contradictory dream-forces: the nation and global capital. But the nation and capital are not univocal agents. Many forms of active and static pressure, human and non-human forces, living and dead labour, have given rise to these 'subjects' that have dreamt up the current Philippine state. The 'subject' that is the Philippine nation, for one, is the consequence of the organization of conflicting, multitudinous desires through the ideals, categories and syntax of the Free World fantasy. That is to say, it is desiring-actions coursed through fantasy-production structures that produce both the national 'subject' and its hegemonic state. On this view, the currently expressed hegemonic dream state — a 'strong republic', whose features are defined by the latest President, Gloria Macapagal Arroyo, as independence from class and sectoral interests and the capacity to execute good policy and deliver essential services[56] — is the very executive decree through which the Filipino subject can be produced anew. The new ideal Philippine state is the corrective to the laxity, indulgence and negligence characteristic of the weak, bulimic state, which reached its apogee in the government of Arroyo's predecessor, Joseph Estrada. Indeed, after the 2001 popular revolt of People Power II, which unseated Estrada, in a manner that so closely resembled the historic 1986 popular revolt, which toppled the Marcos regime, that it was dubbed its sequel, a new Filipino subject was conceived. Its name? Civil Society. As one writer reported it:

> After that successful display of organized collective action, it seems people suddenly discovered that there is such an entity, amorphous yet powerful as to be able to change the course of history. This entity, whose structure, nature and purpose remain vague but whose reality is so compelling was baptized 'civil society'.[57]

Karaos, the writer of this op-ed piece, criticizes the widespread 'misunderstanding' of civil society as a single interest bloc. Civil society is, she claims, rather, the arena of public debate and action where a diversity of interests and perspectives are brought to bear on the government. In spite of her attempt to cast the notion of civil society as a structure of social relations, Karaos nevertheless writes about civil society groups as subjects with values. 'Civic duty and citizenship are the primary values they live by and when they bring these practices to the realm of governance, they are in effect introducing a new way of doing politics.' The Filipino subject is a civic subject, no longer personally entwined in the dirty 'politics of patronage' that Estrada represented, but rather rationally involved in the new 'politics of issues and programs' that People Power II is said to have demanded. Arroyo's 'strong republic' thus appears to have been dreamt by the democratizing, liberalizing Filipino subject ('civil society'), which (retrospectively) brought Arroyo to power and will now be effected via the 'strong republic'. But other forces are at work in the fabulation of the new Philippine state.

Estrada's administration began shortly after the Asian financial currency crisis when foreign investors took flight from the 'crash' that their sudden run had centrally helped to create. It was hence a state mired not only in the economic deficits created by the regional crisis but also in the political-moral deficits of its president, evidenced by his well-known involvement in corruption rackets and his widely publicized excessive habits of lavish public spending and debauched personal consumption. Under what appeared to the transnational business community as a nightmare state, foreign capital investments 'dried up' and the economy 'went under.' No wonder then, given the bleak view for finance capital of this drought-stricken yet sinking place of investment, that the *Far Eastern Economic Review* (the journal for the Asia Pacific business community) should find in Estrada's ouster signs of a 'brightening outlook':

> Last year, the banking and retail sectors were opened to foreign players and some companies, like American retail giant Wal-Mart, have recently shown interest in setting up in the Philippines. If the new administration can convince them that it has what it takes to keep the playing field level and stable, the money might start flowing in again.[58]

The clamour for a 'level and stable playing field' alludes not only to degenerate 'influence peddling,' 'power politics' and 'cronyism' that by themselves present mighty obstacles to a *laissez-faire* global market. It also alludes to the intensifying social crises that have led to the latest presidential unseating.

Arroyo's proposed state must be seen therefore as an appeal to this transnational community.[59] In this regard, 'civil society' is itself a new metropolitan form, like the flyover network, an updated liberal-democratic apparatus for the elite-capital accommodation of demands made by contradictory social movements. Such an apparatus is also intended to serve as a more efficient means of social regulation supporting the deregulated mode of global production. 'Civil Society' would be the new system of representation and medium of desire for the new state, the 'strong republic.' While 'civil society' is a form of dreaming as regulation, a form of governance of social desires, it is also the interim product of other dreams that elude its representational control.[60]

'Big men', 'strong states', followers and usurpers

US political studies scholarship on the Philippines contributes its own share of work in the fantasy-production of the contemporary Philippine state. The bedrock scenario of much of this work consists of two characters: 'weak state', 'strong men'. According to this fantasy, the 'system' of post-war Philippine politics and economics is characterized by a weak bureaucracy or 'weak state' manipulated by local elites or 'strong men' for the aggrandizement of private wealth and power in their own bailiwicks of influence. Historical, comparative and national case studies of Philippine political economy from the colonial times to the present all adhere to this basic theme. The story begins with the US granting of Philippine 'independence' in 1946, when the 'neo-patrimonial' state of the Republic is born, replacing the 'rational, bureaucratic' colonial state of the Commonwealth period.[61] From then on, until the Marcos dictatorship when it experiences a quantitative-turned-qualitative change, the Philippine 'state', which hardly even measures up to the Weberian definition of the state that most of these studies rely upon, serves merely as the appendage of predatory rent-seeking *caciques* or landlords.[62] Post-war politics or what is referred to as 'traditional *pulitika*' (politics) thus consisted of 'big men' in violent as well as 'democratic' electoral rivalry over state control and the economic benefits it guaranteed. What Benedict Anderson has called 'the full heyday of *cacique* democracy' (1954-1972) was put to an end by Marcos's centralization of what was until then a disaggregated power structure into a single 'Strong Man' state. As Anderson writes, 'it was only a matter of time before someone would break the rules and try to set himself up as Supreme Cacique for Life'.[63] The 'big man' became the state, the latter's coffers his personal bank. After Marcos, so the story goes, the state devolved back to 'elite democracy' and traditional 'patronage politics', with the fragmentary oligarchic fiefdoms restored and only a few of the 'crony capitalists' who had benefited from Marcos's largesse left standing.

While this story is undeniably a realist portrayal of the national oligarchy and the peculiar 'mode' of its political and economic operation (including the 'exception' of Marcos who proves the rule by temporary sublation), it is nevertheless still a story, a work of imagination that participates in the Free World fantasy of the developing world.[64] In this fantasy, the symptoms of chronic underdevelopment that erupt in periodic crises are rooted in a flawed 'system'. The flaw in this system is a lack: the lack of a separation between political governance and economic production (or as it is put these days, between the state and the market), between personal relations and political and economic relations. Not surprisingly, the problem identified in the story finds its logical resolution in the ideal of a 'strong republic' articulated by Arroyo.[65] Conveniently, the resulting separation will be mediated by 'civil society', which will serve as the flyover bridging particularist, class interests and the greater political and economic good of the nation.

My point here is that academic imaginations also act as forces dreaming the state, and they do so deploying the categories and ideals of that international imaginary that I have been calling fantasy-production. In this way, they act as projects of social imagineering predicated upon the very Western masculine ideals of autonomous, bounded, sovereign subjectivity that makes for the gender trouble of the post-authoritarian Philippine state.[66] It comes as no wonder that the 'weak state'-'strong man' symbiosis and the long-standing system of 'rent capitalism' and 'clientelist politics' characteristic of the post-World War II Philippine ruling order appears in these analyses as a perverse symptom of the colonial order that sired the Philippine nation-state.[67]

What these scholarly fantasies tend to overlook in their meticulous empirical support of variations on the 'strong man' or 'big man' theme of Southeast Asian political history is the question of social struggles and other contradictory forces of desire, as embodied in this chapter by the urban excess. As they search for adequate concepts/titles to encapsulate the material dreams of the nation's ruling class ('sultan rule,' 'booty capitalism,' 'bossism') and painstakingly track the details of these dreams' operations, they leave no time to explore how such dominant dreams interacted with, shaped and are fueled and determined by the wayward dreams of the nation-state's others. Indeed, while this scholarship has been extremely valuable in tracing the historical origins and transformation of the national elite (its emergence out of and widening distance from the rest of the nation who will come to be known as 'the masses'), this focus and attention to the logic of domination, which they perform, has also proved to be its profound political limit. As I will argue in the last chapter, the project of mapping systems or logics of domination tends to articulate the consciousness of hegemony (often to itself), at the expense of pursuing and extending tangential social practices that escape these logics.[68]

In this regard, I am sympathetic with Resil Mojares's argument that we need to go beyond these scenarios where the 'big men' are the nation's main actors (whose 'dream goes on and on') and to explore 'the realm of followers and nonfollowers'.[69] In this realm of subordinate dreams are to be found the contradictory forces and unruly practices that often find expression in dominant fantasies as debased and devalued forms of feminized and racialized being, such as the fluid, feminine sexuality attributed to informal urban labour. And as these forms of being find concrete embodiment, this 'realm of followers and nonfollowers' tend to be peopled with women. In the next section, I will discuss the two most nationally prominent instances when women were not only the paradigmatic followers in broad movements against the ruling orders of 'big men', but also the followed, that is, the feminine usurpers of masculine authority and power. These two instances are the 1986 People Power revolt against Marcos, in which Corazon Aquino figured centrally as Woman Redeemer with nuns in tow, and the decades-long superstardom of Nora Aunor, the actress who commanded a female following of unprecedented proportions.

For now, however, I want to briefly explore this realm of followers and nonfollowers in the metropolitan context of state dreaming. My contention against the fabulations of political science and developmentalist economics is not that they are fabulations. As I argue throughout *Fantasy-Production*, and illustrate through my discussion of Manila's flyovers, representational practices are inseparably linked to practices of material production. My contention is, rather, that these fabulations provide symbolic ballast for the powers of both 'strong men' and the 'state' (and their relation) to shape the political and social life of the nation. And yet the 'state', to take one of these symbolic figures, is as much a product and means of accommodation of contradictory forces of desire as it is a mere means of the seemingly raw, instinctive ambitions to wealth and power on the part of 'strong men'. Reynaldo Ileto has described the makings of the Philippine colonial state in similar terms of disturbing 'excesses from below'.[70] Roving bandits, peasant uprisings and alternative spiritual communities came to represent the perpetual threat that constitutively shaped the 'state' as an instrument and measure of control.

If we regard Manila's new metropolitan form — what is materialized in an earlier moment in the flyovers and represented in a later moment by 'civil society' — as a state apparatus, that is, as part and parcel of the 'system' that is the state, then we are led to recognize that the unruly social movements that the state sets out to regulate play no small part in shaping the historical forms that the state takes. As a form of dreaming, the state is concretized in the material infrastructures it constructs to serve as regulatory pathways of social desire. Roads and other means of transportation and communication built by the state can thus be read as part of its 'machinery' for the 'exercise of government' over its constituency, or, in the language I have been using, part of its dreamwork.[71] But whether or not this dreamwork works and how also crucially depends on the 'followers and nonfollowers' of its built pathways.

Take EDSA or Epifanio de los Santos Avenue, the major thoroughfare over which most of the original flyovers were built. The building of EDSA was importantly aided by army engineers in the employ of the Marcos administration. In the story of Metro Manila's development, which does not only parallel but serve to paradigmatically represent the story of the development of the state, EDSA's linking of Quezon City and other areas of the metropolis demonstrates the concrete achievement of the integration, consolidation and strengthening of the metropolitan state under martial law.[72] This concrete achievement was part of a general strategy of governmental consolidation that importantly included the creation of an integrated metropolitan-wide police force, with ample advisory and equipment assistance from the US government.[73] In this story, the Metropolitan State of the Marcos regime is the solution to the urban and national crisis of the late 1960s and early 1970s. As Caoili describes this general crisis:

> Manila and other areas of the country were in the grip of fear and lawlessness. As the local police and armed forces were unable to maintain law and order, particularly in Central Luzon, local political leaders strengthened their own private armies; the New People's Army was gaining strength and Muslim dissidents in the south battled with government forces. The specter of anarchy loomed.[74]

Like many of the scholars of the Philippine state, Caoili describes the crises of pre-martial law Philippines as the consequence of the 'anarchy' of warring petty elites and the obstacle 'particularist politics' posed to the solving of urban problems of congestion, inadequate sanitation services, squatting and lack of housing, etc. The concrete achievement of metropolitan integration that the building of EDSA represents, however, is not simply the replacement of 'anarchy' by rational urban planning as the means of a larger project of modern nation building. What the story generally fails to discuss but alludes to in the description above are the unruly, antagonistic movements from 'below' that shape the measures of the new authoritarian state. If we recall the vigorous, formidable student and labour protests and demonstrations that occupied the streets of Manila in the late 1960s and early 1970s and threatened to overtake the ruling order, we can also understand EDSA and other urban developments undertaken by the Marcos regime as technologies of counter-insurgency.[75]

Road building was one of the projects undertaken by US colonialism that spectacularly set it off against the old Spanish order. As was claimed at the 58th Congress, for the new colonial power, 'the road-maker fully as much as the school-teacher must be the evangelist of the Philippines.'[76] The evangelical message of course consisted of two ideals: 'progress' and 'democracy,' later to be combined into the notion of 'development.' While public roads, together with the public educational system, served as the new colonizer's means of 'benevolent assimilation,' it also served as the means of increased communication among disparate communities across the archipelago as well as the means of expression of emergent tastes, emergent values. Like the railway system, which was first laid down at the end of the Spanish colonial regime and developed during the American colonial regime and which it came to finally displace by the 1950s and 1960s, the road system has thus never ceased to be a site of social struggle. Corpuz writes about how the railroad network built by the Manila Railway Company figured in both the Philippine Revolution against Spain in the late nineteenth century and in the Philippine-American War at the beginning of the twentieth. With cars and trucks predominating over trains as the main means of land transportation, roads have not only functioned as extremely profitable investment site, they have also served as an important instrument of counter-insurgent 'development', particularly in the countryside.[77] As such, they have become sites of intense social struggles, such as the vigorous struggles of the Cordillera and other indigenous peoples against the crony state's encroachments on their community lands. Much of the 'encounters' between the revolutionary New People's Army and the Philippine military take place on these roads that are making greater incursions into the forests and mountain areas on behalf of the mining and logging industries.

To return to EDSA then. If, like the flyovers that were built over it, EDSA was a state measure to reconstitute metropolitan order in the face of 'anarchy', it also became the site of emergence of 'people power,' the counter-hegemonic social force that deposed the dictatorial regime of Marcos. Hundreds of thousands of people flocked to EDSA for four days, occupying not only a major stretch of the thoroughfare but also the state television station adjacent to it, as they demanded the resignation of Marcos. State media thus came to be appropriated as a system of alternative representation and the media of expression of counter-hegemonic desires. And an older media, the radio, gained central importance as the means of reorganizing the subject of the nation (see Chapter 5).

Like EDSA, the flyovers were also an attempt to institute a new social order — a new form of dreamwork — in the very spaces where challenges to an older order erupted. Like EDSA, the flyover network itself become a site of social struggle with unexpected consequences. In 2001, the flyovers became the place of staging for another usurping power, 'People Power 2' (Fig. 2.3). Instead of the radio, the cellular

Figure 2.3 People Power 2: Roads to civil society. Photograph courtesy of N-Abler.

phone served as the means of communication of this social power challenging the state.[78] While the cellular phone is a technology that helps to realize the transnational space of capital, it also in this case the means of production of that new national subject called 'civil society.' Beyond being merely the subjects of 'big men' and 'weak states', the 'followers and non-followers' of metropolitan dreams are importantly unpredictable forces of desire altering the very pathways built to channel and regulate them as well as impelling the creation of new pathways, new media, of fantasy-production.

Metro Manila, as it now stands, is a testament to these wayward forces of desire as well as to the fantasies of 'development' and transnational modernity. Far from being entirely the consequence of the failed and haphazard dreams of big men, weak and strong states, or global capital, it is the complex result of a multitude of individual and social desires seeking expression through means of representation and production, which are ultimately owned and controlled by a small few. Other experiences and other tastes, say, the experience of a train ride and the taste of strangely smooth, sweet water, have gotten us here and have contributed to the making of Metro Manila in the shapes it has taken. From the metropolitan view, all these beginnings have found their proper ending, happy or not, or at least their central plot, in the story of the nation, which the urban capital represents. Yet not all our experiences and tastes have been captured by metropolitan dreams. The broad expanse of the sea has other meanings besides the sea of underdevelopment from which we are expected to surface. It has led many of us to other places besides this one. Still, we are continually enjoined to imagine that somehow we are on the same voyage, in the same time, moving forward toward that shared ideal called progress.

Concluding an essay on Philippine values written shortly after the first People Power event, Jaime Bulatao writes:

> ... as the Filipino nation makes its way up the super highway of history, it acquires a full load of experiences from which it chooses what things are most *valuable* in its present stage of journey. In the past stages, Filipinos have developed a particular value and skill in personalistic relationships modeled after family ties. The lower classes and the people of the countryside have kept this value. That forms the rear half of the convoy. But the front half of the convoy, being

exposed to the rapidly developing scenery of a twentieth century world, has developed new values, new tastes of life as it were. And these may be the values of human development, of freedom, and of justice. It may console us to think that the whole convoy is moving forward, though slowly, like a turtle. They say that a turtle does not make progress until it sticks its neck out. Fortunately, we stuck our necks out and we are now moving forward.[79]

'Civil society' makes its early appearance in this construction of the front half of a national convoy. What Bulatao doesn't recognize is that by this time many of those in the rear half of the convoy aren't even on the 'super highway of history' on which the turtle-like Filipino nation is supposedly driving. Sometimes stragglers are not just those who have been left behind, but those who have stepped off the proper timeline, out of synch with the forward march of national history. Just as the urban excess slip in and out of the pathways of metropolitan regulation, so do the bodies of feminized Philippine labour exceed the territorial control of the nation state. They too have developed 'new values, new tastes of life' that are leading them elsewhere, off the path of national 'development' and onto other pathways that have since become central to a new mode of fantasy called 'globalization'.

The bulimic ambivalence of state actions in regulating the metropolitan body at home that I have described in this chapter as a form of 'gender trouble' becomes the mode by which the post-authoritarian state learns to deal with the contradictions arising from people's flight from and refusal of the bodily costs exacted from them. That flight continues on beyond the nation, placing the Philippine state in yet another crisis, unable as it is to control its own boundaries. In the next chapter I discuss the way in which the state attempts to resolve this 'gender trouble' by means of economic nationalism, a new strategy for the regulation and recontainment of the domestic bodies deterritorializing the nation.

3

Domestic Bodies

In the mid 1990s, reports of the exploitation, abuse and torture of Filipina domestic workers working in countries such as Hong Kong, Singapore, Saudi Arabia, Kuwait and the United Arab Emirates increasingly flooded Philippine newspapers. Headlines such as 'Filipina OCW Slain in Kuwait Tortured,' 'Filipino Maid Accuses WHO Exec of Rape,' 'UN Experts: Stop Abuse of OCWs' and 'Maid's body found floating in river after ward drowns' presented themselves almost daily to the news-reading public.[1] These blaring news reports indicate at once the ways in which the physical bodies of Filipina overseas domestic workers are predominantly constructed and sometimes treated by their employers, and the ways in which the diaspora of overseas contract workers (OCWs)[2], in particular, overseas domestic helpers (DHs), is constructed as a national body for a national audience in the Philippines. In this chapter I attempt to sketch out some of the relations between the material and symbolic practices constituting these two kinds of bodies: the individual body of the overseas national (the domestic) and the collective body of the nation. More precisely, I try to delineate some of the contradictions and congruencies among several differential systems of value which shape the emerging transnational fantasy-production of global domestic helpers. This emergent modality of fantasy-production and its new product threaten the hegemonic Philippine nation with a crisis that also serves as an opportunity for the state to reconfigure its role in the changing world order. I restage the quasi-crisis of the nation here to better recognize the greater crisis, which it elides: the creative potential of Filipina women gathering outside their 'home'. Such potential attests to the fact that coursing through the imperative structures of desire within fantasy-production are other dreams bringing this world into being.

Numerous news reports about migrant Filipino workers portray the physical and mental brutality, extreme hardship and misery of their situations abroad. The widespread image of the OCW as 'pitiful, abused and maltreated' has in fact compelled former Labour Secretary Nieves Confesor to deny that this is indeed representative of all Filipino migrant workers.[3] In the face of such widespread 'negative' stories, Confesor's report that 'only a very few — less than one in a thousand — of all our migrant workers ever get into trouble' demanded its own headline: 'Confesor: OCWs are happy.'[4] Nevertheless, the fact that such a contrary view itself makes news demonstrates the ubiquity of the image of the OCW as a suffering body. Moreover, although the category of overseas contract workers refers to both male and female workers, it has begun to acquire a female form. This is what is often referred to as the 'feminization' of migrant labour. While it is apparent that there has been a significant increase in the number of women migrant workers, women still comprise only about 50–55% of the total number of overseas contract workers.[5] In spite of this, and in spite of the fact that overseas contract work is comprised of many kinds of labour, the OCW has taken on a female profile, specifically, the profile of the domestic helper. Other high profile figures of the diasporic population that began to eclipse the figure of the prostitute which was paradigmatic of the nation during the period under the Marcos regime, are the sex worker/ entertainer and the mail-order bride. While these figures continue to hold sway over the national imaginary, it has been the DH, the invariably female domestic helper, who has served as the predominant representative figure of Filipino OCWs.

Several initial questions arise: How are Filipina domestic helpers materially and symbolically constructed? Why has the domestic helper become the symbol of the diaspora of Filipino contract workers? And what kind of community in the Philippines does the figuration of the diaspora through the body of the domestic helper help to create?

THE DH-BODY

It becomes clear that the Filipina DH is first and foremost a physical body. The reports of their abuse and 'maltreatment' all testify to the bodily treatment of domestic helpers at the hands of their employers. Stories of a maid's Singaporean employer 'poking her with a sharp object, spraying insecticide, shouting, pushing, biting and assaulting her [*sic*]'[6] and another maid being sold by her Singaporean employers to men who raped her for five days while a video of the rape was rented out by her employers to their neighbors — such stories demonstrate the way in which domestic helpers are considered bodies without subjectivity, that is, corporeal objects at the mercy and for the pleasure of those who buy them from the recruitment agency. I say 'buy' because domestic helpers are paid not for a specific skill but rather for their gendered bodies — for their embodiment of a variety of functions and services which they are expected to provide at the beck and call of their employers. They are, in a word, labour-commodities. In Veronika Bennholdt-Thomsen's formulation, as women, they 'may not freely dispose of their labour power, like a commodity. Rather, their labour power is sold — or simply appropriated — far from freely, together with their bodies and their sexuality … and hence includes themselves as bearers of that labour power.'[7] The coerced identification of domestic helpers' bodies, sexuality and labour-power is, however, not a structure characteristic solely of their gender constitution, but of their 'race' and class constitution as well, so that we might more accurately say that it is as disenfranchised women from a third world country that domestic helpers are appropriated body and labour.

Such is their condition as posited by the social relations of fantasy-production. Not free to sell their own labour-power but instead themselves sold 'as bearers of that labour power' by others (their family, their recruiters, their government, as well as their employers), Filipina domestic helpers are new-industrial 'slaves'. Expressions such as 'slaving away' when used to describe the work of DHs can thus no longer be seen as mere metaphors. For Filipina domestic helpers are shown to serve as 'modern-day slaves'. As one headline proclaimed: 'Abuse of Asian Maids: Slavery lives in wealthy Gulf.'[8] This is in fact what some of them feel themselves to be. 'I was treated as a slave,' Alice, a Filipina domestic helper who worked for a royal family in Kuwait, recounts. 'In the presence of my employers I had to remove my shoes. If they passed me I had to bow. I could never be seated in their presence. They did not use my name, only bad words like "You, Dog", or "Donkey", or, if I was close by and they wanted something, they just tugged my hair and pointed. The children used to hit me with their toys if I did not do exactly as they wanted.'[9] Alice's slavery consists not only of the withholding of wages and overwork, which comprise the greatest percentage of cases of 'maltreatment', but, just as importantly, her construction as ontologically different, inferior, an animal to be physically manipulated rather than talked to (not even a pet, inasmuch as she did not, for her owners, have a name) — an object with no more value than a toy. The aspects of domestic slavery documented by Human Rights Watch investigations include, in many cases, 'rape and other forms of sexual assault, beating, kicking, slapping and burning' of the workers and, in almost all cases, 'non-payment of salary, passport deprivation, and near-total confinement in their employers' homes',[10] practices which attest to what is often overlooked in discussions of the flux and movement of the present time — that is, forms and conditions of *immobility* in the age of diaspora.

NEW SLAVERY, NEW 'RACE'

While this 'modern slavery' is often attributed to residual traditional cultural practices, and thereby confined to places like the Gulf 'where traditional slavery died out only three or four generations ago',[11] it is rather, I am suggesting, the concrete operation and effect of the gendering and racializing constitution of domestic labour which is carried out in and through the local cultures of both 'sending' and 'receiving' countries, a conglomeration of processes mediated by transnational capital. On this view, domestic slavery is the result of refurbished deployments of old practices through new relations of production. Since it is the case that practices of domestic enslavement obtain usually, but not always only, in newly-industrializing economies, it is perhaps appropriate to call this phenomenon, new-industrial slavery, which should suggest that it is a component part of the conditions of globalization.

The treatment of domestic helpers as slaves and not merely their comparison to slaves can be accounted for by several determining logics. One determination of domestic slavery is the inseparability of 'women's work' and women's bodies, combined with the tendency of production towards the reduction of necessary labour to the absolute minimum (that is, the minimal amount of capital investment in the worker needed for the reproduction of the worker's body), and towards a reliance on devalued, 'natural' *labour*-intensive tasks ('unskilled work', meaning work that is inalienable from the body).[12] The 'flexibilization' of labour refers precisely to the transformation of techniques of appropriation of abstract labour-time, that is, labour-power, into techniques of appropriation of the labourer herself as the embodiment of indefinite labour-time. In the context of labour relations, 'flexible' means, then, that one's labour-power is at the disposal of the employer/ owner.

Another determination of domestic slavery is the intersection of gender and racial systems of differentiation with the logic of commodity fetishism.[13] What I am referring to is the reification and objectification of historical, national-economic relations in and as 'racial' attributes of difference posited in the domestic labour-commodity. This objectification of social relations of dispossession (the domestic helper not possessing her body inasmuch as it is sold in behalf of and to others, the Philippine nation not possessing the bodies of its nationals inasmuch as they have been bought by other nations) is realized through acts of physical violence inflicted on the DH's body. The beating, burning, scratching, as well as sexual violation of DHs are racializing practices that at once are predicated upon and determine the gendered relations of their work.[14] It is possible to conceive of domestic enslavement as part of an on-going process of production of a new 'race', which has as yet no discernible collective identity, but exists only as a changing pool of workers fulfilling class, gender and nationality specifications. We are apprehending a process of racialization that has not congealed into a fully-developed discourse of 'race'. Indeed, there is as yet, as far as I know, no free-floating racial taxonomy or a fully-developed discourse of 'race' particular to the domestic slavery of disenfranchised women from the Philippines, Sri Lanka, Bangladesh, and other still-not-industrializing countries, even though this is already implied and at work in their commodification. The physical as well as verbal practices inscribing domestic helpers' bodies as other and less than human (which is itself in the process of being redefined through the terms of global subjectivity)[15] are in this moment inchoate and unsystematic. They cannot be said to be acts of branding 'race' in any prior ideological sense of a phenotypically-identifiable people, to the extent that they are as much acts of denial of gender, class and sexual sameness (or threat of equivalence within global terms) as acts of 'racial' marking of deviation from any particular norm.

In a succeeding moment, the debased attributes which are a product of this process of creating racial difference become themselves the basis for the overseas recruitment of labour, and hence for the maintenance of the socio-economic systems which manage this transient labour and the crisis which it constantly presents. The 'abdication of responsibility' and 'failure to provide due process and equal protection' to abused domestic helpers on the part of the receiving country's government, for example,[16] are supported precisely by Filipinos' national-racial 'difference' (their subjugating constitution *as* difference) which serves as the social technology for their commodification on a global scale. Accounts attributing practices of slavery to the other culture (of the foreign employers) are in effect responding to this 'difference' by which Filipina domestic helpers are, as Filipinas, exploited and manufactured for exploitation.

DIFFERENCE AND SURPLUS VALUE

'Difference' itself is used to explain the physical abuse confronted by domestic helpers in foreign lands. In the news article which refers to the late demise of traditional slavery in the Gulf to help explain its modern resurgence, a British commentator Roger Hardy is authoritatively quoted: 'The presence of immigrants of over a hundred nationalities has caused a clash of cultures.'[17] The clash of cultures 'caused' by the influx of migrant labour alludes to 'a range of social complications and a pattern of employee mistreatment' mentioned earlier. The violence which is referred euphemistically as 'mistreatment' is thereby seen to be rooted in the difference which migrant labour presents (in its very 'presence'), rather than in a stratifying intolerance of and contempt for difference that is enabled and necessitated by structures of capital accumulation and the relations of power among nations which such structures depend on and effect.

The recourse to cultural difference as a determinative cause of the difficulties suffered by Filipina domestic helpers is demonstrated by anthropologist F. Landa Jocano in his explanation of the 'mental disorders', 'emotional stress', 'suicides' and many other forms of difficulties suffered by Filipina domestics' through the concept of culture shock.[18] As Jocano writes: 'Some are lucky and others are not, whichever is the outcome of their ventures, they all encounter the same initial "shock" in the new cultural setting with which many are not prepared to cope. The term "culture shock" refers to a "form of anxiety that results from an inability to predict the behavior of others or act appropriately in a cross-cultural situation." This anxiety arises because of differences in cultural ways of thinking, believing, feeling and acting that characterize the orientations of people in different cultures.'[19] Apart from ignoring the sustained patterns of assault inflicted on domestic helpers, explaining such experiences away as a matter of 'luck', Jocano attributes the difficulties faced by Filipina DHs to a form of *'inability'* on their part to adjust to and accommodate the ways of their employers. The term 'culture shock' itself, when used to explain acts of abuse, preserves a sense of the equality of subjects that is flagrantly denied by the evidence presented and, moreover, that is denied by locating this malady in a 'fault' on the part of the abused. Such an analysis only repeats and therefore reinforces the historical fantasy-construction of women as beings-for-others — their coerced *di*sposition towards serving the needs of others. It is this construction that enables Jocano to consider sexual abuse as one of the major areas in which the inability denoted by culture shock manifests itself most prominently.

Accounts such as Jocano's fail to consider the congruence of the logics of sexism, racism and commodity fetishism in the creation and maintenance of the Filipina DH as a corporeal object, and the violence endemic to the very structure of domestic labour. Jocano's account invariably abets this violence by constituting the DH as at once the victim and the perpetrator of the abuse it purports to explain. He attributes, for example, the physical and verbal abuse experienced by one domestic helper to her inability to 'handle the language (of her employers) well'. The solution which this way of posing the problem of abuse calls forth can thus only be the improvement of the domestic helper, who is tasked once again with the work of accommodating the difference(s) between her and her employer. The domestic helper becomes, in fact, the objectification of the 'difference' which she accommodates. This is an economic as well as a racial category — performing the necessary labour of her employers (compensating the costs of their reproduction), she represents the difference between her corporeal value, as represented by her wage (or non-wage, as the case may be), and the human worth of employers, as represented by their income. The difference she represents, which is now racially expressed, translates into the value that accrues to her employers. From the perspective of her employers she is, in effect, surplus-labour which they can appropriate directly. She is surplus, in the sense of excess, surfeit human matter, and in the sense of surplus value, which, to the extent that she 'costs nothing', her labour already provides.[20] The difference which she is made to embody and accommodate is thus not only the condition but also the very realization of the surplus of power and value that they have over her.

In conclusion to his analysis, Jocano recommends that 'a pre-departure, cross-cultural seminar be given to the Filipina domestic helpers. This will prepare them on what to expect and how to behave so that they do not become so vulnerable to exploitation and abuse abroad.'[21] On this view, Filipina DHs are products needing further processing before export to other countries. The 'vulnerability' of Filipina domestic helpers is premised precisely on their construction as objects of other people's actions. This is the truth contained in the expression 'warm-body export': domestic helpers' bodies are commodities, corporeal objects for the use of others. It is thus not surprising that prostitution often turns out to be the practical end of domestic workers. What is noted as 'the ease with which contract workers slide into the sex industry' stems precisely from the continuity between domestic helpers and prostitutes and mail-order brides which is based on their constitution as 'feminine' bodily beings-for-others.[22] As a compound of thing and service, product and producer, a commodity which works to produce itself as a use-value as well as to produce other use-values, the domestic helper at once approaches the perfect commodity (indefinitely self-regenerating) and is the revealed truth of all commodities (desubjectified living labour).

The constitution of the DH-commodity as both a 'feminine' and a non-human (dehumanized) body demonstrates the paradoxical continuity and symbiotic relation between the 'feminization' of labour and the desubjectifying and ungendering corporealization of enslavement. Hortense Spillers writes of the 'stunning contradiction' between the constitution of the captive body of the African-American slave as 'the source of an irresistible, destructive sensuality' and its reduction to a thing, 'becoming *being for* the captor'.[23] Spillers notes that with the 'severing of the captive body from its motive will, its active desire', 'we lose at least *gender* difference *in the outcome*'. Reading the testimony of the slave girl Harriet Jacobs, she suggests furthermore that 'the ungendered female — in an amazing stroke of pansexual potential — might be invaded/raided by another *woman* or man'.[24] Although Spillers is writing about a specifically US context, the symbolic operations which she traces demonstrates a techno-logic that has entered and become an integral part of the global economy. In this techno-logic, the DH-body is racialized to the point of her ungendering, but at the same time, her racialization as a *being for* her employer/owner (both male and female) rests upon and intensifies her constitution as a 'feminine' bodily-being-for-others, a captive body that can be and is often 'invaded' or violated.[25]

It is this violence endemic to the gendered manufacture of domestic work(ers) as bodily-*beings-for*-others that, for the Filipino audience, makes the plight of OCWs a women's issue. Ma. Alcestis Abreras writes, 'What separates male and female issues in migration is the use of brutality, force and intimidation inflicted upon women on account of their gender.'[26] It is in part due to this flagrant violence represented on and by the bodies of female migrant workers (as 'low-end labour-commodities') that the image of the exploited, exported OCW takes on a 'female' profile: the DH-body. The violence of exploitation becomes synonymous with the 'feminization' of overseas labour, which is itself grasped in the form of tragedy. 'Another tragic OCW tale: Death by beating in Kuwait,'[27] wailed one headline. 'Tragic tale behind Pinoy maid's death leap in HK,'[28] wailed another. 'A tragic story was behind the death of a Filipino maid who was photographed as she jumped to her death from an eighth floor apartment in Hong Kong last week,' begins the article. The story of the way in which this domestic helper was coerced by her employers into working illegally in a restaurant and then arrested by the police for doing so, however, disappears behind the photographic depiction of her suicide. In fact, in some papers, the only news story consisted of the two pictures of the Filipina maid, one of her perched on an air-conditioning unit outside the apartment window and the other of her leaping to her death. Clearly, the fact that such 'stories' are tragedies has to do as much with what happens to Filipina domestic helpers as with for whom and in what way their 'stories' are told.

TRAGIC TALES, PATHOLOGICAL EXAMINATIONS

The bodily treatment of Filipina domestic helpers in the hands of their employers is intricately related to their bodily treatment in the hands of the media. A report entitled 'Filipina OCW slain in Kuwait tortured'[29] begins: 'The body of a Filipina overseas contract worker (OCW), who died last month in Kuwait, bore severe stab wounds and multiple incisions, with her brain and other internal organs packed and stuffed in her chest, according to the National Bureau of investigation. Dr Ronald Bandonill, NBI medico-legal officer, wrote in his autopsy report that Margie Almogela, 19, was stabbed in the head, right shoulder and trunk and had a massive scalp hematoma at the back of her head.'[30] The report within the report continues with a description of Almogela's 'bruises on her trunk and right abdomen, and a stab wound on her left trunk, which injured the left part of her liver' as well as 'the laceration of [her] genitals, which was a sign that she may have been raped first'. In spite of the fact that the packing of Almogela's internal organs is explained by Bandonill as a common practice in other countries, it is nevertheless described together with the other pieces of bodily evidence of her having been violated, tortured and murdered.[31] Indeed, Almogela is subjected to a second autopsy through narrative — she is bodily taken apart and examined for the experience of being used, which she is no longer around to tell. Often the doubts surrounding alleged suicides of domestic helpers are based on bodily marks which are described by the news reports: 'he saw burn marks on the back of his wife when he viewed her body. There were also bruises on her face that looked like fingernail scratches.'[32] These marks of corporeal difference are both the effect and the instrument of the treatment of domestic helpers as products of consumption.

Discursive autopsies are performed not only on dead maids but on living ones as well. It is as if their bodies can tell better than they can what they lived and live through. Thus it is through the spectacle of the body that the 'tragic tales' are told. These tales typically include descriptions of the nature of the death or abuse of the domestic helper, her age, the number of months she spent abroad, the zero earnings she sent back to her family, followed by a background of the family she left behind who are left with nothing in exchange for her body except for the debt she incurred to go abroad in the first place. What becomes clear from the form of these tales is, the discourse of costs through which the domestic helper's death is processed and through which her body is received. As one mother of a murdered domestic helper expressed: '*Ang gusto lang sana namin, mabayaran naman nila ang pagkamatay ng anak ko para may pambayad kami sa mga utang namin noong umalis siya patungong Kuwait*' [We just want them to pay for our daughter's death so we can pay for the debts we incurred when she went to Kuwait].[33] The domestic helper's body is the embodiment of a certain exchange-value, which the government, purportedly taking the perspective of her family, has a vested interest in. This embodiment of value is blatantly demonstrated by the way in which domestic helpers (their bodies) serve as collateral for the loans they take out to secure employment. As Manang Inday, a domestic helper in Hong Kong, put it, '*Mabuti pa ang kalabaw, hindi niya alam na isinangla siya. Kami, alam naming isinangla namin ang aming sarili*' [Better, the carabao — it, at least, doesn't know when it is put up as collateral. We, though — we know that we put ourselves up as collateral].[34]

Inasmuch as the domestic helper is viewed as the embodiment of a certain exchange-value, she is also the embodiment of a certain labour-time. Indeed, as the commodification of abstract domestic labour-power, DHs do not have time, they are time. Hence their bodies become surfaces for the recording and registering of this time. This is why the tales always mention their age and the length of time of their labour abroad — they are correlates of the time and value they embody. One article concludes: 'Suraya Dalamban had swollen lips, deep scratches on her back and fresh wounds on her fingers. Her five months' work abroad seemed to stretch into a lifetime of pain.'[35] There is an equivalence drawn here between the depletion of Suraya's body and the appropriation of her labour-time, her lifetime. The accumulation of her pain pays for the costs of living of others.

It is precisely because domestic helpers, as gendered and racialized bodies, are already treated as mere bodies — severed from structures of subjectivity and agency — that they can function further as signs. The bodies of domestic helpers have become sites for the construction of and contestation over the national body abroad. DH-bodies serve as objects of the nation's struggle for subject-status on the global scene. In this respect, the verbal bandying of the body is as important as its visual display. This is most clearly exemplified by the case of Flor Contemplacion, the domestic helper in Singapore convicted in March 1995 of murdering Delia Maga, another Filipino domestic helper, and the latter's ward. The furor over Contemplacion's conviction and execution was drawn because this case of what most Filipinos believed to be a miscarriage of justice expressed, for many, the plight of all OCWs and, more importantly, of Philippine labour in general. However, as the efforts to save Contemplacion from hanging were played out in the media, it became clear that the contention that her impending execution sparked was in truth over the role of the Philippine state and its national strength vis-à-vis a developed Asian nation, Singapore, which, in its perceived sterility, cruelty and inhumanity, symbolized the consequences of economic prosperity. In light of the Ramos administration's explicit vision for the country (the development plan called 'Philippines 2000') — that is, achieving NIC status by the turn of the millennium — Contemplacion's body became the contradictory kernel of this construction of the nation, the symbol of those who have been paying and will continue to pay with their lives and remittances for this vision. As the world's largest labour exporter, the Philippines' economic power rests upon the work of those who will not benefit from its further 'development'.[36] Domestic workers pay as well for the global fantasy, of which this 'development' is merely a national version. Besides extending the wages of their host-employers, they also subsidize the below-minimum wages of their families back home, thereby reducing the cost of reproduction of labour for commodity-producing industries world-wide. In this way, domestic workers contribute to the surplus-value expropriated by global capital from both techno-corporate workers in knowledge and information industries in advanced economies and factory workers in commodity-production in peripheral economies (not to mention what they contribute directly as workers in the privatized social services industry).

'SAVING' ACTIONS OF THE STATE

In the presumed absence of agency of domestic workers and of the people who came together in a passion unleashed by the image of Contemplacion languishing in prison, public attention quickly turned to the government. Singapore's disregarding of all the latter's efforts to stay Contemplacion's execution, only served to underscore the weakness of the Philippine state, a weakness already evident in the dependence of its economy on foreign capital, in its indebtedness, and in the dominant role of international agencies in its domestic political affairs.[37] As we saw in the last chapter, such weakness constitutes the 'gender trouble' of the Philippine state, which post-authoritarian administrations have been at pains to resolve. Thus the public clamour over Contemplacion's hanging acted as a catalyst for 'government action', which primarily meant investigative missions, a welfare fund and free legal assistance for OCWs.[38] The showcase of such action was the 'saving' of Sarah Balabagan, another domestic helper in the United Arab Emirates who was convicted soon after Contemplacion's execution of murdering her employer after he attempted to rape her. The saving consisted of the reduction of the penalty from death to a year of imprisonment, 100 lashes, and 'blood money' for the family of her employer. What both cases of Balabagan and Contemplacion dramatized was the nation's battle for sovereignty and dignity on the global stage. Of all the reported cases of abuse and murder of Filipina domestic helpers, none have merited as much 'government action' as these two cases. Both involved dealing with the foreign states' legal systems and thus could serve as sites for the assertion of national power as the power of the Philippine state. National power is, in the case of the Philippines, built on the 'vulnerability' and 'helplessness' of its labour.

The semantic content of this 'feminization' of OCWs is revealed in the government's insistence that the defense counsel should have based Contemplacion's defense on 'diminished responsibility' as well as in the findings of the Philippine team of forensic experts who concluded, after conducting an autopsy on the skeletal remains of Maga, that Contemplacion was, as a regular woman, physically incapable of inflicting the kind of injuries Maga sustained, which could only have been inflicted by 'a man or a very strong woman'.[39] Not only did such pronouncements represent Contemplacion as either infantile or insane and weak, they also served to banish rumors that Contemplacion and Maga were more than 'just friends', revealing the heterosexist imperative shaping the official nation's position.[40] The 'feminization' of Contemplacion was the process of representing her as too weak to have been the agent of violence, and hence too 'feminine' to have been the agent of desire. Furthermore, as the symbol of the national struggle for sovereignty, Contemplacion had to be severed from her relations with other domestic helpers, relations which were beyond the legitimate purview of their roles as mothers, daughters, sacrificing and serving members of the family, in order to preserve her gender and its ideal, normative sexual entailments.

In both cases of Contemplacion and Balabagan, the government's staged efforts did not dramatize the domestic battle, that is, the struggles within the national body: the struggle of disenfranchised women in their constitution as domestic work(ers) even before they become OCWs and the struggle of the majority of the domestic population who are increasingly being thrust into labour relations similar to the relations of domestic labour or homework, which is characterized by low wages, long hours, no security of employment, and no legal protection.[41]

Part of the tremendous cathexis of the nation on domestic helpers stems precisely from the latter's embodiment of the general 'feminization' of the rest of Philippine labour, by which I mean the historical tendency of labour towards relations structuring colonial and women's work[42] (rather than the increasing number of women in what is assumed to be the sphere of men) as well as the national subject's implication in this gendered debasement which it is itself predicated upon. Contemplacion's corpse enabled the people to be manifest to themselves by staging the physics of their absence, and the depletion of their humanity. The compassion for and passionate identification with her was, however, siphoned off and incorporated into a hegemonic national anxiety over the global status of the Filipino people. This anxiety is expressed in two distinct ways which nevertheless predominantly converge: a moral concern for the integrity of the Filipino people, and an economic concern for the progress of the country. One writer expresses both as follows: 'Exporting human labour risks our homes, the very core of our Filipino society. It also threatens the fabric of our labour force, draining it of its brains and brawn, elements vital to our progress. Filipino OCWs are not dregs of our society ... Pushed to leave instead of encouraged to stay by the government, this means the downgrading of our work force at home, lessening our own capability to perform competitively with other countries and pauperizing ourselves of our own people and of their physical, intellectual and spiritual contributions. And if they come home dead, crazed, raped or broken in spirit, we are faced with a segment of a populace that further drains and destitutes us.'[43] The moral concern for Filipino society translates into an economic concern for its competitive advantage on the global labour market.

Clearly, the violence which brings Filipina domestic helpers to the fore as the representative figures of the diasporic population is both the physical violence inflicted on the domestic helpers' bodies and the violence inflicted on the hegemonic nation as it envisions itself. One recognizes a convergence of violating images: the image of the destroyed, drained, destitute labouring body of the nation (a body in debt, in lack), the image of the violated, sullied domestic body, and the image of the shattered and scattered national body abroad. All these images are invoked by the image of Filipinas being taken out of or leaving their home country and selling the labour which properly belongs within that 'home' (the scandal of wives selling their domestic labour outside their conjugal 'homes'). Such an understanding of the problem proposes its own solution: keep them at home. This is in fact what Domini de Torrevillas, a newspaper columnist, asserts: 'What we must do back home is to prevent Filipino women from working abroad to be exploited, raped, and injudiciously treated. This will put an end to the miserable picture that our female OCWs project around the world.'[44] The violence of Filipino domestic helpers abroad, in this account, is also the violence of the image they project of the nation abroad.

One can discern in fact what the hegemonic national subject sees as the nature of the violence — that is, the problem — by looking at the solutions it offers. Keeping Filipino women at home restores the virtuous body of the Philippines, keeps it, and hence, the faculties of the nation, intact. The subtext here is both the mad and mutilated domestic helper and her proximity to the prostitute, a pervasive figure of the 'whoredom' that is the Philippines — the further debasement of an already debased, that is, feminized nation: 'an economy raped and ravaged by foreign powers'.[45] Solutions such as 'the phasing out of Filipino maids working abroad' or even their temporary ban from offending host countries (as in the case of Singapore) do not address the very manufacture of 'Filipino maids' (or 'Filipinas', meaning maids). No one recommends the phasing out of that. Instead, the solutions only confirm that poor Filipino women are considered a national resource requiring government supervision and regulation. Hence the call for more 'protection' of OCWs. The solutions former Labor Secretary Confesor proposed (ironically, after declaring the abuse of domestic helpers to be exceptional) — 'more protective country-to-country agreements, intensified training for OCWs, more focus on welfare and legal assistance and better management of the fund of the Overseas Workers Welfare Administration'[46] — offer no connection between the pervasive sexual assaults against Filipinas 'at home', reported daily on the inside pages of the newspaper, and the so-called 'abuse' of OCWs, reported on the front page — both of whom are considered the nation's 'own'. The problem of OCWs is contained as a matter of state policy, a matter, that is, of 'management'.

On this view, 'phasing out' or regulating the export of Filipino maids is predominantly about regaining control over the Philippine production of labour for the global community, and thereby reasserting the nation's agency and subjectivity in the eyes and terms of the world (as opposed to the objecthood of its labour, which comprises its 'body'). In this fantasy-scenario, the bodies of domestic helpers serve as the objects of that subjectification (which means, for the purposes of labour management, the domestication of the passions and desires of the people). Inasmuch as the racialized national 'sameness' attributed to all Filipinos threatens enfranchised Filipinos with conflation with these bodies, the latter must be alienated from the national subject as the object of its love and concern, and finally, sacrifice. Flor Contemplacion was thus a real martyr to the extent that the sacrifice of her body enabled the nation to mobilize itself and assert its sovereignty as a national subject worthy of respect from other nations. As moral restitution for it's selling out and selling of itself (its body, its own) for 'mere economic reasons', the nation mortified its flesh, not only attaining virtuous agency, but also restoring limited powers to itself in the face of the threat of its dissolution.[47] This was, after all, the state that had to reinvent itself against, even as it was indebted to, the illegitimate, 'strong-man' regime of Marcos. In many ways, the transformation of the metropolitan state as a coordinator of contradictory flows (Chapter 2) prefigures the reformation of the national state in the face of the deterritorialization of the body of the nation.

NATIONAL VS. SUBJECTIVE RESOURCES

Contrary to the belief that global production is transcending and outdating national geographical territories, these territories are resurrected in the feminized form of labour — labouring women are the new bio-geographical territories of the nation, on and over which power struggles are staged. Inasmuch as they are 'the Philippines' prime export commodity' the bodies of Filipina domestic helpers are national territories, unmoored, like the sex workers in Manila, from the naturalized places of their designation. They are resources on which the reconsolidation of a national imaginary and the 'economic assertion of nationalism' can be founded.[48] The clamour for government action is based on an older 'political' model of nationalism, which is redeployed now as an instrument of realizing global state-citizenship (to the extent that this depends on the ownership and management of national property) even as the global public sphere excludes Filipino labour from the privilege of subjectivity in the global imaginary (for which labour amounts to slavery).[49]

The violation of domestic helpers' bodies is understood as a violation of national territory. It is clear then that the 'protection' demanded for OCWs also means the protection of national (that is, state-corporate) interests and correspondingly, a protection of the mode of production which sees to the processing and export of domestic labour, including the socio-cultural structures that are indispensable to the constitution of women as the embodiment of specific kinds of labour. Concern with the consequences of labour migration such as the break-up of the family, the disintegration of values, etc.[50] must thus also be seen to express an anxiety about the destruction of the socio-cultural fabric on which prevailing structures of gender and kinship, particularly those upholding dominant relations of production, depend. This is not to say that families do not suffer but that the change of roles which overseas contract work arrangements bring about (such as the woman being the breadwinner of the family) or threaten to bring about are a cause of anxiety to those who have 'traditionally' benefited from older arrangements. The family is seen as a 'social cost' incurred by immigration. If, however, it is recognized that the family is perhaps the most powerful institution underpinning the production of women, the disruption of this social relation might also be seen, from the side of these women, as a partial liberation. That liberation as well as the possibilities and pleasures of experience not available to them at home can, in fact, account for the 'irrationality' of domestic helpers returning again and again to their overseas work.[51]

The media sees the fate of OCWs, however, from the perspective of the family and thus sees the OCW as the bodily dispossession of the family (to the extent that she is its possession). The proposed solutions to the disintegration of these social institutions is 'proper orientation'. As one analysis states, after concluding that the problems posed by migration result from a lack of education and sophistication on the part of OCWs in dealing with their circumstances: 'The end goal of an orientation regarding the host culture is to enable the migrant worker to use appropriate and effective behavior.'[52] The 'stress management' and the provision of cognitive maps proposed by this analysis would only become part of the improved 'processing' of OCWs desired by those invested in the value that they produce.

The disruption of older social support systems and the creation of new ones (the transformation of the cultural order through cultural displacement) are threatening to the home country as well as to the host countries because of the political potential domestic helpers bear as a group. Carolyn Arguillas, another columnist, senses this potential when she observes:

> Imagine hundreds of thousands more of Filipina domestic helpers in other parts of the globe gather in parks on their day-off yesterday. On weekdays they contribute millions of dollars to the economies of their respective employer-countries by making it possible for the wives of their employers to work and earn. On their day-off on Sundays, they again contribute millions of dollars to the economies of their respective employer-countries by spending for their food and transport to go to Church or 'relax' in the parks and malls. Monthly they contribute millions of dollars to the Philippine economy.[53]

The economic value produced by this group, the sublime proportions of which Arguillas tries to articulate, is the possibility of their political power as well.

HUMAN POTENTIAL

The potential political power of domestic helpers does not lie merely in their collective earning power as labour but just as importantly in their collective creative capacities acquired as women to extend themselves to and care for others. It is this power that some feminists at home have recognized and that has consequently moved them to make Filipina DHs a point around which the struggles of women can crystallize. This power can only be realized through the recognition and commandeering of what escapes these tragic tales and the solutions which they elicit (what escapes the narrative conclusions drawn from such tales): the subjective activity of women. While from the point of view of their consumption they are regarded as corporeal objects of use, this objective condition of domestic helpers can be seen, from the point of view of their self- (rather than mass) production, to consist of their living labour, in the most subjective sense of living. Filipina domestic helpers are not merely objects of other people's practices, objects of better or worse 'treatment', conservation and regulation; they are active producers and creative mediators of the world in which they move, the world which they in fact participate in making through the work of cooperation. The productive function of domestic helpers' subjective cooperation or what I call experiential labour can already be gleaned from the recommendations for orientation seminars, stress management, emotional training, etc. to help streamline their 'processing'. This productive and creative capacity is the living labour of Filipina women — it is their activity which has not yet been objectified and which therefore bears an immanent transformative power — what Antonio Negri calls 'subjective potential'.[54] In seeking to actualize and create access to this potential, Filipina feminists raise the issue of domestic helpers but, I believe, in ways that do not always fundamentally and finally objectify them in behalf of a putative national (even if feminist) subject. In what follows I want to look at two feminist artists' attempts to come into alternative political relation with domestic helpers, that is, to bring domestic helpers into relation with those of us who might see our implication in their plight as the occasion for some form of transformative mediation. Moving away from the public realisms of the government and mass media, these expressive works operate as ways of releasing and tapping women's subjective potential.

One attempt to imagineer the domestic helper is Imelda Cajipe-Endaya's sculptural installation 'Ang Asawa Ko Ay DH' [My wife is a DH (domestic helper)] (Fig. 3.1). The body of the wife/domestic helper is shown to consist of an open suitcase propped up with a broom, a dustpan and a mop, and of an assortment of personal things — a statue of Virgin Mary, an embroidered *panuelo*, books, letters and a voice tape. The only remnants of the human body are her deathly-white appendages which are coextensive with these household instruments and shackled by an ironing cord/ clothesline. Only her right arm escapes this domestic leash — it is pressed against her *panuelo*-covered breast, her fist clenched in resistance against this dehumanizing conversion into a modern, portable maid-machine. If the mass media, the state, and capital treat the DH-body as a unitary thing (as a territorial matter), Cajipe-Endaya deploys this body as a problem, as at once the site of women's oppression and the staging and stating of that oppression. What this assemblage visually expresses is the treatment of woman (asawa/DH) as *kasangkapan* [household utensils or tools], the objectification of subsistence labour or domestic work in and as the instruments and means of subsistence. This objectification as *kasangkapan* is a 'treatment' which the domestic helper experiences in its most acute form. From the point of view of her users/employers, the domestic helper is a *replicant*. Severed from any 'natural' origin, such as her mother country, resembling only other domestic helpers, she is a technological apparatus, an artificial organism designed to perform the work of reproduction otherwise fulfilled by 'real' mothers and daughters. It is in the face (or I should say, facelessness) of this construction that the question of the human — as a matter of who as *creators* 'wives-DHs' are and/or might be — poses itself.

Figure 3.1 'My Wife is a DH', sculptural installation. Photograph courtesy of Imelda Cajipe-Endaya.

Cajipe-Endaya's denatured DH-body is made of many things — it is a heterogeneous assemblage composed of the artifacts of labouring relations constituting the wife/domestic helper. Installed as *kagamitán* — an appliance, equipment, utensils, furniture — the domestic helper demonstrates the logical end of the wife, who is outfitted to furnish the needs of her husband/employer, including the need for sex which women colloquially and appropriately refer to with the word *gamit* [to use], as in *ginamit ako* [I was used].[55] The extent to which the domestic helper is thingified as *kagamitán,* as an object of use, is pointedly expressed by Cajipe-Endaya's explosion of the work 'Ang Asawa Ko Ay DH', a sculptural assemblage still bounded by the familiar contours of the human body, into 'Filipina: DH,' an installation that now occupies and furnishes almost an entire room. Filipina, which becomes commensurate with DH, is exploded all over the room as the room — that is, as the objectification of her labour of accommodation. The found objects which compose this installation are not, as the critic who reviewed this work for *Art in America* understood them to be, 'the objects that fill her life — clothes, suitcases, cleaning implements and room furnishings.'[56] The found objects do not fill her life, they are her life, or I should say, they are her. Without an understanding of the way in which domestic helpers are treated not as persons with possessions but rather as possessions of other persons, as precisely found objects, the critic can only comment on how 'literal' Cajipe-Endaya's commentary on 'the plight of a Filipina maid' is, thereby completely missing the violent literalness with which the domestic helper is made equivalent with the implements and furnishings attached to her. By means of these found objects, Cajipe-Endaya thus evokes the material context in and as which the domestic helper exists, bringing the evacuation of her human subjectivity into skeletal relief.

In this context, the discourse of human rights which feminists have taken up powerfully intervenes. Fused with the discourse of costs in which daily life is conducted, especially the daily life of people living *as* commodities, this human rights discourse enables one to reclaim and liberate one's labour-time as human potential. The economic rendering of 'humanity' as a value that is extracted and can be taken back provides a way of cultivating labouring Filipinas' political potential which is now not merely a function of their economic power. The demand for women's rights as human rights is precisely a demand for women's human potential, the possible power which is taken away from them, extracted from them, but which they might then regain for the first time — as Adora Faye de Vera puts it, these are 'rights inherent in human beings, including those hitherto not experienced but now realizable'.[57] If the discourse of costs is seen as a practical language which structures people's practices and thoughts, this transformed use of such a discourse (using humanity as a value) might also have a transformative effect on dominant social relations of production.[58] Indeed, the fusion of the discourse on human rights and the economics discourse of costs and value is potentially transformative to the extent that the concept of human worth is determined by more than one system of value (for example, by gendered and racial systems of value which are themselves constitutively related to class relations as they are played out through the international division of labour). As value, humanity becomes a form of 'labour-time', where labour encompasses the creative, subjective activity which women engage in to produce life, their own as well as others' — their living labour of life which is at once denied, taken away from and employed against them. To redeem their human potential thus means to redeem the creative power of their lives, in a word, their life-times.

GATHERING TIME

In a poem about a woman who has had a miscarriage, Ruth Elynia Mabanglo, the other Filipina feminist creative artist whose work I want to consider, writes:

> *... batid mo't batid ko —*
> *may alamat ang paglapat ng labi't*
> *pagtiim ng bagang,*
> *may alamat ang kuyumos na palad.*

> [You know and I know —
> there is a tale behind the tightening of one's lips and
> the clenching of one's teeth,
> there is a tale behind one's crumpled hand.]

It is these tales immanent in the bodies of women that Mabanglo tries to articulate, thereby unleashing time from its corporeal reification, from its fusion with women's being — rather than being time, women might then express their own time, the time of their experiences. In Cajipe-Endaya's sculptural installation, this experiential time is trapped inside the suitcase 'body' of the domestic helper — it is contained in the letter, the voice tape, and the books. Mabanglo takes one form of this trapped time, the letter of the overseas domestic helper, and opens up its contents, releasing the subjective activity — the human time of desiring, caring, feeling and thinking — of these women.

If we look at Filipina feminist deployments of corporeal issues, we see that these are always partial means, parts of posing and locating the crises that confront women (the crises that, from the perspective of the nation, women embody). In fact, my own insistence on the body as a lens of analysis, as a tracking object, gives undue prominence and facticity to the body as an effected object. Recognizing the objectification and reification of practices which constitute the body as such demands that ultimately the body disappear or be suspended or be taken apart and reassembled in a way that doesn't merely reconstitute the same body that is violated, beaten and exploited. This is, I believe the transformative possibility offered in Cajipe-Endaya's sculpture. Rather than reclaiming the DH-body as the value-producing equipment of labouring women, it asks for our participation in the dismantling of this body, and of the hegemonic subjectivities we inhabit inasmuch as they are predicated upon this body. Above all, it asks for our participation in the deliverance of the human potential and vitality which this im-mobile dissimulates.

The subjective activity and power of domestic helpers is expressed through the diaries, letters and phone calls they send to their families and each other. Indeed, the power Arguillas sensed in the magnitude of their gatherings also consists of their desire to commune and communicate with one another out of the isolation of their working conditions. In a letter to her parents, Elisa Salem, a domestic helper working in Jordan expresses this isolation and a longing for human connection with which she might contend against the objectifying treatment she receives at the hands of her employer:

Mama, Papa, I am like a prisoner here. I get no rest. I sleep at 2 in the morning and wake up at 4 at dawn. I have been living this way for more than a month. I am forced to wear only bra and panty when I work, and I am beaten all the time by my woman employer. I have no one to turn to, my master is very harsh ... My whole body aches, I am sore all over. She hits me with the vacuum handle, sometimes with iron, she pulls my hair, she kicks me, she slaps me, she rubs my face on the floor. Mama, Papa, my body can't take it anymore. I don't know if I can last till the end of my contract. I beg you to help me, because only you can help me now. I have no one to tell my story to here ... I beg you, Mama, please send me a letter. It will be my medicine for my loneliness here ... Please pray for me always, and give me the strength and courage to go on.[59]

In the last letter she wrote her husband before she died, Salem expresses a source of her desire to continue living and working: her son, Axel.

If not for Axel, whom I think about night and day, I wouldn't care anymore if I came back home a cold corpse. I am really tempted to commit suicide so that I may no longer feel the pain in my body ... You know my plight here. I have no time. Please embrace Axel for me, kiss him for me, my kisses go to both of you. Promise, you will always write me. Please.

Salem's plight is that she has no time, that is, no human time. Letters from her loved ones are doses of human time which help to sustain her life and her desire to live. It is this desiring enacted through writing to reach beyond the confinements of her bodily labour-time that constitutes her vital power.

In her collection of poetry, *Mga Liham ni Pinay* [Letters of Pinay], Ruth Elynia S. Mabanglo attempts to engage and extend this power by writing as and to overseas Filipina women who in turn write to women at home.[60] Writing in the first person, Mabanglo imagines herself in the place of different 'Pinays' (Filipino women) overseas — domestic helpers, mail order brides and a sex worker. The poem-letters are in fact entitled according to the places from where these 'Pinays' write home: '... *Mula sa Singapore*,' '... *Mula sa Kuwait*,' '... *Mula sa Japan*,' and so on. It is this *mula sa* (coming from) which determines

Mabanglo's empathetic occupation of the 'I's of other Filipinas. 'If I were there' becomes 'If I were her'. Placement becomes identity. This subjunctive exercise is not a matter of representing others or speaking in behalf of others. It is, rather, a practice of involving oneself in another. Mabanglo takes the substitutability of women, their exploitative exchangeability within a capitalist, sexist and racist socio-economic order, and turns it into a means of partially experiencing the lives of the women for whom she feels.

Substituting herself for another, another for herself, Mabanglo writes a self and as a self who share in that designation 'Pinay'. The double meaning of 'Pinay' here as at once the general category, 'Filipino women', and the name of an individual woman (signified by *ni*), underscores the duality of the subjective form realized through this writing practice. I experience myself as a unique individual but at the same time, *also always* as an example or instance of the category, Filipina women. On the one hand, Mabanglo demonstrates this gendered and nationalized duality by writing the experiences of different Filipinas as letters of the same 'Pinay'. On the other hand, she uses this duality as the enabling form of her writing/ experiencing the lives of other Pinays. Moreover, in writing as *different* Filipinas, Mabanglo transforms this duality into a multiplicity. As a 'Pinay', 'I' am this other, but 'I' am also this series of others. This practice of taking part(s) is feminist to the extent that it intensifies the subjective being-for-others of women to help create a collective, or multiple, context-being through which Pinays can exercise their historical potential. By mobilizing and commandeering precisely the subjective form through which they are exploited — their extensive self (their being-for-others), which I have elsewhere called syncretic sociability[61] — Mabanglo attempts to gather the creative living power of individual Filipinas into a collective force.

In '... *Mula sa Singapore*,' a domestic helper writes to her family, recalling her mixed emotions and thoughts when she left the Philippines:

> *Sugatan ang ngiti ko nang lisanin kayo,*
> *Malagim ang kahapon at malabo ang bukas*
> *Ngunit kailangang ipakipagsapalaran*
> *Kahit ang mga payak ninyong halik at yakap.*

[My smile was wounded when I left you,
Yesterday was gloomy, tomorrow uncertain
But it was necessary to risk
Even your simple kisses and embraces.]

...

Umalis akong may dawag ng takot
Hatid ng dalita't walang pangalang pagod.
Lumulusot ang kirot sa nakabihis na tapang
Ngunit kailangang makawala sa gapos ng utang.

[I left with a thorn of fear in my side
In the company of torment and a nameless fatigue.
A stinging pain was piercing the courage I was dressed in
But it was necessary to free us from the manacles of debt.]

Pinay tells of her coercion without naming its agents. *'Kailangan'* [it
was necessary] merely points to the demand she responds to and the
pressure she feels. *'Sa gapos ng utang'* [the manacles of debt], however,
alludes not only to the poverty which 'forces' her to leave in search of
a way out, but also to the 'forces' to which her family owes its poverty
— the class from which they are forced to borrow is also the class which
impoverishes them. The objective poverty of Pinay which is the
commonly attributed 'cause' of the vast migration of Filipinas abroad
as domestic helpers, entertainers and mail-order brides is
counterweighed by what she must risk or gamble with
(*ipakipagsapalaran*): 'your simple kisses and embraces'. Bodily tokens
of love are here counterposed to monetary lack. These are both the
symbols and the material of her subjective 'wealth', that is, the as-yet
uncommodified activity of her life. This activity of loving and caring
are what help to produce Pinay's life, and it is this life which
subsequently becomes objectified and obtains value as an exportable
commodity: the domestic helper.

Pinay's ability to care and extend herself in fact does constitute her
labour-power as a *yaya* [nanny], one of her functions as a domestic
helper, and thus from the standpoint of her buyers/employers she can
be seen to be already commodified. However, it is also subjectively
(from her standpoint as living labour) the activity that remains beyond
the purview of exchange. As this uncommodified activity, Pinay's

experience is a power of her own. It is the site of her 'free' activity and thus the site of her potential freedom. Ignoring the pain of leaving, braving the gloom and uncertainty of her past and future, and bearing fear, she demonstrates the emotional work she expends on the way to her objectification. For in fact objectification is what becomes of her: *'Sa among banyaga pagkatao'y itinakwil/ Ipinahamig na ganap sa madlang hilahil'* [I surrendered my humanness to my foreign master/ letting tribulation appropriate it completely]. It is in contradiction to this dehumanisation that Pinay articulates the experiential dimension of her 'processing' as a domestic helper. The repetition of *'Nguni't kailangan'* [But it was necessary] is the means she uses to steel herself for the measures she actively takes. In this way, 'necessity' serves as an important subjective conceit that enables her to try to surmount the 'objective forces' that coerce her, forces that include the daughter's imperative to reproduce the family. 'Necessity' is what she herself helps to make real and effective as the motive principle of women's duties. In other words, by enduring her fear, her torment and her longing, in her willingness and *desire* to free herself and her family from their indebtedness (their bondage), Pinay aids in her own 'processing' as a desirable worker.

Pinay's experience does not only consist of emotionally bracing herself to withstand what is happening to her. It also consists of actively dreaming:

> *Umalis akong may udyok ng pangarap*
> *Makauwi sa galak, maahon sa hirap,*
> *Bugnot na palibhasa sa galunggong at kanin*
> *At palad na meryendang kamote't saging.*
> *Pangarap ko ring maging maybahay*
> *Ng isang ginoong guwapo't ginagalang,*
> *Maligo sa pabango kung Sabado't Linggo*
> *At mamasyal sa parke nang walang agam-agam.*

> [I left, urged by a dream
> Of coming home to cheer,
> Of being removed from hardship,
> From the annoying lot of eating fish and rice
> And a fate of snacking on camotes and bananas.
> I too dreamt of becoming a wife

Of a handsome and respected gentleman,
Of bathing in fragrance on the weekend
And promenading in the park without a worry.]

Pinay's dream of being saved from a fate of 'fish and rice' and 'camotes and bananas' indicates a desire for other tastes, for pleasures beyond subsistence. It is a dream for a life that exceeds her existence as a function of necessity. This uncommodified activity of dreaming is what makes Pinay go, and go on.

Letters are Pinay's means of coping with the pain and suffering imposed upon her — a means of reaching out to loved ones, of expressing what cannot be expressed in any other way, and therefore of proving the truth of one's experience. Letters are a means of realizing her unobjectified experiential activity — a means of realizing meaning to redeem an existence of merely being and functioning for others.

For Mabanglo, words are a matter of taste, expressing the beyond-sustenance. Poetry as a form of expression is thus not the offering up of meanings but rather the exuding of tastes, of sensations of a voice and a life. Words are not vehicles of truth; they do not express — they are themselves what are expressed, tasted and experienced. The experience of Mabanglo's writing can thus be likened to the experience of Pinay (in Brunei) who finds satisfaction in receiving the words of her loved ones ('*Nag-aabang ako ng sulat sa tarangkaha't pinto,/ Sa telepono'y nabubusog ang puso./ Umiiyak ako noong una,/ Nagagamot pala ang lahat ng pagbabasa*' [I wait by the gate and the door for letters,/ My heart fills up through the telephone./ I used to cry in the beginning,/ I didn't know that everything could be cured through reading]). Words comfort and sustain her like the bodily gestures of love Pinay (in Singapore) leaves behind, for they communicate an experiential sense of her loved ones. In the same way, the poem-letters of Pinays are palpable presences reaching out to others, writings of experience meant also to be experienced by another.

Taste is a fitting paradigm for this mode of experiencing inasmuch as it preserves both inner experience (subjective reserves of feeling) and external realities (objective conditions of those feelings) as the poles of one's self-constitution. Mabanglo's writing renders both of these poles, providing a milieu of experience which is at once a construction of a self (Pinay) and a construction of that self's context (her 'fromness' as expressed in '… *Mula sa …*'). Through writing, women can create experiential contexts which they can share with other women, and through this sharing, form potentially transformative involvements with each other.[62] The writing practices of experience engaged in by women are themselves ways of realizing their 'context'. If we understand 'context' to be the form of one's relations with the world, then the active constitution of one's context means the active constitution of one's self.

Each of the letters from Pinay is a placing of Pinay in and as an ensemble of relations. As a contextualization of these various selves, the series of letters is an attempt to place Pinays, both at home and abroad, in involved relations with one another, relations which are at once subjectively liberating and socially empowering. *Mga Liham ni Pinay* is, in a word, a gathering of Filipinas in a socially constitutive context of struggle.[63] Such a gathering takes inspiration from the countless letters written by domestic helpers themselves, many of which have found their way into published books, newspaper columns and women's journals and newsletters. The gathering of these letters and the human times they express in a social imaginary extends the immense subjective potential immanent in the gatherings of domestic helpers on their days off in parks, shopping promenades and prayer meetings. Such gatherings create new contexts for overseas Filipino women, contexts which foster their desires for connection to other women and which mobilize their subjective extendedness and being-for-others, that is, the conditions of their experiential labour, in ways that go beyond 'necessity' and their value for commodity exchange. As contexts for the making of new social relations and therefore of new subjective becomings, these gatherings might then mean the rescuing of the human value of women's times and the liberating exercise of their creative power.

GOING

Nobody knows me. Not even I. That is as good a reason as any to find oneself abroad, far away from all the well-worn paths and currencies of home. Here, away, no one expects of me things I have grown tired of expecting myself, of myself. The day changes as soon as I depart. It is no longer a day like all the days I patiently and diligently live out. It is neither another day nor a particular day because it is not a part of the calendar that has come to take the place of my life.

A Filipina in Japan. It is such a common sight. I think I am here for different reasons. I think I am a different Filipina. And I am. And yet … I wander down these unfamiliar streets, following the direction of my feet, of other feet. I follow the direction of things I take as signs of meanings I as yet do not know, having faith that I will arrive somewhere. The new smell of moist wood gives me pause. It allows me to feel the exhilarating rhythm of my going. Indifference surrounds me, but it is an indifference that doesn't know me and keep me. At least not yet.

Filipinas leaving. It is understood, as so much about me seems to be understood, that what they are leaving is home. They leave that place of common understanding, for what? My own leaving is the afterthought of my going. I have come to talk about gender and empowerment to people who do not already know what it is I am about to say. They do not know that what I have to say means less than this coming. 'To be alone at last, broken the seal/ That marks the flesh no better than a whore's.'[64]

When I return from this extended moment abroad, the world seems large. It is that somewhere that I, in my going, thought I might reach. In another city for another job, I listen to the familiar statistics of Filipinas being trafficked around the world. I give my share of numbers and images of Filipina casualties in the war of everyday life. A sympathetic Filipino high school teacher joins me at a bar, asking to know more. I look at the glass of beer he drinks while he tells me of his suburban life in Virginia teaching the kids of US Filipino navy men like himself and how he is toying with the idea of moving to the city. In Kyoto, I drink a rare glass of beer with others as a Japanese anthropologist among us considers pursuing his passion as a dance instructor in Bohol. We are laughing, and so is he, sensing the seriousness of such playful contemplations of life-exchanges. But everyone pays the bill, and gets on with the business of everyday life.

Some do not return home. Others return only to find their homes destroyed. Many never find homes at all. In New York, people go to work and end up dead. In Afghanistan, villages are bombed to rubble. In Palestine, people remain refugees in their own land. And in the Philippines, more and more people leave their lands for good, becoming part of the

floating populations in the metropolitan sea or in the global sea, or, no
longer part of anything at all. Abruptly and slowly, lives end, while
everywhere, other lives keep going.

DREAMING OTHER WORLDS IN OTHER WAYS

Not all Filipina bodies are domestic workers, but Filipinas abroad alone
will find themselves, at some moment or longer, perhaps eventually
for a lifetime, as domestic bodies. My nation, my body. We wear the
cheap economic value of this territory where we are from on our skin,
on our lips, as the profile of our face, as our physical size. The lack of
geopolitical power of that country of our origin inscribed by all the
borders we cannot freely cross. The limits to our movements posed by
our own embodiments of a suspect nation.

I am reminded by a reader of the limits of the concept of slavery
in its application to migrant domestic workers. After all, they do receive
wages, have Sundays off, not all of them live with their employers.
Many of them engage in petty entrepreneurship, as they perhaps already
did when they were in the Philippines. It would seem that domestic
workers are simply wage workers, some, even microcapitalists. If their
conditions bear similarities to the conditions of slavery, then surely it
is the result of the persistence of older social relations, found in sending
and receiving countries alike.[65] What is 'slavery' but an overblown
metaphor, an ideological hyperbole, bandied about by histrionic people
with a cause.

Like the notion of 'prostitution', which I deployed in the context
of the Philippines' 'sexual economy', however, 'slavery' here is a category
of fantasy-production that I have turned on its head, showing the
material political and economic relations that it issues out of and
symbolically grasps. 'Slavery' is a tendency of labour towards subjective,
bodily and social dispossession, a social technology of control and
extraction that lives on in new forms, in new institutions, supported
by global capital. Angela Davis calls our attention to the fact that
in the US, slavery is constitutionally sanctioned as a form of
punishment enforced by the prison system.[66] She also describes the
intimate links between the expanding prison-industrial complex, in

which slavery is institutionalized as penal servitude, and the globalization of capital:

> As capital moves with ease across national borders, legitimised by recent trade and investment agreements such as NAFTA, GATT and MAI, corporations close shop in the United States and transfer manufacturing operations to nations providing cheap labour pools. In fleeing organised labour in the US to avoid paying higher wages and benefits, they leave entire communities in shambles, consigning huge numbers of people to joblessness, leaving them prey to the drug trade, destroying the economic base of these communities and thus affecting the education system, social welfare — and turning the people who live in those communities into perfect candidates for prison. At the same time, they create an economic demand for prisons, which stimulates the economy, providing jobs in the correctional industry for people who often come from the very populations that are criminalised by this process.[67]

The conversion of organized labour in advanced economies such as the US into penal slave labour thus bears more than the parallel relation to third world labour conscription that Davis's own observation makes: 'Prisons themselves are becoming a source of cheap labour that attracts corporate capitalism in a way that parallels the attraction unorganized labour in Third World countries exerts.'[68] My point here is that 'slavery' is a social technology of dispossession and value-extraction that capital uses and continually refurbishes through the racist criminalization of resident and citizen populations as well as through the economic racialization of immigrant populations.[69] It is for this reason that I have qualified the term with the adjective 'new-industrial' to indicate that the practices it signifies are inextricable from the expansion and development of late capitalism.

To return to the domestic labour industry. Like the discourse of 'traffic' with regard to Manila, the discourse of 'slavery' is not then merely a metaphorical commentary on the deplorable fate of overseas Filipina domestic workers. It is rather effect and shaper of the very material reality that it purports to merely describe. On the one hand, new-industrial slavery is the consequence of the unremitting expansion of capital and its need to combat the falling rate of profit through the conversion of humans into disposable, surplus people. On the other hand, new-industrial slavery naturalizes the social imaginary within which the international labour market is a necessary reality by symbolically serving as the very negation of the fair and rational system of capitalist accumulation. If the racialized penal servitude (slavery in a new form) of the prison system functions 'as a negative affirmation of the "free world"' and as a guarantor of the freedoms and rights of civil society, 'slavery' does the same on a global scale.[70]

In the field of fantasy-production, the 'slave' is at once the binary opposite and supplement of the 'free worker'. As I've already discussed, the discursive, racialized and gendered difference between the two translates into a material surplus of power and value, which is reaped by employers (or 'masters'), recruiters, governments and corporations.[71] In this way, the 'slave' is an economic relation. 'Slavery' is also the symbolic figure against which political freedom and sovereignty for the colony is won. The Propaganda Movement against Spain in the nineteenth century deployed this figure with great frequency. Juan Luna's painting, *Solarium*, for example, allegorically depicts the Philippines as a bloodied, spent gladiator dragged across the coliseum floor by a Roman soldier, the figure of Spain. And José Rizal urges the young women of Malolos to continue their struggle for education by invoking images of enslavement: 'All are born without chains, free, and no one can subject the will and spirit of another ... Ignorance is bondage, because like mind, like man. A man without a will of his own is a man without personality. The blind who follow other's opinion is like a beast led by a halter.'[72] 'Slavery' is the negative image of modern nationhood. Not surprisingly, the image recurs beyond independence, repeatedly invoked by divergent nationalisms trying to determine the form and substance of the nation in a context when the latter's boundaries remain blurred by the intimate ties of neocolonialism. In the early 1990s then Senator Joseph Estrada argued against the retention of the US military bases in these terms: 'In our actions one can trace the pitiful happiness of a slave — who permits and hopes that another human will carry him. It's alien to the dream of a slave that he should use his own powers ...' The 'slave' is thus also a political relation. In both dimensions, economic and political, it functions as the necessary and continuously displaced limit of the free world fantasy.[73]

The discourse of 'slavery' hence grasps the real contradictions of universal capitalism that the Philippines manifests as its continuing crisis. However, the discourse is not merely a symptomatic representation of these real contradictions. It is also a symbolic practice that participates in the displacement and objectification of the Philippines' crisis in the bodies of Filipina domestic workers. Like the 'tragic tales' told by the media and the government, with which it shares a common rhetorical fund, the discourse of 'slavery' also serves as the means of resolving (by transcending) the crisis that the superexploitation of domestic workers represents in the form of a strengthened state. The discourse of 'slavery' is in this way continuous with the violent material conditions that it depicts. It performs the violence inherent to capitalist organization (the bodily price exacted from surplus humans to support its 'universal' system of political and economic value) as an aberration, an abnormal occurrence in the free world. Violence is not, however, a departure from fantasy-production but rather a necessary instrument for the maintenance of its social relations as well as a permanent means of extending its logic of extraction.[74]

When Aquino called Filipino overseas contract workers 'the new heroes' [*mga bagong bayani*] of the nation, she was only performing a logical move within the symbolic field of fantasy-production The hero is the inversion of the slave. The slave becomes the object of sacrifice — the martyr — enabling the heroization of the nation. While in the past martyrs such as Rizal and Gomburza (as the priests, Gomez, Burgos and Zamora were collectively called) helped to found the nation by freeing it from colonial slavery, in the contemporary postcolonial context, martyrs such as Ninoy Aquino and Flor Contemplacion help to reconsolidate and heroize the nation-in-crisis by being restored to it. I will return in Chapter 5 to the martyrdom of Ninoy Aquino and its role in renewing the Filipino people. In the case of Flor Contemplacion, who as a Filipina figures the nation itself (that is, its domestic body), a necessary splitting occurs. The slave figure is split into hero and martyr. The nation as subject performs its 'heroism' by making the domestic body, the repository of the Philippines' continuing enslavement, the object of its 'saving' actions as well as its own sacrifice. This, then, is the state's strategic solution to the nation's 'gender trouble', which I described in the previous chapter. Against the threat of its 'feminization' as a porous nation, the Philippines re-asserts its sovereign state agency by externalizing its crisis in the image of enslaved bodies, the regulation of which expresses the nation-state's renewed (masculinist) self-possession and self-control.

Rosalind O'Hanlon critiques the gendered bounds of the sovereign subject-agent claimed through the heroic ideal: 'It is one of the deepest misconstructions of the autonomous subject-agent that its own masculine practice possesses a monopoly, as the term signifies, upon the heroic: that effort and sacrifice are to be found nowhere but in what it holds to be the real sites of political struggle.'[75] Within the free world fantasy demarcated by the tragic discourses of 'slavery' and exceptional violence, political struggle is often confined either to global juridical reform, which only means greater powers of regulation on the part of states, or to claims made upon bourgeois democratic ideals, which leave the dream-structures of global capitalism intact.

Raymond Williams writes:

> It is a fact about the modes of domination, that they select from and consequently exclude the full range of human practice. What they exclude may often be seen as the personal or the private, or as natural or even as the metaphysical. Indeed, it is usually in one or other of these terms that the excluded area is to be expressed, since what the dominant has effectively seized is indeed the ruling definition of the social.[76]

What all these discourses of tragic slavery and violence exclude are precisely the practices of Filipinas that bypass their meanings for the nation, practices of living that attest to *who* they are as creative forces rather than *what* they might be for others. Scholars like myself write about the suffering, exploitation, and oppression experienced by Filipinas leaving their homes and in this way participate in such discourses at the expense of ignoring the other ways in which their going is also a dreaming of other worlds. Sometimes their actions, from the side of subjectivity, comprise a dreaming in other ways that we fail to co-imagine, a calling that we fail to hear or follow, a beckoning we fail to recognize in our own life-movements because we ourselves are trapped by fantasy-ideals of critically-conscious, sovereign subject-agents of heroic resistance and change. We detach our own comings and goings, our own wayward desires, from the unheroic, everyday dream-actions of people we have set apart from ourselves, even as the limits of our life-possibilities are intimately tied to theirs, even as some of us share in that designation, *Filipina*.

Dreaming in other ways has, however, long been at work in the historical making of this nation that claims Filipinas as its domestic bodies. In the next section, I track the unforeseen and yet invisible ways in which such unruly desires participate in the makings and remakings of Philippine history despite the fact that they are continuously captured and coded by dominant dream-subjects to play merely supplementary, if not altogether reproductive, parts.

PART II

Desiring History, Tangential Pursuits

•

Regimes and Heresies of Transformative Action

In spite of the well-known and highly debated Fukuyama proclamation that we, the world, have reached the end of history, 'history' continues to make its appearance whenever there is talk of or feeling about the nation. Such talk and feeling, in which 'history' figures prominently, are never so fervent, so abundant, as when the nation is in crisis. As the US in the aftermath of the World Trade Center attacks demonstrates, the spirits of nationalism run high whenever the nation appears besieged and history, seemingly forgotten, is feverishly re-dreamt in waking life. Forefathers reappear to remind the citizenry of the nation's founding ideals and of its cherished inheritance, admonishing them to defend what is rightfully theirs; the glorious struggles of the past are rehearsed as models of action for the present; and the voices of dead heroes ring loudly in wakeful ears. Like an attic, 'history' is rummaged for old pictures and medals and dusty words that will revive collective memories, feelings and dreams in a citizenry badly shaken by the crisis event yet at a loss to respond, trapped as it were in the rubble of everyday life. For the most powerful nation on earth, 'history' is a stable resource of sentiment and vision to which its citizenry has unquestioned access, being as it is the nation's own, like a memory-bank storing all of its political-intellectual property, a repository of all its tried and true forms of collective imagination.[1]

For post-independent colonial nations, history is much more problematic.[2] In a permanent state of crisis, postcolonial nations can never take their 'history' for granted and indeed constantly struggle to make lasting claims on it. For the Philippines, as for other postcolonial nations, the very question of its history continues to be the question of its viability and future as a nation. Hence, the question 'whose history?' has continuously dogged the Philippines since the latter's political inception in the late nineteenth century. Or, rather, the question has served and continues to serve as a motive force in the recurrent founding of the Philippine nation. José Rizal's famous and often quoted pronouncement that those who do not look back to where they come from will not reach where they are headed does not therefore only exemplify the new historical consciousness shaping the nineteenth century Propagandist and Revolutionary movements against Spanish colonialism and their aspirations for Filipino nationhood. It also indicates how for the emergent nation the continuing struggle over its own history is a struggle over the very future of its people.

The effort on the part of Rizal and the other Propagandists to refute the historical consciousness bequeathed to them by Spain played a major part in the creation of the 'imagined community' of the Filipino nation. Zeus Salazar describes the historical consciousness introduced by the Spanish colonizers as 'a consciousness that could not help but consider the Indio as the object of historical action by the Spaniard who, in his own self-conscious view of himself, was the conscient subject exercising his political will (through the colonial state) in pursuit of a religious and civilizing mission'.[3] Against this historical consciousness, which espoused a 'bipartite view' of Philippine history consisting of a barbaric pre-Hispanic past and a continuing civilized Spanish present, Rizal, Graciano Lopez Jaena, Andres Bonifacio and other Filipino propagandists and revolutionaries studiously and poetically forged a new vision of Philippine history.[4] In this 'tripartite' view of Philippine history, which espoused a civilized pre-Hispanic native past, a benighted Spanish present, and a free, just and progressive Filipino future, towards which the struggle of the nation was directed, Filipinos ceased to be objects, becoming instead subjects with their own historical will, agency and destiny.

Despite the power of its first appearance, the subject-making potential of the nationalist claim to sovereignty over history has never been realized with any stable guarantee. After all, the symbolic struggle over the representation and interpretation of Philippine history has never ceased to be so directly a part of the material-practical struggle over the organization and control, not to mention the very existence, of the nation. To the extent that, colonialism 'turns to the past of the oppressed people, and distorts, disfigures and destroys it', 'history' serves as the very means of their decolonization and emergence as an independent nation.[5] Almost immediately recolonized by the US after the Spanish-American War in 1898 and the decade-long Filipino-American War (1899–1913), the Philippines found its newfound 'history' wrenched from its control and subsumed by the 'manifest destiny' of US colonialism. As Reynaldo Ileto argues, US colonial textbooks portrayed Philippine history as beginning with the Revolution against Spain, an event that, inasmuch as it led to the formation of a short-lived modern Republic, signified the Philippines' shaky emergence into world history.[6] But this early birth of the Philippine nation was nevertheless considered a failure (a failure, it should be said, realized practically and not just conceptually by the imposition of US colonial rule), its leadership as well as its people considered 'unfit for self-government' and needing American 'tutelage' in the civilized arts of modern nationhood.[7]

Philippine 'history' in the hands of US colonial historians thus prepared the way for the continued political and economic dependence of the Philippine nation-state on the US beyond colonial rule. Recognizing the role that such 'history' played in the support of the Philippines' neocolonial relations with the US after its formal independence in 1946, nationalist historians in the post-Second World War period called for the continued struggle to decolonize Philippine history. As Renato Constantino proclaimed: 'we must unchain not only our culture and our economic and political life, but also our history. It must be subjected to a rigorous examination; we must rewrite it and free it from the myths and assumptions imposed on us for interests other than our own.'[8] Constantino's call for the liberation of Filipino history was answered by the radical activist nationalist movements of the late 1960s and early 1970s, which saw themselves continuing the 'unfinished' revolution against Spain that was to have brought the Filipino nation into being. 'History' itself became once again a rallying cause, an object and means of national liberation. Not surprisingly, it also became a symbolic cause of the dictatorial regime of Ferdinand Marcos, which tried to stamp out these movements by usurping the power of their appeals. The Marcos regime embarked on an ambitious history writing project that espoused 'the Filipino view', a project in which leading nationalist historians were involved.[9] As a 'revolution from the centre', the Marcos project for a 'New Society' consisted not only of this rewriting of Philippine History as a legitimization of authoritarian rule.[10] It also consisted of *making* Philippine History — that is to say, reorganizing the social, political and economic order of Philippine life — in the image of Filipino 'self-rule' that this rewriting was to fashion for Marcos (as the Filipino Self), a rewriting called *Tadhana* [Destiny].

My aim in this brief discussion is to point to the vigorous and violent contestations over 'history' that have taken place in the Philippines as a consequence of the continuing crisis of the nation. 'History' is deeply contested at every moment of its expression down to the very assertion of the 'facts'. Hence numerous controversies over the authenticity of documents, over the dates and places of specific events — not only over the interpretation of historical records and events but of their very existence — plague the writing of Philippine history. The recent controversy over US historian Glenn May's 'exposé' of the posthumous 'invention' of the Revolutionary hero, Andres Bonifacio, by Filipino nationalist historians is only the latest, and perhaps the most telling, of these controversies.[11] It is a controversy that puts into question, yet again, not only the capacity of Filipinos to tell their own history but also the fact that they do indeed have a history to tell. Not only 'whose history?' but indeed 'history'?

Philippine historians comprise an embattled and battling lot. For good reason. What is at stake in all these conflicts over the fact, matter, form and meaning of a 'Filipino history' is no less than the material life of that 'imagined community' of the Philippines itself. Inasmuch as 'history' is one of the key requirements of modern nationhood, it figures centrally in the practical and imaginary constitution of the Philippines as a political and economic unit in the international system of sovereign nation-states. The invocations, instantiations and symbolic enactments of Philippine history by the government and by social movements are, in this view, more than simply representational gestures made to motivate, mask or legitimate material actions and practices — 'real' causes to which one might trace the actually obtaining social conditions of Philippine life. As the uses to which 'history' was put in the projects of the Revolution, US colonialism, activist movements and the Marcos dictatorship demonstrate, the symbolic practices by which 'history' is pursued, constructed and revised are also practical forces shaping the material realities of the nation.

In the first section of this book I examined the imaginary logics at work in the material organization of the Philippine state and national economy. I tried to show, in particular, the subjective dynamics of the political and economic actions of the nation-state and the logics of race, gender and sexuality that such actions heed and participate in realizing. In the following section I focus on the subjective dynamics of the uses and enactments of Filipino 'history'. For 'history', as defined by an alien Western modernity (alienated, that is, from the colonies, which were vital to its production), is the elusive object of desire for postcolonial nations, which by the measure of modern nationhood will always be found to be in a position of lack or of failure. As Partha Chatterjee argues, the 'inelegant braiding of an idea of community with the concept of capital' in the idea of the nation in Western social theory shapes the postcolonial national state's own self-recognition.[12] 'One can see how a conception of the state-society relation, born within the parochial history of Western Europe but made universal by the global sway of capital, dogs the contemporary history of the world.' Attempts to write and make history under the sway of this ideal can thus only perform this lack over and over again. 'The provincialism of the European experience will be taken as the universal history of progress; by comparison, the history of the rest of the world will appear as the history of lack, of inadequacy — an inferior history.'[13] Whence all the fervent protestations, avowals and exhortations on the part of numerous Filipino historians that reveal the desire for a 'true' and 'truly' Filipino history, which is somehow still out of reach. It is not that these historians act in behalf of the nation-state. Rather, their dilemmas in historiography are similarly dogged by the Philippine nation-state's pursuit of and failure to realize this ideal.

As I've already mentioned, for colonials and their descendants, the struggle for a sovereign historiography and the struggle for sovereign nationhood (or put differently, the struggle to write one's own history and the struggle to make one's own history) have always been closely intertwined. At a later moment then in this decolonizing struggle, or at some distance from this decolonization (which some identify with the postcolonial moment), the task of the historian has moved away somewhat from the writing of the unitary nationalist history of the nation.[14] Now the historian turns to the recuperation of those social elements, cultural ways, deeds and life fragments that were repressed, ignored or eschewed in the hegemonic historical narratives of the nation. We can see exemplary realizations of this kind of history in the work of Filipino historians Reynaldo Ileto and Vicente Rafael.[15] For Ileto and Rafael, this move is about recovering lost and overlooked historical agencies. For subaltern studies historians, with whose work both Ileto and Rafael are closely aligned, the recuperation of the underside of nationalist history is also an attempt to understand 'the historic failure of the nation to come to its own'.[16]

My own critical views on history are deeply situated within this trajectory I have just sketched. Indeed, in this book, like Ileto and Rafael, I too am searching for lost and overlooked historical agencies. But as one who writes outside the discipline of history, even if with a similar distance from and keen interest in the Filipino nation, I am a little digressive in this pursuit. Hence, in this section I am rather more interested in how Filipino 'history' figures as the object of desire of the nation as well as the means of desire for the nation.

As that which will fill the lack imputed to the postcolonial nation, a possession that will also mean finally the self-possession of the nation (or even as that which will illuminate precisely 'the historic failure of the nation to come to its own') 'history' serves a subjectifying function. It is, in this aspect, part and parcel of the order of fantasy-production. In the next two chapters, then, I continue my critique of fantasy-production by examining the ways in which 'Filipino history' is pursued, reclaimed, practiced in the post-independence period. Focusing on two revolutionary events as narrated by their national elite victors (Teodoro Agoncillo's history of the 1896 Philippine Revolution against Spain and an oral history of the 1986 People Power 'revolution' against the Marcos regime), I analyse the libidinal dynamics of its telling and of its conscious making. Put another way, I analyse the racializing, gendering and sexualizing effects of the actions made in the name of 'Filipino history'. I also suggest the connections between these dynamics and the worldly contexts they issue out of and effectively shape. In both chapters, I read for the 'rules' by which both hegemonic and counter-hegemonic 'history' is claimed and transformed, and for the persistence of unruly social agencies and transgressive desires beyond the fantasy forms that try to domesticate them.

In the last chapter, I explore another way that history is made, this time in the realm of 'non-history', that is, in a 'non-historical' event: the mass mediated phenomenon of actress Nora Aunor's stardom/ fandom presented in Ishmael Bernal's 1981 film *Himala* (Miracle). In this last chapter, I endeavour to demonstrate the historical, poetic (poiesis as living practice of production) significance of what I call practices of tangentiality, which are paradigmatically enacted by Nora Aunor's massive 'hysterical' following. These socio-subjective practices or practices of imagination are the 'work' of creative agencies seeking their own paths of becoming (paths for coming into other kinds of living) and in the process missing, diverging from and altering 'history'. Beyond this demonstration, however, I also follow these wayward dream-acts to the point where they break away from the subjective structures of fantasy-production, which try to subsume them. In this way, I hope to participate in a heretical mode of rephrasing history.

4

Revolt of the Masses:
National History as Psychology

Over fifty years ago, the historian Teodoro Agoncillo prefaced his just completed work, *The Revolt of the Masses: The Story of Bonifacio and the Katipunan*, with an explanation of the impossibility of writing a biography of the Philippine revolutionary, Andres Bonifacio (Fig. 4.1): 'For the Plebian Hero, the first truly Filipino democrat, suffered from two disadvantages. On the one hand was his lowly and obscure origin, and on the other was the plethora of supposedly reliable documents on his trial and death.'[1] In Agoncillo's view, Bonifacio's 'obscure origin' prevents his contemporaries, including his sister, from remembering his early life with any clarity or accuracy, while the abundance of accounts about his trial and death make it 'sufficiently taxing for a student of the period' to decide which of these accounts are accurate and reliable, and which are not. The obscurity of Bonifacio's life and the unruliness of the accounts of it are hence surmounted by an examination of the revolutionary society that he led, the *Katipunan*. In this way does the *Katipunan* emerge as the medium 'in and through' which Bonifacio must be 'seen and appreciated'. 'To understand him, one must understand the *Katipunan*' (viii). Such understanding is directed toward the final end of understanding the fulfillment of the Revolution initiated by the revolt of the masses.

Figure 4.1 Andres Bonifacio, Philippine hero. Photograph courtesy of the National Commission for Culture and the Arts.

TWO 'RULES' OF HISTORY

In this foreword are evidenced some of the 'rules' of history shaping Agoncillo's work, a work whose significance to Philippine history is at least confirmed by its recent republication on the centennial anniversary of the 1898 end of the Revolution against Spain. At the time of its first appearance Agoncillo's work generated much controversy for what then seemed to be its attribution of inordinate historical agency to the peasant leader Bonifacio and the masses over and above the elite, *ilustrado* (enlightened, educated) leaders and members of the revolution, including its seminal inspiration and founding father of the nation, José Rizal. Out of the heated debates over the decolonization of history, which it undoubtedly fueled, *The Revolt of the Masses* emerged as a lodestar for the founding of a nationalist revisionist rewriting of Philippine history, one that avowed its partisanship to 'the Filipino people' and to the cause of the 'unfinished revolution'.[2] Today, in the wake of recent official centennial celebrations of the purported 'success' of that Revolution, the 'rules' of history set by Agoncillo's work are worth reconsidering. They are worth examining in light of the fact, to which I am drawn, that they continue to hold sway in present attempts to write and make Philippine history. I want to suggest, further, that the hold of these 'rules' over Philippine historical imagination testifies to the powerful imperatives of fantasy-production history, from which they draw their authority and to which they pay tribute.

Let me briefly mention two of these 'rules'. The first rule is that the difficulties facing the historian become the disadvantages of his 'subject'. Put differently, the problems of writing history become the problems of history itself. In Agoncillo's narrative, Bonifacio's lowly origin, which accounts for the paucity of 'reliable' documents about him, turns out to be a principle determinant of Bonifacio's actions and the turn in the Revolution, expressed by the ascendancy of Emilio Aguinaldo to the leadership and the execution of Bonifacio, to which those actions led. In this way does the challenge of Agoncillo's task express itself as the tragedy of Bonifacio's life. The second rule is, biography is sublated by history, by which I mean that while history seems to supplant biography and biography seems to contribute to a history that subsumes and supersedes it, biography persists as the motoring and structuring principle of history. Thus the master narrative of the Revolution at once subsumes and is represented by the Katipunan and Bonifacio, who act respectively as the sum whole and the leading part of the master character of this narrative: the Filipino people. Consequently, in this narrative, Bonifacio's tragedy is the enabling condition of the triumph of the Filipino nation, that is, the triumphant conversion of the underground movement of the Katipunan into the nation-state of the Philippine Republic. Moreover, as this story is biographical in structure, it is also psychological in character. The history of the nation is thus also a work of psychology.

In this chapter, I will attempt to explain these 'rules' and some of their corollaries in more detail and to dwell precisely on the details of Agoncillo's work as proof of their operation. These 'rules' are to some extent expostulated by Reynaldo Ileto in his various critiques of the 'linear developmentalism' that continues to shape much Philippine historiography.[3] Ileto critiques in particular Agoncillo's foundational nationalist construction of the Fall (Conquest), Dark Age (Colonial Rule) and Recovery (Triumph of the Revolution) of the Philippine nation, and the culmination of this history in the founding of the Philippine Republic of 1898. Such a history, which the *ilustrado* and *principalia* (educated and elite) classes subscribed to and propagated, Ileto argues, necessarily suppresses the elements that cannot be incorporated into the developmental narrative, elements such as the irrational, archaic and religious-fanatical views and actions of members of the 'original' illicit association that was the Katipunan. It is according to this developmentalist logic that Bonifacio's purported ambitions to kingship and indulgences in superstitious myths necessitated his execution: 'Bonifacio had to go … A replacement, this time from the *principalia*, was needed to rid the movement of its unsavoury characteristics. Thus, the emergence of a new leader, Aguinaldo, who put the Katipunan in "proper order" as a liberal nationalist movement seeking to form a republican state that would be recognized by all civilized nations.'[4]

With its inexorable narrative movement, the plot of *The Revolt of the Masses* certainly seems to adhere to this progressive logic: 'Starting with the emotive cry of freedom, followed with the instinctive resort to physical force to realize the primitive urge to be free, the *Katipunan* had adopted, first, the political philosophy of the French Revolution — Liberty, Equality and Fraternity — then, the American system of free elections and, finally, the principles of universal freedom of thought, of conscience and of education' (292). The narrative thus reads as the progressive expression of the democratic ideals of Euro-American nationalism through the actions of the Filipinos. In light of these ideals, Bonifacio's refusal to accept the results of the 'free' election of Aguinaldo during the Tejeros convention can only be read as 'a blot in the otherwise glorious record of the Revolution' (231). Instead of being interpreted as a part of a collective act affirming revolutionary authority beyond that accorded by electoral politics, Bonifacio's refusal is transformed, by Agoncillo as well as by the emergent regime which tried and executed Bonifacio, into a threat to the Revolution itself, a threat ultimately attributable to one man, the *Supremo*. This *Acta de Tejeros* is a blot inasmuch as it threatens the fulfillment of Agoncillo's task, as a historian, to produce the coherent, seamless narration of the nation's attainment of sovereignty. Since, however, the blot cannot be erased, it must be converted into a tragedy, and in this way does the biographical principle structure the history of which Agoncillo is the judge and executioner.[5]

As the hero of this tragedy, Bonifacio exhibits, like the blot he causes, a flaw: 'He loved his country *too well*' (emphasis mine). Bonifacio's 'zealous regard for the cause of the Revolution' (231) is his tragic flaw because it is the same trait that catapults him into greatness but brought to excess — his passion for revolutionary Right becomes overbearing and, disabled from listening to Reason, he strays from the political line mapped out by the new Republic. While 'the Revolution inexorably moved towards a climax ... The *Katipunan* had become unwieldy because of its mass and energy ...' (294). As simply 'the moving spirit behind the *Katipunan* and the initiator of the revolt of the masses' (294), Bonifacio had outlived his usefulness: 'When the Revolution broke out in all its fury and tragic implications his services became almost negligible. A new leader in the person of Emilio Aguinaldo had to take his place, for the character of the former was more apposite to the exigencies of the time' (299). Bonifacio was the wrong person to lead to the extent that the passionate 'mass and energy' which he embodied and infused into the *Katipunan*, while necessary to inspire and catalyze the revolutionary movement, had begun to pose a threat to the organization of a modern nation-state. From the moment that he was asked to intervene in the power struggle between the rival factions of the *Katipunan*, 'Bonifacio's personality suffered modifications that were in direct contrast to the character that had made him the unchallenged organizer and leader of the early *Katipunan*' (297). This serviceable character was, in Agoncillo's estimation, 'his modesty, coupled with his tolerance and even temper' (289) appropriate to a man of little education and humble origins. In the enlightened perspective, which by definition recognizes the authority of elections, Bonifacio's refusal to recognize the powers of office elected in the Tejeros convention is evidence that he no longer knew his place. More, that he was too carried away by his own passions and his mistakenly inflated estimation of his capacities to remain serviceable.

Agoncillo's concordance with the historical judgement cast by the ascendant *ilustrado* government thus becomes the basis on which Bonifacio's 'mistake' is clarified: 'His mistake, then, lay in this: that he took everything for granted and, flattered to the limit by the signal honor of having been asked to intervene, he disregarded the psychology of regionalism' (294). Bonifacio can only have been mistaken in light of the 'correct' assessment of his limitations as 'a man so devoid of formal education and family tradition, so simple in his ways, in a word, so common' (288) that his fate could not but lay with the masses with whom he was identified. In keeping with the first 'rule' of history, Agoncillo's difficulties in writing Bonifacio's actions into the 'glorious record' that his narrative aims to approximate are converted into a failing of the latter's character, which itself becomes the 'cause' of his own downfall. In this corrective perspective, Bonifacio 'mistook' himself, to the extent that he took himself at all seriously, as the *Supremo*. In this seriousness lay his overestimation of himself, for from the standpoint of his successors, his power, like the passionate forces of revolt, was meant only for the advent of the Revolution, not for its fulfillment. Only those equipped with proper, rational judgement, a judgement secured by detachment (which purportedly Bonifacio lacked, but Agoncillo had), can recognize the 'truth' of Bonifacio's capacities and his 'historical worth'. Since this worth is measured by degree of conformity to the sovereign, rational citizen who is the protagonist subject and ideal object(ive) of the narrative of nationalism, Bonifacio must be deemed tragic; his tragedy lies in his constitutional incapability to distance himself from 'the people' who, in the time of the Republic, must assume the role of the governed (Fig. 4.2). Disregarding the 'psychology of regionalism' means failing to distance himself from this 'deep-rooted idea and feeling of regionalism that characterize the Filipinos as a people' (300) and therefore allowing it to get the better of his already slight, because so little educated, judgement. What we might read, contrarily, as Agoncillo's 'complex' about Bonifacio's social inferiority appears in Agoncillo's case history as an imputation of Bonifacio's psychological weakness — his 'inferiority complex'. Hence Bonifacio's actions acquire a logic: he is portrayed, for example, as 'probably assailed by doubts and aware of his limitations' (211). In this way does Agoncillo read his class estimation into and as Bonifacio's psychological motivation.

In keeping with the second 'rule', Agoncillo's historical-biographical account of Bonifacio's actions thus proves itself to be a work of psychology. The 'laws of probability' that structure Agoncillo's argument

Figure 4.2 Bonifacio, Plebian Revolutionary. Photograph courtesy of the National Commission for Culture and the Arts.

and the logic of his narrative turn out to be laws of a mechanical, expressivist psychology. Bonifacio's failing is shown to stem from his psychological constitution, which is in turn determined by the social class whose aspirations he is 'by nature sympathetic to' (288). Like Bonifacio, the personality of this class has also suffered untoward modifications: 'The people, because of a sudden exercise of freedom that was won with blood and tears, had acquired habits of thought that were tinged with suspicion. They became jealous of their newfound power and authority and consequently looked upon all modes of actions contrary to their own as a potential danger and threat to their very existence. Out of these jealousies and suspicions arose an attitude that in normal times would have been labeled brutish ... In a critical situation in which the existence of a nation is at stake, the psychology of the people, thinking and acting under the stress of the moment, is impregnated with a virus of distrust that becomes malignant with each passing hour' (310). The trial and execution of the *Supremo* is thus explained as the consequence of the 'abnormal psychology' (309) that held sway over this abnormal time.

Such a time is abnormal because in this developmental history another time has intervened, superseding the time of excitability and plebian passions which, in the beginning of the revolution, met the needs of the movement: 'The spirit of the time, the excited mental state of the people long brutalized and thirsting for vengeance and who by now had found an outlet and an opportunity for sweet revenge, was propitious for the uninhibited release of brute strength' (169). Not only has the time *of* the people, and hence of Bonifacio, passed, the people *as* this time of brutish, libidinal power — that is, the people *as* a character of time (an epoch) no longer apposite to the exigencies of the ascendant time of nationhood — has also become the propellant of that time's, and its *Supremo's*, demise. As Agoncillo argues, 'the very epoch that he created was also one that misunderstood him' (313), predisposed as it was to 'the congenital sentiment of regionalism' (231), by which Agoncillo means sympathetic rather than rational action. Agoncillo thus (psycho)analyses the blot of Bonifacio's challenge as the consequence of the 'abnormal psychology' which temporarily rules, like a slip or a regression, but from which, with the restoration of the proper faculties, the intrinsically rational subject nevertheless quickly recovers.

REPETITIONS OF HISTORY AND UNFINISHED PROJECTS

While all this confirms Ileto's critique of Agoncillo's developmentalism, it also manifests a logic — specifically, a psychology — that shapes Ileto's own alternative history. In place of probing the minds of 'rational' men, Ileto proposes probing the mind of the 'irrational' masses. This project to elucidate 'the mentality that brought disorder to the Republic' demonstrates the persistence of a psychologism which, freed of the developmentalism and heroic individualism that shaped Agoncillo's biographical history, is now directed toward the collective subject, 'the masses'.[6] Before I return to Agoncillo's history, I want to raise three points about Ileto's 'history from below'.

First, it adheres to the principle that 'selfhood is a kind of a priori category of modern historical analysis'.[7] Although the central character of Ileto's history is collective, it nevertheless assumes the form of a unitary self, endowed with driving faculties of thought, imagination and feeling. Ileto's analysis of the mental and emotional structures of this self is predicated upon unexamined psychological assumptions, which become significant principles shaping his historical interpretation.[8] While we might recognize Ileto's work as a form of ideological analysis in its attention to a collective imagination, the grounding of such 'ideology' in a given subject (rather than the constitution of subjects in and through ideological practices) — whence the use of the category of 'mentality' — predisposes his analysis to psychological premises and explanations. In this respect, it is not very different from Agoncillo's history as psychology.

Second, the attention accorded to the masses by Ileto's alternative history is predicated upon a colonial split which Dipesh Chakrabarty convincingly argues is what all national histories perform: 'A historical construction of temporality (medieval/ modern, separated by historical time), in other words, is precisely the axis along which the colonial subject splits itself. Or to put it differently, this split *is* what is history; writing history is performing this split over and over again.'[9] In this case, the subject and object of modernity which comprise 'the Filipino people' are, respectively, the nation's leaders and the masses, or, as they are represented in Agoncillo's narrative, Aguinaldo and Bonifacio. Ileto's focus on 'the masses' reproduces this colonial split between a modernizing elite and yet-to-be-modernized peasantry as well as presumptions of their radically different 'psychologies'. In doing so, Ileto precludes an analysis of the constitutive interactions between these given classes, beyond, that is, the relation between 'rationality' and 'irrationality' or between 'self' and 'other'.

Third, and this point is closely related to the second, Ileto's history presupposes a detachment from and reification of 'the masses' as a sovereign actor. (In the next two chapters I will elaborate further on the process of this detachment as the operation of consolidation of the proper nationalist subject.) Here the detachment of the historian from the historical time of his 'subject' allows two not incompatible scenarios to take place: as a subaltern historian, Ileto 'finds him/herself in the self-effacing role of a facilitator unwilling to articulate a counterhegemonic project that is "extraneous" to the histories unearthed;'[10] and, by elevating the masses to the status of a psychological character, Ileto sets himself up as analyst in relation to the masses, as analysand. In both cases, the separate positions of historian and people are preconstituted: the former as objective theoretical perspective for whom the latter, as a form of subjectivity, serves as theoretical object; each contained in its given, separate historical time.

I have digressed into this brief discussion of Ileto's project because the cogency of its critique of all preceding histories makes it too easy to believe that nationalist histories such as Agoncillo's are hopelessly antiquated (in their developmentalist nationalism) or have now been superseded by the alternative, democratic history that Ileto proposes. It seems to me, on the contrary, that Ileto's work, besides posing new problematics, also 'repeats' old ones. There are more continuities between Ileto's work and the works of the nationalist historians he critiques than we are led to believe. By pointing to these continuities, I have no intention of detracting from the important contributions of Ileto's work to counter-hegemonic nationalist projects. Rather, I want to underscore the power of the epistemological and socio-subjective structures of fantasy-production in shaping postcolonial national histories.

At the same time, I want to emphasize that even if they are bequeathed by a persistent colonial education to 'the students of history', these subjective predicates of a postcolonial national history are as much the accomplishments of their users as they are the products of their purported 'original' inventors.[11] They are accomplishments to the degree that they help to realize the universal import of 'modernity' through its particular application and elaboration. Such accomplishments are, however, always tenuous. Both like and unlike the consolidation of the colonial state, which Ileto shows 'happened' through encounters with images of its 'other', modern structures of self and community that are presumed to have been adopted by an elite class, which is always already identified with the colonizer, are on-going projects, made to happen and yet never fully or finally made. It is this unfinished state which furnishes 'modernity' with its characteristic condition, its progressive temporality and trajectory — in a word, its quasi-cause for 'development'.

My own fascination with Agoncillo's 'accomplishment' lies in his vigorous struggle against this unfinishedness. *The Revolt of the Masses* is the nationalist project of finishing the Revolution, tying up loose ends, and consolidating the bourgeois self in whose image the nation is created. While it is evident that Agoncillo's history is under the sway of developmentalism, it would be a mistake, I think, to assume that this is in fact what it all boils down to, or that it merely fulfills the script of a derivative modern nationalism. I am suggesting, on the contrary, that these nationalist histories can be a source of theoretical knowledge to the degree that they are also original postcolonial *inventions* of modernity that enter the world at large. The Western, colonial, modern structures at the behest of which postcolonial national histories are seen to work are structures of both postcolonial peoples' *doing* and *undoing*. Postcolonial national histories nevertheless always fall short of the ideals that they themselves have participated in creating. I am not saying that these socio-symbolic trusses of post-colonial-national formations can therefore be a source of theoretical knowledge about universal 'modernity' to the extent that, in their unfinishedness, they are what 'modernity' defines itself against. I am proposing, rather, that they *are* the very substance of modernity — they are the abstract modernity risen to the concrete.[12]

This is not, however, the direction of my present interest. My interest lies, as I said, in Agoncillo's vigorous struggle against unfinishedness — a struggle that nevertheless 'results' in a state of unfinishedness characterizing the post-independence nation-state, the petit-bourgeois national subject-citizen and the narrative that links, through possession, one to the other. This hegemonic nationalist 'movement', if you will, cannot make a complete rupture with the colonial order in order to establish the nation's own full and sovereign presence. Moreover, it cannot pacify other movements within and outside of the nation enough to give it the neat semblance of a done deed.

THE MAKING OF SUBJECTS OF HISTORY

Edel Garcellano writes that the history of the revolution 'should not be traced to the alleged moral weaknesses and/or mandated actions of its participants, but rather seen as the collectivistic *behaviour* of interests

— and more specifically, the emergence of classes and the conditions for such emergence'.[13] We might well apply this insight to Agoncillo's history, for it is precisely the open-endedness of the revolution (the unfinishedness of the event) that makes for the latter's radical historical significance. As the continuation of particular strains of the revolution by similar means, Agoncillo's account is part of the making of the class to which the 'finished' revolution is presupposed to belong. Its patent partiality is thus not an effect of a prior class identification but rather the very effort exerted to bring that class-subject into identifiable being. I should clarify here that I understand Agoncillo as a subject-effect of a project of nationalism that contributes to a dominant '*behaviour* of interests' at work in the Philippine formation.

We might thus read Agoncillo's history as a form of making the petit bourgeois or *ilustrado* subject of the nation, which is the cornerstone of the fantasy history it narrates (the arrogation and securing of state power by and for this subject). This making of the national petit bourgeois subject is itself a struggle to the degree that other things, forces and movements work against it. Agoncillo's text is replete with expressions of this struggle: fervent declarations of fealty to principles of rationality; exclamations of indignation and disbelief; insinuations and demonstrations of suspiciousness, bad faith and malignancy on the part of others; defensive moralizings and zealous interrogations of the veracity and authenticity of testimonies — I am tempted to say, expressions of an almost paranoid character. Agoncillo's 'excessiveness' — his hyperenthusiasm for historical truth, his repeated denunciation of 'the play of personal prejudices' in both historical and scholarly action, his severe censure and repudiation of historical reasoning which allows itself to be swayed by fame ('Such mental outlook smacks of hypocrisy and cowardice' (viii), for it fails to stand on its own reason) — all these professions comprise the strivings of one towards an impossibly distant, fantastic ideal as well as give proof of one who is forever 'slipping back' into the excesses which must be renounced and forsaken if this ideal is to be attained. Indeed, it demonstrates that lack always already assumed of the colonial masses. It is of course true that Agoncillo's vigorous protestations were directed at very real critics, but it is the tenor of those protestations that reveals the perceived character of the threat to truth and the very nature of his scholarly ordeal. While Agoncillo therefore 'identifies' with the ideal of universal citizenship, he behaves 'like' the fanatical masses who are its constitutive contradiction.

In sum, Agoncillo's work demonstrates both the performance of the colonial split and its failure. Agoncillo 'himself' is this split subject in whom the 'abnormal psychology' of the masses is contained. I will say more about this 'psychology' as the failure of the colonial split. For now I want to follow Agoncillo's struggle to make this modern subject against its contradictions. The very form of his scholarship is a significant apparatus in the struggle to keep unruly elements at bay:

> No controversial points are discussed in the main body of the book. Only my own conclusions are there set forth, whereas the arguments to support them are sufficiently clarified, I hope, in the Notes. This method, I believe, makes for easy reading and saves the readers from being rudely interrupted in their reading. To include the discussions of doubtful points and the footnotes in the main text would be to make the book a dull and protracted law brief. It is as if in the midst of a lively conversation between two friends, a maid suddenly appeared to tell the host that a salesman was at the door. In the second place, I refuse to argue the positions I have taken in the main narrative, believing, likewise, that it is improper of me to dispute things with my visitor — in this case, the reader — in the sala. I have thought it best to argue in the backroom — in the Notes at the end of the book. (viii–vix)

Both the historian's vocation and what appear as threats to the pursuit of historical truth turn out to have social and material form. The *ilustrado* ideal of civility and domestic ease sought in the spatial arrangements of the modern colonial house, which Agoncillo tries to realize in and as scholarly writing, is potentially disrupted by rude concerns of commerce and petty enterprises represented by the intrusive salesman. The narrative that secures *ilustrado* subjecthood is conceived as a civilized *sala* [living room] conversation between two friends, from which mundane economic concerns as well as politically tendentious arguments must be excluded and relegated to the backroom, the notes at the end of the book. This socio-symbolic organization serves to house the ideal subject of Agoncillo's history, a civic subject who stoops to negotiate dull and worldly business (that is, to behave as a lawyer-politician or as a businessman-executive) only in order to secure the conditions for his real vocation: the writing of the true tragedy of the nation's foundation. While this is not yet the Western house that shapes current metropolitan dreams (see Chapter 2), already we see here the spatial logics that will prevail in the fantasy-production of the nation.

UNRULY BEHAVIOUR, 'IMPERTINENT BOORS AND ALL FORMS OF NOISE'

The *ilustrado* house built by Agoncillo is, however, peopled with others who are themselves part of the apparatus for realizing and maintaining the conditions for this modern vocation. The maid who suddenly appears from nowhere is an invisible protective front, serving in a similar capacity as his nameless Wife to whom he dedicates his work: 'Patient, understanding, and tolerant who has shielded me, in this as in my other undertakings, against impertinent boors and all forms of noise.' Women thus play a similar role in relation to the writing of history as they are said to play in relation to the revolutionary making of history: 'while the men were holding their secret meetings in the backroom, the women, in order to draw away the suspicion of the authorities, were to dance and sing in the sala in full view of passers by' (57). Women do not only constitute a protective front for nationally-significant meetings of men, they also function as indices of the intensity of revolutionary feeling and momentum — they give 'evidence to the growing restlessness of all classes of the social strata' (36). In this respect they are similar to the masses who function as a recording surface over which rumors — the revolutionary media of communication and inflammation of sentiment, idea and social feeling — pass and imprint themselves; as the very condition of time they are in, the masses are 'so ripe for, and sensitive to, the tiniest unsavory whisper' (231). While the masses are invoked to characterize the times, to provide psychological atmosphere, as well as to provide the necessary impetus and conditions for the 'military' triumphs which structure the narrative, women are mentioned to provide paradigmatic demonstration of the revolutionary upheaval of existing social stratifications, as in: 'even women ... readily joined the movement and so gave evidence to the growing restlessness of all classes of the social strata' (36) and 'men and women, driven to desperation ... fought side by side' (189).

Women and the masses thus function as diacritical markers of alterity deployed to define the emerging sovereign, governing nation-subject. They are constituted as such by the very ascendant logic of governance, and are therefore essential both for this ascendance and the founding of the nation by which the revolution becomes subsumed and 'finished'. Women and the masses are not, however, mere narrative devices, the consequences of Agoncillo's given sexual and class biases as an *ilustrado* man. Rather, women and the masses are instrumental by-products of the larger political-economic imaginary, in a word, fantasy, project of producing a nation-subject within the emerging international public sphere. The roles of women and the masses as internal markers of alterity are produced by an ascendant ruling nation-subject in order to assert power and control over creative revolutionary passions and desires which threaten this subject with variant agencies (e.g. the identifiable agencies of 'women' or of 'the masses'). This is abundantly clear in the case of 'the masses' whose millenarian and terrorizing movements, as Ileto has amply shown, were comprehended (and apprehended) by nationalist historians either through categories of 'irrationality' such as 'banditry' or through categories of 'proto-resistance' and 'native' heroism. In this vein, Agoncillo mentions the masses' attacks with 'their bolos and sharpened bamboo sticks' as an example of 'the moral effect of the rebel victory upon the people' (189). In this same example of the height of the people's heroism, 'never before exhibited in such naked boldness', Agoncillo incorporates an 'incident' of a group of women hacking Spanish soldiers to death with a bolo. 'Incidents' such as this become meaningful to the project of the nation-subject precisely to the extent that they 'help' the narrative movement of the Revolution.[14]

Lilia Quindoza Santiago points out that the attempt to define the role of women as 'helpers' is already made by Rizal in his reading of the advocations of the Malolos women for educational reform as evidence that they were 'helpers' in the cause of the Revolution: *'kayo'y katulong na namin, panatag-loob sa pagtatagumpay'* [you are now our helpers, a calming influence in the path to victory].[15] The role of 'helper' into which women and the masses are symbolically incorporated is itself a product of gendered, class relations, which are reestablished in the writing of the Revolution and the consolidation of its privileged *ilustrado* subject. The role of 'helper' is the positive embodiment of 'internal alterity', the abiding condition of modern subjectivity. Although there is a longer history to the cultural construction of 'helper' than that posited here, I want to suggest that with the national aspiration to modern subjectivity the making of 'helpers' becomes an important technology for organizing labour. Indeed, in this particular 'feminization' of 'the masses' exercised in Agoncillo's and Rizal's project to make national history, we can already glean the prefiguration of the gendered and sexualized aspects of dominant social relations of Philippine national production, which, as I've shown in the first part of the book, will obtain much later.

Modern subjectivity is not only the premise of Agoncillo's history but also its objective. As such, the writing of this history is the process of creating the conditions of possibility of a national subject. Central among these conditions is the subordination and subservience of social agencies whose 'behaviour of interests' threaten to overtake and overpower the claims to governance of an emerging ruling class.[16] This class is itself constituted as the national subject by virtue of its management of those unruly agencies. As such unruly social agencies, women and the masses are rendered 'serviceable' through their confinement to a separate, deviant temporal and psychological 'province' ('abnormal times', 'abnormal psychology') internal to a dominant, normative order (History) and its regulating subject (the Nation). In this way are forces and movements of revolution domesticated to secure the governing power of the nation-state.

Another condition of the national subject, inextricable from the first, is the formation of filial attachments that will constitute that subject's cohesive identity. These filial attachments can be seen to have already formed through the activities of the Propagandists and the Katipuneros, particularly in the latter's creation of a society of *'mga anak ng bayan'* [the children of the nation]. Agoncillo's translation (among many others) of these projected non-gendered filial relations of national community as relations among 'sons' symbolically grasps the masculinist dimensions of the secret society's practices of affiliation and, moreover, extends this masculinism to the project of nation-building.[17] However, Agoncillo's writing does not reflect as much as it creates the character of these attachments. This character is evident in his translations of Bonifacio's phrasings of local community (the community of Tagalogs) in national terms: '*ang bayan ng katagalugan*' [the Tagalog nation], '*pusong tagalog*' [Tagalog heart] *and* '*mga tagalog*' [the Tagalogs] become, respectively, 'our land, Filipinas', 'the heart of the Filipino' and 'the Filipinos'.[18] It is precisely for its emblematic interpretation of the power dynamics of Tagalog filiation as national events — the inflated focus on 'Cavite parochialism' and its superimposition on the national struggle for liberation — that Arnold Azurin has criticized Agoncillo's history as a gross instance of 'ilustrado-Cavitismo nationalism'.[19] Azurin attributes Agoncillo's 'myopic vista' to a 'vulgar streak of bias: a clannish fetish' traceable to his 'personal affinities with the personages' who assume a dominant role in the establishment of the nation.[20] In effect, Agoncillo stands accused of the very same 'psychology of regionalism' that he repudiates as the cause of the tragic historical blot that was Bonifacio.

PSYCHOLOGICAL WORK

Agoncillo's history is therefore a work of psychology to the extent that it fulfills the two conditions for the founding of a national subject by recourse to psychological forms. On the one hand, psychology is used as a logic of explanation that contains threatening 'behaviour of interests' in the forms of persons ('Bonifacio', 'masses', 'women'). In this register, 'psychology' is a cause *within* the narrative, determining the behaviour of the characters in Agoncillo's history. On the other hand, psychology is the logic of attachments and sympathetic action that serves as the very 'methodology' of Agoncillo's history. In this register, 'psychology' is a cause *of* the narrative, determining the very mode of inscribing history, which produces its authorial subject ('Agoncillo', 'the nation'). It is not just that Agoncillo is 'prejudiced' by prior regional, gender and class identifications. Rather, it is that Agoncillo symbolically plays out the affective alignments that enable and secure the proper affiliation of the nation with an emergent, privileged class to which he belongs. In this sense, his historiographical-psychological work continues the 'war of position' waged by the proponents of this emergent class within the very ranks of the revolution.

Because Agoncillo's narrative of the national subject depends on the marginalization of potential subjects on psychological grounds, it must disavow its own 'psychology of regionalism'. This disavowal consists of the displaced interiorization of the very forms of affiliation and attachment through which the Katipunan first came into being, indeed of the very social mode of spreading revolutionary sentiment, which initiated and sustained revolutionary movement.[21] As against the formalized, public stagings of Aguinaldo's oath-taking as the 'elected' President of the new Republic and of Bonifacio's trial, the very publicization of which serves to confirm and legitimate the objective fact of Aguinaldo's presidency,[22] furtive practices of winning sympathy and forming sentimental attachments — actions based on feelings of affinity, compassion and personal regard — all these 'backward' practices are psychologistically relegated to the distant interiority of the Revolution, the deep recesses of popular instincts, and the 'backroom' of the main historical narrative. Agoncillo's own failure to distance himself from such 'backward' psychological practices is, however, profusely evident in his almost magical penchant for alphabetical codes and their keys (for auratic symbols and their secret meanings), his fetishism of the written word,[23] his blatant 'literary' embellishments and dramatizations of particular scenes (such as Bonifacio's death), his passionate entanglement in 'intrigues and bad faith', and his 'personalist' contestation of testimonies and sources.[24]

In this history, the 'colonial split' that postcolonial history is fated to perform is never adequately made — whence the continuous intrusive appearance of the maid, indeed, the recurring behaviour of Agoncillo *as* maid protecting his own narrative from boorish suspicions. Hence, in the middle of passionate battle with other historians in the backroom he must declare: 'In presenting the foregoing I should like to repeat that I was motivated not by prejudices, but by my love of what is true ...' (345). Such fervent avowals of love of the true and disavowals of prejudice as 'the bane of history' are jealously made in the seemingly ubiquitous face of counterclaims, suspicions, accusations and 'furious discussions'. (As I mentioned earlier, such controversies continue into the present day.)[25] They demonstrate the difficulty with which Agoncillo tries to maintain a modern self above the tribalist fray. Agoncillo 'himself' is wracked with suspicions, clearly 'motivated' by his high regard for particular embodied authorities, such as Aguinaldo (and not just the disembodied authority of certain abstract principles), and evidently 'courting the favor' of some legitimating ideal Reader whose fairness of mind exemplifies and constitutes the presupposed fairness of mind of Historical judgement. This ideal Reader is embodied by none other than Aguinaldo himself, the 'old man' at the end of the narrative from whom Agoncillo, as a 'student of history', seeks the truth.[26] The 'ringing answer' offered by this old man to the student's quest for truth becomes the very sentimental-correlative of the latter's resulting narrative: Bonifacio is a 'noble plebian', and it is this sentimental truth, with all its inspiration from romantic tales of the 'noble savage', that *The Revolt of the Masses* attempts, ultimately, to convey.

SENTIMENTAL CONNECTIONS

I present the operations of jealousy, personal regard and sentimental forms in this history in order to demonstrate that, contrary to the claims of both Agoncillo and Ileto, *ilustrado* histories are not as rationalist, linear and systematically developmentalist as they aspire to be. While Agoncillo's history proposes that such pre-modern, pre-national, regionalist instincts and feelings were the very cause for the betrayals and temporary failings of the Revolution, in Ileto's account, these 'dark age' modes of action were the very condition of possibility of the formation of the nation-state and all its developmentalist apparatuses. It seems to me, however, that rather than functioning as contradiction or as condition of possibility of modernity (two sides of the same coin holding the universal, ideal value of modernity), the work of 'jealousies' and 'irrationality' are the positive content and form not only of the Revolutionary movement but also of the 'modern' nation. Ileto seems to suggest this but does not pursue it further. He presumes, rather, that the 'irrational' and 'fanatical' faculties fall on the purportedly 'repressed' side of the masses. I am proposing, on the contrary — and this is abundantly suggested by the general zealous tenor and pronouncements of Agoncillo's narrative as well as the jealous character of his disputes — that this 'irrationality' and 'abnormal psychology' exhibited by the masses is very much a part of the behaviour of the *ilustrado* class too.

This view makes the difference between the masses and the elite ('the great cultural divide') less absolute than is often presumed. It is true that part of the making of the *ilustrado* class consists of distancing and differentiating itself from the 'mentality' and practices of the masses, but it is also true that the failure to perform this split completely is as much a part of bourgeois class constitution as the effort to make it. Agoncillo's 'excesses' controvert the persistent presumption of ideological dispositions inherent to given classes.[27] Agoncillo structures his self-possession (as class-possession) as against a likeness to what he attributes to the masses. This self-possession, which is the sovereignty of the bourgeois subject, is rendered precarious by a contradictory form of self, one that is a *medium*, given to speaking and acting in behalf of others with whom she feels akin. The latter is represented as the lack of self-possession of the masses, their disposition to record and react to currents of feeling and ideas, as conveyed, for example, through rumours and suspicions. Agoncillo's construction of the masses as a recording surface for intensities they themselves do not generate or regulate is precisely an attempt to contain the creative and moving power released and realized through socio-subjective modes which he must, as an aspiring sovereign subject, displace and disown. These modes are exemplified by the notion and operation of *kapatiran* [siblinghood], the horizontal affective relation of those who share a common 'origin' or genealogical link, here located in the birthing severance of the nation from Spain. Contrary to Agoncillo's construction, such affiliative, empathetic relations are created by the masses themselves in the very process of revolution. Indeed, the revolutionary movement [*kilusan*] is the social-emotional 'behaviour' [*kilos*] of the people acting in concert as '*mga anak ng bayan*' [offspring of the nation]. The self as empathetic *medium*, as a mode of extensive relations, assumes revolutionary form in the subjectivity of *kapatiran*. Deployed through the notion and operation of *kamag-anakan* [familial blood relations or natural kin], however, it assumes a conservative form through which class interests can be secured and class power aggrandized.

We might view therefore the difference in these classes as a matter of organization of proximate modes of alliances and affiliation — the classes are themselves in the process of being made and maintained through the productive organization of these alliances. 'Cronyism' is, for example, a concept naming economic relations within dominant classes that are structured along lines of fraternal feeling and affiliative ties, of kin and kind. Invariably invoked as an explanation of socio-political processes and relations, the 'psychology of regionalism', might be viewed instead as that which needs to be explained — not as an instance of some enduring tribal traits but rather as a productive structure of socio-subjective practices that emerges out of the revolutionary struggle against colonial rule. The class contradiction palpable in *The Revolt of the Masses* takes national form in the splitting of the political ends and productive organization of these practices into, on the one hand, the various modes of *kapatiran* [siblinghood] at work in and produced out of revolution and, on the other, the prevailing mode of *kamag-anakan* [kinship relations] deployed in the consolidation of national governing power.[28] While the first is open and expanding, the other is closed and monopolistic.

SUBJECTIVE STRUGGLES AS STRUGGLES OF HISTORY

In claiming that there are common media of socio-subjective practices — a common 'psychology', if you will — through which the nation might be said to be created, I am not contending that there are no radical differences in the ideological constitution of contradictory classes. Rather, the processes of interaction and struggle between them are the very processes of creation and maintenance of the relations of production that define class structures and their differences. This is to claim that 'psychological' operations, by which I mean socio-subjective practices or behaviour, also perform 'economic' tasks. That is, they serve as infrastructural tools (or weapons) in the production of 'the Philippines' and the organization of its productive forces.

It is important to see Agoncillo as expending great effort to surmount the contradictions posed by these productive forces in order to recognize that national hegemony consists of concerted acts of expropriation that are never entirely secure. Otherwise, if we view this hegemony as a *state* of domination, we help to consign contestatory forces to the constitutive powerlessness that domination presupposes and is predicated upon. This is indeed how I have interpreted the Philippine state in the post-authoritarian period (See Chapter 2). In a like manner to the state whose behaviour his own will prefigures, Agoncillo exhibits within his work the social contradictions that plague his project of possession (of the revolution, of the nation, of the self) and account for his manifest lack of self-possession. An illustrative scene of this lack of self-possession is contained in three succeeding notes discussing testimonies concerning the 'treachery' of Teodor Patiño, which led to the uncovering of the Katipunan. In these three notes made within five sentences in the main text summing up the treacherous event (in a chapter entitled, 'Let Freedom Ring'),[29] with the last note going on for five whole pages and ending with the denunciation of prejudice as 'the bane of history', Agoncillo sorts through conflicting testimonies, repudiating their authenticity on the basis of 'the laws of probability' which are, in his analysis, evidently laws of psychology.

Although the specific issues of contention which Agoncillo concerns himself with in these notes might seem trivial (Patiño's motivations for revealing the Katipunan to his sister, whether or not this conversation was overheard by Sor Teresa, and whether or not Patiño confessed his secrets to Father Gil within or outside of the confessional), the fact that Agoncillo works himself up into such a state over them provides proof not only of his 'excesses' but also of the operations of 'psychology' by which he defends his own account and authority and through which he constructs his subject. He argues, for example, that Patiño could only have been motivated by vengeance: 'He could not have posed to love his sister more than his own self, since he was aware that revelation of the secrets would cost him his life' (340). The 'laws of probability' regulating 'a normal individual' are here revealed to include the paramountcy of the sovereign self whose individual integrity is underwritten by the juridical signature. This virile, civil self is constructed against the protean, 'lachrymose' feminine self represented by Patiño's sister, whose uncontrollable emotions become the cause for the divulgence of Patiño's secrets to the Spanish authorities.[30] The 'lachrymose' self is not only easily swayed by currents of feeling which she displays and expresses, she can also speak through and be spoken through by her own kin and kind — indeed, 'possessed' by them. She is therefore not so much a source as much as a medium of presence and social-emotional movements. (In the last chapter, I argue for the heretical potential of this 'hysterical' form of subjectivity that women, as media of others' desires, are led to occupy.)

The struggle for the virile sovereign self to prevail over its feminine contradiction is demonstrated in Agoncillo's at once sympathetic portrayal and harsh judgement of Bonifacio as an example of what Resil Mojares calls the vernacular literary archetype of 'a man of feeling', 'a person almost feminine in the delicacy of his sentiments and in his emotional susceptibility'.[31] As equally a work of literature as a work of history,[32] Agoncillo's narrative can be viewed as shaped by both conformity with and struggle against the attitude and method of sentimentalism, which Mojares argues is a 'complex (which) is not at all peculiar to the Filipino psyche'.[33] Mojares's characterization of Philippine vernacular 'tragic' narratives as sentimental is indicative of 'common' socio-subjective modes which, in their constitutive disassociation from the prevailing modern aesthetic faculties now governing the nation, are devalued and yet necessarily drawn upon for the establishment of a capital language and body of expression — a canon, if you will — that takes the name of the nation. The lack of self-possession of the 'man of feeling', which characterizes the 'vernacular' remainder of the nation, might be viewed less as the effect of some historical 'unconscious' contained within the national subject and more as the appearance of the sway of social-emotional movements — i.e., the 'irrationality' in the struggle for liberation — over self-determining individual agency. The capture of such sentimental movements and the expropriation of their creative power is manifested by Agoncillo's historical-psychological narrativization of the revolution through 'character' (including the character of 'the masses'). This method of capture can be seen today in the dominant role of 'personalities' in the realm of politics/entertainment (a realm whose unity, like the unity of Church and State, is crystallized in the recently deposed administration of President-Actor Joseph Estrada). Such 'personalities' are the product of the capitalist subjectification of these social-emotional movements, that is, the alienation and assumption of these movements in money-subject form. As such they can serve to represent and capitalize on the daily instances of struggle and desire embodied by 'the masses' (as exemplified by Estrada's electoral slogan *'Erap Para sa Mahihirap'* [Erap (Estrada's nickname) for the Poor]).

The 'psychology' of the sentimental masses is not some atavistic indigenous cultural trait but rather, is a particular cultural logic of socio-subjective practices and relations (a form of cultural imagination or dreaming) invented out of complex, contradictory transactions of modernization. Agoncillo's history demonstrates the dominant, collaborative side of this transaction and the class, gender and sexual organization of productive forces and movements that is necessary to secure the powers of a privileged national subject who would be equal to the subjects of other free nations. In other words, his subjective struggle expresses and participates in the material, imaginary struggle of the newly independent Philippine nation-state. This raises the question of how these subordinated forces of desiring-production (labour, in its various forms, including 'feminized', 'tribal', 'peasant', as well as 'traditional' male proletariat *labour*) organize themselves socio-subjectively in ways that exceed and counter their organization by the owners of the nation.[34] Feminists have begun to answer this question as well as pose new ones, questions that are not additive but fundamental to questions of revolutionary becomings and alternative dreams, which the dominant present both owes itself to and constantly wages a war against.[35] To understand national history as the work of psychology, and psychology as a system of subjective relations and structures necessary for the reproduction of dominant social relations of production is to enable the forging of a liberative socio-subjective theory and practice of history. This liberative praxis writes into history (indeed, *as* history) the different forms of socio-subjective 'behaviour' that animate revolutionary dreams and yet are continuously quelled and expropriated by the ruling subjects of the nation. By looking into the revolutionary becomings subsumed within dominant Philippine history, such a project participates in the transformation of the very 'rules' of that history. It gives new meaning to the principle that the problems of writing history are the problems of history itself.

Although I have represented Agoncillo's nationalist project as enacting and participating in the project of the postcolonial state, it is also true that his Filipino history was one that ran counter to the ruling views of his time. Those views, which understood the Revolution as the consequence of an elite awakening to nationalist longings, represented the self-understanding and colonial provenance of the oligarchic state. In its populist portrayal of the Filipino 'nation' as the will of the masses, then, Agoncillo's history gave symbolic expression to the social division between the new Filipino elite and the masses, which was rapidly widening as the consequence of colonial tutelage in independent nation-statehood. (By colonial tutelage I mean the ascendance of a native ruling class through the state apparatus bequeathed by US colonialism, which steered the ideals of 'self-government' towards combined US and local comprador interests.) Agoncillo's revisionist history did not only express but also performed this social division, which the dominant, oligarchic history sought to dispel. In this way, we might say, it enacted a proto-bourgeois revolt against the 'traditional' ruling class that would inform and fuel the growing nationalist movements of the 1950s and 1960s. Emerging from and intensifying the widespread social and economic crisis concomitant with US-sponsored patrimonial elite rule, competing Filipino nationalisms in the post-war period confronted each other in a dialectical struggle between radical, social movements and recuperative, state policies.[36] From the anti-colonial armed peasant 'Huk' rebellion, which formed in resistance to Japanese occupation (1941–1946) and later joined forces with the old Communist Party (PKP), to the economic nationalism of President Garcia's 'Filipino First movement', which instituted protectionist measures for an emerging Filipino entrepreneurial class, these contestatory nationalisms set the conditions for the radical undermining of oligarchic power and the subsequent reconfiguration of the state in the interests of an ascendant 'crony capitalist' class, a state pre-eminently realized and represented by the Marcos regime.[37]

Agoncillo's ambivalent nationalist project can thus be seen to express and contribute to the conflicting tendencies of post-war nationalisms, which gave rise to, on the one hand, the re-establishment of the Communist Party of the Philippines (CPP) and its revolutionary New People's Army in 1968, and on the other, the declaration of Martial Law in 1972 and the institution of the authoritarian regime of Ferdinand Marcos. As Ileto writes:

> The fact is, the sons and daughters of well-off families, having been fed a healthy dose of the Agoncillo/ Constantino variant of history, *did* throw down their books and man the barricades in 1970–71; quite a number of them even went to the hills after martial law was declared, and some have been killed by the military. In addition, there can be no doubt that this kind of history subtended (though certainly did not 'cause') the 'EDSA revolution' of 1986, which has been characterized by some as being predominantly middle class.[38]

Ileto argues that the Marcos state adopted the discourse of the 'unfinished revolution' deployed by the insurgent nationalism of the communists, which he traces to Agoncillo, as a legitimating strategy for its authoritarian rule. Although antagonistic to each other, both Marcos and the Communists mobilized a nationalism that saw itself fulfilling the 'unfinished' Revolution of 1896 in a grand progressive, forward march to freedom symbolically identified with a roster of male heroes. In contrast to this hegemonic nationalism, the popular movement against Marcos symbolically led by Corazon Aquino exemplifies a 'feminine' mode of resistance to authority linked to the 'peasant consciousness' at work in other popular movements in the Philippines' historical past.

In the next chapter, I examine more closely the rupture presented by the 'EDSA revolution', the four-day popular revolt in February 1986 that deposed the Marcos dictatorship, as well as the makings of the 'feminine' mode of resistance said to take ascendance during this revolt. I regard this 'feminine' mode of resistance as a process of popular resignification of the state nationalist alignment of gender disempowerment and class disenfranchisement that we saw pre-figured in Agoncillo's symbolic conflation of 'women and the masses'. As we saw in the first chapter, this alignment of gender and class finds full material realization under the Marcos regime as the feminization of labour.

5

'People Power':
Miraculous Revolt

In the last chapter, we saw the limits of a historical imagination that draws its authoritative symbolic forms in accordance to the principles of fantasy-production. These principles, which also serve as strictures on our political imagination, include the privileging of the nation as the paramount unit of world-historical action and the understanding of the nation's actions as determined by the particular character of its internal constitution, that is, by the cultural attributes of its identity. In this worldview, nations consist of individuals whose subjective form serves as a model for that of the nation as a whole. What appears on the level of fantasy political economy, therefore, as an analogical relation between nations and individuals operates, on the level of history, as a homology. To the extent that the historical subject of the nation imagined by Agoncillo took on the sovereign, masculine, civic subject as its ideal, it could not but eschew the sentimental and passionate socio-subjective practices, to which it owed its very emergence, as the 'backward', 'feminine' behaviour of the masses.

In this chapter, I am interested in the event of 'people power', that is, in the subjective emergence of 'the people' out of the feminized 'masses' and its embodiment of the power to change history. The event of 'people power' might be regarded as the unraveling of the imaginary logic of fantasy-production. As such, it is both a replication and alteration of the dominant socio-symbolic practices constituting the fantasy of the Filipino nation. We can see in the unfolding of this event how the problems of writing history that Agoncillo faced and symbolically solved become in another moment the problems of making history.

HISTORY AS EVENT

So much has already been said and written about the 'People Power Revolution' of the Philippines in 1986. It has, as they say, become 'history'. Indeed, it is a piece of history with its own sequel. 'People Power 2', the popular revolt that similarly deposed President Joseph Estrada (1998–2001), was claimed by all to have repeated 'history'. But what 'history' that is, is little touched upon. My own purposes for reconstructing this historical event are twofold: (1) to understand how 'history' is made and experienced, how the antagonisms within a society erupt and are resolved, channelled to preserve (or change) the status quo, how dominance is subverted or challenged through the coding of revolutionary desires into active symbolic forces and how dominance is installed or reinstituted through the recoding of those desires into stabilizing representations; and (2) to foreground some of those very desires that have been effectively elided in the consignment of the transformative event to 'history', to bring to light the contradictions which served as a motor of social upheaval and which subsist even within the homogenized 'history' that supplants this upheaval. In other words, my task is to manifest in the wake of the revolt, that while the 'war' was lost before it was won, the wayward movements of desiring-action coursing through this event continue to insist and might again exert such force (beyond People Power 2) so as to bring about more lasting fruitful socio-political changes.

This analysis is not meant to replace more empirical political and economic explanations of the EDSA revolt.[1] Nor is it meant to take the place of a longer historical and broader sociological view of the conditions that led to the popular uprising, conditions that can account for the 'breakdown' and actual tenuousness of the hegemonic national fantasy supporting the Marcos's regime.[2] These conditions include the mass organizing and underground armed struggle of the Philippine Left, the growth of socially-oriented church movements (which were autonomous from but intimately linked to the Left) and other anti-

Marcos, democratic social movements, the reconsolidation of the political opposition, which Marcos had crushed in the early years of Martial Law, as well as the dynamic, cultural inventiveness of changing labour formations, which I offered glimpses of in previous chapters.[3]

Rather, this chapter is intended to provide an interpretation of the subjective dynamics of the revolt of the people, that is, of the largely unforeseen and unprecedented character or 'style' of its unfolding as history. History is, in this sense, what has gained retroactive unity and homogeneity through the dominant articulated memories of a society. Hence, this event, which has been variously designated as 'the EDSA revolt', 'the People Power Revolution', and, simply, 'February '86', has become an identity inscribed in the hegemonic national imagination through its dominant articulators. It has also become an entity that can be possessed as one's responsibility (in the free world fantasy, history belongs to subjects). Indeed, whose revolution it was immediately became an issue to debate. Even during the time of its actualization, the hegemonic classes were already referring to 'our revolution'. It has become a designable national experience precisely because those whose experience it was (as they possessively claimed to it be) belong to that sector of Philippine society — urban, Tagalog middle class — that defines the national through its own accounts of history.[4] As the possession of a particular class, the 'revolution' repeats itself in a transformation internal to its possessive subject. Thus Bulatao writes, 'the revolution was not only political, a change of rulers. It was also an indication of change and development within persons, at least persons within a social class.'[5]

But the 'event' of People Power took form and content, not simply in the minds of those who did the remembering for the rest of the nation, but through the actions of those who participated in its making — the actions upon which those very accounts are predicated — as well as through the discursive categories that organized both (that is, both actions and accounts).[6] No event is actualized independently of these categories, for there is no historical event that is not a product of people acting upon their experience, that is, upon their cognitive, emotive and bodily apprehension of reality. When Gramsci stated that 'the real philosophy of each man is contained in its entirety in his political action', he implied as much.[7] This is not to assert the primacy of either of these two hypostasized realms of existence, namely symbolic and material reality, as the motor force of history but, rather, to affirm that 'Everything happens on the boundary between things and propositions.'[8] Any event is produced by people acting on and making sense of their conditions of life. History, then, as the collective experience of socio-politically significant events, happens in that dialectical relation between what its actors do to the world and how they perceive it.

This experience, however, is not given; it is created. Experience in general refers to both the process and product of mediation between an individual or collective subject and its environment. As Teresa De Lauretis elaborates, it is '*a process* by which, for all social beings, subjectivity is constructed. Through that process one places oneself or is placed in social reality, and so perceives and comprehends as subjective (referring to, even originating in, oneself) those relations — material, economic, and interpersonal — which are in fact social, and in a larger perspective, historical. The process is continuous, its achievement unending or daily renewed.'[9] If we concur with Jameson's conception of History as the *experience* of Necessity, it then becomes evident how integral the symbolic forms we have at our disposal are to our thinking about historical events, as they are enacted as well as represented. It is largely the significant and necessary character of such events that renders them historical, and the experience of this necessity, as 'the inexorable *form* of events', is made possible through the symbolic means of fantasy-production.

The task I have set for myself is to reconstruct the fantasy-work subsisting in the historical developments now referred to as the four day revolt — the complex and often discontinuous or contradictory processes of coding that gave and continue to give rise to the dominant meanings and facts comprising this event. Vital to the movement of history is the problematic within which its actors orient themselves. The proposed solutions to socio-political crises towards which historical actors are impelled demonstrate the *good sense* directing their active participation in the public sphere (e.g. the proposal, in the wake of increasing reports of abuse of domestic workers, to 'keep them at home' — see Chapter 3). It is on this level that interests and demands are made known and pursued. What I would like to focus on, however, is the *common sense* underlying it — the political imaginary which gives form to these interests and demands, problems and solutions, by making available certain concepts, categories and operations of understanding that have come to wield hegemonic authority over a given population at a particular period of time.[10] None of this is to imply that this imaginary has historical agency. It is to acknowledge, rather, that the dominant historical agency of human beings is inseparable from the fantasy through which history as the experience of necessity is made possible.[11]

To reconstruct this history I have taken much of my material from the book *An Eyewitness History: People Power, The Philippine Revolution of 1986*, a purported 'eyewitness history' — a compilation of stories, anecdotes and commentaries that make up 'an oral history told by the people who witnessed — and made — the events'.[12] Like *Revolt of the Masses*, this is a narrative of a 'revolution' as told by its victors. This 'revolution' was significantly shaped by the mass media, not only because of the extensive coverage it attracted, but also because of the way in which the media ceased to operate merely in its reportorial capacity and instead participated in all the events they were representing — from Benigno Aquino Jr.'s return to the Philippines in 1983 with an entourage of foreign journalists, to Marcos's on-camera decision to call for snap elections (provoked by insistent television journalists), to Radio Veritas's openly partisan coverage of the elections, to Enrile's and Ramos's seeking protection in the company of foreign journalists when they broke with Marcos, to the logistical coordination of military and civilian movements on the radio airwaves. In other words, inasmuch as the mass media were also engaged in the making of history, the texts that serve as bases for knowledge of these events are also visual and auditory. Lastly, as 'one who was there', I have my own experience of the event to draw from. Like those I will be quoting, I too am both historical actor and historian. I am not far removed from what I describe. This reconstruction of history, however, is neither another personal testimony nor another omniscient narration of events, neither a subjective nor objective account of empirically verifiable developments, but rather an interested analysis of the imaginary dimensions of the uprising.

THE EVENT OF PEOPLE POWER

History is not only the experience of Necessity, it is also the experience of a collectivity — it is, in other words, an experience with a wide social purview. That collectivity and social purview may be constructed in varying scales and on varying terms. Hence one speaks of national and cultural histories, as well as histories of peoples bound by religion or faith. Gramsci writes:

> An historical act can only be performed by 'collective man'[sic], and this presupposes the attainment of a "cultural-social" unity through which a multiplicity of dispersed wills, with heterogeneous aims, are welded together with a single aim, on the basis of an equal and common conception of the world, both general and particular, operating in transitory bursts [in emotional ways] or permanently [where the intellectual base is so well rooted, assimilated and experienced that it becomes passion].[13]

The constituency and constitution of this historical subject — here, 'the people' — is dependent on the social formation out of which it emerges and from which it receives that 'common conception of the world'.

Hence, the logic at work in the hegemonic social configuration can be gleaned in the way that the multiple conflicts, contradictions and grievances of Philippine society erupted into the confrontation between Marcos and Cory as the central antagonism of the country. For there were oppositional candidates as well as other challengers to Marcos who, however, never managed to capture the mandate and support of an effective historical collective, to mobilize a broad, national spectrum of forces (including the generally politically apathetic or conservative middle classes) that could act with transformative power. Revolting subaltern groups and underground movements were never popular enough among the emergent 'middle forces' to signify 'the people'. That is to say, if the appellation 'the people' was used before the event of 'people power', it was used synonymously with 'the masses'. Bearing the stamp of subordination and subjection, 'the people' as 'the masses' could not recruit the other, particularly middle, sectors of Philippine society to unite into a collective *subject*, a subject with historical agency.

That the hegemonic significance of 'the people' changed from the election period to the time of the uprising and after does not alter the fact that 'the people' had acquired a historically significant counter-hegemonic power, but rather demonstrates the strength of a ruling social order in diffusing its revolutionary potential.[14] Only Cory could pose a counter-hegemonic challenge to Marcos; only she could bring together the desires undoing the nation and push the latter into crisis by embodying those desires, by becoming the other term necessary to construct an antagonism of national proportions.[15] In other words, Cory managed, as no other oppositional leader had, to become the other half of Marcos, personifying the blockage of his identity, the absolute limits of his embodiment of the Republic of the Philippines.

It is through the construction of this polar confrontation between Marcos and Cory (as much as in its development and outcome) that the presuppositions of authority and power working in Philippine society may be understood. A large part of this construction took place through the rhetoric not only of the two figures, but the rhetoric of all those who publicly participated in debating the issues of Benigno (Ninoy) Aquino's assassination, the severe economic crisis it precipitated (which hit, most dramatically, the business community), the increasingly revealed extent of Marcos's corruption and his deteriorating state of health, and Cory's candidacy as an answer to the country's ills. These issues were brought to the public not only through the media, which were still forcibly constricted in their dissemination of information and opinions that might be damaging to the Marcos regime, but also through the channels of rumour that are acutely developed in politically repressive societies. It might be more accurate to say, these issues began to form a public, inasmuch as the years of repression of civil liberties under martial law had served to eradicate the conditions necessary for a public body to operate vis-à-vis the state (which in a dictatorship assumes for itself the functions and interests that in developed capitalist democracies are at the behest of 'public authority').[16]

Already we see the beginnings of the national subject that would emerge out of 'People Power 2', that is, 'civil society'. In the self-reflective history of this public, the relaxing of these repressive measures under the increasing pressure of international scrutiny and unrelenting local resistance and protest provided some space for the circulation and exchange of information and opinion.[17] Freer communication encouraged the growth of a new community, one increasingly critical of the government, which it identified as 'the US-Marcos dictatorship' and against which it had began to define itself. Thus were the beginnings of the community that would grow and increase its discursive power and which would show its full force in the uprising under the name of 'the people'. The character of this community — meaning, the nature not only of its constituency (whom it was made up of) but also of its constitution (how it held together), as well as of its self-consciousness (how its members conceived of it and of themselves as part of it) — was shaped precisely by the discourses and discursive practices that gave rise to it in the first place. It is not merely coincidental that this community increasingly identified with Cory Aquino, for the affective and perceptive practices that were responsible for constructing her as the antagonistic opponent of Marcos also constructed this new community.

CORAZON OF THE FILIPINO PEOPLE

Since Cory derived her power and authority from 'the people' whose subjectivity her persona helped to define, one cannot speak of one construction without the other. Both are subjects-in-process whose characters became transformed in the course of this short 'history'. The three months between the snap presidential elections to the uprising is generally conceived as a historical, subjective continuum, in which Cory and the Filipino people moved in a linear fashion towards liberation. But I would like to foreground the disjuncture between the two 'events' and the concomitant shift in function and character of Cory as she was constructed by and in relation to the people. Through the making of 'history' out of the four-day revolt, the initial identification of 'the people' with Cory underwent a fissuring process that resulted in 'the people' being conceived and conceiving of themselves in a position of alterity to Cory.

The sexual antagonism performed by the 'feminine' Cory in relation to the hypermasculinist Marcos is best explained by Žižek in his reworking of Hegel's dialectics of the Lord and Bondsman: 'the other itself (the Lord, let's say) is, in his positivity, in his fascinating presence, just the positivation of our own — Bondsman's — negative relationship towards ourselves, the positive embodiment of our own self-blockage … we cannot say that the Bondsman is also in the same way just the positivation of the negative relationship of the Lord. What we can perhaps say is that he is the Lord's symptom.'[18] This is what Žižek calls 'pure antagonism' between subject-positions as differentiated from antagonism as the limit of the social. The Bondsman can free himself from this relationship by experiencing the Lord as the embodiment of his own self-blockage, just as the Woman, as the symptom of Man, can free herself from this sexual antagonism by experiencing Man as 'the reflexive determination of Woman's impossibility of achieving an identity with herself'. In the February revolt of 1986 'led' by Corazon Aquino against Ferdinand Marcos, this is what the Philippines was able to do.

Then, Ferdinand Marcos, the dictator-ally of the US, embodied the blockage of Philippine development and democracy, preventing the Philippines from becoming all that it could be.[19] The country's arrested economic development and incapacity for self-determination, which Marcos guaranteed, of course rendered the country that static element, that *perpetuum mobilé*, responsible for the continued functioning of the US desiring-machine. As the incarnation of the Philippine socius, the substance of its polis, Marcos's decrepit body spoke of the corruption of the State. In fact, his failing health was a well-guarded (but nevertheless well-known) secret. His 'strongman' status was constantly defended and demonstrated, not least by Marcos himself. His immovable anti-communist rhetoric and military offensive (conquering and eradicating evil) as well as his push-ups and body-baring on television were acts to prove to the public his masculine strength and power. Hence, the newsbreak of his loss of an organ (his kidney) not only confirmed what everyone already knew, but also served as one of a series of public blows that steadily emasculated his figure and opened up the space for Corazon Aquino to eventually take his place.

As the widow of Benigno Aquino whose assassination was experienced as the squelching of the country's hope for liberation from the US-Marcos dictatorship, Corazon Aquino embodied the Philippines' national loss. On her figure were displaced an overdetermination of losses. Such explains her immense popularity with the Philippine populace. Indeed, rather than being a disadvantage during the election as some had surmised, Cory's feminine persona was precisely that trait with which the people identified. Frustrated with the country's stagnation, the people saw in her not only the incarnation of loss and subordination rising to challenge the very cause of her incapacity to assert herself, they also saw in her the embodiment of radical desire. She represented, in other words, the possibility of complete change.[20] While Marcos was the objective substance holding the fort, as the incarnation of the Law, Cory, with her political inexperience and girlish demeanor, was the subjective element corroding that structure, the embodiment of transgression.

Cory's femininity was, in other words, the trait with which the nation, as it rose on this occasion, identified. The revolt was itself constructed with profuse feminine images — notably that of the Virgin Mary (who became identified as the patroness of the revolt) and of the nuns — as well as with the voice of June Keithley whose operating of the airwaves was crucial in mobilizing the population and channelling information. The signifying function or the symbolic mandate Cory took up was hence one that bore the stamp of the feminine. This feminine identification does not at all reduce the complexity of factors that informed the overwhelming support she received, including, later, the fundamental support of the US government. It is however to demonstrate the metaphoric surplus she embodied, which enabled her to act as the counter-hegemonic subject challenging the prevailing order. Only this figure who brought God to earth in man, whose loss bore the seeds of discontent and promise, could carry 'the historical moment, pregnant with heterogeneous and contradictory possibilities' into an explosion of popular will.[21] Cory was, in other words, a signifier of the desires of a nation whose people came to conceive of it in terms of lack and loss with the murder of her husband. This function would not remain the same over the course of developments. Later she would serve to channel those same desires, under the Law of the Father (God) — no longer the transgressive element corroding the authority of the Marcos regime, but now the instrument of a higher order, bearing a greater (because moral) authority. In a sense, the shift from bearing the promise of national redemption for the losses made palpable by Ninoy's death to being the deliverer of the nation's Providence is not a shift. In many ways, the shift can be understood in terms of the contradictory tendencies inherent in the ambivalent persona of the Virgin Mary who was not only the avowed patroness of Cory but also whose role as the mother of Christ greatly influenced people's perception of Cory and her own role.

Cory's symbolic power was, however, in no way simply given. It had to be created by means of materials (facts, categories) provided by 'history' and continuing traditions of social practice. Put differently, her identity had to be constructed within the field of the prevailing national fantasy. 'Insofar, in other words, as symbolic action … is a way of doing something to the world, to that degree what we are calling 'world' must inhere within it, as the content it has to take up into itself in order to submit it to the transformations of form.'[22] Thus, the way Ninoy was killed — coming home on a plane from America, wearing all white — for example, presented material that took shape as it was used symbolically. Ninoy's death was crucial in the molding of Cory's figure, and it was time and again invoked, especially by Cory and Ninoy's mother, who also joined in protest rallies and actively campaigned for her daughter-in-law during the election period, as symbol and parable. The image of Ninoy's fate was engraved in the imagination of the community that had begun to form. For Ninoy's death to be experienced as a national trauma and to generate the massive outpouring of sympathy and rage that it did, it had to be thought through the categories of a collective fantasy. Within this collective fantasy intersect the ideological sign-systems of nationalism and Christianity. Thus the subjective experience of one witness is expressed in these terms:

> What struck me about the assassination of Ninoy was the animal savagery and the brutality. It was like an ominous scream, something that you had never heard in this country. You're so mad. Shot in the tarmac! It was not in accordance with anything that a Filipino was ever used to. We're Christians. Whatever our enmity, whatever our rivalry, whatever our differences, there are some limits to what we can do.[23]

The death of Ninoy, who was known primarily and more popularly as an opposition politician and only later constructed by his mother and wife (as well as the sympathetic Catholic Church) as a man of God, derived its metaphorical significance from the discourses of nationalism/patriotism and Christianity. As Cory preached: Ninoy was 'a man for whom love of country was only the other face of his love for God. And I think this is the truest and best kind of patriotism. It is only on this plane that patriotism ceases to be, as they say, the refuge of scoundrels and becomes, instead, the obligation of a Christian.'[24] The gap between the secular subjectivity of a nationalistic perspective and the sacred objectivity of the Christian worldview is bridged through familial terms. Filipino and Christian, Ninoy was thus conceived as at once a son of the nation and a son of God. The metonymic and metaphorical corollaries derived from this symbolic condensation would not, however, produce a coherent structure of meanings or a unified order of allegorical figures. There would be overlapping, inconsistency and contradiction among the paradigms used to organize people's experience of events and the values conveyed by them. Hence, Cory could alternately be Christ and the Virgin Mary (just as the people could be the people Christ died for as well as Christ himself), and the metaphorical significance of each personage could shift in meaning and emphasis depending on the situation of its realization.

In spite of this agonism within the ideological-fantasy field, there is a level of compossibility among the categories of meaning and scenarios offered by the fundamental discursive systems configuring Philippine society. The different meanings read in Ninoy's fatal return could thus meet on a ground of sense held in common by many people — the sense of the familial, the national, and the divine. One man expressed his reading as follows:

> I recounted the words of one old woman: 'They are so cruel. He was returning to his country; they did not even let him step on the soil of his native land.' There was a symbolism there. They were in such a hurry to kill him, they did not even allow him to see his native land, his mother.

And Ninoy's mother recalled:

> Before Ninoy was buried, a sculptor came to do his death mask and
> this man told me: 'It is very significant that Ninoy came down from
> the plane to meet the people. He had to do that because he is a man
> of the people.'[25]

While the first reading bears the patriotic symbolism of the country
and 'the native land', and the second reading bears the Christian
allegory of the man descending unto his people, the two readings are
reconciled in the equivalences made among a number of terms, namely,
land, people and mother. The condensation of all three terms to signify
'the Filipino' as the nation would ultimately be secured in the person
of Cory Aquino.

The rallying cry that emerged out of the assassination was a phrase
known to have been uttered by Ninoy: 'The Filipino is worth dying
for.' This quotation circulated rapidly and served as a *point-de-capiton*
(the Lacanian signifying 'quilting point') for the construction of Ninoy
as a patriot and Christian martyr. The loss experienced with his death,
or rather, through his death (to the extent that his death only
symbolized a prior loss, which was the real crisis of the nation) was
thus overdetermined in its manifestation in the collective fantasy as a
national trauma.[26] The trauma of Ninoy's not having been allowed to
return 'to see his native land, his mother' could be perceived as the act
of breaking the bond between mother and child, a concept which Ileto
shows to bear significantly on the Philippine imaginary: 'The
preoccupation with the mother-child separation theme has left a strong
imprint on Tagalog literature. In the *pasyon's* development through the
centuries, for instance, the dialogues between Christ and the Virgin
Mary grew all out of proportion, making the *pasyon* just as much an
epic of Mother Mary's loss.'[27] Placed in the context of this intersection
of nationalist, Christian and familialist discourses, Mother Mary is the
motherland [*Inang Bayan*]; the Filipino 'worth dying for' is the people
for whom Christ died, a people to be redeemed; the death of Ninoy as
a Christ figure is thus the loss of his people, who are his brothers and
sisters in the eyes of *Inang Bayan*. The metaphorical equivalence made
between Ninoy and Christ[28] can in part explain the overwhelming

identification of 'the Filipino people' with Cory, for she embodied the place of grief that the people had come increasingly to realize and experience as their place as Filipinos. It is important to clarify that this mode of interpretation is not intrinsic to 'the people' experiencing history. Rather, it is precisely the mode of producing 'the people' as the subject of historical experience.

The mourning for 'a returning son/ Whose fate rocked umbilical with the motherland'[29] hence took on the form of mourning for Christ, which as Ileto shows was made familiar to the lower classes through the *pasyon* (the ritual reading and dramatization of the passion of Christ during Holy Week).[30] Thus explains the penitential behavior of the mass of mourners as it was described by those privileged to articulate history:

> People were there shouting: 'Ninoy!' They stood in the rain and in the sun. For them, it was an expiation for having allowed this to happen. Even Marcos said that Ninoy's assassination was a 'national shame'. For me, this was the evidence: between one and two million people of Metro Manila out there in the streets, not just for ten minutes but for hours; some of them marching for many hours. There was thunder, lightning, and rain that afternoon. But people stuck it out; they didn't leave. They stood, they waited, they shouted, and they clapped. 'Put down your umbrellas. Only Imelda carries an umbrella.'

As another put it:

> The people who went would not give up and leave, no matter how tired or uncomfortable they were. It was as if they had made a vow or thought of what they were doing as penitence.

Vicente Rafael observes that in the writings of José Rizal, who is generally considered 'the First Filipino', 'the love one feels for the *patria* is conveyed by what we might call a rhetoric of mourning. Mourning implies a process of working through, then setting apart one's memories of a lost object or person from one's experience of them while still alive. In doing so one is able to reconcile oneself to the fact of loss. Such a reconciliation is accomplished through the idealization of the person or object. Put another way, mourning succeeds when what one remembers is an image of what was lost, no longer the lost object itself.

Mourning thus entails the reproduction of stereotypical images of the lost object. In such a context, memory attaches itself not to direct experience but to its mediated versions'.[31] Hence, the allegorical translation of Ninoy's death was crucial for it to be experienced as a national loss.

The outpouring of emotion during the funeral was a moment of epiphany for many in the middle classes whose Christianity and latent national consciousness enabled them to identify with 'the people' as the Filipino 'race' waiting to be redeemed through the mercy of God ('who gave his only son to save the sins of the world'). As one middle-class housewife recounted:

> The entire experience with its outrage, its shame, its confusion, its restlessness and insecurity, its questioning — was also cleansing and a tremendous opportunity for faith and trust in God.
>
> Tomorrow I will visit the grave of Senator Aquino, as people continue to do so with prayers and flowers all of this week. Tomorrow it will be a week after his burial and I know that there, after all these days, I will at last cry — because we have lost an alternative.
>
> And yet I will also cry out of joy and pride for our race, for the Filipino people who in these recent days have shown themselves people of faith and of heart, people who mourn and weep, people who pray. In all, it is the Filipino people who emerged triumphant and whole from Aquino's death — open, free, unashamed, and unafraid to grieve and to mourn.[32]

The *jouissance* or libidinal joy felt by this mourner reveals the desire behind the need for national restitution and redemption. The impelling desire that finds satisfaction in the glorification of the Filipino 'race' is the shame of being Filipino, the shame of the nation, which would be condensed into the Marcoses (without their military machine) and purged from the Filipino identity it bears. The shame stems from being a violated people, an object of another's pleasure, the shame of a 'prostituted' and debased nation (see Chapters 1 and 3).[33] To glory in being a people of faith and of heart is to reveal their being a people of lack (of faith, of courage, of love); to triumph in wholeness is to reveal their being a divided people — a people in crisis with itself (experiencing separation from itself, lacking integrity). That heart would be Corazon, who would thus not only become Corazon of the people, but more importantly, Corazon, the People.

To many it was precisely those qualities which comprised Cory's weakness — her being a woman, her political inexperience, her girlish demeanor, her marital loss, her gentle manner — that inspired people's faith in her. Cory was quite aware of this advantage. As she told her mother-in-law when she decided to run: 'The people will believe me, Mommy. I am a victim; we are victims of this regime. We have suffered a lot. I can say that I am with them in their sufferings. My sincerity will be real and will make people free from fear.'[34] People voted for Cory for the very reasons that others rejected her. The trait-of-identification by which she was known and recognized was construed as her strength as well as her weakness. This trait was none other than the meaning of her name, Corazon: heart.

One joke circulated by those who were against her winning was just such a play on her name: *Si Corazon Aquino* [(in Tagalog, simply the way of designating a person] became *Si, Corazon* [in Spanish, 'Yes, heart'], pointing to the head, *Aqui, no* ['Here, none']. In other words: yes, she has a heart, but she has no brain. The same is expressed more explicitly by a Marcos loyalist who asserted after Marcos had been deposed and Cory installed as President that she wanted Marcos back because 'He is so intelligent. Cory has done nothing, and she is only a girl. She doesn't know the ins and outs of politics. Marcos has so much experience', and preferred even Imelda because 'she is more brainy than Cory', who 'has too soft a heart'.[35] But to the great majority, it was this woman's heart that the country badly needed. Cory was aware that her appeal lay precisely in her lack of political experience. As she would repeatedly ironically confirm, 'I have no cheating experience. I have no "salvaging" experience. I have no experience in arresting and terrorizing people.'[36] Thus was she able to reverse the objections to her softness of heart. Indeed, it was those qualities which constituted her femininity that made her challenge against Marcos in such an act of defiance. As Cardinal Sin, the head of the Philippine Catholic Church, expressed: 'If Cory wins, it would be the greatest humiliation of Marcos. Imagine, a housewife, not a politician at all, winning over him. That would be the greatest vindication of Ninoy.' But underlying this confidence in Cory's victory was the desire for redemption for

Ninoy's death, and the faith in a greater power, that of God. In this sense, Cory could be conceived as an instrument of a higher authority, from which she received hers. One who wielded great influence over the reading of events, Cardinal Sin, interpreted her role as such:

> 'All right, kneel down,' I said. 'I will bless you. You are going to be president. You are the Joan of Arc.' At that moment I thought God answered the prayers of our people. He chooses weaklings. And why weaklings? Why a weak woman? We have never been gifted with a president who is a woman. That is how the Lord confounds the strong. When Our Lady appeared in Lourdes, she appeared to a girl who was weak. And in Fatima she appeared to three children. 'This is what will happen. And you will win. We'll see the hand of God, one miracle after another. God bless you,' I said to Cory.

But this is the reading sanctioned by the Church, one of the institutions which would eventually serve to re-channel the desires released by the figure of Cory, and bring them back into the fold of the Law. What this account elides is the identification with Cory, herself — the feminine persona, without the authority of God the Father — experienced by a great number of people, a significant part of which were women. As the following excerpt from a poem by Marne Kilates attests, 'the people' was a construction against the masculine persona of Marcos and his dictatorial regime,[37] an identification with women and children marked by loss and violence:

> O Scheming father, O Patriarch of Greed,
> O Merchant of Hunger,
> Behold us now linking arms ...
>
> Behold us now
> Who have long kept our peace,
> Behold us now
> Who have long postponed our rage,
> Behold us now
> Mothers who grieve our missing sons,
> Wives who lost husbands,
> Women oppressed by Gender and your insults,
> Children of the Snarl
> Who have known only the violence you have done
> To their minds ...

The People are here. We are your People.

The People are here and we command you now:

Begone! Begone! Begone![38]

CHRIST AND THE VIRGIN

With Ninoy identified with Christ in this popular Philippine imaginary, Cory came to be identified with the Virgin Mary. But the attributes and qualities securing that identification did not remain the same throughout, for the Virgin Mary herself is not a stable sign with a single meaning. As in the case of the Lady of Guadalupe in Mexico, she can serve a subversive function as well as the conservative function she traditionally plays in many Catholic societies.[39] Although the spectre of Mother Mary hung above her, Cory was sought not as a symbol but as an active medium of people's desire. In the next chapter, I trace the origins of this radical reworking of the Virgin Mary as *Inang Bayan* to a prior 'event' in the sphere of popular culture.

In the language of 'the people', the hope was for Cory to act as Joan of Arc rather than to remain the symbol of the mourning motherland. The popular movement to draft her into presidency was launched in hopes 'that this still sorrowing widow will shed her mother's garments for the battle tunic of a political warrior'.[40] When she did decide to run, Cory herself declared:

> Some who support my candidacy say that if I am elected my role will be that of Mother of the Nation. I am honored by the title, but I am campaigning to be president of our country. It is in that capacity that I shall serve. And as president, I assure you, I shall lead. If elected I will remain a mother to my children, but I intend to be Chief Executive of this nation. And for the male chauvinists in the audience, I intend as well to be the Commander-in-Chief of the Armed Forces of the Philippines.[41]

It was in no small measure that this refusal to be relegated to being a mere symbol of the nation's desires led many to her side. The boldness of her leadership inspired a devotion that was not passive but that on the contrary brought with it an eagerness to participate and act:

Through Cory, we have found expression for all our wishes and desires and values. My husband asks me why I go to rally after rally. It isn't the speeches that I want to hear. *It is the spirit that I seek. I want to be part of the hope and the reaching out for sincerity, for honesty, for truth. I want to be part of the jubilation* because we have at last a spokesperson, a rallying point, a champion. *I want to be counted. I want to be part of the protest as much as I want to be part of the affirmation.* (emphasis mine)

This spirit was what would impel 'people power', a substance configured in terms of the Holy Spirit, Christ and the Filipino, and inspirited with love of woman, nation and the Virgin Mary. What the people needed was this faith or love (experienced as 'jubilation') that would enable them to act on their own behalf, in order to affirm a new identity as a people of the nation and of God. A faith in self and love of self made possible in the same of the nation and the Virgin Mary. Because the hegemonic desires of the nation were configured within the imperialist fantasy in such a way that the Filipino became repulsed by itself — detached from that debased feminized self which was the 'symptom' of the free world fantasy (see Chapter 1) — the people needed to protest this dominant identity and affirm another, one with which it could reconcile itself to mend the crisis producing this self-alienation. It needed, in other words, to become loveable to itself in the gaze of another that was not the First, Free World (inasmuch as this was the gaze that produced it in its present identity). This other that would arouse the faith and love of the people because it let them have faith and love for themselves as the Filipino people would be a condensation of the Filipino nation and the Virgin Mary.

Thus the desires that Ninoy's death triggered manifested themselves in the form of a fervent Catholic nationalist mourning. 'Nationalism as a kind of mourning is built on remembering as a reciprocal act'.[42] After the assassination, the opposition launched full-force into remembering, insisting on the symbolic significance of Ninoy's death. As his widow, Cory led and shaped much of this process, recounting stories and anecdotes about her husband, giving her interpretation of past events, and so on, in political rallies, prayer meetings and various group gatherings (of businessmen, sororities, etc.). Cory was thus shaping national memories into a history understood in folk Catholic terms. But Cory was not doing this single-handedly. Aside from the Church, the media and other influential opinion-making institutions and apparatuses, the operation of which is in the control of the religiously Catholic middle and upper classes (who would become Cory's staunchest supporters), joined in this foregrounding of the nation's historical consciousness and informing that consciousness with the categories of Catholicism.

The result of this process of remembering current events through religious scenarios was a transmutation of the new community's sense of temporality — the infusion of divine or biblical time into historical time. This is clearly evidenced in the Messianic rhetoric of Cory, the influence of which in shaping her followers' experience of history, their conception of themselves as a people and their consequent collective action:

> I say to Mr Marcos what Moses said to the cruel, enslaving Pharaoh — Let our people go! The nation has awakened. I, like millions of Filipinos, look on this awakening as the dawning of a new day ...
>
> The people are crying for change ...
>
> I have crisscrossed the length and breadth of the nation. I have traveled by air, by plane and by helicopter; I have traveled by land.
>
> I have seen the devastation wrought by a policy built on a mountain of lies.
>
> I have seen the broken bodies of men, women, and children buried under promises of peace and progress. I have heard the anguished voices of victims of injustice answered only by hypocritical pledges of retribution
>
> I have been kissed by the poorest of the poor, and have felt the warmth of their tears on my cheeks. I have been emboldened by the eager embrace of throngs determined to put an end to this regime.
>
> I have heard them shout that I must win. I have been electrified by their every cry for freedom, and inspired by their every clasp of hope.
>
> I cannot shut my ears to them. I cannot turn my back on them.[43]

The inflection of the testimonial form of this speech with the biblical voice of a Moses-Christ also demonstrates Cory's self-placement in a Judeo-Christian Messianic tradition that shores up the people's identification with the people of God awaiting Christian redemption.

For the middle classes, the death of Ninoy was the awakening of their sense of moral responsibility. Feeling accountable for their passiveness, they were beckoned by Christian and patriotic duty to redeem themselves and the country with whom they now so strongly identified as a victim of injustice and evil. Duty was the way in which the indebted status of the Philippine socius as symbolized by Ninoy's death manifested itself. The cynicism that had pervaded the populace, keeping it subjected because resigned to the realities of the country by diffusing its desires (in irony, sarcasm, self-deprecating jokes), could not hold much longer. Indeed, overcoming this cynicism was crucial in overcoming apathy. Only by grasping the Catholic nationalist fantasy-scenario with utter seriousness and belief, that is, as reality, could the population rise forth to act and to transform it. No longer confronted with fictions but with 'truth', the people could feel impelled to respond to it with conviction and commitment. It is this recovery of faith that, as I will argue in the last chapter, that overcomes the debilitating effects of irony on radical action.

The abandonment of irony, however, is not the same as the abandonment of humour.[44] For the former works with depths of repressed truth, the latter with surfaces of fantasy-reality. Indeed the entire revolt was played out on the surface of fantasies; the battle was fought on the terrain of the sign.[45] During these four days almost no bullets were fired — the deadly arms of war were waived for other gestures and the 'encounters' and confrontations were hardly ever physical and mainly symbolic. As in love and faith, the conquest was effected through rhetoric (coaxing, appealing, reprimanding) and other expressions of emotion — images, sounds, and music: horns blaring the chant 'Co-ree, Co-ree', hands flashing the L-sign, statues of the Virgin Mary carried down the streets, patriotic songs played on the radio and sung in the face of army tanks, food, cigarettes and flowers being offered, and the inundation of the color yellow:

> *Yellow was the color of this longing and this warmth,* yellow like the ribbons tied around old trees, not oak but mango, acacia, and *banaba* standing along Ninoy Aquino's homecoming route, yellow like the sun and stars of the Philippine flag vanished in the black of mourning, always that black of mourning, where Marcos and the military ruled in viselike grip.

> In this campaign, Cory always wore yellow, radiant Child of the
> Sun returning to the Land of Morning and yellow the towels and
> dishcloths, umbrellas, dried leaves, raincoats, fans the people waved
> back at her in *a rising tide like light* ...[46]

The color yellow was significant because it came to symbolize the
unfulfilled promise, the aborted coming (of Ninoy, as the answer to
the nation's ills), as well as a new hope (a second coming, in the person
of Cory, not yet the Virgin Mary, but the Messiah) — a symbol of loss
and future fulfillment. The color itself was significant because of the
atmosphere of jubilation it helped to create, a jubilation that was
peculiar to this unique revolt. The brightness of yellow contributed to,
by affirming, the joy of 'people power', the triumph and fulfillment
experienced by the people in their inner transformation, in their newly-
found subjective freedom (even before the ouster of Marcos). It signified
the spirit the religious middle-classes wanted to be a part of and the
fervor of their national desires, which took shape through the discourse
of liberation and deliverance from oppression expressed in terms of
truth and lies, sin and redemption.

SUBVERSIVE DESIRES OF WOMEN

It is not coincidental that after Ninoy was killed, an unprecedented
number of women from many sectors, significantly from the middle
classes, became politically active, even militant.[47] Many of the
organizations formed in support of Cory's candidacy were led and
composed by women. And many men were drawn into the struggle
against Marcos by their wives.[48] The feminine aspect of Cory, the Virgin
Mary and the Filipino nation with which the women identified was
not, however, submissiveness and obedience but rather the courage of
conviction, initiative and self-determination. During the revolt wives
acted independently from their husbands, sometimes against them. June
Keithley remembers: 'My husband was out on EDSA when he heard
my voice. He didn't know where I was but he got to a phone, called
our maid and asked her to give me a message. The maid got to me
and she said: "Ma'am, Sir just called. He said you should go home." I

said: "I can't go home," and I hung up.' Another 'wife and mother' relates the liberating experience of participating in the making of history, the subjective freedom that comes with the decision to act, which was shared by not only many women but by most of those who counted themselves as part of 'people power':

> 'Please stay at home because it's dangerous. You have to think of the children,' my husband said. I got angry. Precisely it was for the children that I was going to risk life and limb — so that they could hope for a better future. *I had to be where the action was.* My younger children were safe with a trusted nursemaid. I had encouraged the older kids to go and join the crowd. It was Cardinal Sin, no less, who had exhorted people to come to defend the military and to pray. How could I now not practice what I preach?
>
> For a second I sat down on the sofa; *I was immobile and close to tears.* I heard on the radio that people were being urged to man the barricades and that they were arriving even from the provinces. Here I was in White Plains, just a stone's throw from the barricades, and I was being kept in the house.
>
> The decision did not take long to make. *I was going out there to do my share. This was the relevance I had been searching for: to be able to express my faith in God,* who is sometimes so near and yet often so far away. He was here, right now, asking me *to prove myself by going out to be counted.* I couldn't stay put in my comfortable home while thousands from the depressed areas were doing their share to fight for me.
>
> With towels and lemon juice to lessen the sting of tear gas, I walked out into the early dawn alone, out of the house into the street. I walked out of grace — from my marriage, so I thought at the time — into independence and into freedom.[49]

The freedom experienced by this woman in her decision did not derive from a renouncement of her feminine identity but from taking independent charge of that identity, from becoming responsible for defining her role as a wife, and especially as a mother. A freedom from the immobility and passivity she was being confined to and constricted by. The fulfillment of a need to be part of something larger, the need to 'prove (one)self by going out to be counted' — a self-affirmation in a community holding together in faith and love and determining its own history. This experience was the experience of 'the people' as well as the women who signified and organized their desires.

'And the women!' exclaimed Cory shortly before the election. 'They have cast caution to the winds to campaign and lead in the people's crusade. They are determined to prove that people power is mightier than all the men and money of the crumbling dictatorship.' Constructed against 'the men and money of the crumbling dictatorship', people power is implicitly an ascendant feminine power. The identification of people power with Cory and the Virgin Mary indeed determined its feminine construction. The meaning of feminine, however, was not given — it emerged or achieved definition in the exercise of people power. The ambiguity of the 'we' in the following account of people power in action may be seen to signify the overlapping of meanings of the women and the people demonstrated in actuality:

As I was leaving home for a second day at the barricades, I heard Minister Enrile on the radio: He wanted women and children to come into the camps, for their safety. It sounded like the echo of a bygone era. How many would take him seriously, I wondered? I certainly didn't intend to, nor did any of my women friends, I felt.

We were fighting not with physical strength but with unarmed courage, and so our women's efforts could certainly count as much as men's.

A scene that showed this conviction coming alive was small compared to events happening around the camps that day. Although it must have been played out elsewhere by thousands of others, being part of it made me proud to be a Filipino — and a woman.

… An hour before we had confronted the naked steel of fixed bayonets, Armalites ready to fire, and the grim stare of a Marine commander who, when we refused to give way to his truckload of troops, had warned the priest leading us that he was quite used to killing. Seeing that he was ready to do it, *we gave way, of course — frustrated, angry, shaken, yet knowing that we hadn't failed,* since our aim wasn't to make martyrs but to avoid bloodshed, delay the loyalists, and show them our determined vigilance.

The incident had lasted some twenty frightening minutes. 'This can't really be happening!' I thought as I saw the barrel of a rifle appearing over the heads of the massed, crouching crowd. It was outlined against the sky, only a few feet from our faces. But *nobody panicked, screamed or ran away. All I heard were appeals to the soldiers for compassion, songs and prayer to keep up our spirit. For that, at least, we felt we could be proud.*

As the group sat on the road after the incident, calming down, preparing for the next encounter, a marshal announced our new formation: women volunteers were needed for the front line of the human barricade, together with a few marshals. This would appeal to the Marines' feelings, we hoped. The tactic had worked in other areas the day before. Come stun them with your beauty, he joked. But the women responded seriously — even while he was speaking, some were standing up and moving forward.[50]

The power of the people that made this woman proud to be a Filipino and a woman is construed as inner strength, 'unarmed courage', 'determined vigilance' and compassion. The triumph of women lay not in military-like recalcitrance or physical resistance, not even in sacrifice but rather in spiritual endurance, in an immovable and collective will, and in unwavering faith. And the beauty that the marshal had joked was the weapon of women would come to be experienced by many in the course of the events as 'people power' — the overwhelming mixture of emotions that would move men and stop tanks:

The military are powerful because they have their Armalites, 38s, 45s, shields, truncheons, tear gas, protective masks, smoke grenades, so on and so forth. Courage comes easy with them because of what they possess.

For my part, I discovered an inner quality I did not know I possessed, the inner spirit of courage without outside, material support. Consequently, I have begun to feel less burdened and to be filled with Christian forgiveness for the uniformed aggressors because I know I have come out the victor.

While this expression of the triumph of the spirit bears the strains of Christian righteousness, it does reveal the way 'people power' is constructed against the power of the military, that is, against the power of 'mere men' and their weapons of control and repression. Because 'the people' took on a feminine construction (through the system of equivalences made with the polarization of Marcos and Cory, the identification of the Filipino and the motherland), the strategy it employed not surprisingly took feminine form as well. What is important is that while 'the people' took on feminine contours, it was nevertheless associated with (and more than that, it bore) power.

The people power strategy of appealing to feelings was, however, also determined by the Christian practice of evangelization or conversion. Love of fellow citizens, love of country and love of God as it was conveyed through women became the foundation of 'people power', the overdetermined motivation of people acting selflessly in the face of danger. The nuns who were always at the battlefronts on the streets epitomized as well as demonstrated this motivation. As an organized group of women, they acted 'for the people, for the exploited ones and for justice. Even if we would have to risk our lives, we should follow Christ who had died for us. Wasn't it the rule of our young order that we should manifest our love and remind the people of our love for each other, for the poor, the rich, and also for the NPA [the New People's Army, the military arm of the Communist Party]? Here was a chance to prove this all-embracing love.'[51] It is important to note that the nuns, like many other women including Cory, were not merely symbols but, more importantly, *organizers of desire*. Their role was not merely inspirational but directive. Through them the forces impelling 'people power' took on the contours of patriotic and Christian love and duty.

SEXUAL ANTAGONISM, PATRIOTIC LOVE AND CHRISTIAN DUTY

In his widely-read book on nationalism, Benedict Anderson asserts that '*amor patriae* does not differ … from the other affections, in which there is always an element of fond imagining … What the eye is to the lover — that particular, ordinary eye he or she is born with — language — whatever language history has made his or her mother-tongue — is to the patriot.'[52] This language that produces the imagined community, however, is not to be thought only in its linguistic sense. For this language, as the product of history, comprises the figurative media responsible for the constitution of a society's imaginary. The experience of Christian faith and patriotic or nationalistic love rests on the fantasy of sexual relations. Indeed, 'there is only desire and the social. Beneath the conscious investments of economic, political, religious, etc., formations, there are unconscious sexual investments, micro-investments that attest to the way in which desire is present in a social field, and joins this field to itself as the statistically determined domain that is bound to it.'[53]

During the revolt, people courted Marcos's soldiers into conversion. With cigarettes, food[54] and flowers, people, mostly women, approached the 'errant brothers', hoping to gain their love — their Christian, patriotic, but also sexual love.[55] The people endeavoured to release the love that they believed to be immanent in these men (but which was blocked by the military uniform, by the symbolic weight of Marcos to whom they had pledged their loyalty and to whom they were therefore in debt). With the nation put asunder by the polarization of the Marcos (masculine) forces and the revolting (feminine) people, it was all a question of (heteronormative) reconciliation. This strategy was predicated upon the assumption of primordial heterosexual unity under the gaze of the family, the nation and God. The theme of reconciliation is thus overdetermined by the familial, nationalistic and Christian ideals of unity, which is in turn underpinned by the heterosexual fantasy of love as the ideal fulfillment of unity.

Whether of country or of God, love pertains to the experience of wholeness or completion, which Freud traces to the subject's primary narcissism. The ego ideal, which determines the object of love or the ideal ego (in the case of narcissistic love), 'has a social side; it is also the common ideal of a family, a class or a nation'.[56] As the ideal ego of the nation constituted by lack, Cory was the object of the narcissistic love of 'the people' — narcissistic because 'the people' had developed as the group ego ('the Filipino') as a result of the separation symbolically experienced by Ninoy's death and as such had constructed Cory for its ideal. The ego ideal which determined Cory's construction, that is the point from which she would be constructed as loveable, is a product of the ideals of family, nation and God, as they were historically articulated, ideals that would finally regulate the sublimated libidinal desires of the Philippine socius.

The love, then, that people were filled with, that impelled them to act with such courage in their bid to reincorporate the loyalist military (which was now seen as being that extrinsic element serving as a source of antagonism) into the socius, was largely narcissistic. In love with its own unity with the motherland, the Virgin Mary/Cory, as the ideal image of itself, the people offered to the loyalists this wholeness that they guarded and celebrated and experienced as their redemption. In turn, what they attempted to arouse in these grim, fearful men was the desire to share in their libidinal joy by loving *them*, the Filipino people. Freud looked upon this latter mode of loving as masculine — 'Complete object-love of the attachment type is, properly speaking, characteristic of the male' — while he looked upon the former narcissistic love as characteristically feminine'.[57] Within this conceptual framework of the heterosexual fantasy, one can recognize the antagonism between Marcos and Cory being played out by their followers as a sexual antagonism.

Once the subjected, subordinated symptom of the fantasy-production of the US-Marcos regime, 'the people' transformed itself into a desiring subject and turned the loyalist military into the object of its own desire, in Lacanian terminology, into an *objet petit a*. In other words, the positions were now reversed. Thus explains the mixture of feelings people had for the loyalist military, for an *objet petit a* is 'a hard core embodying horrifying *jouissance*, enjoyment, and as such an object which simultaneously attracts and repels us — which *divides* our desire and thus provokes shame'.[58] One recalls that, in the court of public opinion and in the halls of the Agrava commission assigned to investigate the case, the military was found to be responsible for the assassination of Ninoy. The military was thus deemed the cause of the 'national shame' that provoked the massive sympathy which would culminate in 'people power'. In this sense, too, can the military be conceived as 'the object causing our desire and at the same time ... posed retroactively by this desire'.[59] They became the surplus object blocking the newly conceived identity of the nation (embodied by 'the people' rather than by Marcos).

The people then strove to love these erring soldiers and, by doing so, bring them back into their fold. 'And the soldiers were so grateful. All of us were deeply touched with the way the soldiers talked to us. "We were supposed to protect the civilians and now it is the other way around," they told us ... People were able to see the soldiers as their brother Filipinos. Before, people had a dislike for the PC constabulary.

Now, there were no soldiers, there were only Filipinos.'[60] To these people, Marcos was now the soldiers' surplus object, preventing the soldiers from being Filipinos — hence the protection people afforded them. It was up to the people to relieve the soldiers of their command, and in this way, to liberate them as well. In addition to *laban* [fight], the acronym of Cory's political party and the slogan of the revolt, the 'L' shape people's fingers formed in their bid for freedom was now said to mean love. This double meaning encapsulates the strategy of 'people power': conquest by love (as Christian lore has it, 'love conquers all'). And the effectiveness of this strategy resulted in the glorification of the nation and God for the love of whom the Filipino people arose in unity.[61]

What the soldiers experienced then was nothing less than the euphoria of love: 'when finally on Tuesday night the news of Marcos's departure were confirmed, we enjoyed one of the proudest moments of our lives. People considered us heroes. There was joy, but, above all, there was the feeling that people really loved us.'[62] To the extent that the people acted in the capacity of Christ who strove to love even the soldiers who crucified Him, the military felt that love of Christ in 'the Filipino', which was their redemption. Hence the apparent humility and willingness with which they submitted to the will of the people.

FEELING REVOLUTION AS SUBJECTIVE FREEDOM

The experience of that intangible, inner quality identified as 'people power' was, not surprisingly, highly spiritual in nature. One man recalled: 'All the time we were out there, we felt spiritually high. We didn't feel that we were tired. We mingled with the crowd who didn't look at us as Chinese. Everybody was like a part of one big family.'[63] This experience of blending into the crowd speaks of the dissolution of the boundary between the ethnically marginalized identity of this Filipino-Chinese man and the dominant social world of the nation, a dissolution that simulates the imaginary wholeness of primary narcissism. Feeling a part of 'one big family' stems from this unity with the hegemonic ideal of family or nation, which depends on the transcendence of its particular others, those who are made to figure the internal excess of the nation (such as racially embodied by the Chinese).[64]

The *jouissance* of 'people power' can be discerned in the following recollection of a market vendor:

> There were plenty of people, plenty of children and babies. It was so nice in EDSA. *Whatever you felt, there were plenty who shared it with you.* You wouldn't worry what would happen to you, because there were so many others who would eventually suffer the same fate. I was standing close to the tanks. People had built barricades. The nuns were there and they would give food to the military. We would pray all together and kneel down in the street in front of the tanks. The nuns were always first when the tanks came. 'Let's love each other. We are Filipinos,' they told the soldiers.[65]

As evinced in this account, the *jouissance* of the people did not derive from 'winning' the holy battle between Cory and Marcos, but from the experience of community. This experience of *communitas* was not yet definitively interpreted in nationalistic or Christian terms (although, as the last sentence indicates, the nuns had already begun to stabilize its meaning), but rather was only known as an experience of 'plenty'.[66] Marcos and Cory were no longer in the forefront of the consciousness of the vast majority:

> Watching them, listening to them, feeling them, I suddenly realize that these millions have already transcended Cory, Enrile-Ramos, and Marcos. Cory, Enrile-Ramos, and Marcos have, in fact, become incidental to the situation.
>
> These people are here to assert themselves, to declare their freedom, to reclaim their dignity after a generation of silence, of fear, of self-deprecation. And even though this pure moment, this pure feeling, cannot last, I have seen it and felt it. If only for this, I feel my whole life has been worth it.[67]

This is the moment of subjective freedom, the moment of pure becoming in which the Filipino people find themselves empowered as historical actors, not subjected to the actions of their leaders. But the social machinery that had produced the antagonism, for which they were a response (the antagonist turned protagonist), had not ceased to channel desires. Thus, this was also the moment in which Cory's shift in function from instigating signifier of desire to comprehensive signified of desire was clinched. For transcendence of the people also meant their separation from their leaders, which would enable the latter to eventually regain the power the people had hitherto assumed. Equalized by their difference from the people, Cory and the 'new' military (now calling itself the Army of the Filipino People instead of the Armed Forces of the Philippines, as it was known under Marcos) now united in rivalry for the power and control of the State, which together they recomposed.[68]

When the rebel military faction tore away from the Marcos apparatus, this symbolized the breaking apart of the identity of the nation that was increasingly recognized as the forced fiction of the regime. Marcos had constantly invoked the unity of a country that was torn by divisions and antagonisms, and put forth his strongman image to embody the staunchness and strength of the nation triumphant over its corrosive internal elements (such as the communists and the Muslim liberationists). He was the (Martial) Law of the land. As the lies began to unravel, the threads of the fiction fraying and coming undone — exposés of his hidden wealth, fraudulent war medals, deteriorating health — so did Marcos begin to witness his own undoing. Indeed, for many it was the lies that led them into revolt and to the side of Cory as the bearer of truth.

With the disintegration of the nation well underway yet upheld like a screen of denials and fabrications, the defection/separation served as a point from which a new nation could be founded — a new nodal point around which to unite. Thus began the effective, patriarchal usurpation of Cory's subversive power. From this point on, the movements began to take on the tenor of reconciliation, which actually meant the re-consolidation of the military and in some measure the Church (whose lower echelons had turned against the conservative dogma and put themselves at the service of the people, thus reversing the flow of power — reaping the spirit from the suffering, rather than sowing the spirit of suffering).

This glorified reunion could only come to be accepted by the people with the expiation of the country's ills (including, for some, the military's atrocities) in the form of the Marcoses. In this way did the

Marcoses become a family driven out as the source of pestilence so that a new family, a new nation of figures might reign. The shouted greetings to one another of 'Happy Birthday' and 'Happy New Year' when news of Marcos's departure had spread expressed the feeling of gaining a new lease on life — the experience of rebirth. The long-awaited resurrection of the nation after the death of Ninoy finally came when the embodiment of the Philippine fault (the internal fissure of the nation) was expelled, purged of its own evil. As the decaying, corrupt body of the nation, Marcos symbolically condensed all that impeded the community from coming into being.[69] He was the bearer of Death, which the people could overcome through the fantasies of family, nation, and God. The inexplicable ecstasy of Filipinos celebrating Marcos's departure could be said to derive from the feeling of immortality conveyed in these ideals, ideals for which many have laid their lives down at other times, impelled by the image of something greater and beyond their own mortal existence. One might then see that the experience of people power was the experience of the power over death. The libidinal force that moved men and women to act without thought of self-preservation, and which later came to be hegemonically interpreted as the hand of God, was no less than this power over death exerting itself as the power of life (as against the power *over* life that the repressive Marcos regime had for so long held) expressed through the fantasy of love.

In truth, the revolt was a revolt of the Filipino against itself — that is, against the quasi-cause of its shame. The freedom it secured was the freedom from 'the Filipino' as it had been historically constituted — without courage, dignity, independence or integrity: a veritable compound of lack. Whence the character of joy expressed by Cory upon 'liberation':

> It is true: the Filipino is brave, the Filipino is honorable, *the Filipino is great.*
>
> I have never felt prouder to be a Filipino. I am sure I share this feeling with millions of Filipinos. I am told that in other cities, when they learn that you are a Filipino, they shake your hand and praise the nobility of your race. In the streets of New York, I am told that Filipinos are being stopped and congratulated for moral courage as a people. *The Filipino stands proud before the whole world.*

And by the local media:

> *Every Filipino in the world today stands a little taller and a little prouder.*
> *No longer the butt of jokes and the object of pity or derision, Filipinos*
> *can take their place in the council of nations* because they are one of
> the few races who have done the impossible.
>
> They have deposed a dictator without the help of anyone but
> themselves, and they have unshackled their country from a decade
> of bondage with minimal bloodshed.
>
> When Filipinos first voted out Marcos and their will was
> frustrated, it seemed as if the depths of degradation as a people had
> been plumbed. *Years of being the world's prostitutes, coolie labor,*
> *international criminals, apathetic subjects of a repressive ruler had made*
> *the Filipino a laughingstock in the international community.*
>
> But redemption was forthcoming.
>
> … Filipinos have regained not only their liberty but their pride,
> not only freedom but dignity, not only honor but the respect of other
> men.[70]

Having long lived with the realization of being a subordinated
country, a body of people exploited for the power and pleasure of
another nation, the identity of the Filipino race was constructed as a
symptom of US imperialism — suffering the 'prostitute' constitution
of a neo-colony. Ideologically produced by its ego ideal — the
international community (as represented by the US) — the Philippines
could thus only attain redemption in the eyes of this Other. Hence the
importance of the international gaze in the making of Philippine history,
a gaze that was incarnated by the foreign media.

But in addition, the Filipino race found itself glorified, for it had
itself taken up the cross of Christ to save itself.[71] Heeding the call of
the Bishops who advocated 'active resistance of evil by peaceful means
— in the manner of Christ',[72] Filipinos took out the thorns in the crown
of thorns it had worn for so long, and thereby transformed it into a
crown of freedom:

> We did not feel tired anymore when we heard that Marcos had left.
> We laughed, we shouted and we danced, all at the same time … *we*
> *felt as though a thorn had been pulled out.*[73]

In fact, one of the most widely-toted emblems of the revolution was a piece of barbed wire, which people tore off from the barricades protecting Malacañang palace, shaped into a circle with a yellow ribbon attached to it. As one poet inscribes, 'The winner smiles/ As now he waves a crown of thorns — / Barbed wire, bloodied yellow ribbons — / He dares the skies.'[74] But this identification with a resurrected Christ also signified the rift between Cory and 'the people', for it was the latter who took up the cross in the name of the former.

The equivalence made between Ninoy and 'the people' in the image of Christ, which is signified by Cory's declaring, 'My courage and strength will come from Ninoy and all of you,' puts Cory in a category separate from both, thus making it possible for her to be reconstructed in the symbolic likeness and role of the Virgin Mary. This reconstruction was clearly evidenced (and perhaps clinched) during the revolt. Note the similar ways in which her name and the image of the Virgin were used by the people:

> All around us, the horde of people that stretches far back to the intersection a block away begins to chant angrily. 'Co-ree! Co-ree!' as if the name alone and the *laban* sign had the power to stop arrogant men and metal.[75]
>
> We then spotted a van with the image of the Blessed Virgin on top. We decided to use this as a shield as we proceeded to the Channel 9 transmitter. We believed that the snipers would not shoot because they still feared God.[76]

MEDIATION, REPLICATION AND DIFFERENCE

Inasmuch as television was tightly controlled by the government, Cory had little access to mass visual representation. The spirit of revolt expressed by the opposition to Marcos thus had to take mainly auditory routes of dissemination — through radio and word of mouth. On the one hand, these auditory channels assured widespread, democratic access to Cory, reinforcing the horizontal linkages of the community. This was amply demonstrated at EDSA by the crucial role played by Radio Veritas and Radio Bandido in mobilizing people as well as military troops.[77] People were able to share in the making of history not only by listening and receiving instructions as to where to go and what to do, but also by phoning in information, making appeals to the loyalist soldiers to join them, and thereby participating in the deployment of forces.[78] The multilateral channels of communication that linked the dispersed sites of the revolt thus formed a community that could have a 'democratic' experience of itself.

On the other hand, people needed to see Cory, and since they could not do this through the television, they gained visual access to her by going to see her in person in campaign rallies. For reasons already touched on before, these rallies took on the form of pilgrimages, which thus reinforced the vertical filial structure of the despotic regime. Indeed, even during the revolt, people from the provinces were seen to be pilgrimaging to Manila to join in the holy battle. In this sense, Cory was being groomed for the same position Marcos was being expelled from — the position of President as the King of the nation:

> About fourteen generals and colonels were standing around Enrile as he put on his bulletproof vest and buckled on his pistol. Enrile did not plan to make a speech. He was just talking to the men as he finished dressing. He said: 'I just spoke to the President.' Cory had already been inaugurated, so I thought he was talking about her. But he was not. To Enrile, 'the President' meant Marcos. He said: 'He is willing to negotiate for a graceful exit. I promised that we would not harm him, or his family ...'
>
> He had finished dressing and was now standing still. Suddenly it was a real message. He said: 'Gentlemen, we can no longer offer allegiance to our old commander-in-chief. If you watched the inauguration this morning, you saw that the people really want Cory. Our allegiance is to the people. And the people are represented by Cory.'
>
> Everyone was standing stock-still. There was a hushed silence. It was like a funeral. 'The King is dead. Long live the King!'[79]

What this account demonstrates is that the position of power that Cory was bound to occupy had come to be constructed in patriarchal terms.[80] For this position, which Marcos had possessed for so long, was completely identified with, supported and embodied by the masculine position of the military. While Cory's power and authority were initially secured by the people, the glorification of the military in its reconciliation with the latter and its consequent re-empowerment resulted in the transference of her mandate from the people to the military.[81]

Cory's invisibility and silence during the first two days of the revolt can be viewed as signifying as well as reinforcing this patriarchal pre-empting of her power, a process that was already well underway with the military defection of Enrile and Ramos (Fig. 5.1). The fraternal shape that the reconciliation of the military factions began to take was congruent with the paternalistic role the Church was playing. Together, military and Church began to re-institute the Law, which Cory came to incarnate, rather than redefine.[82]

Figure 5.1 Ramos and Enrile with Virgin Mary: Patriarchal usurpation of People Power. Photograph by the *Philippine National Inquirer.*

After the uprising, the revolutionary potential of the defiant Virgin was diffused. Instead of acting the part of subversive desire, that is, of the desiring subject, Cory was reduced by dominant interpreters to *being* the representation of the desired. Rhetorically, she was stripped of her power to make history, and only allowed to serve as a mere emblem of what had already been decided. Thus, was she conceived in the retrospective interpretation of the 'Marian revolution'. Note the following example of the hegemonic interpretation of the revolt:

> The Filipino's victory was a Marian victory. During those three shining days of courage, Our Lady was a Filipino ... The Filipino was never more Christian than when he [*sic*] won fighting his most precious battle — the battle for freedom, democracy and peace.
>
> Let no one write the history of this brave, noble revolution and forget that God was with his Filipino children and Mary led the battle. Our Lady begged and pleaded for us. And God pulled the stops and the flood of graces was like a tidal wave sweeping us to victory, overwhelming and leaving us breathless and speechless at the suddenness and the magnitude of it all.[83]

Seen from this perspective, Cory is reduced to the role of Mother Mary, Mother of the nation, a role that she had once explicitly refused. Vessel and instrument of God's power, she thus lost her claim to 'people power'. In the mythical rewriting of the 'essence' of EDSA in the hands of the dominant sector, Cory functions to confirm the patriarchal foundations of Christianity. Now she is once again equated with the country — the motherland — in the eyes of one poet, renewed as 'an unforeknown bride/ free of the rags of old loves/ and older emblems of easy thoughts,/ easy tongues and easy hearts.'[84] Thus does patriotism also reveal its patriarchal foundations: now Cory and the country are the freed terrain on which the patriot proves his masculinist love, as well as being the object of that love (which is also his reward for liberating 'her'): 'There sits now our bride/ who shall be our passion's shape/ and chronicler.'[85] In other words, the patriot is the historical actor for whom the country, like a lady in distress, is the cause, the terrain, and the reward of his struggles and his passion. Cory, the country, the Virgin — muse of patriarchal patriotism and Christianity.

The interpretation of 'people power' as God's power erased the people as a historical subject, reducing them once again to that inert substance sometimes called the masses, whose shape and role is determined by greater or stronger forces transcending them. The transference of power and affection from people to nation to God is one effected to patriarchal ends, to the extent that the faith moving men and women now assumes the form of 'a continuity or fusion with an Other that is no longer substantial and maternal but symbolic and paternal.'[86] In other words, when the nation as an ego ideal took on the form of God the Father, shedding its Virgin Mary garments, the people could resubmit themselves to patriarchal authority.

By the end of it, the EDSA revolt was a defensive movement that resulted in reconfirming the conceptual universe of the middle and upper classes, securing the ruling hegemony, and bringing back into the fold all the unruly signifiers of desire that erupted. Hence the offensive challenge Cory posed, not only to the political regime, but more importantly to the political imaginary, turned into a carnivalesque revolt (with the institutions of Church, military, bourgeois classes prevailing with their own laws of reading, and therefore with their directives for corresponding action). New territories of meaning could not emerge, all the old holdings seem to have remained the same and the terrain of socio-political significance left largely unchanged, and even unmoved. The awareness of world opinion, this identification with the gaze of the international community informed the Aquino government's subsequent actions, as evidenced by its preoccupation with the democratic process (acting according to the rules of 'democracy' when the conditions and structures of the state apparatus were in fact 'clientelist'). As shown by the accounts of the middle-class participants, this awareness and identification underpinned the interpretations of the event and the definitions of the Filipino character that emerged as dominant.[87] Nowhere is this imaginary identification and its material consequences better demonstrated than in the Aquino government's decision to abide with the international agreements that supported the Marcos regime, which meant servicing the massive fraudulent international debts incurred by the latter, a burden ultimately borne by the working masses, particularly overseas Filipino workers.

As I have suggested in earlier chapters, changes did occur as a consequence of this event. A new regime of power with new strategies of production and regulation emerged out of this historical rupture, precisely through the containment of the unruly desires of 'the people'. Something of a 'coalitional' government continued to obtain well beyond the Aquino administration, which in some ways allowed a certain contingency to remain within the state.[88] Indeed, the ambivalences and contradictions of the contemporary Philippine state, which I discussed at length in the first section, can be partially attributed to this uneasy predication on 'people power' and the coalitionist accommodation of popular and social democratic forces within it. This incorporation of some of the social elements of the uprising within the government as well as the imaginary precedent set by the uprising itself can thus be seen as the conditions of possibility of the latest eruption of popular desires into the space of metropolitan dreams (See Chapter 2).

But this revolutionary moment did not produce lasting radical changes. The international community re-emerged as the ego ideal of the nation. This symbolic identification with the international was clearly manifested in the necessary eagerness of the nation-state for international recognition and acceptance and materialized in its honoring of Marcos's debts to the World Bank and the IMF and in its continued reliance on the political, economic and military authority of the US.[89] The restoration of order was expressed furthermore by the ascendance of a Marianist interpretation of the event. This Marianist view, as I will show in the next chapter, subsumes the radical potential of *Inang Bayan*, whose historical undercurrents can be traced to the Revolution of 1896 but also to the more recent 'revolt' and national exodus of feminized labour.

With the EDSA experience essentialized in terms of feminized loss and patriarchal redemption, that is, as a masculinist enactment of the passion of Christ, came the foreclosure of history and the deprivation of people of historical agency. Within this fantasy-scenario, the revolt occurred in the divine time of the ruling orthodoxy. In this time, it was thus an event from which moral lessons could be learned and about which parables could be told. In fact, many of the accounts in the hegemonic text (such as *People Power*) took on biblical forms; they were told as parables, testimonies, juridical witnessings, and exegeses. And the entire revolt is told as a parable of a Church-sanctioned miracle.[90]

As the filling of a lack (Ninoy's death), the fulfillment of a promise (national redemption), and the expulsion of a surplus object of antagonism (Marcos), the EDSA experience served to encapsulate the crisis that *is* the nation as the crisis *of* the nation, which had now been dealt with and overcome. Thus the nation building that came afterwards could not be founded from another point radically different from the point from which it had been hitherto constructed and maintained. As I argued in the first chapter, the fantasy upon which the Marcos regime had been founded was still in place, even if the state would undergo alterations in the process of accommodating the excessive desires of the people. Viewed in terms of Ninoy's death in the hands of the Marcos-military regime, the debt that marked the nation's constitution was seen then to have been paid or recompensed (such that even the military's complicity came to be overlooked). Rather than being seen within the context of the international fantasy of imperialism, it was seen only as an internal, domestic problem. In other words, the national crisis was not addressed within this larger context, outside the grasp of the Free World fantasy. Dependence was seen as a symptom of only an internal national failure rather than as the product of international dreamwork. Thus the emphasis on inner strength and transformation, thus the spiritual solution — 'reconciliation' — to the antagonisms that pervade the Philippine socius. No doubt, these are the 'empty gestures' by which we assume our subjective freedom as a community. But that subjective freedom is the condition of struggle, not its end. In order to transform our concrete 'reality', we must also undo the fantasy-scenarios that organize it and dream other realities into being.

The political imaginary that needs to be transformed to revolutionary ends, however, subsists in concrete social relations — in the world men and women make with the instruments of their lives as well as with their minds. In the words of Sékou Touré, 'the world is always the brain of mankind [sic].'[91] Hence, any struggle to transform the fantasy-reality of our society must also be a material struggle to transform the socio-political structures and institutions it regulates. For history is made on the fantastic terrain that stretches between a society's objective institutions and its living imaginary. More importantly, it is made by the people who ply that terrain, who are no longer willing to be resigned to the possibilities of life 'reality' affords, and who decide to act, to heed other callings and make 'reality' yield to their desires. This is where true 'people power' or, as some have put it, 'people's power', lies.

6

Himala, 'Miracle':
The Heretical Potential of
Nora Aunor's Star Power

It is difficult to attempt to depict, much more to explain, the magnitude of Nora Aunor's star power — the immense draw of a following that commands its own analytical category.[1] In movie critics' conversations, the most expressive sign and irrefutable evidence of the spectacular power of this greatest Filipina actress of all time is the hysteria of her fans. The 'hysteria' is as much about the formidable size of her following as it is about the imputed excessiveness of their devotion. It is not, therefore, surprising that Ishmael Bernal's 'critically acclaimed' film, *Himala,* is in these circles widely understood to be about the star of the film, Nora Aunor. *Himala* thematizes mass hysteria through the story of a young rural girl, Elsa, who achieves both divine and celebrity power as a faith healer. In the middle of darkness cast by a solar eclipse over the desolate, impoverished town of Cupang, Elsa has a radiant vision of the Virgin Mary that leaves her with the miraculous capacity to heal. In awe of Elsa's blessed power, friends and acquaintances are converted into her devoted attendants, and soon droves of ailing people from all over the country flock to her to be touched by her healing hands. Cupang becomes a national mecca and Elsa its holy star. However, the holy miracle, which is also a phenomenal commercial success, rapidly breeds greed, lust, crime, corruption, and disease. Suffering, alongside her own flock, the blight of these 'developments' that her own powers have wrought, Elsa calls for her vast following to gather on the sandy dunes where she first receives the sacred gift of her calling. It is before this teeming mass of followers that Elsa performs her final, revelatory act of redemption: the return of divine power to the people.

Describing the film's ambition in terms of the 'theatrical potential' of its setting, the 'histrionic stylizations' of its actors, and the 'hysterical audience' before whom the climactic scene was to be played, Joel David concludes: 'It was truly a great actress's opportunity of a lifetime, and Nora Aunor seized it and made it not just her role, but her film as well.'[2] *Himala* was Nora's film inasmuch as it represented the seizures of spectacular power, which she herself (as the superstar, Nora Aunor) embodied, and performed. Elsa, whose poor origins, humility, and unearthly talent for healing capture the zealous devotion of an unruly multitude, *was* Nora — the 'poor, small, dark-skinned, and barely educated country girl' revered and idolized by millions as much for her miraculous rise to spectacular power as for her beautiful contralto voice that first elevated her from the common lot.[3]). And Nora, in her intense portrayal of Elsa as a medium of divine power and the religious mass, brought her performance of her own life role as the Superstar, the worshipped medium of mass desire, to sublime heights.[4]

In this chapter, I write about the popular constitution of Nora Aunor's star power and its vital role in bringing about a new national as well as global political and economic order. I argue that in many ways the event of Nora Aunor's star power prefigured the event of People Power, which we saw in the last chapter. This is another story of 'the people' who helped to unravel the national fantasy of the strongman state. I make a serious attempt to deploy the imaginary dimensions of historical transformation in ways tangential to the aims of fantasy-production. I claim that the social movement mediated by the persona of Nora Aunor bears a living heretical political potential. This claim is at the same time a calling to follow and further this heresy, a calling to which cultural criticism must respond if it is to participate in the transformation of history that this movement has already begun.

STAR POWER AS MASS HYSTERIA

Many hold the view that *Himala* is as much about the popular hysteria mediated by the idol, Nora Aunor, as it is about the mass hysteria endemic to colonial Catholicism. The film blurs, as they say, the line between real and reel life. And that blurring, because it falls on the side of the 'real', gratifies and exhilarates the critical sensibilities. The aesthetic gratification and sublime experience provided by *Himala's* exceeding of the film's narrative boundaries is opposed to the mass enjoyment of another kind of blurring, intrinsic to the very films that helped to establish Nora Aunor's superstardom. In these films, Nora always plays 'herself' — a poor, young girl who suffers many hardships but finally stumbles into good fortune. Benilda Santos criticizes one such paradigmatic Cinderella film, *Atsay* [Maid] (1978), precisely for this blurring: 'Myth extricates the *atsay's* story from the temporal and the dialectical, and elevates it to the archaic, thereby blurring the gap between the past and the present and dulling the critical impulse of the moviegoer. The injustice suffered by the *atsay* is no longer important. She comes out of it unscathed and doubly blessed anyway.'[5]

In Santos's analysis, the 'aura of apparent invincibility' that accrues to the *atsay*-heroine in *Atsay*, a quintessential Nora Aunor movie, 'and the legendary life of superstar Nora Aunor, almost a carbon-copy of the script, makes of film the perfect genre for the elaboration of the image of the Filipina as a stoic, suffering victim'.[6] The 'life' of Nora Aunor is simply another script; her 'aura of apparent invincibility' is written over and over again in the filmic adaptation and elaboration of the script which her life copies. There is no Nora Aunor film that does not script her 'own' life. That script, as others have pointed out, invariably resolves the mythical suffering of the proverbial *babaeng martir* [female martyr] through some escapist 'fantasy' or religious, almost superstitious, belief.[7] Nora Aunor herself is a myth that, like other myths propagated by popular movies, serves to perpetuate and legitimize the existing social order by satisfying the desires and fulfilling the beliefs of the masses. Attempts by the rationalist, critical faculty to account for Nora Aunor's phenomenal appeal typically invoke the explanatory power of 'identification': '[Nora] gains new ground with every rotten tomato, every sour grape thrown her way. The more of it, the more she earns sympathy from the common man. It sharpens her image as their tiny Dolorosa, not unlike the many who are poor and abused in this country. To the fans, *she is just like them*, a victim of derision in a society that refuses to concede success to one who comes from the masses' (emphasis added).[8] Inasmuch as she performs the life of the oppressed as seen through the gaze of their imputed desire, Nora Aunor is the hysterical symptom of the masses, a symptom that is their enjoyment to consume.

This enjoyment of the masses of their own symptom is at once pathologized and gendered. Nora Aunor's following is gendered as female not only because of its large (but not exclusively) female composition; more importantly, it is gendered because of its perceived disposition for suffering [*pagpapakasakit*] and for taking the suffering of others as its own [*pagmamalasakit*]. The fans' identification with their idol — more specifically, with the trait of the *martir* that she embodies — is hysterical inasmuch as it is an act(ing) executed on behalf of an Other: the colonial, Catholic God for whom suffering is a virtue. And Nora Aunor is the hysterical symptom of the masses, from whose ranks her fans issue, inasmuch as she is both a part and a symbol of their collective, suffering being. Like Christ, she takes on the suffering of the people. She suffers in behalf of them, and thereby sacrifices herself. And like Christ, her aura as a Superstar derives from her status as simultaneously being *beyond* the common *tao* [person] and being *of* the common *tao*. The religious comparison is deliberate, for the superlative function Nora performs in relation to the masses is part of a religious delusional-structure to which the masses, in their feminine disposition, are considered to be innately susceptible.[9]

Nora Aunor movies are faulted for indulging in this religious delusional structure by filmically participating in (by mimicking) the masses' hysterical identification with their *babaeng martir* idol. Thus, in her contrastive analysis of *Insiang* (dir. Lino Brocka, 1976), Santos approvingly describes how 'the camera as a voracious but true recorder of environment … deliberately moves from scene to scene, forthright and direct, without hysteria'. Santos repeats this phrase, 'forthright and direct, without hysteria' three times, twice in reference to the camera, once in reference to the female character who is, in this respect, 'like the camera'. In Santos's view, it is the absence of hysteria in both camera and character, and the nonhysterical identification of the latter with the former, that makes possible the emergence of a true and revolutionary consciousness in the character/camera and, by extension of this medium, in the audience.

While in *Himala*, the female character, Elsa, makes a hysterical claim to divine power (assuming the healing powers of Christ as well as his stigmata), the film's very representation of that hysterical claim and the hysteria of the mass following that Elsa's claim creates demonstrates the 'critical distance' — or, one might say, 'critical difference' — between the filmic gaze and its delusional subject (the subject-complex of the masses and their symptom). This 'critical distance' between the filmic gaze and what thereby becomes its representational object makes *Himala* similar in form and content to the rational, demythologizing, psychoanalyzing accounts of Nora Aunor's spectacular power. Like these accounts, *Himala* provides a nonhysterical picture of the religious, delusional structure of the masses' subjectivity and critiques the mass media's parasitic and exploitative relation to the latter's fanatic tendencies. In the film, the mass media's efforts to capitalize on the mass hysteria generated by the spectacular figure of Elsa/Nora are shown to be themselves hysterical, at once mimicking and reproducing the very structure of desire the media claims merely to represent and satisfy. Newscasters, reporters and cameramen ripple with excitement as they wait for Elsa/Nora to emerge out of her house. As she descends the stairway, they rush to her in a frenzy, falling over one another, almost indistinguishable from the throng of her zealous fans, all of them uncontrollably drawn to her, nearing to the touch of her body, screaming her name for one moment of her regard. The elevated, wide panning action of the camera in this scene establishes precisely the 'critical difference' between the film and the mass media industry. Like the myth-ideology critiques of Tagalog movies whose acclaim for the film might be read as an exclamation of satisfaction at the happy correspondence between the film's critical consciousness and their own, *Himala* undoes the myth of spectacular power. The film, in fact, performs and represents the demystifying gesture of such critiques in its famous climactic scene, when Elsa/Nora reveals to her fanatical congregation that there were and are no miracles, that it is the people, not God, who makes miracles ('*Walang himala! Tayo ang gumagawa ng himala!*').

While *Himala* might hence be compared to ideological criticisms of the colonial Catholic, capitalist mythical structure undergirding the spectacular power of Nora Aunor, it also goes further than these criticisms to the extent that it theorizes the constitution of Nora Aunor's superstardom in relation to the particular historical, socioeconomic conditions of her possibility. Moreover, as a practical theory, *Himala* works to transform those very conditions, a project that Nora collaborated with and actively pursued.[10] In deploying Nora to explicate her spectacular power, the film attempts to actuate the imaginary it represents, not, however, to reproduce the prevailing social order but rather to disrupt it.

THE NORANIAN IMAGINARY

This chapter gropes for an understanding of this imaginary, which I am calling the *Noranian imaginary*, and of the social order that it is said to reproduce. To grope for an understanding of a social imaginary is not to describe, from a critical distance, the collective consciousness or mass subjectivity of a particular group of people. Neither is it to delineate, also from a critical distance, a system of signification or a sociosymbolic order that constitutively structures the subjective processes and relations of those caught within its regime. To grope for an understanding of a social imaginary is, rather, to feel for a constellation of sociosubjective practices that are at work in the co-operative production of a form of sociality and an economic assemblage. This is not the same as explicating the regulatory principles of a fully constituted 'economy' from which one can be removed.

In my view, the Noranian imaginary is a historical experience that is at the same time a collective constitution, a form of 'class' and 'gender' in the making in the 1970s and 1980s in the Philippines, whose paradigm is the fandom of Nora Aunor.[11] The Noranian imaginary consists of sociosubjective practices and relations that are mediated by the figure of Nora Aunor, but its operation is not limited to her actual fans. What I am calling the collective constitution of Nora Aunor's following is part of a process of making, a historical process out of which emerged a new form of sociality — domestic labour — whose exploitation has become the basis for the founding of a new political-economic order.[12] The collective constitution at once exemplified and instantiated by Nora Aunor's following might hence be viewed as a passage in a historical movement. It is this movement that *Himala* theorizes and re-mediates. It is a movement that is not merely represented and critiqued by the film but one that exceeds and traverses it. In looking for an understanding of this movement by way of the film, I am not looking at the film as a text to be read for its truth content — that is, I am not making an ideological critique of the film. I am looking at the things in and about the film that partake of the process of constitution of both Nora Aunor and her following, in an attempt, on the one hand, to bring this process back into vital relations with the prevailing mode of production and social struggle in the Philippines during the height of Nora's spectacular power and, on the other, to reconnect this process to the situation that now weighs upon us as the inescapable global present.

It may seem that, in my qualified use of the concept of the imaginary (as 'Noranian'), I am merely demonstrating a specific historical and cultural instantiation of what is a globalizing (if not universal) 'economy of desire' that operates in cinema.[13] In much US feminist film theory concerned with questions of the relation between spectatorial subjectivity and social domination, the 'imaginary' is conceptualized as precisely an 'economy of desire', a psychical-libidinal order of signification at work in cinematic representation. The female image is seen as fundamental to the operation of this psychical-libidinal economy, which shapes and regulates the desires of cinema's spectatorial subjects. More particularly, the female movie star (unmarked by race, nationality, or culture) is viewed as the paradigmatic fetish object of cinema, whose critique unveils the economy within which it operates.[14] The female movie star thus becomes the object of a deciphering action, and what is deciphered is precisely the system of signification in which she operates as a key signifier.[15]

While using the concept of an imaginary, my own approach departs from those of filmic critiques seeking to represent the 'economy of desire' or signifying system underlying the production and operation of the female star. It also departs from the approach of US cultural critiques seeking, more generally, to represent or 'map' the fields of power within which both images of social identity and negotiations over their meanings and effects are determinately shaped.[16] I will return at the end of this chapter to the stakes involved in refusing the *representation* of logics of domination (or, comprehensive knowledge of dominant logics through their adequate representation) as the proper end of cultural analysis. In this project, while I consider it expedient to begin with the notion of a social imaginary as a determining logic, I also consider it to be crucial to 'end' elsewhere — to move towards its undoing. That undoing entails following modes of acting that are fundamental to a social imaginary beyond their constitutive role in a dominant logic. In this case, it means following the practices of 'hysteria' in precisely their tangentiality not only to a dominant social imaginary but also to a full knowledge of its operations, the will to which constitutes one of the orthodox imperatives of cultural criticism today. By following 'hysteria' to the point where it breaks away from, and perhaps even breaks down, the hegemonic structure within which it is read — that is, by following the waywardness of its action — we approach what I discuss below as the heretical dimensions of Nora Aunor's superstardom. The important thing is to be theoretically swayed by (and not just politically aligned with) heretical ways of acting that make history. Like the film, I am attempting to create a moving picture of a concrete historical moment that has not yet fully passed, a moment in which the Noranian imaginary obtains as a constellation of vital processes of subjective experience, political expression, and economic production. To the extent that such processes are vital still, the picture I am trying to make begins to get caught in and extend their movement.

HERETICAL MEDIATORS

When Nora/Elsa declares at the end of the film, '*Tayo ang gumagawa ng mga sumpa at ng mga diyos, tayo ang gumagawa ng himala*' [It is we who make curses and gods, it is we who make miracles], she unveils the alienation of the people's creative power and its deposit in the spectacle that she has become. What she unveils, however, does not exist before the unveiling. Rather, it is through this revelation that Nora/Elsa finally realizes herself as the fetish object of the mystified masses, which the undeluded modern classes have always believed her to be. A moment later, she is shot for the blasphemy that she utters against the order of God and the ruling strata, her concrete bodily life confiscated for all time.

The fatal bullet, however, only fixes the truth of her disclosure. She is irrevocably converted into an image without self, a bodily specter bearing the value and power conferred upon her by her followers whose desperate supplication is the means of their own divestiture. Nowhere in the film are the people more 'the masses' than in this scene of arrest, in which Nora/Elsa is taken from their midst and exalted to the condition of the spectacle-form;[17] the ailing people are simultaneously amassed and devalued to the degree that she is made into the icon of their collective labour of suffering. The chaos and tumult of countless limbs and trunks and heads, which ensue when the arresting shot is fired, are then brought to ruling order. The masses are herded into the fold, their eyes directed to the firmament, waiting for the vision of the answer to their prayers.

Ironically, then, the 'heresy' of Nora/Elsa's climactic confession spells the end of the immanently greater heretical movement that she begins. Nora Aunor's emergence as 'the biggest and the brightest star to rise and shine in the firmament of Philippine entertainment'[18] was, as it is often told, a miraculous defiance of the racial and class ideals of the Hollywood-patterned star-system of Philippine film, and of Philippine society in general. That defiance expresses the subversive potential of Nora's following, a constituency that this defiance was itself an affective instrument in creating.

Early in her career, entertainment journalists recognized the political significance and possible threat of Nora's *popularity* (by which I mean both her belovedness and the 'populace' which came into being in and as this be-loving) in the comparisons they made between the size of the crowds she drew and the size of the crowds at political demonstrations mounted against the government. Such comparisons were not idle ones. Later in her career, Nora would lend her star power to the Marcos regime by supporting the dictator's post-Martial Law 'snap' re-election campaign, a decision that would cost her dearly in terms of her 'mass' following and for which she has since attempted to atone.[19] We could very well say, in fact, that the subversive potential of Nora's popularity, of her defining common countenance, found realization in the role of the insurgent woman Redeemer that, in the wake of Nora's relinquishment of her mandate, Corazon Aquino took up during the February Revolt of 1986 immediately following the 'snap' elections. For, contrary to most views, Nora's power did not lie in her personification of the *babaeng martir* as powerless victim of suprahuman forces, but rather it lay in her acting as the blessed *atsay* who is able to capture and enact the power and grace of those forces. This capture and enactment — that is, the seizing of the suprahuman forces that constitute the agent-source of worldly blessing to bless oneself (and therefore to act as and in behalf of these forces of blessing, to be one's own Redeemer) — is the greater heresy that Nora performs — a heresy she performs 'herself' in her life and career and as Elsa in *Himala*.

As Elsa, Nora demonstrates the gendered and sexual characteristics of this heresy and the 'social movement' that it actuates and is actuated by. Elsa proclaims that 'what was of the Father has passed, now it is with the Mother [*lumipas na ang sa ama, ngayon naman sa ina*].' Invoking the Virgin Mary as the source and object of her holy vision and miraculous gift of healing, she attracts an entourage of female attendants, women who neglect their other sanctioned roles as wives, girlfriends to men, sisters and mothers, to minister to the calling of Elsa and to the want of the people, which receives Elsa's response [*sagot*]. Elsa's answering [*pagsagot*] of her calling becomes their responsibility [*pananagutan*] and thus the answer to their own calling. In this way is the Catholic virtue of bearing responsibility for one another [*Lahat tayo'y may pananagutan sa isa't isa*] overturned into a liberative taking of divine power into one's own hands.

The ostensible coincidence of callings and answers among Elsa, her attendants and the people is not, however, the consequence of an identification, much less an identity of desires. If Elsa's calling becomes the calling of her attendants, it is not because those callings are the same; nor is the want of the people (seeking healing, restoration, revival) the want or calling of either Elsa or her attendants, at least not in any identical or clearly identifying way. Rather, there is a measure of missing in each meeting of calling and answer. There is a tangentiality to the correlations of desires among all these persons that is not the effect or the expression of an unqualified situation of transference or displacement.[20] This tangentiality is the condition of singularity and difference that enables the sway of persons on each other and, together, on the world — the sway that, appearing as sheer contingency, allows the making of history. Each one is a medium of the others' desires but is also a mediator, an interactant, not only moved but moving of her own accord [*kusang-loob*]. The movement that Elsa sets off is however a collective one — one that coordinates people's inner loci of will, feeling, and action [*loob*] in a socially significant and disruptive (and disruptive because socially significant) way.

As the focal medium of her female attendants' desires, Elsa personifies the disturbance of the prevailing gendered and sexual order brought about by their accordance. She is a woman alone, orphaned, adopted, single, without natural kin or naturalized heterosexual ties, and therefore 'it's as if she isn't a woman, as if she isn't human' [*parang hindi siya babae, parang hindi siya tao*].[21] Pilo, the sexually-frustrated boyfriend of the most zealous of Elsa's attendants, Chayong, utters this fearful presentiment of the danger Elsa poses to the sanctioned social order. While the town priest expresses the danger Elsa poses as a danger to the holy, hierarchical order of the Church, catechizing Elsa on the dire consequences of just anyone claiming to have these miraculous visions (what if miracles were so easy to come by?) and on the devil's deceptive posturings [*pagpapanggap*], Pilo enacts the masculinist character of the many efforts made to exploit and destroy the subjective power that Elsa claims and that, through her, others like Chayong come to claim too. Chayong defers her refusal to 'give herself' to Pilo to the sacred authority of Elsa. Although within the Church-sanctioned social order virginity is the oppressive exaction of moral purity from and sexual containment of women, here it is the expression and means of a sacred subjective sovereignty [*kapangyarihan*], which Chayong embraces.[22] Elsa is the pretext for this empowering embrace, just as she is the pretext for the newfound 'work' of her attendants. That work of devotion that Elsa and her divine cause inspire serve to legitimate not only Chayong's self-possessing repulsion of the desires of the men who claim her body and her labour but also Sepa's nonsacrificing negligence of her wifely and maternal duties and Saling's (Elsa's adoptive mother) full-time devotion to her unnatural child. As opposed to the oppression and alienation of waged employment and the sacrificial impositions of familial responsibility, this cooperative mission affords Elsa's attendants personal pleasures, collective joy and a vital sense of meaning and empowerment (Fig. 6.1). Elsa is the crucial instrument for the liberation of such passions from the naturalized ties and confinements of the ruling sociosexual order.

Figure 6.1 Elsa and her attendants, Chayong and Saling. Film still courtesy of the Film Center of the University of the Philippines.

One of the stories told as part of the myth of Nora Aunor recalls an afternoon in a wealthy subdivision in Manila: chaos and crisis suddenly erupt in the peaceful homes of the rich — children are crying, 'housewives' are helplessly stranded, pots are boiling over. It turns out that all the maids working in these households have abandoned their wards, female employers and domestic duties to watch a 'shooting' of a Nora Aunor movie in the neighborhood.[23] Like Elsa, Nora is the 'event' [*pangyayari*] bringing about but also made by an insurrection of poor women against their domesticating 'masters' [*amo*]. The subversive power [*kapangyarihan*] that she portends for the ruling classes lies precisely in her 'eventfulness' — her capacity to arouse her followers to act out their passions and to do as they desire rather than as others desire (to 'follow' their *kalooban*, their inner motivation), which is precisely the realization of their own capacity [*kapangyarihan*] to make things happen [*mangyari*]. This is the power that Elsa claims is with and of the Mother, the heretical power of the Virgin as *Inang Bayan* [Mother of the people] that Nora's popularity had helped to express and shape but that, in aligning herself with the authoritarian patriarchal order of the Marcos regime, she betrayed and thereby 'allowed' Corazon Aquino (and the Church, the military and the class for which she stood) to usurp and reform, effectively turning it from a revolutionary people's power to a conservative and stabilizing majestic Marian rule. This structure of the 'event' that the Noranian imaginary articulates enabled the 1986 revolt.

The heretical power of *Inang Bayan* consists of people acting on their collective own, acting neither as mere symbol nor instrument of a more primordial and real power but rather acting on and acting out their self-authorization and Truth. Marian rule, on the other hand, represents and serves the supreme power from which it derives; it is an intercessionary order installed in behalf of the good of the people, which is first and finally the Good of God. Two different maternal figures inspire these two different powers: one, the Virgin Mary, submitting to the Maker who creates her as a holy vessel and to the Child whom she begets in His image; the other, the adoptive mother-child [*mag-ina*], self-realizing as well as fortuitous, the mother finding and claiming the child who calls her into being, the child decisively choosing to embrace the mother's mandate as her own calling, child and mother together [*ang mag-ina*] begotten by the will and intent in this foundational claim that has no natural or divine guarantee. The difference between such figures is not absolute but is rather diacritical — it marks the contradiction between the conservative, 'reproductive' dimension of feminine power and the heretical, creative dimension of feminist power. I can refigure this contradiction as the conflict between Nora/Elsa as a spectacular medium (functioning in the form of a fetishized idol/commodity) and Nora/Elsa as a vital and vitalizing mediator (acting in the capacity of the *babaylan*, the indigenous female, or cross-dressed male, shaman, or faith healer/blessed actor).

As a medium, Elsa is a non-causative actor whose ostensible cause is the Virgin Mary (herself a non-causative actor moved by the First Cause, God). It is no accident that, when her healing powers take leave of her, she thinks about becoming a domestic helper [*katulong*]. For the latter is the paradigm of the non-causative actor.[24] It is in this moment of being a medium of an action initiated by another that Elsa serves as an object of both identification and desire, lending herself precisely to commodity fetishism or what Marx calls the 'religion of everyday life'.[25] Her spectacular value is created by the audience, which confers it on her. Indeed, it is to the camera of the documentary filmmaker who has come to 'shoot' her that Elsa gives her most Nora Aunor-as-star-like smile. But just as the Virgin Mary is here also her own cause, moved by her own bullet-inflicted wound which is at once the infliction and affliction of the people, so is Elsa also moved by her own wounds and ambitions which are shaped by the taunts and wants of the *baryo* people. She is in this moment an active mediator exercising, not merely serving, effective power. The immaculate conception and causation of oneself as the actor — that is, the acting as both 'actor (initiator)' and 'actor (agent)' — such is the heresy of Elsa's claim. The heresy does not lie in her false pretensions [*pagpapanggap*]; Elsa does not remember if she made it all up or not. Rather, the heresy lies in her *acting* the role of redeemer (the *adopted* child of the Virgin Mary), a performance that is not a matter of appearance but of subjective becoming. In this sense, Elsa's acting is not the masking of a truth or reality (such as of objective social relations); it is, rather, the performance of truth, the truth of the people's capacity to take [*angkinin*] as one's own this power to which one is otherwise subject — that is, the truth of the people's capacity to *act*, to take action.

Elsa's avowal of her own ambitions (at ten, she wanted to be president) demonstrates the active part she plays in her becoming a *kasangkapan sa panggagamot* [healing 'medium']. Inasmuch as she assumes the character of this human-acting instrument (the character of the *babaylan* who prefigures it), she embodies the characteristics of both social actor and object medium of social action. It is in her performance of the character of this subjective object that Nora Aunor generates so much commotion in and among those whose lives are defined for them by their use for others. Treated as mere utensils — that is, as objectified *kasangkapan* [household tools] (as I argued in Chapter 3) — domestic workers (who figure but do not wholly constitute Nora's wide following) are drawn to Nora not simply and primarily because they identify with her as the portrait of the suffering *atsay*.[26] Certainly, as an empowered servant, Nora/Elsa is an inspiring example. In this respect, her personal ambitions do not detract from her aura of blessedness, for the blessed power she exercises is precisely the result of both her choosing and her chosenness, of having decidedly and decisively taken a chance. She inspires, by her example, the potential of these women to act on their own claims (claims that assume the form and force of a suprahuman mandate). She inspires, in a word, the taking of a chance in faith. In this heretical moment, faith is less a belief in something (less a creed) than *acting as believing itself.* This assumption of a power that is both bestowed and claimed, a power that is the product of both ambition as absolute destiny and 'chance' or opportunity as radical contingency, undoubtedly characterized and constituted the 'popularity' of Corazon Aquino. In making this heretical assumption, Nora acted as a point of reference and release for the people's own assumption of power. Like the apparition of the Virgin Mary, the firmamental image liberating and authorizing Elsa's calling, Nora mediated this process of subjectivization of the people, their coming into empowered, human, vital being through truthful acting.[27]

As in *Himala,* Nora emerged out of the people's and her own hopes for a miracle to save them from the continuing curse upon their collective existence. Nora thus played the invention of a liberative movement. She performed the role forged by a common longing: the true artist/actor [*artista*] whom she embodied as the very potential of the people (and in serving as its embodiment, proved the immanence of that potential). The true artist/actor is one whose exercise of her creative capacities is the very act of her empowerment. Her performance is creative and truthful to the extent that it realizes, authorizes and deploys a power which precedes and overflows her, a power that is no more but no less hers than it is the power of those whom it inspires (those who, by recognizing it, participate in its realization). It is this form of political agency that links Noranian 'popularity' to 'people power'.

Nora/Elsa is therefore not an example apart from those who view her as such. As a social mediator, she is also part (and not just a metaphor) of the people, and hence she can *act* for them, not just *represent* them in another realm of power nor represent power to them (as a medium of symbolic action). She can act, in other words, as an intercessor, a role that merges and recreates the roles of the Catholic saint and the indigenous *babaylan*.[28] At the same time, she exceeds this intercessional role. Recognized by and addressing others as a 'common person', Nora/Elsa lives and moves among her followers and hence cannot be reduced to an image conjured by and detached from them. It is in fact a crucial part of Nora's persona that to this day she employs the honorific *po* in speaking to people, thereby asserting that she has retained her common, humble stature. In the film, while Chayong manifests an ecstasy in emulating Elsa, she also manifests an ecstasy in drawing close to her, being with and being near her. 'Approaching' Nora/Elsa is not simply a matter of approximating an ideal. It is also a matter of physical, social and emotional proximity and intimacy. Unsurprisingly, Nora's relation to her fans consists not only of her opening her house to them and celebrating her birthdays with them, that is, of keeping the borders between her public career and her private life open; this relation also consists of her fans touching, embracing, kissing and holding her. The devotion of Nora's fans for her is not a form of idolatry, if by idolatry we mean the veneration of an inhuman or objectified figure of power. This devotion, and the power that resides in and results from it, is love.

'I love you, Nora!' shout her fans. Loving names a mode of relational activity that is not reducible to two terms, even in a triangulated scenario, or to a subjective state that makes of another the object of one's desiring action. I am suggesting that the libidinal energies aroused and liberated by Nora exceed the notion of desire implied by the logic of fetishism. Moreover, they course through sociosubjective structures that do not respect the form of individual bourgeois subjects on which such a logic is predicated. This activity of loving consists of what might be inadequately described as indigenous or creatively persistent sociosubjective relations and forms, experiential modes revitalized and 'invented' by the women who engage in this loving. It is a loving that cannot be separated from the practice of power and the production of life.

THE WORK OF *SAMPALATAYA*, 'FAITH'

Raul Pertierra writes that '[i]n societies such as the Philippines, where structures of power and authority involve the close articulation of spheres of technical control, moral imperatives, and interior experiences, religion serves as the ideal vehicle both for the conception and the practice of political action'.[29] In his view, religion provides 'an important idiom and a range of concepts for articulating significant relationships and interests', which can thereby be deployed by political movements that seek to radically challenge the prevailing social order.[30] Pertierra cites the 1986 revolt as an example of this political efficacy of religion and furthermore links it to what he calls the radical tradition of religiopolitical protest, a tradition that has historically drawn inspiration from both indigenous and Catholic sources. While my own discussion above attempts to demonstrate how Nora/Elsa's heretical appropriation and interpretation of the sacred power of the Mother is brought into play in the revolt of 1986, I do not see the practices and structures of the Noranian imaginary in a realm set apart from the everyday realm of socioeconomic life, such as in the realm of political action.[31] The forms of political articulation that surfaced during the revolt of 1986 and that I have been designating as part of the Noranian imaginary can certainly be viewed in relation to Ferdinand Marcos's project to invent a new national imaginary (the 'New Society'). After all, sociofamilial forms that allow a 'super'-member of the community to embody and mediate power in behalf of the rest are deployed by both the Marcos regime and the popular movement opposing it in the scenario of antagonism between the authoritarian Father and the liberative, redemptive Mother. However, I think it is important to recognize the infrastructural (i.e., 'economic') significance of these religious-ideological forms beyond their symbolic-representational function. This is more than a matter of seeing culture as the performance of political meanings within a dominant sociosymbolic field commensurate with the ruling order. It is more than a matter of reading culture as a practical language of resistance and negotiation, providing idioms and forms for the articulation of otherwise inarticulate experiences of struggle and protest, for which the cultural analyst becomes a privileged interpreter or, in current academic usage, translator. Such a view relegates the activities and inventions of the people, and in particular of women, to a secondary, 'feminine' status — as overdetermined, complex responses to the more fundamental structures that determine them and their 'meanings'.[32]

We might be able to see the ways in which the 'religious' or 'cultural' practices and structures of the Noranian imaginary create and transform 'economic conditions' — that is, how they are 'productive' in a historically significant way — if we translate the notion of 'economy' to an understanding of *kabuhayan,* which encompasses livelihood, ways of living, as well as life-producing activities. To understand the activities of the people-event actuated by Nora as *pangkabuhayan,* as vital, value-bearing and life-producing activities — as conditions of and for life — is to recognize that the joys and pleasures, the healing and inspiration, that Nora's followers experience in their following — this loving that they engage in — cannot be separated from their 'work' or from their class constitution as domestic labour. As Enrique Dussel writes, 'Work is the very substance of culture, its ultimate essence, its basic determination, in the sense that its very being, as *actualization* of the human being, is a *way of producing human life.* Work is the self-production, the creation, of human life. Before being objects, indeed before being "modes of consumption" of these cultural objects, culture is a *way of working*' (emphasis added).[33]

To view the phenomenal power of Nora Aunor solely in terms of commodity fetishism, to see her as a spectacular form of the commodity, is to be blind to this way of working, the creative activity, that goes into both the consumption and production of her objectified image. Indeed, it is to occupy the position of the transcendental subject whose unconscious is the 'real abstraction' at work in exchange, the abstraction that supports objective-universal scientific knowledge.[34] This subject position is given figuration in Orly, the unbelieving documentary filmmaker, whose compulsion to reveal the truth about Elsa is, to my mind, itself hysterical in that it stems from an identification with the masculinist gaze of modern progress (the gaze of capitalism as well as of an enlightenment anti-capitalism), the point from which the practices of faith of Elsa's following appear to be misplaced desires. In this case, Nora/Elsa is a fetish to the filmmaker as ideological critic, inasmuch as Elsa can only be seen as a fetish from the perspective of disenchantment (just as the modern category of the fetish in both Marxist and Freudian usages is created out of disenchantment).[35] My point here is to question not the commodity form of the spectacle of Nora Aunor, but rather the immediacy of objectification — that is, the direct conversion of complex practices of production into commodity forms and, moreover, the analytical presumption of that conversion as a given. 'Before being objects, indeed before being "modes of consumption" of these cultural objects, culture is a *way of working*.'

Cultural critiques that understand film and film stars as, before anything else, representational objects, and the relation of fans to such representational objects in terms of consumption (and, in turn, of identification as consumption), only succeed in masking, with their own explicating representations of the imaginary as an abstract system, those ways of working and relating that precede and exceed the commodification process.[36] Put another way, to the extent that they confront cinematic phenomena as image signifiers on the level of ideology (with the 'imaginary' on the level of a representational 'economy'), such critiques only succeed in reinforcing the field of abstraction on which commodity fetishism depends. They succeed in imposing on creative and wayward practices the logical framework of the dominant order that they critique.[37] To recognize other dimensions of Nora's phenomenal following, beyond and before objectification, we must take her seriously, that is, we must be swayed by her blessed power. The power of the Nora/Elsa phenomenon is in the mode of her claim; it is in the form of her event (the miracle). To understand this power means to take Nora/Elsa at her word. It means to partake of this openness, which is miscoded as hysteria, an openness to forces and claims beyond one's ken of what is real.

In this spirit, we must believe that 'the internationalization of capital ... also renders capitalism open to subaltern pressures, to the pressure exerted by the forms and forces it subordinates', here pressures exerted by women to make their living, to make life amidst the curse of impoverishment and social oppression.[38] For women are mediators, creatively assembling relations between 'tradition' and new structures of exploitation, regulation and order, in ways that allow them, and 'others' to whom they extend their selves, to produce, live and enjoy life. We must believe that the characteristics of capital (such as its flexibility, mobility and creativity), as accumulated, objectified labour, are fundamentally shaped by the characteristics of labour. This labour consists of women who will, in a succeeding historical moment, depart in unprecedented numbers from their territorially bound roles as mothers, daughters, sisters and girlfriends, to lend themselves out as domestic workers in households outside of their communities. It is the inventive practices and activities of these women that give them their life force, a life force that is only subsequently integrated, assimilated, subordinated and extracted — in a word, exploited — by others through various apparati of capture.[39] These are dream acts that are later held hostage to the belief structures of global fantasy production.

What I have identified as the experiential practice of taking a chance in faith, which informs Noranian popularity, can be recognized as what is already at work in the 'reckless actions' of women freeing themselves from their families and communities to find ways of living elsewhere and otherwise. This taking a chance is denoted by practices of *pakikipagsapalaran* [destiny playing or adventure]and *pagbabakasakali* [chance-taking], the concepts with which they express their actions. As one overseas domestic worker says: '*Kami ay nagbabakasakali upang kumita at makaginhawa naman sa hirap ng buhay sa ating bansa*' [We take our chances in order to earn and at least find pleasure and relief from the hardness of life in our country].'[40] This action of chance taking is an *acting in faith*. In *Himala*, the power and strength that Elsa and her followers wield lies in their having faith or, more accurately, *sampalataya*, a 'quality' that the men, in their pursuit of the idol of money, are accused of having lost (Fig. 6.2). The concept of *sampalataya* is predicated upon sociosubjective forms and practices that I am suggesting are revitalized, recreated and transformed by women (inasmuch as within the logic and system of modernization women become the repository of 'religion' and 'indigenous tradition'). 'According to the *baylans* and the indigenous healers, "*sampalataya*" is the primary motive force behind the rituals they want to take place. It means that some miraculous powers told them to carry out and develop their capacities so that they can be of help to the members of the group. "*Sampalataya*" incarnates the unarticulated relations among people — feelings, respect, hope and belief.'[41]

I have tried to describe the way in which the 'indigenous' — that is, creatively persistent — form of agency encapsulated in the figure of the *babaylan* and in the grammatical form of non-causative action is revitalized and reinvented into a heretical form of power, whereby a 'medium' of another's action, a *kasangkapan*, is transformed into an active mediator through an unnatural, unorthodox claim, a claim the prevailing social order does not sanction. The power founded on this

Figure 6.2 Heretical following. Film still courtesy of the Film Center of the University of the Philippines.

claim is one that inspires and passes on to those who have *sampalataya*. Elsa's healing practice of passing her hands over the ill, of healing through touch, depicts the notion of the self as a permeable medium.[42] This practical notion enables not only the spread of her power but the very claiming and creation of that power. It enables the flow of libidinal energies that constitute Noranian popularity. This sociosubjective form of the active mediator (the self-motivating medium of action) is, however, also invented through those libidinal energies, energies that are part and proof of the life-producing activity of loving performed by what can now be recognized as domestic labour.

Both the power of this constituency and the exploitation of this power are evident in the restructuring of the Philippine economy into a global manufacturer of domestic (and, more broadly, service) workers. By this I mean to claim that the forms of acting in love and heretical faith paradigmatically depicted in and by Nora/Elsa's popularity are 'economic' forms that people in servitude have invented in the production of their lives. They are 'economic' forms to the extent that they are life- and value-producing activities. To see forms of loving and faith in this way is to recognize the ways in which they have been captured and exploited by capital. It is to recognize that these passions of the people have fueled the restructurations that state, corporate and household institutions have made precisely in order to appropriate the life and value that they themselves do not produce. These restructurations are now said to be constitutive of a historical shift, a shift characterized by, for example, the diasporicization of Philippine labour and the conversion of the Philippine state from an employer-overseer of a national industry of natural and semi-processed goods to a labour-recruiting and resourcing agency for transnational capital. Contrary to the history of global capital, which views this shift as its own effect (viewing itself as its own as well as the world's cause), I am claiming a historical, poetic (*poeisis* as production) power for the passions of this domestic labour. *Himala* renders this historical shift and the role of such passions in bringing about this shift in its depiction of the growth and demise of the tourist-, export-oriented industry, which builds on and around Nora/Elsa's popularity, and the evacuation of the town as a consequence of the demise, or, more accurately, the evisceration, of the heretical power of that popularity. The diasporicization of domestic labour, its value for capital, is predicated upon the objectification of those passions as the people's — more particularly, as labouring women's — capacities for suffering, for relieving suffering for others, for using their selves as the instruments of others' relief — in a word, as poor people's nature to be *mapagmalasakit*. It is in the moment beyond and before their objectification and alienation, however, that the people who live these passions exercise an immense historical potential.

The claim that such a trivial affair as Nora Aunor — a 'gimmick' of the entertainment industry, a media event — should be bestowed with this historical significance may seem to be itself somewhat of a hysterical claim. It is indeed a claim that gives in to the sway of Nora's spectacular power. It is a claim that is 'out there'. But it is precisely this excessiveness and its worldliness (in people taking and acting this excessiveness in the world) that express *sampalataya* — here, a faith in, in the very act of exercising, one's creative capacity to make history.

THE FATAL TRAGEDY OF IRONY

Does *Himala* have *sampalataya*? The answer to this question lies in the answer to another question: Who kills Elsa? In the film, who fires the fatal shot is an unanswered mystery. It is a shot out of the crowd. And yet the narrative provides some clues: Pilo holds Elsa responsible for Chayong's suicide as well as for the frustration of his masculinity, which has already led him to murder; drug-crazed teenagers rape Elsa and Chayong as an act of profanation — a 'testing' — of Elsa's divine charm; shortly before Elsa's revelation, the mayor directs his chief of police to arrest anyone who speaks out against him, the government, or God. Together the clues point to a dominant masculinist, religious-political order threatened with the revitalization of the heretical movement, which it believed it had already domesticated. This domestication is carried out through the expropriation of its power — the commodification of Elsa's healing power in bottled holy water and religious articles, the selling of her presence and popularity as mass spectacle, television image, tourist site and fashion event.

Elsa's powers begin to fail when she and Chayong are raped. Elsa is stripped of her divine charm, not only by the rapists, but also by Orly, the documentary filmmaker, who records the rape as evidence of Elsa's all-too-human, all-too-female, powerlessness. In effect, a profound disbelief or, more accurately, the power of the reality of the ruling order to command belief, disempowers Elsa. Deaths ensue because of the objective reality of social opprobrium, fatal disease and money met with fear, ignorance and desperate greed. These deaths do not, however, spell the end of Elsa. She regains strength and emerges out of her confinement to issue another call to her followers.

When Elsa utters her revelation, it signals both the end of her heresy and the beginning of a new one. Impregnated through violence with yet unknown possibility, as Elsa has been through the rape, this moment is put to an end by the fatal shot. We see the fatal shot fired from the position of the camera. Formally, the smoking gun leads to us, the viewers, in alignment with the cinematic apparatus. If the camera 'kills' Elsa, it is in its capacity as an objective means of representation, as the detached purveyor of the truth about Elsa — and Nora. This shot, which stops the threat of Nora/Elsa exceeding her role as fetish, indicts the disenchanted, representational, filmic gaze. For while the decoding of fetishism results in the waning of the power of the fetish, it is only when it is a dead body that the fetish can be recognized as such, that it can be arrested as a fetish. In proving the fetish character of Nora/Elsa, the film intensifies the process that cinema — as an apparatus of capitalist enchantment — engages in, even though for different ends. The draining of life from the forces of production through their products is here turned toward the draining of life from the product as a way of returning it to the producers. Nora/Elsa's confession, finally extracted from her through this progressive disenchantment, enacts her self-identification as a commodity form, which is, of course, fatal. It is in this sense that the death of Nora/Elsa is the result of the film's perspective, one that is without *sampalataya*.

Bienvenido Lumbera asserts that the absence of the logic of irony in many directors accounts for the failure of so many Philippine films to achieve the respectability of an art form. Irony is 'that double-awareness which detaches the creator from his material and allows him to discover a pattern in the incongruities of experience. Its logic, therefore, would be inimical to the naive, the romantic and the sentimental, qualities that indicate the creator's inability to comprehend in its totality the experience he aims to translate into art.'[43] There is no doubt that with *Himala*, as well as with many other films, Ishmael Bernal achieved the artistic ideal that, for Lumbera, kept the Tagalog film a 'scorned stepsister' to the other performing arts, 'understandably' disdained by the intelligentsia for gratifying the moral and emotional tastes of its similarly disdained audience. Bernal is, in fact, one of the directors whose works made the 1970s and 1980s the 'Second Golden Age' for Philippine cinema. It is widely acknowledged that the initial 'Golden Age' of the 1950s fell, along with the studio system, in the 1960s, making way for the emergence of 'commercial' formulas and the 'superstar syndrome', with these transformations understood to have been brought about as a consequence of the influence of parallel transformations in the US Hollywood system.[44] What is less recognized is that the closing down of the studio system, which brought with it such 'artistic decline' and 'rampant commercialism' was also the consequence of an intensifying labour movement.[45] Nora Aunor's spectacular rise in the late 1960s must hence be seen as part of the social ferment that the declaration of martial law in 1972 was a state effort (backed by international governance and capital) to arrest. Her sudden and unmatched box office power did not only epitomize the 'superstar syndrome'; her 'superstar' status also challenged, subverted and sublated the masculine beginnings of 'superstardom' in the male actors-heroes of the new commercial genre, the 'action-film', and in what was touted as the exceedingly popular presidency of the dictator-to-be, Ferdinand Marcos.[46]

Himala thus fulfills Lumbera's notion of an artistic film to the extent that it comprehends the larger sociohistorical conditions of Nora Aunor's 'superstardom'. It provides not only a theory of the spectacle form but also a history, told in fable form, of the specific 'personality cult' that constituted her popularity. The 'miracle' of Elsa conveys the subversive as well as symptomatic dimensions of Nora Aunor's status within the spheres of politics and entertainment, which converge in her figure (consequently bringing mass cultural production and government together). Heresy and orthodoxy are mixed in Nora Aunor's *himala*. In the film, this mixedness is evident in the heterogeneity of Elsa's following. Rich city patients cut through the throng of ailing, rural poor women, men and children to see her. Independent filmmakers, television broadcasters and reporters, foreign tourists and other curious onlookers join in the production and enjoyment of the spectacle. The local economic and political elite invests in her and grows protective over their investments. Panning shots of the crowd show irreducibly diverse kinds of fans and admirers, making different claims on her, calling to her with different forms of want and desire.

In its thinly disguised depiction of Nora Aunor's 'life', it would seem then that the film follows the form of 'traditional' Philippine cinema, which Nicanor Tiongson describes as occupied with the presentation and approximation of reality rather than, as is true of the New Cinema (another name for the Second Golden Age films), with the *representation* of a hidden reality, or 'the *faithful* depiction of truth' (emphasis added).[47] However, the film does in fact succeed in detaching itself from the passion of Nora Aunor as lived by her following and in establishing an ironic distance from her popularity in order to represent her historical 'truth'. In this way it is able to convert the melodrama of Nora Aunor's 'life' into a realistic tragedy of the 'superstar syndrome'.

Naomi Schor shows how, in Flaubert's work, irony serves as a trope of fetishism in its double act of negation and preservation, recognition and denial, of the 'truth' of femininity (the 'truth', that is, of women's castration, which for Flaubert is embodied in Romanticism). Fetishism is, in this analysis, an 'exclusively male perversion' that defines the limits of realist description, to the extent that what is disavowed cannot be described.[48] In arguing that fetishism falls on the side of the ironic filmmaker, and that this masculinist mode, predicated on the disavowal of the knowledge of Nora's heretical power and its replacement with the *belief* in her commodity-function, enables the film's project of demystification, I am not so much moving towards the conception of an alternative fetishism as pointing to the deadly consequences of irony as a mode of political critique. As an approach with belief but without *sampalataya*, ironic fetishism is what kills Nora/Elsa.

Like Orly, the film recognizes its culpability in the disempowerment of Nora/Elsa through disenchantment. Orly's confession to Elsa of his complicity, his expression of concern that perhaps he was no different from those who would use anyone and anything without veneration [*na walang pakundangan*], as well as the indicting shot, which places *Himala*'s filmmaker alongside Orly, attest to the film's ambivalence towards its project of demystification and the detachment on which such a project is predicated. Like Orly, the film wants to 'follow' Nora Aunor to a place where she might take us, the audience — a place where we have never been. There is, in this 'following', an attraction that is being worked through to some as yet unseen, but nevertheless presupposed, end.

The film's writer, Ricky Lee, expresses a similar desire in a short story written more than a decade earlier during the very height of Nora Aunor's fame. In 'Si Tatang, Si Freddie, Si Tandang Senyong at Iba Pang Mga Tauhan ng Aking Kuwento' [Tatang, Freddie, Old Senyong and Some Other Characters of My Story], an ambitious writer sets out to shake up an incomprehensible and uncomprehending world through his individual art. But he finds himself embarking on an unexpected path when he witnesses the police constabulary gun down the amulet- and sacred machete-bearing followers of a religious political sect called the *Lapiang Malaya* as they make their way to the presidential palace to demand the surrender of President Marcos.[49] Abandoning all his previous attempts to write about the world from a distance, he decides to investigate and write about the sect's mysterious leader, Tatang, who is committed to a mental hospital. His investigation leads him to greater and greater involvement in the lives and stories of his would-be 'characters' and consequently to a greater understanding of the oppressive structures that distort their perceptions and misshape their actions into impotent, protesting gestures of madmen. Moved by the suspicious murder of Tatang, he abandons the paralyzing and paralyzed world of coffeehouse writers and joins the workers' movement. Thus, while Lee's writer is drawn to and follows the enigmatic figures and paths of peasant irrationality, he awakens to a place already believed to be there: the real world struggles of the revolutionary proletariat.

The deadly consequences of the ironic fetishistic mode of the film are, as I have been trying to argue, inflicted through the fatal abstraction of Nora Aunor's popularity. In Lee's story, it is precisely the death of Tatang that compels the narrator-writer to take political action. The detachment of the filmmaker/writer as the subject-coming-into-(political) consciousness is not so much an attitude as much as it is an operation performed on the experience of 'following' [experience as passage, *pinagdaanan*] — whereby *'following'* Nora is alienated and hypostatized as Nora's *'following'* — to enable this coming into consciousness. Through the objectification and abstraction of Nora's popularity, the subject of the film/story emerges as an awakened [*mulat*] subject with the potential for political action. Disavowing his own attraction, by professing his intent to decipher a 'truth' believed to be behind the superstar, this critical subject is produced in the cleavage between him and the 'masses', the thing that now stands for both Nora's spectacular power and his alienation. In effect, to the critical subject, the 'masses' are *just like him*.

The ambivalence expressed by the film, in its identification with Orly, would appear therefore to be but the oscillations of the fetishist. Indeed, we might view the scenes of Elsa's praying body on the hill, stigmata on her hands and blood running down her arms, and of the prostitute Niña's body, which she bares and twirls around on the hill for the pleasure of the town's young boys and then wraps with a Virgin Mary-like shroud — we might see these reverent scenes as 'memorials' for a 'denied and longed-for female body',[50] inextricable from a denied and longed-for materiality as spiritual truth (or material embodiment of spiritual truth). I want to aver, however, that the ambivalence of the film exceeds the ambivalence of ironic fetishism. Nora's own overcoming of her symbolic role causes a palpable sway. There are unlocalizable moments in the film when Nora overpowers her fictional persona and comes across as 'herself'. I maintain this not only to profess to 'know' her (as her fans 'know' her) and therefore to respond to her appeal. As the downtrodden one who miraculously rises, she is, after all, always playing 'herself'. I maintain this, more importantly, to begin to entertain the suggestion of a new heresy.

Himala evinces the elements of a radical political model or, better, the features of another heretical movement coursing through it and the history it tries to make, another movement besides the political movement it believes will make that history. In Nora's overpowering of her instrumental role for the purposes of political critique, we find evidence that Bernal and Lee are themselves swept up by her superstardom. Actuating the 'personality cult' they set out to critique, using the superstar herself to dismantle the syndrome of which she is the highest instance, Bernal and Lee allow her to exercise her persona fully and give in to the sway of that power. She is directed but also directing. She *is* playing herself in a melodramatic way. And the film *does* present the reality for which she stands for her fans (the barrio lass, the movie fan, the *babaeng martir*), except here she does not find happiness, she is not released from her curse, she is not finally blessed.[51]

It is, indeed, the duration of suffering, of the passion, on which the film lovingly dwells that makes for the film's faith. Scenes of Elsa's attendants dwelling on her dress and of Elsa rapt in prayer reverently linger on beyond their place in the well-paced narrative, replaying some of the intensity of the first dramatic scene. This first scene, in which Elsa first beholds the apparition of the Virgin Mary, is a prolonged dwelling on the longing and ecstasy expressed by Elsa/Nora's face and body as she is bathed in the increasingly luminous glow of the sun emerging out of the eclipse, a dilation of time and light that is inseparable from the veneration-suffused regard of the film itself. Even as it works towards disenchantment, the film abides awhile by the mythical reality of Nora Aunor, whose appeal comes across and through, in spite of the film's abstraction. The power of that reality of

Nora Aunor over the film's representational objective is manifested in the weakness and irrelevance of the charge that this film was nothing but a copy of a Cuban film made some years earlier.[52] While the film's representational objective to critique the dominant social relations of the spectacle would depend on the abstraction, or, we might say, transcendence, of the Nora Aunor phenomenon, it is precisely the inseparability of the representation of the superstar syndrome from the presentation of Nora Aunor herself that attests to the powerful sway of Noranian popularity. The film's relinquishment of its own heretical political potential lies in its failure to sufficiently abide by Nora's belovedness, to stay with her 'following' and move according to its sway (rather than to the progressive perspective with which the 'critical' subject identifies) — in a word, its lack of *sampalataya*.

FASCISTIC, FETISHISTIC POWER VS. A HERETICAL POLITICS OF EMPOWERMENT

When I make such a claim, I am aware that it draws the fear of fascism. There is plenty of reason to believe that the superlative role in which capacity Nora Aunor served is a fascist structure. Both Ferdinand Marcos and Corazon Aquino secured their populist authoritarian power precisely through the spectacular structure of identification mediated by her. I want to argue, however, that it is the subsumption of Noranian popularity by the logic of fetishism as a logic of identification that allows for the support of fascism. Claude Lefort holds that 'At the foundation of totalitarianism lies the representation of the People-as-One.'[53] This representation of the social body 'breaks down into the image of a whole, and a part that stands for the whole', a part that, detached from the social whole, constitutes the whole it represents. The logic of identification that such a representational constitution of 'the people' entails underpins the *realpolitik* fantasy-critiques of Nora as the image of the Masses-as-One. This same logic governs the fetishistic system of capital: 'Commodities and capital goods, wageworkers and capitalists, money and credit … are members of the body of Capital, whose value-essence transcends and yet incarnates itself in these material beings like the divine salvational power of Christ in the faithful members and sacramental objects of His church.'[54] But just as Elsa's power exceeds the form of the sacrament of the Eucharist (the logic and form of value under capital), in its transmission through touch rather than through consumption, so also does Nora exceed her commodity function, and in particular her role as idol-image of the masses.[55] To the extent that the critiques of Nora attempt to capture all that is tangential to the presumed totality of her 'popularity', they fail to recognize, much less be moved by, 'the social relations that elude the grip of power'.[56] It is these relations that will spell the difference between a fascist/fetishistic structure of power and a heretical politics of empowerment.

In *Himala*, Niña faults Elsa for her detachment from people, for having 'followers' but no friends. This reprimand recalls the friendship between them that is itself left behind when Niña is driven out of Cupang because of an affair with a married man. When Niña returns from Manila where she is engaged in prostitution work, Elsa is already engulfed by the success of her own profession. Yet each continues to bear a palpably tender regard for the other, a regard that is both knowing and seeking. In this scene, where Niña confronts Elsa after the police shut down Niña's cabaret at the behest of the town's moral majority, sparks fly and Niña's accusation bears the hurt tones of one once loved and spurned. The relationship between Elsa and Niña is a fundamental symbolic axis of the film. Niña is the other Mary, Mary Magdalene, the prostitute, who is cast out by a moralistically blinded people. We wait to see if she will arouse the compassion of Elsa, as Mary Magdalene did of Christ. But the film plays with this relationship in ways that exceed its parable function. For besides Mary Magdalene and Christ, they are also, as Niña tells Elsa, both whores. They meet on common earthly ground. They are two women whose value for the world is produced by meeting the needs of others with their bodies. This objective condition is not, however, the sole determinant of their common ground. They also share a subjective history — a long duration of knowing each other — replete with childhood hope and play and love, only later split by the world into sexual desire and sacred passion.

On this earthly ground, another renewed relation is explored that eludes the logic of identification predicating Nora/Elsa's representation of the People-as-One. At the funeral procession for the deaths of Chayong, Sepa's children, and the baby of the town's pariah, Elsa's step begins to fail, weighed down as she is by profound grief and the suffering that she now cannot heal but can only experience in her own being and, more, as her own doing. Watching from the sidelines, Niña steps in to catch and hold her. This image-relation of them walking together in an embrace is contemplated further when, finding themselves together at Chayong's tomb after the funeral, Elsa asks if she might join Niña in the city to work as a maid. There is in this moment of objective disenchantment with Elsa's power an affirmation of the faith that brought Nora Aunor into stardom. But here faith in acting is revived within the Noranian fan, the maid. Brought down from the cinematic firmament and into the earthly relation with Niña, this renewed, altered faith tries to break out of its alienation and isolation in orthodox apparati of power and to reconnect with the world. But the moment and its promise of a new relation between Elsa and Niña, of a different future together, does not last, for Elsa is recaptured by her own spectacular function for 'the people'.

Crying both 'There is no miracle!' and 'The miracle is in our hearts', Nora/Elsa announces a new heresy in the making, one in which objective disenchantment and subjective faith coexist [Fig. 6.3]. But

Figure 6.3 'Walang Himala!': A new heresy in the making. Film still courtesy of the Film Center of the University of the Philippines.

Bernal and Lee cannot follow it, even if they have helped to present its possibility. They cannot do so because they decide to pursue the critique of fetishism to its end, and hence they abandon what seems to be tangential to the totality they aim to critique: the sociosubjective modes and relations that do not develop into the proper national subject of history.[57] In doing so, they also abandon the heretical potential of Noranian popularity, a potential they themselves recognized to the extent they did not take full command of it but rather allowed it to sway and direct the movement of the film.

That new heresy, while abandoned in the film (as well as by Nora Aunor herself), is taken up in history. The heresy in which objective disenchantment and subjective faith coincide is carried out by the millions of Filipinas who have left the national community to fulfill their own wishful prophecies by acting as domestic workers all over the world. The profound emphasis on religious spirituality made by the Aquino regime in its recentering of the 'Filipino Ideology' formulated by the Marcos regime demonstrates not only the state's recognition of the significance of the living faith practiced by people (evidenced by the role of this faith in the deposing of Marcos) but also the state's need to interpret that faith as a way of containing and capturing its heretical potential.[58] While domestic workers 'made' history by causing their own calling, by subverting their role as non-causative media and taking on a heretical assumption, the Aquino regime tried to take their claims away by proclaiming them the new 'heroes' of the nation — as representatives of the Filipino People, they were enjoined to sacrifice themselves, Christ like, as the Christ-like, Eucharistic body of Capital, to be consumed by the nation. But what continues to go unrecognized is the fact that these women did not act Christ like; they were not obeying a truth that transcended them nor were they heeding a sacred call that they themselves did not make (up). In effect, they reinvented Nora/Elsa as themselves — they were their own superstars.[59]

The distinction between the spirituality of the state and the faith of the people is neither fixed nor essential. Rather, it is a critical difference between a totalitarian structure of power and a heretical politics of empowerment, both of which are strains present in the social phenomena I am trying to describe. What enables the sway of Noranian popularity to be mobilized for the fascist regime (indeed, to find its mirror-image in Marcos/Aquino) is the detachment of the image of heretical potential (Nora) from the heretical movement that she articulates and is generated by. This detachment requires the transcendence of Nora Aunor's own earthly positivity, which is precisely the unglamorousness (the classed/racialized genderedness) of her body as well as of the worldly practices of loving that are inextricably involved in that positivity.

The heretical politics of empowerment therefore demands not only *sampalataya*, this faith whose truth lies in the acting; it demands not only a 'following' of the sway of a radical claim against the orthodoxy of belief. It also demands a reconnection of that *sampalataya* to earthly desires and to the movements those desires inspire. This reconnection means an involvement in, not a capture of, the powerful sway of women's loving claims. Rather than a substitute for, a symptom of, the People, Nora/Elsa has to become mundane, a worldly thing or *bagay* [a thing that is always already attached and relevant to, a nonabstractable part of, a worldly context]. In this way, she becomes no different from — though certainly not the same as — all the individuated parts of the movement that involves her (rather than that she represents).[60] And the devalued, gendered experiential mode of *pakikiramay* [extended feeling] constitutive of women's 'hysteria' becomes a mode of historical action and empowerment.

In emphasizing the importance of this gendered involvement in the sway of women's loving claims (claims as practices of loving as well as claims to loving), I refer neither to a loving without knowing and knowledge nor a loving without antagonism. Both Elsa and Niña are moved by a loving that is mixed with the pain of resentment and jealousy. And both are joined finally by an objective disenchantment that translates into knowledge as well as by an understanding that comes from a long duration of familiarity (a knowing that is different from knowledge). It is, however, the absence of objective *faith* that makes the film an inadequate approximation of a radical political-expressive form that, on the one hand, would 'submit', in the way that Nora/Elsa and her fans do, to the sway of socioemotional movements that claim one as much as issue from one's own claims and, on the other, would compel a knowledge of the world, its logics and structures from which this movement draws its momentum and course, precisely to elude its grasp. Elsa's vision of the Virgin Mary, which is the seeing of a called witness as unorthodox adoptive child, provides a figure for a heretical witnessing that needs to inform any cinematic vision attempting to become a radical political mediator (the heretical potential of Nora/Elsa). It is 'a question of leaving a testimony and not any more of providing information', where information refers to a knowledge of things as God knows them, 'knowledge that can be obtained from a human viewpoint by a God who does not get caught in finitude'.[61] Moreover, it is a question of acting in faith upon a heretical claim, of testifying to a release from the orthodox forms of this finitude. A radical cinematic movement would hence involve both faith (which is also knowing) and knowledge, rather than, in the case of fetishism, knowledge and belief.

REPHRASING HISTORY

My own movement in this chapter, as well as in this book as a whole, has been an attempt to mobilize both elements of faith and knowledge. The politics of this movement in cultural analysis is based not on 'identification' with a preconstituted, pregiven people in whose behalf one writes. It is based, rather, on *sampalataya*, a faithful acting on one's own claims in concert with others to help in the reclamation and realization of the impeded heretical potential of a becoming-people from whom one cannot be removed. The knowledge that this politics calls forth is no longer the objective, comprehensive knowledge of an analytic perception. It is, rather, a 'partial' knowledge, which means that, more than being embedded and situated in a particular location, one is already caught up in the claims that others act out. It is a form of commitment that extends beyond a conscious decision to align oneself with a particular, preconstituted group. In this way, it is a knowledge moving towards faith.[62] Very importantly, this knowledge is also a knowledge of duration. It is a knowledge that accounts for the history on which it is based from the perspective of one caught within it. It is a 'knowing' that means another kind of relation to its 'object', which is never quite an object but rather always already a subjective mediator whose relation to the knower is as much her doing as it is her knower's and as much an undoing as it is an accomplishment.

We do not only need both faith and knowledge for a heretical politics of empowerment. We also need to place these elements in creative relation, where creative means the capacity to make things (*bagay* such as Nora Aunor) happen as history. This can be done if we understand history as the tension between what could have been and what is now, and, understanding this, if we know what was otherwise and what now might become. Such is the rephrasing of history accomplished by Elsa/Nora when she claims, 'what was of the Father has passed, now it is with the Mother'. To follow the heretical mode of this rephrasing of history means to extend the structure of the 'event' instantiated by Nora's popularity to the realm of cultural criticism. It means acting against the formal and real subsumption of women's practices of loving by apparatuses of capture, which include but are not limited to capital and its theoretical supplements. It is the belief in the real world *fantasized* by capital — indeed, the belief in the power of capital to subsume the world — among many other orthodox beliefs, that we must suspend if we are to participate in the making of other 'truths'. To make things happen as history as well as to make history as something yet to happen, we need to bear heretical witness to those other truths that are tangential to the ones we have comprehensive knowledge of. This is a faithful claim I make and throw out into the world in order to see if it will be taken up by another (if it has not yet, but I know it is already out there) and, if so, if that will make one motion in, I hope, a larger movement.

Conclusion:
Hope

In Donna Haraway's critical description of the tropic role of the gene in the reality games of technoscience — the gene as 'the alpha and omega of the secular salvation drama of life itself' — we can recognize the workings of much larger units of human life.[1] Nations, states, peoples, cultures — these are the privileged authors of and actors in the dramas of the present world, the things-in-themselves shaping destinies in our times. Not open futures, just a fixed array of possible outcomes. Like genes, replicators travelling across evolutionary time in living organisms as their bodily vehicles, nations, states, peoples and cultures are the subjects dreaming us.

There appears to be a mistake. Us humans, the agents *par excellence* of a universal modernity, the object of these abstract things' dreams? Indeed, there is a 'mistake' but one proper and fundamental to the global capitalist world we live in: fetishism. As Haraway puts it, 'Fetishism is about interesting "mistakes" — really denials — where a fixed thing substitutes for the doings of power-differentiated lively beings on which and on whom, in my view, everything actually depends.'[2] This practice of 'mistaking', here, principally, geopolitical and social categories as real, self-moving, acting entities, is not of course a matter of false consciousness, any more than the national and international dreams that *Fantasy-Production* tracks are mere illusions. Marx discussed fetishism as a practical operation crucial to the functioning of the system of capitalist exchange and not merely as an ideological effect of that system. As William Pietz writes of money and capital, nations, states and peoples are representational forms of material social relations that have become *universal*: 'they are fetishes insofar as they have become necessary functional parts that are privileged command-control points of a working system of social reproduction'.[3] It is the hold of political and economic *realities* (for the increasingly pragmatic, worldly citizens of the present, the real itself) over all our lives — the power of command they exercise over our practical imaginations of the possibilities and limits of social organization and collective happiness — that makes for the fact that nations, states, peoples, not to mention money and capital, are dreaming us.

Describing the 'belittling' view of Pacific islands and peoples with which he once wholeheartedly agreed and even participated in propagating, seemingly based as it was 'on irrefutable evidence, on the reality of our existence', Epeli Hau'ofa expresses the bleakness of the prevailing geopolitical-economic realist perspective for his community: 'What hope was there for us?' If indeed we — those of us who share in the daily indignities, unacknowledged pain and monumental violence that the realities of our countries' and our peoples' 'smallness' spell for us — are in dreams not of our own making, how can we dream other (our own?) dreams? What hope is there for us?

I find Haraway's irreverent, critical joking approach towards 'life itself' — the seemingly non-tropic, purely referential world of natural reproduction encapsulated by the gene — to provide a great measure of relief from the relentless reality-dreaming in which we are caught. Her 'diffraction' of the concrete facts of nature can be seen as a theoretical supplement to practices of other dreaming, which invisibly shape and yet might transform the 'real world' that serves as the place of our commandment.[4] Replacing the terrain of technoscientific fetishism, 'life itself', with a notion of 'liveliness', where 'contingency, finitude and difference' inhere, Haraway reminds us who ply the terrain of geopolitical-economic fetishism not only of the inescapably imaginary, figurative dimension of even the most 'serious' (scientific) claims of reality.[5] She reminds us, following this realization, also of the (cultural) conventionality and mutability of the shapes that that 'hard' reality takes. In these reminders we glean some glimmer of hope.

It is of course true that a simple, voluntarist will-to-thinking differently will not change the facts. Political scientists and economists are aware that nation-states and national economies are analytical categories. They themselves periodically remind each other of the dangers of hypostasizing such concepts, and yet ... They know very well that these are conceptual categories and yet they nevertheless refer to them as if they were real things in order to account for the facts. That is to say, in analytical practice they exercise the very belief that they theoretically disavow. What is this curious balancing act between theoretical knowledge and practical belief if not the very act of fetishism? While this analytical act is what helps to produce the facts, it does not do so either on its own or outside of the world it takes as its object. Fetishism is not simply hypostasization. Political science and economic discourses that attempt to provide an adequate theoretical account (a map of correspondence) for the way things are in the dominant terms of their organization only serve to support the actual social practices that make for this institutionalized reality.[6] My point here is that while the material world is profoundly imaginary, acts of analytical imagination and theoretical invention will have material effect only to the extent that they are connected to worldly social practices.

It is for these reasons that I do not see 'critical consciousness' or, for that matter, any idealist instantiations of counter-imaginations and oppositional fantasies to be adequate sources or means of hope. Instead of aspiring for new dreams, new romances, to reshape our real worlds, we can begin living creatively, acting differently, making other worlds to found new dreams.

But I have not yet said what I mean by hope. At the opening of the People's Plan 21, a gathering of people's organizations from all over the Asia Pacific region, held in Japan in 1989, Muto Ichiyo announced: 'The slogan at the beginning of the twentieth century was progress. The cry at the end of the twentieth century is survival. The call for the next century is hope.'[7] Against the images of 'progress' and 'development' where people have placed their desires, Muto sees a new picture of the world forming out of the interactions of people's movements. In the actual movements of Asia-Pacific peoples, indigenous peoples, women and ecological activists, he sees not the romantic dream but rather the practice of alternative futures. He witnesses 'people-to-people relations' regulating the economy in place of relationships between things regulating the relationships between human beings. What he calls the Alliance of Hope does not rest on the system of states that I have argued constitutes the very imaginary field of fantasy-production. The Alliance of Hope is made possible by 'peopleness', which is the living, dynamic relations of cooperation and interaction among peoples in struggle, working across and through their differences without eschewing them:

> Peopleness is not an idealist construct. It is what is actually at work in the existing solidarity movements among seemingly very different groups of people. It is what is behind the real sympathy and compassion for other people's struggles. It is what is behind the sacrifices being made for the people's cause everywhere. Denying the working of peopleness would be to deny the reality of these movements — or to render them incomprehensible. Peopleness represents our radical equality and our equal radicality.[8]

Departing from twentieth-century approaches to real social change, which were predicated on the seizure of state power, Muto sees in these movements a new kind of hope that does not rest on a remote future but rather on a possible future in the here and now: 'When social movements start changing the existing relationships here and now, they are already building an alternative society here and now.'[9]

My own sense of hope is close to Muto's. Hope to me lies in the daily exercise of our creative capacities to remake the world, in the acts of living in ways that depart from the orthodox dreams of our world-historical, real-politik time. It means, as I argued in the last chapter, both faith and knowledge against the regime of belief that presently reigns over the 'free' world. While Muto attends to the actions of organized social movements, I find that his insights apply not only to them but also to the broad range of actions on the part of socialities-in-the-making, that is, on *de facto* social movements seeking routes of escape from the fantasy structures of dominant orders. It is for this reason that I have argued in this book for cultural criticism coming under the sway of the non-realist logics guiding and created by the tangential and heretical pursuits of love, happiness, freedom and possibility embodied in these de facto social movements. To get caught up in the unorthodox faithful actions of others, including our own, has been my call.

I began *Fantasy-Production* by gesturing towards the limits of irony as a mode of critique and the borders that it sets up in the very process of putting them in question. Haraway similarly points to the reassuring and normalizing effect of the 'comic' mode, which 'does not recognize any contradictions that cannot be resolved, any tragedy or disaster that cannot be healed'.[10] Far from abandoning the comic mode, Haraway persists in it without, however, restoring its implied harmonies. Letting the contradictions stand as a practice of producing difference in the world, instead of self-sameness, and situating her own claims in intimate relations with the worlds she criticizes but continues to deeply care about, Haraway's method reads as 'feminist irony', which Naomi Schor defines as 'an irony peeled off from fetishism'.[11] In much of this book, I have attempted to put this 'feminist irony' into practice. It can be heard in the tone I adopt when speaking about 'prostitution' and 'slavery', calling the Philippines 'she', referring to the entire nation as a 'symptom' of American as well as global capital desire. I am practicing 'feminist irony' when I mimic these fantasy categories and the syntax of their racialized, gendered and sexualized phrasings but at the same time foreground the social contradictions on which they depend. I am practicing 'feminist irony' when I perform the fantasy-critique of this place called the Philippines without being able to remove myself from it and its consequences. I am, after all, one of those consequences. But more than that, it is of great consequence to me — it is a place which continues to shape my life, a place with which I have absolutely vital, living, material relationships, a place that remains a source, a means and an end of many of my most passionate attachments.

It is in light of the devastating masculinist implications of ironic critique, which I discussed in the previous chapter, that I have come to recognize the great importance of what I would call feminist hope, a hope that is at work in the practice of 'feminist irony' but that also goes beyond this practice. This hope is precisely that creative acting on faith exemplified by people power and the heresy of Filipina women leaving their homes. It is what cultural criticism would do well to be moved by in the making of its claims. In the face of an expanding global regime of pervasive cynicism and revanchist belief, I see the political need for intellectual producers to make faithful claims. Faithful claims enact and extend desiring movements that escape the debilitating, life-taking dreams of the New World Order. They are creative acts that 'follow' — pursue, supplement, submit to — other life-mandates coursing through history, other practices of imagination that are already making the world different or making different worlds out of this one by defying the orthodox truths of fantasy-production.

In 'following' the heretical actions of others, we cannot, however, assume that these actions constitute an *a priori* 'correct' political course or strategy. To do so would be to romanticize the people and their spontaneous philosophy in ways that have proven disastrous at other places and other times. Our claims must be our own even as they are in concert with others. And as we need knowledge as much as we need faith, knowledge (as the product of 'critical consciousness') must be part of our claims, which cannot only act under the sway of others' claims but rather must also exert a sway on others. Balibar's interpretation of the significance of Althusser's conception of ideology might well apply here. As he writes, 'Very much in the line of Gramsci's notion of "hegemony", it [Althusser's conception] implies that the importance of "science" in revolutionary practice is not so much to "explain reality", even less to forecast future history, but above all to transform the masses' ideology, therefore the proletariat's *own* ideology.'[12] I would only add that 'we', who are on the side of 'science', and the knowledge we proffer cannot remain detached from that transformation we hope will take place in others. 'We' and the particular mode of critical thought that defines 'us' must be in the very process of transformation that we would expect of the people with whom we find ourselves intimately, painfully and promisingly linked. Let me quote Muto once more:

> Interactions, if properly stimulated and organized, can cause mutually liberatory changes in the practices and cultures of the communities involved, and the community with a modified internal culture, by deepening its understanding of the partner communities, will certainly improve its relationships with them. This is what I would call an alliance building process. When this unraveling of the imposed mutual relationships occurs inducing internal transformation, we already see a process of an alliance of hope being built. As is obvious, this is a dynamic, ever-self-renewing, cross-fertilization process. But isn't this a mere wishful thinking?

In fact, it is not. The Alliance of Hope building process is partly
a description of what is happening on a significant scale and partly a
new context whereby what is happening is to be understood and
oriented.[13]

The knowledge we produce has to be informed by the heterodox logics
of people's liberative actions and pursuits. Otherwise, while we seek
to change prevailing dreams, we decline the transformation of our own
practices of imagination.

In this book I have tried to 'follow' the re-imaginings of the nation
and the world that are already happening in order to expand the
horizon of my own truth-claims about the Philippines and the global
order within which it is placed. While I have endeavoured to hold on
to and heed the particularities of Philippine life, which I at once
intimately know and am far away from, I have also learned to heed
claims and ways of struggle in other social contexts, which I have come
to know. I have learned that to change prevailing social relations here
and now means to directly address the cultural logics of difference that
organize them — to address racism, sexism and homophobia in their
everyday social effects and actions. It means to attend to the cultural
resources that people have drawn upon and invented in their daily
struggle to prevail over the small and grave, intermittent and relentless
acts of repression, debasement and dispossession directed against them.
This attention has, in my view, been one of the most important
contributions of the movements of multiculturalism and their demands
for and claims of heterogeneity, diversity and difference.

At the same time, to make a different world here and now means
to peel these cultural resources from the structures of fantasy-
production that subsume them, including categories of national or
social 'identity', possessive subjectivity and representational democracy.
To make culture matter beyond 'culturalism' we have to take seriously
the role of cultural practices of imagination in the material production
and organization of our given worlds and, moreover, to put those
practices to work in the creation of new political and economic forms
of collective life. Such vital work depends on the freeing of our
imaginations from the hold of existing realities, which naturalize the
presence and necessity of all the apparatuses of social regulation and

expropriation supporting the global order, from states and prisons to military forces and labour markets.[14] It is in this spirit that Ngugi Wa Thiong'o dedicates his work with 'the message of my hope for a world without prisons and detention camps. It is the hope, in other words, for a world which will have eliminated the necessity of prisons, detention camps, the army, and police barracks, in short, eliminated the conditions which make the state as we have known it necessary in the organization of human life.'[15] As I have suggested, that freeing is already happening in the actions of people dreaming other worlds. The predicament for many of us is how to grasp and be theoretically swayed by those dreams and, furthermore, communicate in them to others. I have only begun in this book to suggest ways of doing so, ways of reconceptualizing people's historical agency by recourse to the languages of their transformative actions.

If it is true that the present world experiences 'not so much a scarcity of hope and imagination but an unbounded incommensurability of hope between different regions and cultural spaces', then it seems to me that the task of intellectual work is to participate in bringing those different regions and cultural spaces into conversation with one another.[16] If fantasy-production sets veritable limits to what of other dreams it is possible to convey, then we are enjoined to actively create, together with other cultural producers, new figurative means, new inter-cultural languages, by which some of that incommensurability of hope might be bridged.

In the present dire context of global war, we are called upon to bear vital witness to other dreams against and beyond the current global-US fantasy of world security, which returns with a vengeance to the shores of anti-imperialist Filipino struggle. In April 2002, at a teach-in, cultural protest and activist congress called 'Culture Against War: Philippines on the Axis of Empire', several hundred others and I experienced a radical hope that already spans great cultural distances.[17] This event was organized by a multicultural group of students, activists and teachers as a public counter-cultural stance to the dominant culture of war supporting the joint US-Philippine military deployments in the Southern Philippines. Both the process of organizing the event and the event itself were powerful testimonies to the lively imaginations that are moving to make new worlds of socially just and joyful communities.

A new generation of politicized, culturally creative youth here in the US joined music, rhythms, images and words with new and older generations of revolutionary struggle in the Philippines to make faithful claims to an 'axis of resistance' that exceeds the geopolitical coordinates of the global-militarist crusade. In the inspiring cultural performances of JUICE, a multicultural student guerilla theater troupe at the University of California at Santa Cruz, the Bay Area cultural activist band Diskarte Namin, the hip-hop artists Kiwi and DJ Owl Boogie, other independent artists and cultural performers and in the congress of activist organizations that followed, I heard new languages, new feelings and new social relations being created that celebrated and practiced peoples' power and peoples' love against the pieties of patriotism everywhere extolled and against the state powers to which all feeling for human life is required to pay tribute.

While this protest dream-action was a small one, it nevertheless heeds a call to which so many innumerable others have also responded and continue to respond, a call that people have, by means of their faithful actions, themselves 'caused'. In these acts of hope and in the unorthodox ways that people are speaking their tangential dreams to one another and being swayed by each other's claims, we bear active witness to a new heresy in the making. No miracles, just hope.

Walang himala! Tayo ang gumagawa ng himala![18]

Notes

INTRODUCTION

1   We might even say, in the contemporary context when the West's right to world hegemony has never been more besieged, it is also the enjoyment of seeing the afterlife of one's old possessions, no longer the pleasure of imperialist nostalgia but rather a certain *jouissance* in watching the tragic-comic play of 'dispossessions of empire.' 'For the foreigner, romances/ of "Aloha,"/ For Hawaiians,/ dispossessions of empire.' Haunani-Kay Trask, 'Writing in Captivity: Poetry in a Time of Decolonization' in *Inside Out: Literature, Cultural Politics, and Identity in the New Pacific*, ed. Vilsoni Hereniko and Rob Wilson (Lanham, Maryland: Rowman and Littlefield Publishers, Inc., 1999), p. 22.

2   Arjun Appadurai, *Modernity at Large: Cultural Dimensions of Globalization* (Minneapolis and London: University of Minnesota Press, 1996), p. 29.

3   Ibid., p. 30.

4   See for example the portrait of the Marcoses drawn by James Hamilton-Paterson who writes, 'if nothing else is clear, we at least have to recognize the centrality of *fantasy* to their regime. Onto Ferdinand's and Imelda's carefully edited pasts were grafted various myths and fragments of myths, ranging from the conquering hero to Cinderella, from cosmogony to Camelot, which in turn encapsulated snippets of the Abe Lincoln log-cabin-to-President mythology that Lyndon Baines Johnson also laid claim to James Hamilton-Paterson, *America's Boy: The Marcoses and the Philippines* (London: Granta Publications, 1998), p. 359. While Hamilton-Paterson sees fantasy as a general condition and practice of the heads of nation states, recalling how Ronald Reagan for example 'was equally deep

in a fantasy that had come to him via Hollywood, his "Star Wars" or Strategic Defense Initiative,' this example becomes the measure by which the Marcoses particular fantasies appear to be 'small beer, even quite touching' (p. 360).

5 Appadurai, *Modernity at Large*, p. 31.

6 Ibid., p. 31.

7 The conflation between imagination as analytical category and as historical object in the above formulation of imagination's 'newness' is telling. Distinguished from older analytical notions of cultural practice (in Marxist, Freudian, modernization theories), imagination is not only a new concept (no longer 'fantasy' as false consciousness) but also a new thing (a form of work). While this conflation might be true of all paradigm-shifting efforts, this account obscures the participatory role of scholarly discourse in the making of real things, in this case the objectification of imaginary practices as labour. Instead, the analyst emerges once again as one who is merely finding theoretical adequation for a changed reality that he or she has no role in making. Appadurai argues that imagination's new importance in social life is due to two features of our present day world: electronic mediation and mass migration. Technology and diasporic movements are the privileged forces that have brought about this historical rupture in global conditions. We might say, they are the ultimately determining instance in his theory of historical transformation.

8 Appadurai differentiates his theory of a rupture from older social theories of the ruptures of modernization by recourse to the negative: it is not teleological, not a project of social-engineering, not prognostic and not national (p. 9). Nevertheless, these differences do not seem to me to override some important shared modernist features such as the notion of a radical break and the privileging of technology as historical determinant and signifier of this break.

9 For a discussion of the value-productive activity of spectatorship (as a dominant form of social imagination), see the important work of Jonathan Beller, especially 'Cinema, Capital of the Twentieth Century,' *Postmodern Culture*, Vol. 4, No. 3 (May 1994): 'The Spectatorship of the Proletariat', *boundary* 2, Vol. 22, No. 3 (Fall 1995): 171–228 and 'Numismatics of the Sensual, Calculus of the Image,' *Image [&] Narrative 6: Medium Theory* (2003).

10 They do not only become the new object of economic and political ventures, they also serve as the new object of scholarly inquiry.

11 As Appadurai represents their performance. My own view is that these songs are not performed in the mode of nostalgia. If there is a nostalgic resonance, it issues out of a sensibility of the 'lack' and 'loss' in Filipino

life that the performance of US plenitude and power implies. For an excellent critical exegesis of a contemporary Filipino popular song's parody of this 'lack', see B. Carlo M. Tadiar, '"Picha Pie," Marx and Freud,' *Philippine Daily Inquirer Interactive* (http://www.inquirer.net/issues/aug2000/aug21/lifestyle/entertainment/ent_6.htm)

12   'It is precisely as *value-creating* that living labour is continually being absorbed into the valorization process of objectified labour. In terms of effort, of the expenditure of his life's energy, work is the personal activity of the worker. But as something which *creates value*, as something involved in the process of objectifying labour, the worker's labour becomes one of the *modes of existence* of capital, it is incorporated into capital as soon as it enters the production process.' Karl Marx, *Capital: A Critique of Political Economy, Volume 1* (New York: Vintage Books, 1977), p. 988.

13   It is to obey one of the fundamental axioms of fantasy-production, which posits that, like individual subjects, nations and peoples are their own causes, their lived conditions determined by their own internal constitution. This axiom is closely related to the first of two axioms that Samir Amin argues underwrites the Eurocentric vision of the world: 'The first is that internal factors peculiar to each society are decisive for that comparative evolution. The second is that the Western model of developed capitalism can be generalized to the entire planet.' *Eurocentrism* (New York: Monthly Review Press, 1989), p. 109. For the role of the international media system, see Edward W. Said, *Covering Islam: How the Media and the Experts Determine How We See the Rest of the World* (New York: Vintage Books, 1997). Said argues that the consensus, which US-dominated international media 'feel themselves to be clarifying, crystallizing, forming,' works by setting limits and maintaining pressures rather than by dictating content (pp. 52–3). The global order of dreamwork works similarly. As I argue below, the limits and pressures that it sets appear in the shared language of international political and economic exchange.

14   Marx, *Capital*, p. 988.

15   Many scholars, following the activists, have argued this. See for example, the work of Saskia Sassen, who argues, 'that most global processes materialize in national territories and do so to a considerable extent through national institutional arrangements.' ('Spatialities and Temporalities of the Global: Elements for a Theorization', paper presented at the conference on 'Place, Locality and Globalization', University of California, Santa Cruz, 28 October 2000).

16   Chatterjee's task is to demonstrate the creativity of anti-colonial nationalist imagination before the expression of nationalism in proper political movements and, more, the inhering of these other, subaltern forms of

imagination within universal forms of modern regimes of power. As he writes, this task 'might allow us the possibility not only to think of new forms of the modern community, which, as I argue, the nationalist experience in Asia and Africa has done from its birth, but, much more decisively, to think of new forms of the modern state.' *The Nation and Its Fragments: Colonial and Postcolonial Histories* (Princeton, NJ: Princeton University Press, 1993), p. 13.

17 As Arif Dirlik argues, 'Because Marxism is crucial to any critique of capitalism, no consideration of the future can afford to overlook the critical premises within the theory. Marxism as a guide to the future, however, is another matter entirely from Marxism as critique of capitalism. The Marxist vision of the future has been distorted by its internalization of capitalist spatiality and temporality; thus Marxism, as we have known it, however effective as a critique of capitalism, does not promise a viable or a desirable alternative to the capitalist mode of production.' *After the Revolution: Waking to Global Capitalism* (Hanover and London: Wesleyan University Press, 1994), p. 15.

18 Slavoj Žižek, *The Sublime Object of Ideology* (London and New York: Verso, 1989), p. 33.

19 Revisiting Althusser's invocation of Pascal's 'Act as if you believe, pray, kneel down, and belief will come by itself,' Žižek clarifies the relationship between 'knowing' and 'doing' or conscious belief and practical ritual as a matter of 'an intricate reflective mechanism of retroactive "autopoietic" causality, of how "external" ritual performatively generates its own ideological foundation: kneel down, *and you shall believe that you knelt down because of our belief*—that your kneeling was the effect/expression of your inner belief.' 'Class Struggle or Postmodernism? Yes, please!' in Judith Butler, Ernesto Laclau and Slavoj Žižek, *Contingency, Hegemony, Universality: Contemporary Dialogues on the Left* (London and New York: Verso, 2000), p. 118.

20 Appadurai, p. 7.

21 Žižek, *Sublime Object of Ideology*, p. 34.

22 This is one of the insights of Michel Foucault's *History of Sexuality*, trans. Robert Hurley (New York: Vintage Books, 1980) with regards to psychoanalysis. Psychoanalysis is one of the technologies that constitute the repressed desiring subject.

23 This is also Althusser's position. See his famous essay, 'Ideology and Ideological State Apparatuses' in *Lenin and Philosophy, and Other Essays*, trans. Ben Brewster (New York, Monthly Review Press, 1972).

24 On other scales, such as that of the nation or of the individual subject, this history nevertheless continues. By this I mean that the political, economic, social and subjective structures and technologies of domination

that emerged out of Western imperialism continue to be 'internally' deployed by postcolonial nation-states in relation to their subaltern classes, and by individual postcolonial subjects in relation to their own residual affective and psychical subalternity.

25 See my 'The Dream-Work of Modernity: The Sentimental Education of Imperial France,' *boundary 2*, vol. 22, no. 1 (1995): 143–83.

26 *Fantasy-production* is precisely about production as signification and signification as production. While Marxism has often separated these questions, foregrounding the determinate character of production and, among literary and cultural critics, secondarily linking it to questions of signification, notably through the categories of ideology, aesthetics and politics, Marx himself, most famously in his analysis of commodity-fetishism, critiques their inextricably intertwined operation (money as sign, commodity as representation).

27 My thinking on the inextricable relation between production and signification, and the role of desire as a force coursing through both is also indebted to the work of Gilles Deleuze and Félix Guattari, especially *Anti-Oedipus: Capitalism and Schizophrenia*, trans. Robert Hurley, Mark Seem and Helen R. Lane (Minneapolis, MN: University of Minnesota Press, 1983) and *A Thousand Plateaus*, trans. Brian Massumi (Minneapolis: University of Minnesota Press, 1987).

28 Arturo Escobar, *Encountering Development: The Making and Unmaking of the Third World* (Princeton, NJ: Princeton University Press, 1995), p. 59.

29 In tracing the dominant logics of gender, race and sexuality to histories and cultures of imperialism, I do not wish to imply that these have effectively wiped out local systems of gender, race and sexuality. I merely want to emphasize the cultural power that international political and economic systems exercise, before and beyond the particular contents of what would be conventionally understood as forms of cultural imperialism. Under the sway of international capitalist culture, local gender, race and sexuality practices become subaltern practices. How such subaltern activity persists in the interstices of capitalist social relations is a concern that I am currently addressing in the work that follows this one, entitled *Things Fall Away*.

30 Rey Chow, *Woman and Chinese Modernity: The Politics of Reading Between West and East* (Minneapolis and London: University of Minnesota Press, 1991), p. xiii.

31 Ngugi Wa Thiong'o, *Penpoints, Gunpoints, and Dreams: Towards a Critical Theory of the Arts and the State in Africa* (Oxford: Clarendon Press, 1998), p. 20.

32 Carlos P. Romulo, *My Brother Americans*, excerpted in Liana Romulo and

Marivi Soliven-Blanco, ed. *The Romulo Reader* (Manila: Bookmark, Inc., 1998), p. 48.

33 Excerpted in *The Romulo Reader*, pp. 49–52.

34 Ibid., p. 50.

35 See Amado Guerrero, *Philippine Society and Revolution* (Manila: Pulang Tala Publications, 1971) and Renato Constantino, *A Past Revisited* (Quezon City: Tala Publication Services, 1975).

36 Philippine Congress managed to pass this act only by ousting eleven Democratic Alliance senators and congressmen who opposed its passage. Supported by the HUKBALAHAP, the anti-colonial people's army founded under Japanese occupation, these senators and congressmen were accused of electoral fraud.

37 Nick Cullather, *Illusions of Influence: The Political Economy of United States-Philippines Relations, 1942–1960* (Stanford, CA: Stanford University Press, 1994), p. 37.

38 'Romulo shuttled between New York and Washington, keeping close touch with American officials and speaking with them on various topics: the politics of the United Nations, France's troubles in Indochina, the rehabilitation of Japan. Romulo often reminded the Americans of Filipinos' attachment to "our common ideology." He missed few opportunities to stress the "urgency" of the Philippines' financial situation. But most important, Romulo tracked the blood pressure of [US Secretary of State Dean] Acheson and others in the American administration, and he issued warnings to Manila when apoplexy approached. The accuracy of his analyses was reflect in the fact that for all their fulminations the Americans always stopped short of pulling the plug on aid.' H. W. Brands, *Bound to Empire: The United States and the Philippines* (New York and Oxford: Oxford University Press, 1992), p. 235. Brands' history is in the service of the tenacious argument that 'America's treatment of the Philippines, at least after the suppression of resistance to annexation, was gentle and well received' (p. 353). Hence, it tends to underplay the pernicious, violent side of US involvement in Philippine affairs.

39 The 1949 presidential election that brought Quirino to power was one of the bloodiest and most terroristic in Philippine history. It was during Quirino's regime that the formidable peasant Huk rebellion was crushed (with the crucial help of CIA counter-insurgency intelligence and logistical support) and the US-Philippine Mutual Defense Treaty ratified.

40 Joseph Y. Lim, 'Our Economic Crisis: A Historical Perspective,' in *Synthesis: Before and Beyond February 1986*, ed. Lilia Quindoza Santiago (Quezon City: The Interdisciplinary Forum of the University of the Philippines, 1986).

41 Quoted in 'Salonga: No State of War, No Use of Air Space,' *Philippine Daily Inquirer* (17 September 2002) [http://www.inq7.net/nat/2002/sep/17/nat_3-2.htm]

42 'The Global Situation,' paper presented at the conference on 'Place, Locality and Globalization', University of California, Santa Cruz, 28 October 2000. The features of globalist fantasies which are critically described by Tsing, namely, futurism, geographical and ideological conflations and the valorized focus on circulation, can be seen to be shaped by the assumption of a common field, which Tsing calls attention to in asking, 'what is this thing we call the globe?' In a related vein, Kuan-Hsing Chen has commented on globalization as a structure of feeling. Inter-Asia Cultural Studies Conference 2000, 1–3 December 2000, Kyushu University, Fukuoka, Japan.

43 There is hardly any serious questioning of the 'real time' in which we live. Exceptions include Fatima Mernissi's discussion of the imperialism of secularist, Western time, the universal time standard instituted by the atomic clock. Mernissi suggests that this temporality is the military-secured temporality of global capitalism. For discussions of history as encounters between conflicts of time, see Enrique Dussel, *The Invention of the Americas: Eclipse of "The Other" and the Myth of Modernity*, trans. Michael D. Barber (New York: Continuum, 1995) and Dipesh Chakrabarty, 'The Time of Gods and the Time of History' in *The Politics Of Culture In The Shadow Of Capital*, ed. Lisa Lowe and David Lloyd (Durham, NC: Duke University Press, 1997).

44 Economists have begun to recognize the ways in which their theories help to make the worlds they describe. See Donald MacKenzie, "Fear in the Markets" in *London Review of Books online* [http://www.lrb.co.uk/v22/n08/mack2208.htm] and Michael Perelman, *The Invention Of Capitalism: Classical Political Economy And The Secret History Of Primitive Accumulation* (Durham, NC: Duke University Press, 2000). Perelman describes the agency of classical political economy in the furthering, not merely the explanation, of the development of modern capitalism. This was, of course, already a crucial insight of Marx.

45 See Patricio J. Abinales, *Making Mindanao: Cotabato and Davao in the Formation of the Philippine Nation-State* (Manila: Ateneo de Manila University Press, 2000) for an insightful discussion of the making of the Philippine colonial-state in the periphery as a prehistory of the 'strong' state inhabited by the Marcos regime.

46 See Anthony Giddens, *The Consequences of* Modernity (Stanford, CA: Stanford University Press, 1990). A considerable body of postcolonial work argues that such 'reproductions' are not in fact 'reproductions' but

'alternative' forms of modernity. See, for example, Dilip Parameshwar Gaonkar, ed. *Alternative Modernities* (Durham, NC: Duke University Press, 2001).

47 See Aihwa Ong, *Flexible Citizenship: The Cultural Logics Of Transnationality* (Durham, NC: Duke University Press, 1999).

48 I use 'universal' here in the sense of money as a universal, where a generalized abstraction has reached a level of operational effectivity as to make it a fundamental though invisible (i.e. transparent) 'command-control point' of dominant systemic practices and relations. The software categories and hardware components of fantasy-production are precisely ideologically authoritative and politically and economically forceful bids to 'universality'. We might liken them, respectively, to 'the window-icon-menu-pointer (WIMP) interface of the Mac and Windows, a culturally specific and, in the event, interculturally normative visual vocabulary as powerful as colonial English' and the USB port. Sean Cubitt, *Digital Aesthetics* (London: Sage Publications, 1998), p. 2.

49 Quoted by Judith Butler, 'Restaging the Universal: Hegemony and the Limits of Formalism' in *Contingency, Hegemony, Universality: Contemporary Dialogues on the Left*, ed. Judith Butler, Ernesto Laclau and Slavoj Žižek (London and New York: Verso, 2000) p. 38.

50 Deconstruction has shown the limits of the dialectical mode but at the same time has perhaps given it short shrift, by not recognizing the creativity 'internal' to it. It has also overestimated the power of the agencies of this creativity (or rather, assumed too quickly that their potential was already power, ignoring the very fields of meaning and order which determine what effectively can act powerfully, and therefore *be* power). As a consequence, it has largely been content to point to their presence, and to remain theoretically unswayed by the acting claims of such creative agencies. Moreover, by conveying a generalized subjection, it helps to realize the new religion of fantasy-production through a human predication on the artifices (linguistic, social, epistemological) of its own making. As Wlad Godzich's extolling of the merits of deconstruction makes clear: 'The epistemological ground favored by deconstruction permits the assertion of an equality between all human beings by virtue of their dispossession from the domain of meaning. The insistence on aporia, undecidability, the fact of the dependence of our thought processes upon language and its tropological games, all convey the same sort of human powerlessness that obtained within religious thought, without any of the latter's transcendental dimension.' Wlad Godzich, *The Culture of Literacy* (Cambridge, MA: Harvard University Press, 1994) pp. 243–4. It is this generalization of dispossession and the concomitant

undertheorization of peculiarity (not particularity) that makes the deconstruction of nationhood and of other hegemonic forms of postcoloniality the theoretical supplement of globalist fantasy-production. Or, more accurately, as the endpoint of cultural analysis, the generalization of subjection (advanced by expansionist theories) marks the limits set by fantasy-production, limits beyond which we must go if we want to do something else besides give the new globalist fantasy-production a symbolic adequation of itself (what might have once been called a 'consciousness'). While I recognize that deconstruction, like historical materialism, (whose symbolic technologies I draw heavily upon) still crucially enables political action and social concern, I am also arguing that these theories need to connect, through the mediating involvement on the part of cultural analyses, to the wayward theoretical claims performed in people's actions as well as articulated by intellectuals becoming-people. See Walter Mignolo's related argument about the imperative to act on colonial difference in 'Dussel's Philosophy of Liberation: Ethics and the Geopolitcs of Knowledge' in *Thinking From The Underside of History*, ed. Linda Martín Alcoff and Eduardo Mendieta (Maryland: Rowman and Littlefield Publishers, Inc., 2000). As interpreters, we must go closer to the creation of meaning (rather than remain its discoverers), if we are to participate in the breaking of new paths taking place all around us. I elaborate on this point in the conclusion.

51   As Michael Hardt and Antonio Negri write, in their critique of Satrean cultural politics: 'The power of the dialectic, which in the hands of colonial power mystified the reality of the colonial world, is adopted again as part of an anticolonial project as if the dialectic were itself the real form of the movement of history. Reality and history, however, are not dialectical, and no idealist rhetorical gymnastics can make them conform to the dialect.' *Empire* (Cambridge, MA: Harvard University Press, 2000), p. 131.

PART I

1   There is, I believe, a Latin American (probably Mexican) version of this joke. The origin is less important than what it illuminates in its dissemination.

2   Inasmuch as he is perceived to have been portrayed as a pacifist and a reformist desiring integration into the West, in contrast to Andres Bonifacio who has been generally portrayed as a revolutionary who called for an armed separatist struggle (see Chapter 4). Nevertheless, Rizal is generally credited with ideologically spearheading the revolutionary

struggle against Spanish colonialism, and therefore acknowledged to have been central in the making of Philippine nationhood.

3   The gender indexes a particular social moment in the struggle against US imperialism. As I will show in the chapters that follow, gender both shapes and is produced out of the libidinal political economy of international relations.

4   Lauren Berlant, *The Queen of America Goes to Washington City: Essays on Sex and Citizenship* (Durham & London: Duke University Press, 1997), p. 4.

5   It is not of course the only colonial territory that has served in this capacity. Which is why the joke is told from other places as well (other former Spanish colonies incorporated into the US empire).

6   Kuan-Hsing Chen, 'America in East Asia: The Club 51 Syndrome,' *New Left Review* 12 (November–December 2001): 73–87, pp. 85–6.

7   Arturo Escobar, *Encountering Development: The Making and Unmaking of the Third World* (Princeton, NJ: Princeton University Press, 1995).

8   This vision was articulated in Truman's 1949 doctrine of a 'fair deal' for the whole world. As Escobar describes it, the intent was 'to bring about the conditions necessary to replicating the world over the features that characterized the "advanced" societies of the time — high levels of industrialization and urbanization, technicalization of agriculture, rapid growth of material production and living standards, and the widespread adoption of modern education and cultural values. In Truman's vision, capital, science, and technology were the main ingredients that would make this massive revolution possible ... This dream was not solely the creation of the United States but the result of the specific historical conjuncture at the end of the Second World War. Within a few years, the dream was universally embraced by those in power.' Escobar, *Encountering Development*, pp. 3–4. The historical blind spot of this universal dream is contained in the very object of its desiring-action: the Third World. For all those features of 'advanced' societies that were to be extended to the rest of the planet were themselves the historical product of colonialism and imperialism.

9   Anne McClintock, *Imperial Leather: Race, Gender, and Sexuality in the Colonial Contest* (New York and London: Routledge, 1995), p. 23.

10 For a full discussion of these dynamics, see my 'The Dreamwork of Modernity: The Sentimental Education of Imperial France,' *boundary 2* vol. 22, no. 1 (1995): 143–83.

11 There has been a considerable amount of scholarship on the ideological confluences between nationalisms and sexualities, much following on the heels of Benedict Anderson's underscoring of the analogical relations

between nationhood and gender. See Andrew Parker, et al. *Nationalisms and Sexualities* (New York: Routledge, 1992); Rey Chow, *Woman and Chinese Modernity: The Politics Of Reading Between West And East* (Minneapolis, MN: University of Minnesota Press, 1991) and the critiques of nationalist narratives in third world feminist anthologies such as M. Jacqui Alexander and Chandra Talpade Mohanty, ed. *Feminist Genealogies, Colonial Legacies, Democratic Futures* (New York: Routledge, 1997), Inderpal Grewal and Caren Kaplan, ed. *Scattered Hegemonies: Postmodernity and Transnational Feminist Practice* (Minneapolis, MN: University of Minnesota Press, 1994) and Caren Kaplan, Norma Alarcón, and Minoo Moallem, eds. *Between Woman And Nation: Nationalisms, Transnational Feminisms, And The State* (Durham, N.C.: Duke University Press, 1999).

12   This is supported by the argument of international feminists that the international division of labour in the New World Order depends on at the same time that it promotes a sexual division of labour. Maria Mies, *Patriarchy and Accumulation on a World Scale: Women in the International Division of Labour* (London: Zed Books, 1986).

CHAPTER 1

1   Samir Amin argues that the Gulf War inaugurated a new historical era, proving that the new world order would be imposed on all peoples of the global South and that US military superiority trumped not only the military credibility of the former Soviet Union but also the economic and financial power of Europe and Japan. 'In this sense, the Gulf War was a world war — the North, commanded by the United States (subordinating Europe and Japan), against the South — played out regionally.' 'US Militarism in the New World Order,' *Polygraph*, no. 5 (1992): 13–37, p. 14.

2   As I explain in the introduction, the concept of fantasy which I employ here derives from Slavoj Žižek for whom a fantasy-construction 'serves as a support for our "reality" itself: an "illusion" which is structuring our effective, real social relations and which is masking thereby some insupportable, real, impossible kernel' ('The Real in Ideology,' *PsychCritique* 2: 3 (1987): 265). In the global fantasy, that impossible kernel would be the third world, that is, the non-industrialized, residually feudal, pre- or anti-capitalist sectors of the world.

3   The possibility of grasping the actions of nations as citizens or international subjects is founded precisely on the historical colonization and decolonization of the world. The entire debate on imperialism since

the turn of the century might be seen to turn on the issue of world citizenship, that is, whether the colonial peoples were fit for self-government and thus inclusion in the world community of nations. As global divisions in the New World Order show, however, inclusion did not in any case mean equality with imperial nations. The divisions of the world into First, Second, Third, also signify a hierarchy among nations in the eyes of the Free World. There is no room for me here to elaborate on the historical process of oedipalization of nations, that is, in the creation of nations as modern subjects. But the strong identification peoples have with their nation and the state actions and popular movements that are predicated upon this identification should point to a shared process of identity-formation for individuals and nations as subjects in the modern world. Hence there is more than metaphorical truth in the observation not only that nations act like men and women, but also that men and women act like nations. Inasmuch as sexuality is a central axis of subject-identities, nations are configured sexually. Sexuality is endemic, however, not only to the individual modern subject, but to the modes of production which have produced him (the modern subject is configured as masculine) as such, other individuals who do not quite qualify as modern subjects (women, colonials, ethnic and sexual minorities, the masses), as well as all modern nations, and countries that do not qualify as international subjects. These modes of production of modern identities to which sexuality is endemic include patriarchy, colonialism, orientalism, imperialism and global capitalism.

4   'The New Asia-Pacific Era: A Perspective from an International Nation Building for the 21st Century,' *Britannica Book of the Year 1986* (Chicago: Encyclopedia Britannica, 1986), p. 14.

5   Senator Alfred J. Beveridge, 'Our Philippine Policy' in *The Philippines Reader*, ed. Daniel B. Schirmer and Stephen Rosskamm Shalom (Boston: South End Press, 1987), p. 24.

6   Purificacion Valera-Quisumbing, 'Towards an Asia- "Pacific Community": Varying Perceptions,' in *The Pacific Lake*, ed. Jose P. Leviste, Jr. (Manila: The Philippine Council for Foreign Relations, 1986), p. 81. Abrino Aydinan also asserts this US-Japanese parentage of the Pacific idea: 'The idea of organizing the nations lying along the basin or rim of the Pacific is a Japanese and American notion which has been embraced by the Association of Southeast Asian Nations (ASEAN), with the United States and Japan only too willing to yield the cares of paternity' ('Doubts Plague Pacific Basin Organization' in *The Pacific Lake*, p. 119). It is interesting to note that this expression of lineage or history is one used in the discourse of law (Quisumbing is a law professor) as well as in the

discourse of business (Aydinan is a writer for a business-economics review).

7   Edgardo B. Maranan, 'Peace, Development and Solidarity Through Initiatives from Below,' *Diliman Review* 37, 4 (1989): 21.

8   Philippine Government, '*New York Times* Advertisement' in Schirmer and Shalom, eds. *The Philippines Reader*, pp. 227–9.

9   Nelson Navarro, 'Accidental Saints of Filipino Nationalism,' *Malaya* (13 May 1990). The fantasy is one maintained by Americans as well. George Bush's ludicrous toast to Marcos after the latter effected his re-election in 1981 ('We love you, sir') attests to this. The US Government's support of the popular ousting of Marcos five years later also attests to the inconstancy of that love.

10   Schirmer and Shalom, *The Philippines Reader*, pp. 23–6.

11   Quoted by Epifanio San Juan, Jr., *Crisis in the Philippines* (Massachusetts: Bergin & Garvey Publishers, Inc., 1986), 18.

12   Luz del Mundo, 'Disadvantages of a Pacific Community,' in *The Pacific Lake*, p. 116.

13   Aida Fulleros Santos and Lynn F. Lee, *The Debt Crisis: A Treadmill of Poverty for Filipino Women* (Manila: Kalayaan, 1989), p. 16.

14   Ibid.

15   'Hospitality girl' and 'hostess' were euphemisms for sex workers. They were later replaced by 'GRO' or 'Guest Relations Officer'.

16   Lolita, quoted by Joseph Collins, *The Philippines: Fire on the Rim* (San Francisco: The Institute for Food and Development Policy, 1989), p. 271. This was her response to the question of whether she wanted to marry an American, which was posed to her during a discussion of her illegitimate child whose father is American. Two significant things come out of this contextualization: first, the option of marriage is a question posed to Lolita by an American, that is, the form of her desire is predetermined by a dominant logic; second, the wish expresses the need for legitimation and financial support, both of which mean the same thing and are the result of a pre-existent relation. In other words, the desire to marry is the consequence of already 'being fucked'.

17   Emmanuel S. de Dios, 'The Philippine Economy: A Conspectus of Recent Developments' in *Diliman Review*, 37, 2 (1989): 5.

18   Raffy Rey Hipolito, 'Japanese Economic Power, Philippine Setting,' *Diliman Review*, 37, 3 (1989): 23.

19   This possibility is one that Aydinan (*The Pacific Lake*, p. 121) sees as necessary if Japan is to serve as a model for other Asian countries.

20   This successful defense has, however, roused Japan's international partners to action, into forcing her open: 'The yearly trade surpluses of Japan with

the US and European Economic Community members have angered the latter. Japan has been subjected to strong-arm tactics by her Western allies to open her economy' (Hipolito, 'Japanese Economic Power', p. 22). The leverage that the US and the EEC. have, of course, is the 'international community', a global super-ego over which they exercise dominant control through ownership of greater symbolic shares. As an American political economist asserted: 'If there is one country that is criticized for not playing by these emerging global rules, it is Japan. But the logic of the global web is so powerful that the Japanese will either be forced to comply over time or else face a stiff penalty from the marketplace, the talent pool, and competitors and governments' (Robert B. Reich, 'Who is Them?' *Harvard Business Review* [March-April 1991]: 81).

21 Leviste, Jr., *The Pacific Lake*, p. 19.

22 Emmanuel S. de Dios, 'The Philippine Economy', p. 5.

23 Hence the regular deployment of the specter of sodomy in the management of US foreign relations. For a trenchant and illuminating analysis of US national fantasies, see Lauren Berlant, *The Queen of America Goes to Washington City: Essays on Sex and Citizenship* (Durham and London: Duke University Press, 1997). In this regard, the 'rape' of Kuwait that served as a pretext for the Gulf War was not only a depiction of that nation as a female body but also an emasculated, sodomized male body. The imagined punishment for this infraction unsurprisingly takes the same form as the offense. Thus, 'In a gesture both homophobic and misogynist, US bombardiers obliged by inscribing the message "Bend Over, Saddam" on the ordinance they dropped on Iraq.' 'Introduction' in *Nationalisms and Sexualities*, ed. Andrew Parker, Mary Russo, Doris Sommer and Patricia Yaeger (New York and London: Routledge, 1992), p. 6.

24 As Walker, the central character in Gillo Pontecorvo's film, *Burn* (1969) [Italy], who argues for and effects the transformation of the fictional colony Quemada into a neocolony (that is, the transformation of a slave-labour economy into a wage-labour economy), asks its colonizers, 'Gentlemen, which would you rather have? A wife whom you must clothe and feed even when she is no longer of any use to you? Or a whore who you need only pay for so long as she pleases you?'

25 Liza Maza, 'Equity in the Philippines: Development Strategies and the Impact on Philippine Women,' *Gabriela Women's Update* 7, 3 (July-September 1990): 15.

26 Santos and Lee, *The Debt Crisis: A Treadmill of Poverty for Filipino Women*, p. 36.

27 In the 1970s, about 200,000 Japanese visited the Philippines annually, 90% of whom were male. (*Japan Christian Activity News*, [29 August 1980])

28   A. Lin Neumann, 'Tourism Promotion and Prostitution' in Schirmer and Shalom, *The Philippines Reader*, p. 182.

29   Walden Bello, David Kinley and Elaine Elinson, *Development Debacle: The World Bank in the Philippines* (San Francisco: Institute for Food and Development Policy, 1982), pp. 13–39. The authors argue that the World Bank emerged as a central influence in Philippine affairs as a consequence of an economic and political crisis. 'In the late 1960s and early 1970s, Philippine society underwent a fundamental crisis. In its economic dimension, the crisis was precipitated by the intersection of three developments: the failure of the strategy of import substitution as a path to sustained industrialization, the increasing inability of agriculture to meet the country's basic food needs, and the growing pressure from foreign capital to "open up" the economy more completely.' Added to this was a growing class and national consciousness, the breakdown of patronage politics and the intensified competition within the oligarchy for political power. With the declaration of Martial Law and the blessing of US business whose interests the World Bank represented, Marcos reconsolidated his position and centralized power, commandeering the state for the desires of capital.

30   Ibid., p. 198.

31   Ibid., p. 28.

32   Quoted in Ibid., p. 14.

33   Quoted by Paul A. Gigot, 'Manila's Economic Revolutionary,' in Schirmer and Shalom, *The Philippines Reader*, p. 375.

34   'Under Marcos, promotion of tourism resulted in Manila's competing with Bangkok for the title of "International Sex City"; Manila's reputation has become well-known, particularly to the Japanese' (Yayori Matsui, *Women's Asia* [London: Zed Books, 1987], p. 70).

35   This division of the land into prostitution colonies also occurs with beach resorts, a 'domestic' practice that might be traced to the libidinal-economic practice of keeping mistresses' salons in late nineteenth century Europe. In the Philippines, these brothels, and other owned land and businesses, are generally acquired by expatriate men marrying a Filipino wife or adopting a Filipino child under whose name the property is registered.

36   Karina David, quoted by A. Lin Neumann in Schirmer and Shalom, *The Philippines Reader*, p. 185.

37   'In the Philippines, Chile, and Uruguay — all countries renowned for long-standing democratic traditions — there emerged from the wreckage the same formula pioneered by the Brazilian junta in the late 60s: a military or presidential-military dictatorship "sanitizing" the social situation with massive repression, justifying its existence with the ideology of controlled

modernization with the indispensable participation of foreign capital, and resting on a social coalition of technocrats, officers, local bureaucrat-capitalists, and foreign investors' (Bello et al., *Development Debacle*, pp. 35–6).

38   Vicente L. Rafael, 'Nationalism, Imagery, and the Filipino Intelligentsia in the Nineteenth Century,' *Critical Inquiry* (Spring 1990), p. 602.

39   Schirmer and Shalom, *The Philippines Reader*, p. 453.

40   Philip Shenon, 'How Subic Bay Became a Rallying Cry for Philippine Nationalism,' *The New York Times* (15 September 1991), p. 2.

41   Santos and Lee, *The Debt Crisis*, p. 23.

42   Sr. Mary Soledad Perpiñan, 'Philippine Women and Transnational Corporations,' in Schirmer and Shalom, *The Philippines Reader*, p. 239.

43   Many of these men find employment and the opportunity to regain lost masculinity in the army or vigilante groups, both run rampant over the countryside. Extreme militarization is evidenced by the creation of the Citizens Armed Forces Geographical Units in 1987 by the executive order of President Aquino and other vigilante groups (Arnel de Guzman and Tito Craige, 'Counterinsurgency War in the Philippines and the Role of the United States,' *Bulletin of Concerned Asian Scholars*, 23, 2 [1991]: 41). The Armed Forces of the Philippines plans to have 80,000 'combat-ready forces' in the CAFGUs when the master plan is fulfilled. The human rights abuses (including torture, mutilation and cannibalism) of the 600 vigilante groups that exist at the present are well documented. Given that the insurgency movement is also growing steadily, absorbing the dispossessed, the unemployed and the abused — all refugees of the state of political and economic war being waged to motor international capital — the military is a secure occupation. The regional community proposed by the Asia-Pacific can only exist in its present form through the maintenance of this war. That 'the United States provides 83 percent of the procurement, operations and maintenance budget (excluding salaries) of the Philippine military' (p. 46) attests to its interests in this community.

44   The figure of the 'prostitute' is in a continuum with the figure of the 'housewife'. See Colette Guillaumin and Maria Mies.

45   M. Dueñas, 'Filipina as Japayuki-San,' *Philippines Free Press* (4 April 1987), p. 40.

46   '"Mopping up excess liquidity" was the term Central Bank (CB) Governor Jobo Fernandez, currently the CB head and former Marcos government official, used to justify an increase in domestic rates, which made credit hard to come by. Small companies and factories with little capital had to close down and hundreds of workers were laid off. By IMF standards, but with extreme hardship for the people, the "mopping up" resulted in

improved financial capacity so the Philippine government could better service its foreign debt obligations' (Santos and Lee, *The Debt Crisis*, p. 9). The analogy is accurate inasmuch as the export of women is directly tied to the debt-servicing policy of the government — not only as an outcome but also as a necessary function of this policy. Not only does the policy result in inadequate funding for local income-generating activities which forces the women's seeking employment abroad, but also, the earnings abroad which they remit are used for debt payments. (p. 40)

47 This qualification is important when we consider the phenomenon of forced child-prostitution, which manifests that feminization, cuts across biological and age differences and depends primarily on the bodily tractability and economic dependence of the feminized subject.

48 Yayori Matsui, *Women's Asia*, p. 52

49 'Asian Migrant Women Working at Sex Industry in Japan Victimized by International Trafficking', *In God's Image* (June 1990): 6.

50 Mainichi Shimbun, quoted in *Philippines Free Press* (4 April 1987), p. 15.

51 The economic and ideological contradictions of the harmonious Asia-Pacific community become most visible in the fate of the third world, an appellation that increasingly refers to peoples marked by poverty, infantilization and feminization, in other words, in the fate of the poorest of the global poor, notably indigent, non-white women and children. The feminization and infantilization is unambiguous and intensified in the case of third world Asian nations because of the combination of two independently feminized units, that is, Third World and Asia.

52 Quoted in Edward Said, *Orientalism* (New York: Vintage Books, 1979), p. 187. Flaubert was one of the more notable writers who contributed to the simultaneous idealization and debasement of prostitution in nineteenth century France. I discuss elsewhere the relation between this representation and the role of France in the age of imperialism. Suffice to say that prostitution as a mode of discourse of international relations was already evident in France at the time because of the latter's particular 'sentimental relations' with the colonies until then — relations defined more by capital investments rather than by physical and military presence.

53 Quoted in Bello et al., *Development Debacle*, p. 153.

54 Marlyn, quoted by Brenda Stoltzfus, 'The Sale of Sexual Labor in the Philippines: Marlyn's Story,' *Bulletin of Concerned Asian Scholars*, 22, 4 (1990): 19.

55 Matsui, 'Asian Migrant Women', p. 8. Compare this with another assessment: 'Filipinos, mostly women, accounted for about 70 per cent of all offenses committed by Asians in Japan in 1985, followed by Thais, 20 per cent, and Koreans, 9 per cent, a dubious distinction consistently

maintained by Filipinos since 1982 — a phenomenon which a top official of the Japanese immigration office perceived as an indication of the depressed Philippine economic condition' (Tono Haruhi, quoted in *Philippines Free Press*, p. 15).

56   In the next chapter I analyse the racialized predicates and racializing consequences of these national ideologies.

57   Matsui, 'Asian Migrant Women,' p. 12 and Tono Haruhi of AMPO Japan-Asia Quarterly Review (Vol. 18, No. 2–3), quoted in Schirmer and Shalom, *The Philippines Reader*, p. 15.

58   M. Dueñas, 'Filipina as Japayuki-San', p. 42.

59   V. G. Kiernan, *The Lords of Human Kind: Black Man, Yellow Man and White Man in an Age of Empire* (New York: Columbia University Press, 1986), p. 182. In other words, Japan had to show it was man enough to be treated like an imperial nation. Again, this is a 'Western' interpretation of Japanese actions, which can only cover over the complex, and most likely contradictory, meanings such actions held for the Japanese.

60   Matsui, 'Asian Migrant Women,' p. 9.

61   Compare this with the perception of Filipinos as bearing diseases. It is not merely coincidental that AIDS has been represented as having spread in the Philippines mainly through the US bases. The 'tainted' relation between the Philippines and the United States only legitimates and aggravates the system of exploitation that Japan engages in. This is achieved, however, not only through representation but actual practice. For Japan's mode of relation with the Philippines is built upon or made possible through the system of exploitation that the United States had already established in its 'special relations' with the Philippines.

62   Quoted in 'Debt Crisis Burden Heaviest on Children,' *Daily Globe* (30 December 1989).

63   Ibid.

64   Maranan, 'Peace, Development and Solidarity', p. 4. Needless to say, ASEAN has failed to heed such advocates, intent as it is on supporting APEC.

65   For the first scholarly discussion of the Asia Pacific as an ideological invention, see Arif Dirlik, 'The Asia-Pacific Idea: Reality and Representation in the Invention of a Regional Structure,' *Journal of World History* 3 (Spring 1992): 55–79. See also Dirlik's *What's In A Rim? Critical Perspectives on the Pacific Region Idea*, 2nd Edition (Lanham, Maryland: Rowman and Littlefield Publishers, Inc., 1998), in which Dirlik's article as well as the first part of my chapter appear. For a discussion of the historical and ideological genealogy of the Pacific Rim idea, see Christopher L. Connery, 'Pacific Rim Discourse: The US Global Imaginary

in the Late Cold War Years' in *Asia/Pacific as Space of Cultural Production* (Durham and London: Duke University Press, 1995): 30–56. Connery argues that the idea of the Pacific Rim emerged in the mid-1970s and remained dominant in the US geo-imaginary until the late 1980s, at the onset of the New World Order.

66 See 'Introduction' in *Globalization: Displacement, Commodification and Modern-Day Slavery of Women* (Proceedings of the Workshop on Women and Globalization, People's Conference Against Imperialist Globalization, 23 November 1996, Quezon City, Philippines).

67 Epictetus E. Patalinghug, 'The Philippines in a Global Economy: Competition Policy and APEC' in *Coming to Grips with Globalization*, ed. Cayetano Paderanga, Jr. (Quezon City: University of the Philippines, 2000), p. 227; and 'Introduction' in *Globalization: Displacement, Commodification and Modern-Day Slavery of Women*

68 Epeli Hau'ofa, 'Our Sea of Islands' in *A New Oceania: Rediscovering Our Sea of Islands*, ed. E. Waddell, V. Naidu and E. Hau'ofa (Suva, Fiji: School of Social and Economic Development of the University of the South Pacific, 1993): 2–16.

69 Hau'ofa, 'Our Sea of Islands,' p. 97.

70 Of the current rewriting of nationalist histories into oceanic ones, Connery warns, 'perhaps there is a danger in working within the dominant conceptual category of the ocean, given that it is capital's favored myth-element'. Instead, he proposes, 'let resistance write its own geography'. Connery, p. 56.

71 The joint military 'exercises' between US and Filipino forces, called 'Operation Balikatan 2002', was portrayed as the 'second front' in the global war on terrorism, after the war on Afghanistan. Gary Leupp, 'The Philippines: "Second Front" in the US's Global War,' *Counterpunch* (21 February 2002). US military forces have withdrawn once again after six months of 'training' and the botched Philippine rescue of US hostages held by the Abu Sayaaf, the paramilitary criminal group purportedly linked to the Al Qaeda network. They are, however, expected to return for another round of training exercises in October of this year (2002).

72 In 1995 and 1998, the US Department of Defense issued 'Security Strategy Report for the Asia-Pacific Region,' which states the need to maintain a 'credible power projection' within the region through the deployment of 100,000 US troops. Another Pentagon planning document, 'Joint Vision 2020', designates Asia as the key focus of US military strategy in the early twenty-first century. In 2000, there were 37,000 US military personnel in Korea and some 63,000 in Japan. Including troops based in Guam, Hawaii and other islands in the Pacific, there are up to 300,000 US troops in the

region. 'US Military Power in the Asia-Pacific' in *Ang Bayan* (January-February 2002), p. 15 and Gwyn Kirk, Rachel Cornwell and Margo Okazawa-Rey, 'Women and the US Military in East Asia,' *In Focus* 4, no. 9 (July 2000): 1–4.

73   Ruth Gilmore tracks the demise of US military Keynesianism and its succession by a US militarist state built on prisons as shaped by the growth of national and international resistance movements and liberation struggles. 'The more that militant anti-capitalism and international solidarity became everyday features of US anti-racist activism, the more vehemently the state and its avatars responded by, as Allen Feldman puts it, "individualizing disorder" into singular instances of criminality, that could then be solved via arrest or state-sanctioned killings rather than fundamental social change.' Ruth Wilson Gilmore, 'Globalisation and US Prison Growth: From Military Keynesianism to Post-Keynesian Militarism,' *Race and Class* 40, 2/3 (1998/99): 171–88.

74   Peter Schwartz argues that it is the US attempts to counteract the challenge posed by the European union, paradigmatically represented by the introduction of the euro as a serious rival of the dollar, by means of its military superiority that serves as 'the underlying logic of the repeated eruptions of American militarism over the last 10 years, which have found their momentary climax in the present war in Afghanistan'. 'Europe on Rations: The Afghan War and the Dilemma of European Capitalism,' *World Socialist Web Site*, 19 March 2002. (http://www.wsws.org/articles/2002/mar2002/lect-m19_prn.shtml). Of the new economic complex of military and security firms that the business press has labeled the 'Fear Economy', Mike Davis writes: 'The current globalization of fear will accelerate the high-tech dispersal of centralized organizations, including banks, securities firms, government offices, and telecommunications centres, into regional multi-site networks. Terror, in effect, has become the business partner of technology providers like Sun Microsystems and Cisco Systems, who have long argued that distributed processing (sprawling PC networks) mandates a "distributed workplace".' 'The Flames of New York,' *New Left Review* 12 (November-December 2001): 44.

75   Rosalind P. Petchesky, 'Phantom Towers: Feminist Reflections on the Battle Between Global Capitalism and Fundamentalist Terrorism,' Presentation at Hunter College Political Science Department Teach-In (25 September 2001).

76   Val Moghadam, 'The Neopatriarchal State in the Middle East: Development, Authoritarianism and Crisis' in *The Gulf War and the New World Order*, ed. Haim Bresheeth and Nira Yuval-Davis (London and New Jersey: Zed Books Ltd., 1991): 199–207. Arundhati Roy, 'The Algebra of

Infinite Justice,' *The Guardian* (29 September 2001) [http://www. guardian.co.uk/Saturday-review/story/0,3605,559756,00.html]. For feminist critiques of Eurocentric representations of 'traditional' fundamentalist patriarchy in the Middle East and the collusions between Arab 'tradition' and Western, capitalist 'modernity' in the contemporary shaping of gender relations in Middle East societies, see Lila Abu-Lughod, ed. *Remaking Women: Feminism and Modernity in the Middle East* (Princeton, New Jersey: Princeton University Press, 1998).

77   Gavan McCormack, 'Breaking the Iron Triangle,' *New Left Review* 13 (January-February 2002): 5.

78   Compare with de Dios, 'The Philippine Economy', p. 22.

79   Judith Butler, *Gender Trouble: Feminism and the Subversion of Identity* (New York: Routledge, 1990).

80   'US-Asian Treaty Targets Terrorism,' *San Jose Mercury News* (2 August 2002). The US provided $50M in aid to Indonesia and another $55M to the Philippines (in addition to the $100M already allocated soon after the proclamation of the war on terror.

81   At a news conference in the Philippines, after meeting with the Philippine President, US Secretary of State Colin Powell proclaimed 'we have to work with our friends and allies, we have to connect our intelligence systems, connect our law enforcement systems …' 'Powell: Asia Increasingly Aids War On Terror,' *San Jose Mercury News* (4 August 2002).

82   'It was a good break after all this talk on terrorism,' said Syed Hamid Albar. 'Powell's Serenade: Secretary of State Finds His Voice,' *San Jose Mercury News* (2 August 2002). While the US is providing financial aid to these Southeast Asian nations, the latter are seen as 'aiding' the war on terror by means of local intelligence and law enforcement systems and local military forces. This exchange of 'aid' is what is meant by 'mutual commitments'. 'Powell: Asia Increasingly Aids War On Terror,' *San Jose Mercury News* (4 August 2002).

83   This masculine emergence within the US cultural imaginary can be traced in the spate of new orientalist literature and film from the 1970s to 1980s, the generic ideological features of which Christopher Connery keenly describes. Connery, 'Pacific Rim Discourse,' in *Asia-Pacific Cultural Production.* As Connery depicts, from James Clavell's novel *Shogun* (1975) to Ridley Scott's movie *Black Rain* (1989), Japan is transformed from feminized setting for the new American male *bildungsroman* (a prize location for re-humanizing in the wake of domestic and international challenges to American masculinity) to a complementary 'partner' of the American cop figure, each contributing to the other's moral and psychic regeneration as the new masculine heroes for the changed times.

84 Donna J. Haraway, *Modest_Witness@Second_Millenium.FemaleMan ©_Meets_OncoMouse™: Feminism and Technoscience* (New York and London: Routledge, 1997), p. 11.

85 Quoted in Filomeno S. Sta. Ana III, 'So Much, But So Little to Go Around: The State of the Philippine Economy,' *Human Rights Forum* 7, 2 (January-June 1998): 51.

86 Raul V. Fabella, 'East Asia Will Again Lead the Charge. Can the Philippines Keep Apace?' and Emmanuel C. Lallana, 'Philippine Foreign Policy at the Century's Turn' in *Philippines Yearbook 2000*.

87 Emmanuel S. de Dios, 'Between Nationalism and Globalization' in *The State and the Market: Essays on a Socially Oriented Philippine Economy*, ed. Filomeno S. Sta. Ana III (Manila: Action for Economic Reforms, 1998).

88 Liza Largoza Maza, 'Strategies of the Women's Movement in Fighting Imperialist Globalization' in *Issues, Challenges and Strategies: Selected Speeches and Articles on Globalization* (Quezon City: GABRIELA, A National Alliance of Women's Organizations, 1999), p. 10.

CHAPTER 2

1 This mode of orientation is necessitated by the widespread practice of locating through contiguity (with concrete landmarks) rather than through transcendent vectors and abstract signs. In Manila, generally unused street signs are often obscured or absent. Also, large monuments and landmark buildings built by the US colonial 'developers' lose visual prominence as one becomes buried in the density of one's surroundings. In any case, all Manila's major centers of activity (government, commercial, residential) have nomadically changed locations periodically while many historic structures have either deteriorated beyond recognition or have been completely destroyed by natural and human forces so that attempts to represent the city with any single monument invariably fail. A greater collective signifier might be the experience of moving through the thickness of the city, through its crowds and traffic, its dirt and pollution, and its relentless assault on one's senses.

2 F. S. Cruz, the company contracted to build the flyovers was the same company in charge of Imelda Marcos' project of reclaiming land from Manila Bay mainly for the purpose of erecting international cultural centers.

3 Neil Smith, *Uneven Development* (Oxford: Blackwell, 1984), p. 77.

4 Anthony D. King, *Urbanism, Colonialism and the World-Economy: Cultural and Spatial Foundations of the World Urban System* (London: Routledge, 1990), p. 1.

5   Ma. Isabel Ongpin, 'Traffic, Traffic, Traffic,' *Manila Chronicle*, 17 June 1993, p. 5.

6   Arturo Escobar shows how the 'imaginary of development' through which planners and economists in the Third World have inscribed and produced their reality has been subjected to numerous critiques: 'Development has been the primary mechanism through which these parts of the world have been produced and have produced themselves, thus marginalizing or precluding other ways of seeing and doing' ('Imagining a Post-Development Era? Critical Thought, Development and Social Movements,' *Social Text* 10, 2–3 (1992): 22). Many such critiques, however, focus on 'the ways in which the Third World is constituted in and through representation. Third World reality is inscribed with precision and persistence by the discourses and practices of economists, planners, nutritionists, demographers, and the like, making it difficult for people to define their own interests in their own terms — in many cases actually disabling them to do so' (p. 25). Aside from ignoring the incredible scale of systematic violence used to underwrite these 'discourses and practices', such critiques also ignore the efforts and activities of 'the masses', that is, the nationally marginalized, in shaping or influencing the policy actions of the 'people', that is, the global representatives of the nation-state.

7   Manual A. Caoili, 'Metropolitan Manila Reorganization,' *Philippine Journal of Public Administration* 29, 1 (1985): 8.

8   Manila: National Planning Commission, 1954, pp. 638–40.

9   Aprodicio Laquian, 'Manila,' in *Great Cities of the World: Their Government, Politics, and Planning*, ed. William A. Robson and D. E. Regan, vol. 2 (London: Allen & Unwin, 1954), p. 644.

10 Jurgen Ruland, 'Metropolitan Government Under Martial Law: The Metro Manila Commission Experiment,' *Philippine Journal of Public Administration* 29, 1 (1985): 28.

11   Ruland, 'Metropolitan Government under Martial Law,' p. 30.

12 John F. Doherty, *The Philippine Urban Poor* (Honolulu: Philippine Studies Program, Center for Asian and Pacific Studies, University of Hawaii, 1985), p. 25.

13 Doherty gives a comprehensive account of the systematic oppression of squatters in spite of Imelda's avowed concern for the urban poor, and the numerous projects intended to benefit them. The meaning of this exclusion, of course, is that the poor are not members of the race of 'Man'. The gendered humanity for which Manila is built aligns the urban poor with a femininity that must be contained in order that the metropolitan body can be enjoyed by those to whom it belongs.

14 Ricardo G. Abad, 'Squatting and Scavenging in Smokey Mountain,' *Philippine Studies* 39, 3 (1991): 284.

15 The Ramos' administration's obsession with reaching NIC (newly industrialized countries) status is clear evidence of this identification.

16 This is in no way to characterize Manila, a city of what used to be known as the Third World, as postmodern. Rather, because the particularity and significance of Manila as a socio-historic-economic formation threatens to disappear in the face of Third World cities discursively realized as such in First World nations (such as L.A. — the quintessential postmodern, third world *and* global city), it is all the more important to show that such categories and their discursive power, the desires upon which they are predicated as well as their material hardware, are reproduced rather than found in places like Manila. To argue this differentiation is important not only to engage the specificity of Manila but also to show that this specificity reveals a certain aporia in First World theories (that is present especially when these attempt to analyze the internal third world as a way of understanding global phenomena), an aporia that stands in for conditions endemic but invisible to late capital societies.

17 Smith, *Uneven Development*, p. xiii.

18 Michael Sorkin, 'Introduction: Variations of a Theme Park' in *Variations of a Theme Park*, ed. Michael Sorkin (New York: Noonday, 1992), p. xi.

19 Sorkin, 'Introduction,' p. xiii.

20 Daniela Daniele, 'Mapless Cities: Urban Displacement and Failed Encounters in Surrealist and Postmodern Narratives', Ph.D. diss. (New York University, 1992), p. 133.

21 Alfredo F. Lim, 'A Vision for Manila,' *Panorama*, 20 June 1993, p. 5.

22 Smith, *Uneven Development*, p. xi.

23 See Richard P. Appelbaum and Gary Gereffi, 'Power and Profits in the Apparel Commodity Chain,' manuscript.

24 A. R. Samson, 'Traffic and the Economy,' *Manila Chronicle*, 23 February 1993, p. 5.

25 Ibid.

26 As Jonathan L. Beller writes: 'transnational industry attempts to narrow the people's choices until democracy means acquiescence to the world-economic system, that is, until it means nothing at all' ('Winning the Heart of the Military-Industrial Complex,' *Manila Chronicle*, 8 June 1993, p. 15).

27 'Social movements constitute an analytical and political terrain in which the weakening of development and the displacement of categories of modernity (for example, progress and the economy), can be defined and explored' (Escobar, 'Imagining a Post-Development Era?' p. 28). Thus, the

urban excess and its structuration of Metro Manila can also be viewed as displacing or at least challenging the dominant epistemological categories of metropolitan experience, as well as of prevailing epistemological categories of gender and sexuality.

28   'Our city's monument is decay' (Augusto F. Villalon, 'Manila Malaise,' *Manila Chronicle*, 17 June 1993, p. 16).

29   Ricardo V. Puno, 'Southexpressway Revisited,' *Philippine Star*, 6 June 1993, p. 11.

30   Rafael A. S. G. Ongpin, 'Fascist Tack to Traffic,' *Manila Chronicle National Weekly*, 25 December 1992, p. 1

31   That the 4 cities and 13 municipalities have been called 'fiefdoms' manifests the political structure of the metropolitan government. In other words, metropolitan politics has reverted to the fragmentation and particularism that Laquian deplored before martial law. Clearly, however, this kind of 'feudal' politics is now completely compatible with the prevailing mode of transnational production.

32   Lim, 'A Vision of Manila,' p. 30.

33   Sigfried Giedion, *Space, Time and Architecture* (Cambridge: Harvard University Press, 1982), p. 824.

34   Giedion, *Space, Time and Architecture*, p. 825.

35   EDSA (Epifanio de los Santos Avenue), the main thoroughfare stretching across the entire metropolis and now overlaid with the most flyovers, is in fact the product of this modernist valorization of movement, as well as of modernization itself. Constructed by the Americans (as Highway 54), it was a later partial realization of the 1904 urban plans for Manila drawn up by Daniel H. Burnham, the Chicago architect who worked on designs for Washington, DC, Cleveland, San Francisco and Chicago. The plans for Manila included a system of broad thoroughfares, diagonal arteries and rotundas (rather than traffic lights) superimposed on the medieval narrow streets built by the Spanish colonial government. The great emphasis Burnham's urban designs placed on monuments and expansive avenues demonstrated his own participation in and support of the imperialist project of his government to the extent that they were predicated on the belief in the civilizing influence of artifacts of power. As he asserted: 'Make no little plans, for they have no power to stir man's minds' (Quoted by Lewis Mumford, *The City in History* [New York: Harcourt, 1961], p. 402). Flyovers are not so much modeled on an imperialistically imposed metropolitan form as much as produced by an identification with a compelling metropolitan desire: the desire for modernization and capitalist development. However, this infrastructural form is not merely produced by particular desires but more importantly, is constitutive of those desires.

For a discussion of the role EDSA played as a site of the People Power revolt in 1986, see Chapter 5.

36 Giedion, *Space, Time and Architecture*, p. 826. 'Our period' refers to the age of monopoly capitalism of first world nations, and hence its 'space-time feeling,' to the experience of modernity. Therefore, what Filipinos (as the bourgeois nationalists proudly assert themselves to represent) experience in their own period is, rather, a space-time feeling *for* the modernity of capital. It is not accidental that urban life in Manila is pervasively characterized by its own residents as modern. On the other hand, what makes it postmodern is the conscious relation it maintains to an already realized and extant modernity, that is, to the ideology of modernity and modernization imported from advanced capitalist nations.

37 Larry J. Cruz, 'Dream House,' *Metro*, July 1992, p. 16.

38 Ibid.

39 Gaston Bachelard, *The Poetics of Space* (New York: Orion, 1964), p. 6.

40 As I have tried to argue, these are what flyovers *attempt* to accomplish. The height afforded by these structures, however, might also enable the emergence of other subjectivities. The significance of this consciousness-formation for subaltern subjects cannot be underestimated. In 'Oberpas' [Overpass], a short story by Tony Perez, a young gay man mired in depression and self-loathing after his love is rejected gains the desire to continue living as he contemplates the expanse of his life and of his self from the top of a pedestrian overpass (in *Cubao 1980 At Iba Pang Mga Katha: Unang Sigaw ng Gay Liberation Movement sa Pilipinas* [Manila: Cacho, 1992], pp. 184–9). Metropolitan forms such as flyovers and overpasses become new sites of experience, spaces in which one can lift oneself out of the mire of one's existence to reflect upon one's life or to dream of alternative ones. Perhaps because of the slower movement, pedestrian overpasses might be more conducive to such reflections.

41 Mark Wigley, 'The Housing of Gender,' in *Sexuality and Space*, ed. Beatriz Colomina (New York: Princeton Architectural Press, 1992), p. 352.

42 *Philippine Daily Inquirer*, p. D-8.

43 Sally Ann Ness, Body, *Movement and Culture: Kinesthetic and Visual Symbolism in a Philippine Community* (Philadelphia: University of Pennsylvania Press, 1992), p. 53.

44 Lindablue F. Romero, 'Fear and Loathing in Ermita,' *Philippine Daily Inquirer*, 6 June 1993, p. D-8.

45 George Yúdice, 'Postmodernity and Transnational Capitalism in Latin America,' in *On Edge: The Crisis of Contemporary American Culture*, ed. George Yúdice, Jean Franco, and Juan Flores (Minneapolis: University of Minnesota Press, 1992), p. 3.

46   Elizabeth Grosz, 'Bodies-Cities,' in *Sexuality and Space*, ed. Beatriz Colomina (New York: Princeton Architectural Press, 1992), p. 243.

47   Smith, *Uneven Development*, p. 86.

48   Wigley, 'The Housing of Gender,' p. 335.

49   Ibid., pp. 352–3.

50   This is characterized by the 'stress on export development … , the liberal importation of foreign goods, the attraction of more foreign investments, unhampered repatriation of profits and capital, unhindered access to foreign exchange, and free or floating exchange rate for the Philippine peso' (Maria-Luisa Canieso-Doronila, 'Educating Filipinos for the World Market,' *Manila Chronicle*, 20 June 1993, p. 8).

51   The profitability of this porousness and its relation to commodified female sexuality can be gleaned from a caption accompanying an article on global prostitution: 'Poverty, political chaos and porous borders have turned prostitution into a global growth industry' (*Time Magazine* 41, 25 [1993]: 1). The similar construction of women and children as porous — obedient orifices open to sexual exploitation — shows the complex relations between national identity and sexuality. I discuss some of these relations in Chapter 1.

52   This is in no way to suggest that the oppressive structures of capitalism, patriarchy and homophobia are the same or equivalent, merely that on the level of the nation-state, they are cooperative or at least compatible. But even on that level, the contradictions between economic profit and state morality demonstrate the tenuousness of that cooperation. The equivalences made from a dominant perspective (for example, between femininity and class) are undone in specific contexts of oppression, in which particular lines of differentiation or systems of value (for example, the sex-gender system) are deployed over and above others.

53   The other part of the reason for this urban excess's continued and pervasive presence is of course its own desire. In other words, the state's bulimia is also induced by the *resilience* and *will to survive* of the informal sector, which constantly defies state injunctions and state terrorism to return to the streets.

54   Wigley, 'The Housing of Gender,' p. 388.

55   Ness, *Body, Movement and Culture*, p. 41.

56   Teddy Casino, 'Gloria's Strong Republic,' *Business World* (26–27 July 2002).

57   Anna Marie A. Karaos, 'Civil Society in the New Politics,' inq7.net (4 July 2001) [wysiwyg://128/http://www.inq7.net/opi/2001/jul/04/opi_commentary1-1.htm]

58   Deidre Sheehan, 'Brightening Outlook,' *Far Eastern Economic Review* (8 March 2001) [http://www.feer.com/_0103_08/p054econmon.html]

59   As Arthur Woo, an economist at HSBC in Singapore, makes clear, Arroyo's appeal to overseas capital is personal/political (as the head of state) and national: 'Her ability to market herself and the Philippines as a whole is vital for attracting foreign money, because it looks like they will need foreign money to cover the budget.' Quoted in Deidre Sheehan, 'A Fine Balance,' *Far Eastern Economic Review* (8 February 2001) [http://www.feer.com/_0102_02/p044money.html]

60   As a form of dreaming, the state is an attempt to manage the desires of its constituency (the body of the nation) through representation in and as the national subject.

61   Alfred W. McCoy, 'Rent-Seeking Families and the Philippine State: A History of the Lopez Family,' in *An Anarchy of Families: State and Family in the Philippines*, ed. Alfred W. McCoy (Manila: Ateneo de Manila University Press, 1994), p. 434.

62   Paul D. Hutchcroft, *Booty Capitalism: The Politics of Banking in the Philippines* (Ithaca, NY: Cornell University Press, 1998). See also the other essays in *An Anarchy of Families*, ed. Alfred W. McCoy.

63   Benedict Anderson, *The Spectre of Comparisons: Nationalism, Southeast Asia and the World* (London and New York: Verso, 1998), pp. 206–9.

64   As Achille Mbembe writes of the literature of political science and development economics in Africa: 'In spite of the countless critiques made of theories of social evolutionism and ideologies of development and modernization, the academic output of these disciplines continues, almost entirely, in total thrall to these two teleologies. This thralldom has had implications for understanding the purposes of these disciplines in Africa, for the conception of their object, and for the choice of their methods. Mired in the demands of what is immediately useful, enclosed in the narrow horizon of "good governance" and the neo-liberal catechism about the market economy, torn by the current fads for "civil society," "conflict resolution," and alleged "transitions to democracy," the discussion, as habitually engaged, is primarily concerned, not with comprehending the political in Africa or with producing knowledge in general, but with social engineering.' *On the Postcolony* (Berkeley: University of California Press, 2001), p. 7.

65   As the conclusion of a review of Hutchcroft's book makes clear, the 'end' of this story is invariably reform: 'Booty Capitalism is a solid history that makes clear why a fully functioning Philippine economy with sustained growth requires reform in both economic and political sectors.' Alan Berlow, 'Taming the Oligarchy,' *Far Eastern Economic Review* [http://www.feer.com/9905_13/p41inreview.html] It would seem, in reading these accounts, that all anyone and everyone wants and are motivated by in

the Philippine formation are the intertwined ends of state power and private wealth. The naturalization of rapaciousness that occurs in these pathologizing accounts of the Philippine political-economic 'system', is perhaps an attempt to counteract the tendency in earlier scholarship to explain away the problems and crisis of Philippine life via notions of 'culture'.

66 It is no accident that women hardly figure, if at all, in these US political historians' stories of the 'big men' of the Philippines. These political historians who focus on third world examples of 'failed' modern state masculinity bear an uncanny resemblance to mainstream Western feminists who find in less advanced economies (the third world) traditional forms of patriarchy that presumably the West has left behind. For a critique of Western feminism, see for example Chandra Talpade Mohanty, 'Under Western Eyes: Feminist Scholarship and Colonial Discourses' in *Third World Women and the Politics of Feminism*, ed. Chandra Talpade Mohanty, Ann Russo and Lourdes Torres (Bloomington and Indianapolis: Indiana University Press, 1991) and Uma Narayan, *Dislocating Cultures: Identities, Traditions, and Third World Feminism* (New York: Routledge, 1997).

67 Here the 'weak' state is heteronormatively theorized as a queen surrounded by sycophantic rent-seeking courtiers, the local 'strong men' currying 'her' favor. James Buchanan provides this parable to illustrate the theory of rent seeking. His description of the courtiers' behavior shows their rather effeminate constitution (from the point of view of twentieth-century masculinity): 'They will invest effort, time, and other productive resources ... to shift the queen's favor toward their own cause. Promotion, advertisement, flattery, persuasion, cajolery — these and other attributes will characterize rent-seeking behavior.' Quoted in McCoy, 'Rent-Seeking Families and the State,' in *An Anarchy of Families*, pp. 430–2. It is of course evident from this theoretical fantasy-scenario that the King, who represents the ruling dispensation on which these peripheral arrangements ultimately depend, is none other than the ideal state embodied by Western bourgeois democracies. Is it any wonder that the Supreme 'strong man' himself should so identify with this monarchic example that, as the button on the intercom system at the presidential Palace clearly showed, he had himself designated as 'the King'? Mark R. Thompson, *The Anti-Marcos Struggle: Personalistic Rule and Democratic Transition in the Philippines* (New Haven: Yale University Press, 1995), p. 54.

68 In the interest of change, such projects expect that 'resistance' would take the form of a full rational consciousness of and direct opposition to the logic of hegemonic power.

69   Resil B. Mojares, 'The Dream Goes On and On: Three Generations of the Osmeñas, 1906–1990' in McCoy, *An Anarchy of Families*, p. 321.

70   Reynaldo C. Ileto, *Filipinos and Their Revolution: Event, Discourse, and Historiography* (Quezon City: Ateneo de Manila University Press, 1998), p. 137.

71   As Nira Yuval-Davis and Flora Anthias write, 'the state is neither unitary in its practices, its intentions nor its effects … The term refers to a particular "machinery" for the exercise of "government" over a given population, usually territorially and nationally defined, although the definitions of what constitutes these boundaries etc. will shift and change depending on what it is government or power over and what is being managed or negotiated.' 'Introduction' in *Woman–Nation–State* (London: The Macmillan Press, Ltd., 1989), p. 5.

72   Manuel A. Caoili, *The Origins of Metropolitan Manila: A Political and Social Analysis* (Quezon City: University of the Philippines Press, 1999), p. 134.

73   Caoili, *The Origins of Metropolitan Manila*, p. 135.

74   Ibid., p. 141.

75   To be fair, Caoili does mention these protest movements though as part of his description of the general 'anarchy' of the decade before Martial Law. There are other ways that these infrastructural projects helped to guarantee state power. It is well known that Marcos surpassed all previous administrations in the building of public works. This was as much a matter of ideological promotion (as slogans such as 'Marcos means more roads' attest) as it was a matter of tapping into foreign aid and investments oriented towards 'development' and 'modernization.' Caoili, *The Origins of Metropolitan Manila*, pp. 135–6. See also Gary Hawes in Ruth McVey, ed. *Southeast Asian Capitalists* (Ithaca, NY: Southeast Asia Program, Cornell University, 1992).

76   Quoted in Arturo G. Corpuz, *The Colonial Iron Horse: Railroads and Regional Development in the Philippines, 1875–1935* (Quezon City: University of the Philippines Press, 1999), p. 27.

77   See Walden Bello, David Kinley, and Elaine Elinson, *Development Debacle: The World Bank in the Philippines* (San Francisco: Institute for Food and Development Policy, 1982) on rural development as counter-insurgency.

78   See Vicente L. Rafael, 'The Cell Phone and the Crowd: Messianic Politics in the Contemporary Philippines', *Public Culture* 15, 3 (2003): 399–425.

79   Jaime C. Bulatao, 'Another Look at Philippine Values' in *Manila: History, People and Culture*, ed. Wilfrido V. Villacorta, Isagani R. Cruz and Ma. Lourdes Brillantes (Manila: De La Salle University Press, 1989), p. 330.

CHAPTER 3

1   In *Philippine Daily Inquirer* (15 July 1995), *Philippine Daily Inquirer* (9 February 1996), *Philippine Daily Inquirer* (28 May 1996), and *Today* (16 February 1996), respectively.

2   Although this term has now been replaced by the more nationalist category of Overseas Filipino Workers (OFWs), I use it here to indicate the continuities between the mode of this work and the strategy of private subcontracting adopted by the Philippine state.

3   Natasha Vizcarra, 'Confesor: OCWs Are Happy. Abuses Are Few, Dismissed Labor Secretary Reports,' *Philippine Daily Inquirer* (22 May 1995). Confesor was dismissed by the government to appease public outrage over the hanging of Flor Contemplacion, a domestic helper in Singapore who was convicted of murdering Delia Maga, another domestic helper, and the latter's ward. I talk about Contemplacion as a public symbol later.

4   Confesor, 'White Paper on Overseas Employment,' quoted in Vizcarra, 'Confesor: OCWs Are Happy'.

5   '[B]y 1991 ... 50.6% of the estimated 742,700 Filipino OCWs were women. Recent reports from government and NGOs reveal, however, that the proportion has increased to 55% ...' Ruby P. Beltran, Elena L. Samonte, and Sr. Lita Walker, RSCJ, 'Filipino Women Migrant Workers: Effects on Family Life and Challenges for Intervention' in *Filipino Women Migrant Workers: At the Crossroads and Beyond Beijing*, ed. Ruby P. Beltran and Gloria F. Rodriguez (Quezon City: Giraffe Books, 1996), pp. 15–6.

6   'Court Acquits S'porean Who Blinded Pinay,' *Philippine Daily Inquirer* (29 June 1995). The particular attention paid to the situation of Filipina DHs in Singapore came in the wake of the Flor Contemplacion execution, of which more examples are listed below.

7   Veronika Bennholdt-Thomsen, 'The Future of Women's Work and Violence Against Women,' in *Women: The Last Colony*, Maria Mies, Veronika Bennholdt-Thomsen and Claudia von Werlhof (London and New Jersey: Zed Books Ltd., 1988), p. 114. I have omitted the phrase 'that is, their distinctiveness as women' to the extent that this formulation essentializes the condition of women without any regard to the ways in which other systems of differentiation (race, sexuality and class systems being only among the most prominent) are involved in the constitution of 'women's labor'.

8   *Philippine Daily Inquirer* (8 July 1995).

9   From Bridget Anderson with contributions from Anti-Slavery International and Kalayaan and the Migrant Domestic Workers, *Britain's Secret Slaves: An Investigation into the Plight of Overseas Domestic Workers in the United*

Kingdom, quoted by Eden Casareno, 'Of Aprons and Bikinis: Filipinas as Modern Slaves of the World,' *Laya: Feminist Quarterly* 3, no. 2 (1994): 12.

10 *The Human Rights Watch Global Report on Women's Human Rights* (New York, Washington, Los Angeles, London and Brussels: Human Rights Watch, 1995), pp. 274, 284.

11 'Abuse of Asian Maids: Slavery Lives in Wealthy Gulf,' *Philippine Daily Inquirer* (8 July 1995). The same behaviour exhibited by employers in other Asian countries towards their Filipina maids is, curiously, not considered slavery but instead 'abuse' and 'maltreatment'.

12 'In the case of men, labour power becomes a commodity; in the case of women, the whole person becomes a commodity.' Veronika Bennholdt-Thomsen, 'The Future of Women's Work,' p. 121. Bennholdt-Thomsen herself makes the comparison between slaves and housewives (who are, in effect, amateur or unpaid domestic helpers). This is in no way to posit any form of commensurability between the two. It is merely to point out the relations of continuity (rather than analogy) between their respective structures of labour relations. The inseparability of women's work and women's bodies is fundamental to the capitalist tendency towards the reduction and devaluation of necessary labor through its naturalization, a tendency eclipsed by the increasing reliance, especially evident in post-industrial spheres, on capital-intensive labour (or what has been touted as the immaterial labor of knowledge-production).

13 Cf. Aihwa Ong's 'Cultural Citizenship as Subject-Making: Immigrants Negotiate Racial and Cultural Boundaries in the United States, *Current Anthropology*, 37, 5 (December 1996): 737–62, in which she demonstrates what she calls the 'racializing of class logic'. My own analysis, while similar to Ong's in its emphasis on the dynamic character of 'race' and 'ethnicity' (i.e., their construction out of everyday practices), considers gender as a constitutive part of this racializing process, which is, in my view, less a matter of class logic than of commodity fetishism. The context of OCWs demands an analysis of commodity relations, rather than an analysis of class subjects. While the logics of class and commodity fetishism are clearly related moments, they are not the same. The conflation of the two moments is a principle problem of Harry Chang's illuminating analysis of the practices of reification of race as obeying the logic of commodity fetishism. 'Toward a Marxist Theory of Racism: Two Essays by Harry Chang,' ed. Paul Liem and Eric Montague, *Review of Radical Political Economics*, 17, 3 (1985): 34–45. I am indebted to Donna Haraway for suggesting the article by Ong.

14 Domestic helpers are often sexually violated by their male employers and mutilated or physically abused by their female employers, a sexual division

of sexualizing and racializing violence that is determined by the imperatives of heterosexist masculinity, as well as by the threat of a disenfranchising sameness.

15   For an account of the postmodern reconfiguration of the human, both as species and as individual being, through the human genome project and immunological discourse, see Donna J. Haraway, 'The Biopolitics of Postmodern Bodies: Determinations of Self in Immune System Discourse' in *American Feminist Thought At Century's End: A Reader*, ed. Linda S. Kauffman (Cambridge, MA and Oxford, UK: Blackwell Publishers, 1993): 199–233. Also see, Donna J. Haraway, *Modest_Witness@Second_Milliennium.FemaleMan©_Meets_OncoMouse*™ (New York and London: Routledge, 1996).

16   *Human Rights Watch Global Report on Women's Human Rights*, pp. 296–305. Apart from domestic helpers' national-racial difference, it is also their gender that enables the ratification of their abuse. The exclusion of 'domestic servants and those having their status' from Kuwait's Private Sector Labor Law No. 38 of 1964 (n. 31, p. 285), for example, should be viewed as a discriminatory act against female or feminized work.

17   'Abuse of Asian Maids: Slavery Lives in Wealthy Gulf,' *Philippine Daily Inquirer*.

18   F. Landa Jocano, 'Culture Shock: The Case of Filipina Domestic Helpers in Singapore and Hong Kong,' *Solidarity*, no. 143–4 (July–December 1994): 61.

19   Ibid.

20   Her embodiment and provision of surplus is determined and expressed by her 'race' and gender. As Maria Mies asserts, 'the definition of what is "necessary" and what is "surplus" is not a purely an economic question, but a political and/or cultural one' (*Patriarchal and Accumulation on a World Scale* [London and New Jersey: Zed Books Ltd., 1986] pp. 65–6). Mies defines surplus as what is stolen and appropriated. One must read the food deprivation, even starvation, of domestic helpers as attempts to keep them 'costing nothing' and therefore to increase the surplus-value expropriated from them.

21   Jocano, 'Culture Shock,' p. 66. As I try to show later, many of these kinds of analysis which result in some policy recommendation indirectly participate in the state efforts to defuse the contradictions and potential antagonism produced by these new labor relations, by helping to streamline and improve the process of production and distribution of cheap Philippine labor.

22   Ninotchka Rosca, 'The Philippines' Shameful Export,' *Nation*, quoted in Jerry Esplanada, '"RP Delights" in HK: Women sold in body parts'. That

ease stems from women's embodiment of domestic labor, that is, 'feminine' activities demanded of them (including the provision of sexual services) as fulfillment of the needs of the family as these are defined by masculine power. Prostitution and domestic labour are thus two forms of commodification of women as bodily beings-for-others. 'Supply cannot meet demand for women in reunified Germany,' '"RP Delights" in HK: "As simple as ordering pizza"' and 'Women sold in body parts' are only some of the headlines that tell of the reduction of Filipina women to corporeal products by the sex and mail-order bride industries (Roby Alampay, 'Supply cannot meet demand for women in reunified Germany,' *Today* [12 June 1995]; Jerry Explanada, '"RP Delights" in HK: "As Simple as ordering pizza"' *Philippine Daily Inquirer* [26 May 1996]; and Jerry Explanada, '"RP Delights" in HK: Women sold in body parts' *Philippine Daily Inquirer* [27 May 1996]).

23 Hortense J. Spillers, 'Mama's Baby, Papa's Maybe: An American Grammar Book,' *diacritics* (Summer 1987): 67.

24 Ibid., p. 77.

25 Spillers observes that, in fact, 'the quintessential "slave" is *not* a male, but a female' (Ibid., p. 73). Spillers demonstration of the vestibular function of black females in relation to the dominant understanding of gender — 'black women do not live out their destiny on the borders of femaleness, but in the heart of its terrain' ('Interstices: A Small Drama of Words,' in *Pleasure and Danger: Exploring Female Sexuality*, ed. Carol Vance [Boston: Routledge & Kegan Paul, 1984] p. 95) — points to the ways in which racializing practices are integral to but not registered by the process known as the 'feminization' of labor. 'Feminization' is, in this view, a partial misnaming of the practices and symbolics producing domestic labor, inasmuch as it doesn't acknowledge the racializing practices of colonization, which are repeated and refurbished under present conditions of post-industrial and newly-industrial capital.

26 'UN experts: Stop abuse of OCWs,' *Philippine Daily Inquirer* (28 May 1996). As Rosca puts it, 'This exchange-system exploits both men and women, but women exploitation comes with a thick overlay of violence, from murder to battery to sex trafficking' (Quoted in Jerry Esplanada, '"RP Delights" in HK: Women sold in body parts").

27 Gabriel Cardinoza, 'Another Tragic OCW Tale: Death by Beating in Kuwait,' *Philippine Daily Inquirer* (3 July 1995).

28 Juliet M. Labog, 'Tragic tale behind Pinoy maid's death leap in HK,' *Philippine Daily Inquirer* (30 May 1995).

29 Gabriel Cardinoza, 'Filipina OCW Slain in Kuwait Tortured,' *Philippine Daily Inquirer* (15 July 1995).

30 Ibid.

31 Whether this is true or not, lies outside of my knowledge. I merely want to highlight the contradiction in the article between an attempt to explain this bodily treatment by gesturing toward national-cultural locations where it might be logical/natural and an attempt to heighten suspicions of 'foul play'.

32 Edward Pelayo, 'Maid's Funeral Rites Set Today,' *Today* (6 February 1996). Suicide as the unsignifiable.

33 Quoted by Cardinoza, 'Filipina OCW Slain in Kuwait Tortured.'

34 Quoted in Carolyn O. Arguillas, 'Mabuti pa ang kalabaw,' *Philippine Daily Inquirer* (3 July 1995).

35 Mary Ann Benitez, 'Maid's Body Found Floating in River After Ward Drowns,' *Today* (16 February 1996). Dalamban is not the maid found floating in the river. She is mentioned at the end of this article as 'another entry in a long list of abused Filipino contract workers'.

36 'The Philippines is the world's largest labor exporter, and remittances are Manila's principle source of foreign currency. Economic migrants sent home $2.6 billion in the first eleven months of 1994, the government says, a 29 percent jump over the same period a year earlier. And that's just what came in through the banking system.' 'A New Kind of Hero,' *Far Eastern Economic Review* (30 March 1995), cited in *The Human Rights Watch Global Report on Women's Human Rights*, p. 275. According to the Philippine Overseas Employment Administration, in 1995, remittances from overseas contract workers amounted to US$4.9 billion. Lito Etulle, 'The Exodus to Money Meccas continues,' *The Manila Times* (2 April 1997).

37 The Philippines is a country with one of the lowest per capita GNPs in the Asia-Pacific region, and one of the most heavily indebted in the world Asian Development Bank, cited in *Women of a Lesser Cost: Female Labour, Foreign Exchange and Philippine Development*. Sylvia Chant and Cathy McIlwaine (Quezon City: Ateneo de Manila University Press, 1995), p. 45. The 'weakness' of the Philippine state is characteristic of its instrumentality not only for foreign capital but also for local capital.

38 Domini de Torrevillas, 'Violence Against Filipina OCWs: The Flor Contemplacion and Sarah Balabagan Cases,' in *Filipino Women Migrant Workers: At the Crossroads and Beyond Beijing*, ed. Ruby P. Beltran and Gloria F. Rodriguez (Quezon City: Giraffe Books, 1996), p. 49.

39 Torrevillas, 'Violence Against Filipina OCWs,' pp. 54–5.

40 For a scintillating discussion of the role of gossip and mourning in the construction of OCWs, in particular, in the case of Contemplacion, see Vicente L. Rafael, '"Your Grief Is Our Gossip": Overseas Filipinos and Other Spectral Presences,' *Public Culture* 9 (1997): 267–91.

41 Malou Talosig, 'More Home Workers Being Abused — ILO,' *Today* (7 July 1995).

42 Claudia von Werlhof sees this situation to be 'the real character of our mode of production': 'What is involved here is an unfree, "femalized" form of wage labour, which means: no job permanency, the lowest wages, longest working hours, most monotonous work, no trade unions, no opportunity to obtain higher qualifications, no promotion, no rights and no social security.' Claudia von Werlhof, 'The Proletarian Is Dead: Long Live the Housewife!' in *Women: The Last Colony,* p. 169. Werlhof asserts that 'the organization of housework will determine our future' (p. 174). Feminization also means for me the negation of a dominant structure or category (and its systemic entailments) based on the repression and repudiation of the feminine, which the structure or category itself configures as its constitutive contradiction. Thus the phrase 'the feminization of labor' points to the intrinsic significance of the category of the feminine in the constitution of the category of labor. This is not merely conceptual but also practical (that is, it is realized through the practices of constitution of the socio-individual being defined as labor). Feminine is the ideal expression of the gendered social relations in labor-exchange, as well as the historical metaphor for those groups who are viewed as existing outside of the civil society premised on relations of exchange.

43 Evelyn Miranda Feliciano, 'OCWs: Counting the Cost,' *Patimos: A Vision For Our Times* 11, 1: 3–5.

44 Torrevillas, 'Violence Against Filipina OCWs,' p. 66.

45 Tonette Raquisa, p. 222.

46 Quoted by Vizcarra, 'Confesor: OCWS Are Happy.' Confesor's recommendation for deregulation so that migration could become 'strictly a matter between the worker and his [sic] foreign employer' belies the fact that this relation is already privatized, and as such not perceived to be a social problem

47 'The saddest part is that the sacrifice is for mere economic reasons,' Lucy V. Arboleda, 'Taking the OCW Phenomenon at Its Roots,' *Patimos: A Vision For Our Times* 11, 1: p. 17. To the extent that the bodies of domestic helpers serve this capacity of fulfilling the needs of others, they are martyrs. Women as martyrs (as bodily-beings-for-others) is religious-cultural construction as much as an economic structure — bodily sacrifice for a spiritual cause (for transcendent value). Indeed, the other side of slavery is martyrdom. The upholding of sovereignty as an ideal and its implied practices has in some ways been accountable for the continued production of the domestic body (the corporeal entities on which the national voice

is predicated). Without attention to social and economic production (domestic and international), the desire for sovereignty takes part in the modernization of the Philippines and thereby reinforces the oppression and exploitation of disenfranchised Filipinas (the disenfranchising of Filipinas) which this project of modernization entails and produces.

48   This is a phrase from U. P. Plan 2008, the centennial plan of the University of the Philippines, which takes inspiration from the Ramos administration's plan of development for the whole country, 'Philippines 2000'.

49   The contradiction between desiring as subjects and being treated as objects in part accounts for the public clamor for more assertiveness on the part of the state (since it is the state that acts as the national subject in the arena of representation, even through it is corporate capital that acts as the point of subjectification for nations).

50   Beltran et al., 'Filipino Women Migrant Workers,' p. 27.

51   It is important to point out that the liberation from the family, which I suggest, is not because there is a 'traditional family' obtaining in the Philippines that is inherently oppressive (the family is itself invaded by dominating conscriptions and prescriptions of behaviour according to and benefiting economic structures such as the labor market). Nor is it adequate to assert that domestic helpers return abroad because they are 'pushed' by poverty. It is equally important to take into account the particular contents of their desires and pleasures. See, for example, Jane A. Margold, 'Maid/Made in Hong Kong: Beauty Pageants and Other Cultural Revisionings of Filipina Selves,' Paper presented at the SSRC-ISEAS Conference on Diasporas in Southeast Asia, 5–7 December 1997, Singapore. For an early account of the joys as well as tribulations of overseas domestic workers, see Jo-Ann Q. Maglipon, *Primed: Selected Stories, 1972–1992* (Pasig, Metro Manila: Anvil Publishing, 1993).

52   Beltran et al., *Filipino Women Migrant Workers*, p. 35.

53   Arguillas, 'Mabuti pa ang kalabaw'.

54   See Antonio Negri, *Marx Beyond Marx: Lessons on the Grundrisse*, ed. Jim Fleming (South Hadley, MA: Bergin & Garvey, 1984).

55   The recent rejection of the Anti-Rape Bill of 1997, the amendments to extant laws on rape which implied the possibility of marital rape, only underscores the widespread belief that 'every act of sex between husband and wife, even when "force, threat or intimidation" is used, is consensual because a marriage contract stipulates free and unlimited access to a spouse's body'. Editorial, 'Women Are Unhappy,' *Philippine Daily Inquirer* (14 June 1997).

56   Eleanor Heartney, 'Asia Now,' *Art in America* (February 1997): 74.

Heartney's review of the works from Korea, Thailand, Indonesia, India and the Philippines included in the exhibit, 'Contemporary Art in Asia: Traditions/Tensions' demonstrate precisely the ethnocentrism the show was intended to challenge. Even as she notes that 'the particular social contexts of the work in [the show] may be unusual,' she decidedly sees 'how perfectly it meshes with the trend toward identity art which has permeated American institutions in the 1990s' (pp. 70–1). In an astounding disregard of the 'social and political factors which underlie these works,' Heartney concludes that '"Traditions/Tensions" serves a useful purpose in widening Western knowledge of developments in contemporary Asia' (p. 75).

57 Adora Faye de Vera, 'The Struggle for Human Rights: Beyond Vigilance' in *And She Said No! Human Rights, Women's Identities and Struggles*, ed. Liberato Bautista and Elizabeth Rifareal (Quezon City: National Council of Churches in the Philippines, 1990), p. 142.

58 The discourse on human rights stipulates women's protection (from violation of these rights) and their treatment as workers whose union is the ILO, constructing women within a liberal-democratic model of citizenship. While the defense of such rights is important in enabling them to organize themselves, and supporting their struggle to live, these rights in themselves do not transform or challenge the social relations of production that determine the contracting of disenfranchised Filipino women for domestic labor (the structure and character of their commodification). However, I am arguing that the focus on the human, which this discourse generates, has a transformative capacity that exceeds liberal-democratic objectives to the extent that it mobilizes subjective desires. I want to thank Florence M. Tadiar and Thea M. Tadiar for making me look more closely at the significance of the focus on the human within the Philippine women's movement.

59 Quoted and translated by Conrado de Quiros, 'Two Letters,' *Philippine Daily Inquirer* (14 August 1996).

60 Elynia S. Mabanglo, *Mga Liham ni Pinay* (Manila: De La Salle University Press, 1990). All subsequent references to this text are my translation.

61 This is the concept used by Merleau-Ponty to describe the child's relations with others. In 'Prostituted Filipinas: The Crisis of Philippine Culture,' *Millenium: Journal of International Studies* 27, 4 (1998): 927–54, I argue that this 'infantile', 'underdeveloped' subjectivity is what women are socialized into inhabiting as part of their gendered structuring for the purposes of capital, that is, in their capacity as 'traditional' producers of subsistence. Virgilio Enriquez theorizes this syncretism through the concept of *kapwa* [fellowbeing] and shows it to a positive, residual core

concept of Filipino psychology that has great transformative possibility. Virgilio G. Enriquez, *From Colonial to Liberation Psychology: The Philippine Experience* (Manila: De La Salle University Press, 1994.

62 For Mabanglo, writing is contrasted with, and therefore constituted through, domestic activities. In *'Ngayong Umaga'* [This morning] she ignores the pot that is waiting to be put on the stove and the water that is waiting to be swirled around with a rag to 'float a poem/ on my tears'. In *'Pagkamulat'* [Upon awakening], writing replaces her expected female duties: *'Bakit pluma ang kuyom ko/ sa halip na ari ng isang lalaki?/ Bakit papel ang aking binibihisan/ sa halip na anak kong/ nagdaramdam?'* [Why is it a pen that I clutch/ instead of the sex of a man?/ Why is it a piece of paper that I dress/ instead of my moody child?] And in *'Ibig Mong Ihabi Kita ng Tula'* [You wish I would weave you a poem], she likens writing a poem to weaving, and words to substances to color one's coffee and soften one's food.

63 'What seems to constitute "women of color" or "third world women" as a viable oppositional alliance is a *common context of struggle* rather than color or racial identification.' Chandra Talpade Mohanty. 'Introduction: Cartographies of Struggle' in *Third World Women and the Politics of Feminism*, ed. Chandra Talpade Mohanty, Ann Russo, Lourdes Torres (Bloomington: Indiana University Press, 1991), p. 7.

64 Angela Manalang Gloria, 'Revolt from Hymen' in *Songs of Ourselves: Writings by Filipino Women in English*, ed. and intro. Edna Zapanta Manlapaz (Manila: Anvil, 1994).

65 In spite of their intentions, scholarly works that demonstrate the continuing persistence of pre-colonial 'debt-bondage' relations in present-day 'cultures' may be held as evidence of the role of 'tradition' in the perpetuation of slavery.

66 'The abolition of slavery thus corresponded to the authorisation of slavery as punishment. In actual practice, both Emancipation and the authorisation of penal servitude combined to create an immense Black presence within southern prisons and to transform the character of punishment into a means of managing former slaves.' Avery F. Gordon, 'Globalism and the Prison Industrial Complex: An Interview with Angela Davis,' *Race and Class: A Journal for Black and Third World Liberation* 40, 2/3 (October 1998-March 1999): 151.

67 Ibid., p. 148.

68 Ibid.

69 See Aihwa Ong, 'Cultural Citizenship as Subject-Making' and Lisa Lowe, *Immigrant Acts: On Asian American Cultural Politics* (Durham: Duke University Press, 1996).

70 Angela Davis, quoted in Avery Gordon, 'Globalism and the Prison Industrial Complex,' p. 151.

71 While corporations profit directly from employing prison slave labor, they profit in a more indirect way from domestic labor, which serves to reduce the cost of reproduction of formal white-collar workers, thereby extending the latter's wages and reducing the capital costs of corporations.

72 José Rizal, *Political and Historical Writings (1884–1890)* (Manila: National Historical Institute, 1963), pp. 13–6.

73 'If capitalism is the exterior limit of all societies, this is because capitalism for its part has no exterior limit, but only an interior limit that is capital itself and that it does not encounter but reproduces by always displacing it.' Gilles Deleuze and Felix Guattari, *Anti-Oedipus: Capitalism and Schizophrenia*, trans. Robert Hurley, Mark Seem and Helen R. Lane (Minneapolis, MN: University of Minnesota Press, 1983), pp. 230–1.

74 The violence signified by 'slavery' can be understood as the process of primitive accumulation. 'So true is it that primitive accumulation is not produced just once at the dawn of capitalism, but is continually reproducing itself.' Ibid., p. 231.

75 Rosalind O'Hanlon, 'Recovering the Subject: *Subaltern Studies* and Histories of Resistance in Colonial South Asia' in *Mapping Subaltern Studies and the Postcolonial*, ed. and intro. Vinayak Chaturvedi (London and New York: Verso, 2000), p. 111.

76 Raymond Williams, *Marxism and Literature* (Oxford and New York: Oxford University Press, 1977), Quoted in ibid.

PART II

1 See Lauren Berlant, 'The Theory of Infantile Citizenship' in her *The Queen of America Goes to Washington City: Essays on Sex and Citizenship* (Durham and London: Duke University Press, 1997), for a discussion of this access to national history performed in the pilgrimage to Washington.

2 In the US as in all first world nations of the West, there are of course contestatory histories, which the house hegemony disavows, that those marginalized within the nation try to bring to light, like skeletons in the closet. To the extent, however, that such minority histories are brought to the nation to be owned up to, they only confirm that history is indeed the nation's own. There are of course more radical deployments of repressed histories, in which case not only the borders but also the material organization of the nation are put into question.

3 Z. A. Salazar, 'A Legacy of the Propaganda: The Tripartite View of

Philippine History' in *The Ethnic Dimension: Papers on Philippine Culture, History and Psychology*, ed. Z. A. Salazar (Cologne: Counselling Center for Filipinos, Caritas Association for the City of Cologne, 1983): 109.

4   Ibid. See also John N. Schumacher, S. J., *The Making of a Nation: Essays on Nineteenth-Century Nationalism* (Quezon City: Ateneo de Manila University Press, 1991).

5   Frantz Fanon, *Wretched of the Earth*, trans. Cosntance Farrington (New York; Grove Press, 1965), p. 210.

6   Reynaldo Ileto, *Filipinos and Their Revolution: Events, Discourse, and Historiography* (Quezon City: Ateneo de Manila University Press, 1998), p. 241.

7   As President McKinley explains his God-given reasons for colonizing the Philippines: '(1) that we could not give them back to Spain — that would be cowardly and dishonorable; (2) that we could not turn them over to France or Germany — our commercial rivals in the Orient — that would be bad business and discreditable; (3) *that we could not leave them to themselves — they were unfit for self-government, and they would soon have anarchy and misrule over there worse than Spain's was;* and (4) that there was nothing left for us to do but to take them all, and to educate the Filipinos, and uplift and civilize and Christianize them, and by God's grace do the very best we could for them, as our fellowmen for whom Christ also died' (my emphasis). Quoted in Horacio de la Costa, S. J., *Readings in Philippine History* (Manila: Bookmark, 1965), p. 219. See also Vicente L. Rafael, *White Love and Other Events in Filipino History* (Durham and London: Duke University Press, 2000).

8   Renato Constantino, *Dissent and Counter-Consciousness* (Quezon City: Malaya Books, 1970), p. 97.

9   See Caroline S. Hau, *Necessary Fictions: Philippine Literature and the Nation, 1946–1980* (Quezon City: Ateneo de Manila University Press, 2000), pp. 126–7.

10   Ferdinand E. Marcos, *Revolution From the Center: How the Philippines Is Using Martial Law to Build a New Society* (Hong Kong: Raya Books, 1978).

11   Glenn May, *Inventing a Hero: The Posthumous Re-Creation of Andres Bonifacio* (Quezon City: New Day Publishers, 1997). See Reynaldo Ileto's critique of May's work in *Filipinos and their Revolution*.

12   Partha Chatterjee, *The Nation and Its Fragments: Colonial and Postcolonial Histories* (Princeton, NJ: Princeton University Press, 1993), p. 237.

13   Partha Chatterjee, *The Nation and Its Fragments: Colonial and Postcolonial*, p. 238.

14   See Neil Lazarus, 'Disavowing Decolonization: Nationalism, Intellectuals and the Question of Representation in Postcolonial Theory' in his

Nationalism and Cultural Practice in the Postcolonial World (Cambridge and New York: Cambridge University Press, 1999). See also E. San Juan, Jr., 'Postcolonial Theory Versus the Revolutionary Process in the Philippines' in his *Beyond Postcolonial Theory* (New York: St. Martin's Press, 1998).

15   Reynaldo Ileto, *Pasyon and Revolution: Popular Movements in the Philippines, 1840–1910* (Quezon City: Ateneo de Manila University Press, 1979). Vicente L. Rafael, *Contracting Colonialism: Translation and Christian Conversion in Tagalog Society Under Early Spanish Rule* (Durham and London: Duke University Press, 1993). To some extent this kind of history writing is also the mode of Ambeth Ocampo, although Ocampo's 'style' is more naturalist (in the literary sense). As Rafael describes his work: '[T]his act of communing with the deadweight of the past tends to focus on an obsessive, one might even say fetishistic, delight in the details of everyday life. This brings us to the third quality of his essays: the careful attention they devote to the common, the overlooked, the ordinary, what we might think of as the splendid *basura* (trash) of the archives — the *sari sari*, the *tira-tira*, the *anu-ano*, as well as the *diumano* of the past.' Vicente Rafael, *White Love*, pp. 195–6.

16   Ranajit Guha, 'On Some Aspects of the Historiography of Colonial India' in *Mapping Subaltern Studies and the Postcolonial*, ed. Vinayak Chaturvedi (London and New York: Verso, 2000), p. 6.

CHAPTER 4

1   Teodoro A. Agoncillo, *The Revolt of the Masses: The Story of Bonifacio and the Katipunan* (Quezon City: University of the Philippines Press, 1996), p. vii. Originally published by the College of Liberal Arts, University of the Philippines, 1956. All subsequent references to this work will be indicated by page numbers in the main text.

2   Reynaldo Ileto, *Filipinos and Their Revolution: Event, Discourse, and Historiography* (Quezon City: Ateneo de Manila University Press, 1998). See also Caroline S. Hau, 'Literature and History' in *Necessary Fictions: Philippine Literature and the Nation, 1946–1980* (Quezon City: Ateneo de Manila University Press, 2000).

3   Reynaldo C. Ileto, *Pasyon and Revolution: Popular Movements in the Philippines, 1840–1910* (Quezon City: Ateneo de Manila, 1979); 'Rizal and the Underside of Philippine History' in *Moral Order and Change: Essays in Southeast Asian Thought*, ed. D. Wyatt and A. Woodside (New Haven: Yale Southeast Asia Studies 24, 1982); 'Outlines of a Non-Linear Emplotment of Philippine History' in *Reflections on Development in*

Southeast Asia, ed. Lim Teck Ghee (Singapore: Institute of Southeast Asian Studies, 1988). The second of these 'rules' is implicit in the later nationalist historians' critiques of the 'great men' approach to history exemplified by Agoncillo's work. See Renato Constantino, *The Philippines: A Past Revisited* (Quezon City: Tala Publication Services, 1975) and 'Partisan Scholarship'; Amado Guerrero, *Philippine Society and Revolution* (Manila: Pulang Tala Publications, 1971). Ileto's subsequent critique of the 'subtle elitism' and progressivism of Constantino and the NDF, while 'correct', too quickly classifies their own histories of the people and of the masses in the same category as Agoncillo's history simply on the basis of their 'common historical emplotment'. Ileto argues that the reason the linear-developmental framework appeals to 'most educated Filipinos' (by which he means those from the *ilustrado* class, to whom he credits the emergence of the progressive, linear and 'purposive' writing of Philippine history) is because it 'puts *them* at the forefront of the development process. Whether as apologists or activists, they are able to recognize themselves in a comfortable way in the past, and they are assured of a primary role in the fulfillment of the end towards which history moves.' 'Outlines of a Non-Linear Emplotment of Philippine History,' p. 136. It seems to me that to lump 'apologists and activists' together in this way disregards significant differences in their deployment of the 'linear-developmental mode'. These include differences in their respective interpretations of the culmination of history (while the 'apologists' celebrate the de facto founding of the nation-state, the 'activists' affirm the continuation of the revolutionary struggle and posit the triumph of the people as the climax of this history as struggle) and, moreover, differences in the place and strength of their respective *mythos* in present relations of power. Ileto's claim that in an alternative history *ilustrado* constructions of reality have 'the same status as the world of the Tres Cristos and Dios-Dios' (as examples of illicit associations), since they are all viewed as constructions, ignores the apparatuses of state power that give some constructions more 'historical value' than others (or as it was said of the Marcos's cronies, 'some are smarter than others').

4   Ileto, 'Outlines of a Non-Linear Emplotment of Philippine History,' p. 152.
5   'Unity — this was the leading imperative of the Revolution, and everything, including justice itself, was sacrificed at its altar in the interest of a larger, deeper issue: freedom. The Revolution, therefore, must be judged in its totality, not in separate and isolated incidents. To judge it properly, one must be equipped with an understanding of the forces that breathed life into it.' Agoncillo, *The Revolt of the Masses*, p. 279. Agoncillo is not too far from Ileto to the degree that both are equipped with this

understanding of 'the masses.' Inasmuch as 'justice' can only be realized 'in time of peace and plenty', it is reserved for the historian who enjoys this time and thereby eschews the continuing as well as different war against the peoples who are marginalized in and by these dominant historical narratives, peoples who serve as the libidinal force and diacritical marks which make such narratives possible and meaningful. I discuss this further below.

6 Ileto, 'Outlines of a Non-Linear Emplotment of Philippine History,' p. 153. For a full elaboration of this mentality, see Ileto, *Pasyon and Revolution*.

7 Lynn Hunt, 'Psychoanalysis, the Self, and Historical Interpretation,' *Common Knowledge* 6, 2 (Fall 1997): 10–19.

8 Ileto's later essays focus on structures and processes of social constitution (e.g. the constitution of the *pueblo* and the State). His critique of developmentalist historians, however, is still predicated on the category of the self as the agent of psycho-ideological operations.

9 Dipesh Chakrabarty, 'Postcoloniality and the Artifice of History: Who Speaks for "Indian" Pasts?' *Representations* 37 (Winter 1992): 13. Chakrabarty shares a similar framework and project with Ileto to the extent that both want to restore the repressed of modern history. Chakrabarty's own objective, to enable the world to 'once again be imagined as radically heterogeneous' (23), seems to me to advocate a multiculturalist agenda for heterogeneity similar to that proposed by David Theo Goldberg in his introduction to *Multiculturalism: A Critical Reader* (Oxford, UK and Cambridge, MA: Blackwell, 1994) as well as by Ella Shohat and Robert Stam in their book, *Unthinking Eurocentrism: Multiculturalism and the Media* (London and New York: Routledge, 1994). While I think such projects are indispensable interventions and challenges to the subjects of monoculturalism and Eurocentrism, I feel there is much more to be done — more and different history to be made — than that which valorizes 'narratives … [which] entail subject positions and configurations of memory that challenge and undermine the subject that speaks in the name of history' (Chakrabarty, 'Postcoloniality and the Artifice of History', pp. 10–1), or put another way, that writes subaltern narratives into significance *for* and *to* the very subject which impedes the knowing and acting of such 'other narratives of human connection' (Ibid., p. 23).

10 Madhava Prasad, 'On the Question of a Theory of (Third) World Literature' in *Dangerous Liaisons: Gender, National, and Postcolonial Perspectives*, ed. Anne McClintock, Aami Mufti and Ella Shohat (Minneapolis: University of Minnesota Press, 1997), p. 147.

11 Or as Chakrabarty argues, the equation of Europe with 'modernity' is the

work of both Europeans and third-world nationalisms. 'Postcoloniality and the Artifice of History', p. 21.

12　In the vein of this thought-experiment, we might read a famous passage of Marx in reverse, reading colonial-national society in place of 'bourgeois society' and Western, colonizing formations as 'vanished social formations': 'Bourgeois society is the most developed and the most complex historic organization of production. The categories which express its relations, the comprehension of its structure, thereby also allow insights into the structure and the relations of production of all the vanished social formations out of whose ruins and elements it built itself up, whose partly still unconquered remnants are carried along within it, whose mere nuances have developed explicit significance within it, etc ...' Quoted by Chakrabarty, 'Postcoloniality and the Artifice of History', p. 4. It is quite accurate to view the imported symbolic and material technologies of the advanced industrialized nations by third world nations as 'ruins' of vanished social formations, not only because they are artifacts wrenched free from their original systems but also because the West as it persists is the vanishing point of third world, post-independence development.

13　Edel E. Garcellano, *Interventions* (Manila: Polytechnic University of the Philippines Press, 1998), pp. 98–9.

14　An 'incident' is what helps the main narrative, which is composed of proper 'events.' What constitutes an 'event' is thus a fundamental issue of history.

15　Lilia Quindoza Santiago, 'Ang Salaysay ng Babae, Pagkababae At Kababaihan Sa Rebolusyon Ng 1896' [The story of woman, womanhood and women in the Revolution of 1896] in *Ulat sa Ikatlong Pambansang Kumperensya sa Sentenarya ng Rebolusyong 1896: Ang Papel ng Kababaihan at Katutubo sa Rebolusyong 1896* [Proceedings of the Third National Conference on the Centennial of the 1896 Revolution] (Baguio: University of the Philippines at Baguio and Benguet State University, 1993), p. 35.

16　In this regard we can view Agoncillo's subsumptive inclusion of female agency in his narrative in light of the growing strength of women's liberative movements. See Belinda A. Aquino, 'Philippine Feminism in Historical Perspective' in *Women and Politics Worldwide*, ed. Barbara J. Nelson and Najma Chowdhury (New Haven and London: Yale University Press, 1994).

17　Santiago notes this as a problem of sexist historiography: 'Just think about the exclusion of women that was accomplished when historians beginning from Zaide to Agoncillo translated the Highest, Most Respected Society of the Children of the People as "*Most Supreme, Most Esteemed Society of the Sons of the People*"' (translation mine, italics originally in English). 'Ang Salaysay Ng Babae, Pagkababae At Kababaihan Sa Rebolusyon Ng 1896',

p. 34. The masculinist project articulated in historiographical practices are constitutively linked to the masculinist project of nation building.

18 These are phrases from Bonifacio's poem, 'Pagibig sa Tinubuang Bayan.' The gender of the land/nation as mother is given by Bonifacio himself at the end of the poem. However, it is in Agoncillo's translation that the people and their tribulations are particularly and repeatedly personified as a woman and 'her suffering', — the Filipinos thereby become separate from the people whom, as a woman in distress, they, heeding the heterosexist imperative, must chivalrously rescue. Fe Mangahas makes a similar point in arguing that in the prevailing historical view, 'The community of men in the Revolution and its humanity are one. In contrast, the humanity of women is dismissed or separated from production and revolution. Although the official image of the people or nation is Mother Nation, this is nevertheless fought for and given freedom by men. In that case, the liberation of the people does not mean the liberation of women' (translation mine). Fe B. Mangahas, 'Ilang Tala Hinggil Sa Teorya O Perspektiba Sa Papel Ng Kababaihang Pilipino Sa Rebolusyon' [Notes toward a theory or perpsective on the role of Filipino women in the Revolution] in *Ulat sa Ikatlong Pambansang Kumperensya sa Sentenarya ng Rebolusyong 1896*, p. 15.

19 Arnold Molina Azurin, *Reinventing the Filipino Sense of Being and Becoming* (Quezon City: University of the Philippines Press, 1995), p. 73. Azurin cites Glenn May's criticism of the ways in which Agoncillo juggled data and analysis 'to suit his bias'. My own interest in Agoncillo's 'bias' is not as 'his', that is, not as a personal bias but as a socio-historical behaviour which continues to shape the specific relations of production of the Philippines.

20 By 'personal affinities' Azurin means Agoncillo's blood relation to Aguinaldo. Azurin adds that it is not only the focus on the Tagalog provinces at the expense of other regions that constitutes the myopia of Agoncillo's vision but also the limitation of the struggle to the period between 1896 and 1898, 'As though the succession of rebellions among non-Tagalogs did not matter in history, nor in the political configuration of the colonial government. As though, and this is the saddest swindle of all, the so-called key revolutionary leaders did not turn their backs so quickly on the revolutionary cause and their comrades to get the annual pensions and the privileged positions dangled by the Americans — while the fight would yet continue in various uprisings sparked by the oppressed around the country.' Azurin, *Reinventing the Filipino Sense of Being and Becoming*, p. 101.

21 Ileto's *Pasyon and Revolution* has been foundational in illuminating this affective movement in the Revolution.

22 Agoncillo regards Aguinaldo's presidency as a 'fait accompli' (*Revolt of the Masses*, p. 228), and judges Bonifacio's actions by this accomplished fact (a fact her participates in accomplishing): 'Bonifacio had no right to arrest the *Magdalo* men, especially when it is considered that Aguinaldo *was* the President of the Republic at the time ...' (p. 232, emphasis mine). It is by writing Aguinaldo's presidential claim as a 'done deed' that Agoncillo can then conclude that 'If Bonifacio was guilty, *as indeed he was* ... It is not the punishment meted out to him that demands a reconsideration of historical judgement, but the irregular method employed by his accusers in making him expiate for his errors' (*Revolt of the Masses*, p. 314, emphasis mine). Hypothesis serves as the presupposition of a foregone conclusion.

23 Agoncillo devotes considerable space to the Katipunan's different secret codes, symbolic uniforms and flags, to facsimiles of 'original' documents, authenticating signatures, 'living' personal testimony. While he dismisses the 'historical significance' of rumors, he nevertheless includes them in the main text to demonstrate the auras of Rizal and Aguinaldo. His own awe-filled and fetishistic relation to the written word is a combination of the mystified elevation of the writing apparatus characteristic of a colonial bureaucratic and educational system and akin to the 'common people's' relation to *anting-antings* (amulets) and other material-symbolic embodiments of metahuman power.

24 In his notes, Agoncillo accuses 'some people' of malignancy in 'twist(ing) historical facts', others of insincerity, 'bad faith', a 'subconscious wish' to 'make up' for past betrayals, motives of vengeance, etc. 'Personalism' is a concept used within a modern, secularly enlightened framework to understand actions overdetermined by affective attachments and associated with a purportedly archaic reverence for embodied agencies. Such 'personalism' continues to characterize current debates about history, such as Azurin's criticism of Agoncillo's 'clannish fetish' and ulterior personalist/familialist motives. 'Regionalism' is often invoked as an explanation rather than as something that requires historical explanation. When it is 'explained', it is attributed to some pre-colonial 'ethnic rivalry'.

25 See the interviews of Agoncillo and other historians in Ambeth R. Ocampo, *Aguinaldo's Breakfast and More* Looking Back *Essays* (Manila: Anvil Publishing, 1993).

26 The real Aguinaldo, it turns out, is also the friend in the sala with whom Agoncillo conceives himself having a lively conversation. Of course the Reader/friend in the sala, the master to whom Agoncillo is an apprentice, is the victor of history, the one who lives, whose prevailing is not deemed the product of domination but the evidence of moral right. Agoncillo evidences the behaviour of the adherents of historicism whom Walter

Benjamin points out as empathizing with the victor. 'And all rulers are the heirs of those who conquered before them. Hence, empathy with the victor invariably benefits the rulers.' Walter Benjamin, 'Theses on the Philosophy of History,' in *Illuminations*, ed. and introduction Hannah Arendt (New York: Schocken Books, 1968), p. 256.

27 This presumption is often held in cultural analyses of Filipino class struggle. Agoncillo's own analysis is premised on given classes and their innate predispositions. Thus all identifications are foredained. Rizal, for example, could not understand the masses because 'he was not one of them' (Agoncillo, *Revolt of the Masses*, p. 114). Bonifacio could because he *was*. For Agoncillo, 'the intricate psychology of the middle class of the period' predisposed them to inaction, not having 'the courage and abundant hope, the dash and the careless abandon of the masses whose unsophisticated mind could not see the various possibilities that might accompany a mode of action' (*Revolt of the Masses*, p. 43).

28 Alice G. Guillermo, 'Interpretations of the Revolution of 1896,' *Diliman Review*, 40, 1 (1992): 4–11. Guillermo argues that the 'class aspect of revolutionary discourse was not fully developed and radicalized' and thus easily dropped out of the official nation's programme. It was however articulated in the *kapatiran* movements of various peasant uprisings, which persisted well after the formal end of the revolution.

29 'Treachery' is the triggering event of the revolution. Secrecy, as a 'subjectively' selective telling replete with emotional-political intimacy and significance, is the very mode, not just condition of possibility, of the eruptive, expressive acts (physical and symbolic) constituting the revolutionary movement.

30 The authenticity of a man's testimony, and therefore his integrity as a man of his word is verified by writing, by his signature; the testimony of his sister can be uttered by her daughter, that is, can pass through another like and linked to her, but as such ultimately remains unverifiable. Agoncillo suggests this eternal dubiousness of women's testimonies when he asserts: 'If Honoria herself could not tell a story that is consistent with the story of Sor Teresa, since both were leading *dramatis personae* in that vast drama, *how could her statement, any statement, be relied upon as final and conclusive*? Or was it Sor Teresa who was not telling the truth?' (343, emphasis mine). 'Honoria herself' is constructed through the testimony of her daughter, which Agoncillo asserts 'may be taken as that of Honoria' (342).

31 Resil Mojares, 'Aspects of Sentimentality in Philippine Vernacular Fiction,' *Philippine Quarterly of Culture and Society*, 4, 4 (1976): 243–9, 245. I have in mind Vicente L. Rafael's useful formulation of the vernacular 'as that

which simultaneously institutes *and* subverts colonial rule' and 'as the uncanny crossroads formed by and formative of the intersection of the local with the global.' *Contracting Colonialism: Translation and Christian Conversion in Tagalog Society Under Early Spanish Rule* (Ithaca: Cornell University Press, 1988), p. xv.

32   In light of his view that there is no great Filipino literature and, moreover, the structuring of much of his 'history' through both Filipino and Western literary references (the former as instances of revolutionary expression and the latter as the standards by which he judges Filipino works as mediocre but powerful), Agoncillo might be seen as attempting to write the great Filipino novel in which the creative powers of the Filipino can finally be showcased. 'As a symbolic structure, the historical narrative does not reproduce the events it describes; it tells us in what direction to think about the events and charges our thought about the events with different emotional valences.' Hayden White, 'The Historical Text as Literary Artifact' in *Between History and Literature*, ed. Lionel Gossman (Cambridge, MA: Harvard University Press, 1990): 52.

33   Mojares, 'Aspects of Sentimentality in Philippine Vernacular Fiction,' p. 243.

34   Ileto's work is an important answer to this question. His attempt to give full subjectivity to 'the masses' provokes more and difficult questions about the gendered and sexual dimensions of the organizing movements of the masses, such as how the *babaylan* powers deployed in these movements come to be dominated by men and how women realized *kapatiran* through their own actions. See also Vicente L. Rafael's very important work, *Contracting Colonialism*, which demonstrates the Filipinos' 'evasion of the totalizing grip of Spanish colonialism'. See especially his discussion of the colonial project to institute the 'internalization of an exterior hierarchy' (p. 101) through the confession and, moreover, the Tagalogs' 'hollowing out (of) the Spanish call to submission' (p. 135).

35   In 'Ang Kilusang Feminista at ang Katipunan' [The Feminist Movement and the Katipunan], Lilia Quindoza Santiago outlines the feminist historial project in the following way: 'one should focus attention on the significant role of women in the realization of the principles and the founding of the Katipunan as a revolutionary collective ... one should consider more deeply the development of a "feminist movement", both inside and outside the Katipunan and the revolution in the last part of the nineteenth century' (translation mine), *Diliman Review*, 40, 1 (1992): 13.

36   This post-war crisis is discussed widely. See, for example, *Dictatorship and Revolution: Roots of People's Power*, ed. Aurora Javate-de Dios, Petronilo Bn. Daroy and Lorna Kalaw-Tirol (Metro Manila: Conspectus, 1988) and

Joseph Y. Lim, 'Our Economic Crisis: A Historical Perspective' in *Synthesis: Before and Beyond February 1986*, ed. Lilia Quindoza-Santiago (Quezon City: The Interdisciplinary Forum (IDF) of the University of the Philippines, 1986): 15–26.

37 For a discussion of the role of the 'Filipino First movement' and political negotiation over the US bases in preparing the state for 'crony capitalism', see Nick Cullather, 'Filipino First' in his *Illusions of Influence: The Political Economy of the United States-Philippines Relations, 1942–1960* (Stanford, CA: Stanford University Press, 1994). For a discussion of the racialization of the Chinese as 'alien capital' as a fundamental operation of this state nationalism and its consequence in the post-authoritarian period, see Caroline Hau, '"Who Will Save Us from the 'Law'?"; The Criminal State and the Illegal Alien in Post-1986 Philippines' in *Figures of Criminality in Indonesia, the Philippines, and Colonial Vietnam*, ed. Vicente L. Rafael (Ithaca, NY: Cornell University Southeast Asia Program Publications, 1999). For a discussion of these competing nationalisms, see Amado Guerrero, *Philippine Society and Revolution* and Renato Constantino, *The Philippines: A Past Revisited.*

38 Reynaldo C. Ileto, *Filipinos and Their Revolution*, p. 197.

CHAPTER 5

1 See, for example, *Dictatorship and Revolution: Roots of People's Power*, ed. Aurora Javate-De Dios, Petronilo Bn. Daroy, and Lorna Kalaw-Tirol (Metro Manila: Conspectus Foundation, 1988), as well as *Synthesis, Before and Beyond February 1986: The Edgar M. Jopson Memorial Lectures*, ed. and intro. Lilia Quindoza Santiago (Manila: Edgar M. Jopson Memorial Foundation, 1986).

2 See Benedict J. Kerkvliet and Resil B. Mojares, ed. *From Marcos to Aquino: Local Perspectives on Political Transition in the Philippines* (Honolulu: University of Hawaii Press, 1992).

3 See Vince Boudreau, *Grass Roots and Cadre in the Protest Movement* (Quezon City: Ateneo de Manila University Press, 2001); Mark Thompson, *The Anti-Marcos Struggle: Personalistic Rule and Democratic Transition in the Philippines* (New Haven: Yale University Press, 1995); and Permanent Peoples' Tribunal Session on the Philippines, *Philippines: Repression and Resistance* (Philippines: KSP Komite ng Sambayanang Pilipino, 1981). In the book that follows this one, *Things Fall Away*, I track the cultural contributions of the revolutionary movement to the force and 'style' of the EDSA uprising.

4   The ruling classes' hegemonic taking over (that is, managing, controlling, and defining) the events is encapsulated by June Keithley frantically exclaiming, 'They (the communists/leftists) are trying to steal our revolution.' This disjunction between 'they' and 'our' signified (and in some measure secured) the redivision of 'the people' — a split homologous to that which would occur between Cory and the people. Monina Allarey Mercado, ed. *An Eyewitness History: People Power, The Philippine Revolution Of 1986* (Manila, Philippines: J. B. Reuter, S. J., Foundation, 1986), p. 192. From hereon, references to this book will be cited as *People Power*.

5   Jaime C. Bulatao, S. J., 'Another Look at Philippine Values,' in *Manila: History, People and Culture*, ed. Wilfrido V. Villacorta, Isagani R. Cruz and ma. Lourdes Brillantes (Manila: De La Salle University Press, 1989), p. 325.

6   In discussing the relation between the two in *Alice Doesn't: Feminism, Semiotics, Cinema* (Bloomington: Indiana University Press, 1984), Teresa De Lauretis observes that 'For Pasolini, human action, human intervention in the real, is the first and foremost expression of men, their primary "language"' (p. 49), which renders discourse, such as historical discourse, products of a secondary mediation.

7   Antonio Gramsci, *Selections from Prison Notebooks*, ed. and trans. Quintin Hoare and Geoffrey Nowell Smith (New York: International Publishers, 1971), p. 326.

8   Gilles Deleuze, *The Logic of Sense*, trans. Mark Lester with Charles Stivale, ed. Constantin V. Boundas (New York: Columbia University Press, 1990), p. 8.

9   de Lauretis, *Alice Doesn't*, p. 159.

10   In his critique of the Left's decision to boycott the snap elections, E. San Juan, Jr. alludes to this common sense as an inherently conservative imaginary: 'By withdrawing from involvement in the "sham election", the leadership of BAYAN left the masses to be guided by "common sense", which means essentially the beliefs and value-systems and life-goals of the traditional ruling classes.' *Only By Struggle: Reflections on Philippine Culture, Politics and Society in a Time of Civil War* (Quezon City: Kalikasan Press, 1988), p. 103.

11   In the words of Michel Pecheux: 'History is there where there is a logic *within* contingence, a reason *within* unreason, where there is a historical perception which, like perception in general, leaves in the background what cannot enter the foreground but seizes the lines of force as they are generated and actively leads their traces to a conclusion. This analogy should not be interpreted as a shameful organicism or finalism, but as a reference to the fact that all symbolic systems — perception, language,

history — only become what they were although in order to do so they need to be taken up into human initiative' (p. 98).

12 From the book jacket of *People Power*. The accounts are classified under five headings representing the stages leading to the uprising:

  I.   The Assassination of Benigno S. Aquino, Jr., 1983
  II. Rallies, Marches, And Demonstrations, 1983–1985
  III. The Election Campaign, 1986
  IV. The Election and Ballot Watch, 1986
  V.   The People's Uprising, February 22 to 25, 1986

  The organization of the accounts clearly manifests the hegemonic historical time framework of the 'revolution'.

13 Gramsci, *Prison Notebooks*, p. 349.

14 The subterranean role of the revolutionary movement in creating the conditions of possibility for the popular revolt is a topic I reserve for another time.

15 My use of Marcos's last name and Aquino's nickname to designate these opponents stems from popular usage. This practice was in part a means of distinguishing them from their spouses (Imelda and Ninoy), which contributed to the way in which they were publicly constructed. That the male personages in this national drama were generally designated by their last names while the female personages were designated by their first names manifests the discursive operation of gender in the staging of the crisis.

16 'Citizens behave as a public body when they confer in an unrestricted fashion — that is, with the guarantee of freedom of assembly and association and the freedom to express and publish their opinions — about matters of general interest.' Jurgen Habermas, 'The Public Sphere: An Encyclopedia Article', in *Critical Theory and Society*, ed. and intro. Stephen Eric Bronner and Douglas MacKay Kellner (New York and London: Routledge, 1989) p. 136. Habermas shows that 'the public sphere as a sphere which mediates between society and state, in which the public organizes itself as the bearer of public opinion' (p. 137) emerges under particular historical conditions that determine its manifest form. He also shows the important role communicative structures play in the creation of the public sphere as a realm of society, and in its operation as a principle of social activity, especially the mass media which 'free communication processes from the provinciality of spatiotemporally restricted contexts and permit public spheres to emerge, through establishing the abstract simultaneity of a virtually present network of communication contents far removed in space and time and through keeping messages available for manifold contexts' (Habermas, 'The Tasks of a Critical Theory of Society', also in *Critical Theory and Society*, p. 303).

17   See, for example, Armando Malay, Jr., 'The Politics of *Kaluwagan*' in *Marxism In The Philippines: Marx Centennial Lectures* ed. Third World Studies (Diliman, Quezon City: Third World Studies Center, University of the Philippines, 1984).

18   Slavoj Žižek, 'Beyond Discourse Analysis,' p. 8.

19   A popular joke was that the Americans wanted to protect the dictator to protect the bases so that they could protect democracy.

20   Her political slogan, *Tama na, Sobra na, Palitan na* (Enough already, Too much already, Change already), bore this promise. In contrast, Marcos's slogan, *Marcos pa rin* (Marcos just the same), bore the assurance of stasis. The combined slogan used as a joke but also evincing the cynical apprehension of the opposition between the two, is the paradox that marks the antagonism the Philippines bears: *Tama na, Sobra na, Marcos pa rin!* (Enough already, Too much already, Marcos just the same!)

21   San Juan, *Only By Struggle*, p. 105.

22   Fredric R. Jameson, *The Political Unconscious: Narrative as A Socially Symbolic Act* (Ithaca, NY: Cornell University Press, 1981), p. 81.

23   Teodoro Benigno, *People Power*, p. 17.

24   It is important to note that this was from a speech delivered on 10 March 1984, long before Cory's candidacy was even a possibility. Her lack of personal political ambitions was crucial to the meaning her rhetoric held for the community she was helping form. For her authority would rest upon this disinterest in the petty affairs of jockeying for power in traditional *pulitika* (politics).

25   *People Power*, p. 14.

26   This encounter with Ninoy's death occurs in 'the place of the real, which stretches from the trauma to the phantasy' [Jacques Lacan, *The Four Fundamental Concepts of Psycho-Analysis,* ed. Jacques-Alain Miller, trans. Alan Sheridan. (New York: Norton, 1988), p. 60]. Lacan elaborates on the real as trauma and on the dream as the place of its eruption: 'Desire manifests itself in the dream by the loss expressed in an image at the most cruel point of the object. It is only in the dream that this truly unique encounter can occur. Only a rite, an endlessly repeated act, can commemorate this not very memorable encounter' (*Four Fundamental Concepts*, p. 59). How this recurrent fascination with martyrdom (Christ, José Rizal, Ninoy Aquino) is a symptom of the socio-historical configuration of the Philippines would have to be studied elsewhere. Ileto points out that 'at several points in Philippine history, there have appeared extraordinary individuals who were perceived by the masses as embodiments of the Christ model' [*Pasyon and Revolution: Popular Movements in the Philippines, 1840–1910* (Quezon City: Ateneo de Manila

University Press, 1979), p. 63]. However, this is explained mainly as the resulting influence of the *pasyon*. In any case, the fantasy through which this trauma is symbolized is what is important to the extent that it structures and regulates the social reality people experience and act upon as they make history. As Žižek posits: 'The real is an entity which should be constructed afterwards so that we can account for the distortions of the symbolic structure. All its effectiveness lies in these effects, in the distortions it produces in the symbolic universe of the subject: the traumatic event is ultimately just a fantasy-construct filling out a certain void in a symbolic structure' ('Beyond Discourse Analysis', p. 3).

27 Ileto, *Pasyon and Revolution*, p. 130.

28 The equivalence is made in the imaginary of Philippine society, with only the sketch of the comparison experienced in actuality. However, many writers from the middle classes consciously represented the imaginary analogy between Ninoy and Christ, thus demonstrating the ideological content of the prevailing fantasy of patriotism, as in the following excerpt from Gemino Abad's tribute to Ninoy, called 'The Dead Man's Tale': 'Surely he knew beforehand/ at the charmed womb's portal/ his abrupt and giddy mortality/ Upon this tarmac, / before our comforting lies, / the final object of grief/ and an endless tale — / 'Ecce Homo!'/ In old Jerusalem too, / city of fickle crowds. / Someone was lifted up at noon/ upon dead wood — / the rude breakneck letters/ of One skywriting long ago.' What is most striking in this portrayal is its steeping of events in divine time, fusing current and biblical events in 'One skywriting'. This temporality will be shown to be characteristic of the hegemonic transformation of history into myth.

29 Victor Jose Peñaranda, 'Assassination', in *Kamao: Tula Ng Protesta, 1970–1986*, ed. Alfredo Navarro Salanga et al. (Manila: Cultural Center of the Philippines, 1987), p. 389.

30 In *Pasyon and Revolution*, Reynaldo Ileto gives an insightful analysis of how 'the masses experience of Holy Week fundamentally shaped the style of peasant brotherhoods and uprisings during the Spanish and early American colonial periods' (p. 15).

31 Vicente Rafael, 'Nationalism, Imagery, and the Filipino Intelligentsia in the Nineteenth Century,' *Critical Inquiry* 16, no. 3 (1990): 600.

32 *People Power*, p. 32.

33 For a discussion of 'the politics of shame' in the everyday life of the poor, see Michael Pinches, 'The Working Class Experience of Shame, Inequality, and People Power in Tatalon, Manila' in *From Marcos to Aquino: Local Perspectives on Political Transition in the Philippines*, ed. Benedict J. Kerkvliet and Resil B. Mojares (Quezon City: Ateneo de Manila University Press, 1991).

34 *People Power*, p. 48.

35 *The Turning Point: Twenty-Six Accounts Of The February Events In The Philippines*, ed. Marilies von Brevern (Manila, Philippines: J. B. Reuter, S. J., Foundation,1986), pp. 138–139

36 *People Power*, p. 56.

37 KAAKBAY (a nationalist organization led by former Sen. Jose W. Diokno) asserted in its statement of support of Aquino, 'the two principal opponents of the Filipino people today are American imperialism and the dictatorial regime of Ferdinand Marcos. Their defeat is the key to the attainment of genuine national independence and sovereignty, popular democracy and real development' [*The Philippines Reader*, ed. Daniel B. Schirmer & Stephen Rosskamm Shalom (Boston: South End Press, 1987), p. 348].

38 'The People's Carnival', in *Kamao*, p. 358.

39 René Jara shows how the Virgin was adopted and appropriated for purposes of revolt rather than obedience: 'Guadalupe meant nothing less than a deconstruction of the patriarchal system of colonization and conversion undertaken by the Europeans in the Indies' ['The Inscription of Creole Consciousness' in *Re/discovering Colonial Writing*. René Jara and Nicolas Spadaccini, Eds. Minneapolis: The Prima Institute, 1989) p. 361].

40 Joaquin Roces (chairman of the Cory Aquino for President Movement), *People Power*, 45. It is important to note that while there have been many women national leaders, Cory Aquino was the first to be nominated by the people rather than by a party. One of her conditions for running was the gathering of a million signatures in support of her candidacy, a condition that was easily fulfilled.

41 *People Power*, p. 53. An interesting look at Cory's resolution is afforded by her vice-president, Doy Laurel: 'I talked to Cory about eight times. We had eight meetings. I tried to convince her that she should not run, that she should allow me to run, she should allow me to take the brickbats. *She should remain the symbol, like Gandhi, and I would play the role of Nehru. I said: "Be the lady in distress and let me be your Lancelot.* I am battle-scarred and trained for this. I have the political party, the party that has been declared as the dominant opposition party. I am like a knight with the armor, a shield, a horse and a sword, ready to do battle, let me fight for you. If I lose, only I will lose. But if you run and you lose, even Ninoy's heroism may be affected." But she was very stubborn. Her mind was also made up. To her, losing was nothing. She didn't mind losing' (*The Turning Point*, p. 14). This kind of patriarchal logic, which posits woman as symbol and inspiration, man as actor, however, would eventually win out over Cory, beginning with the military usurpation of the 'people power' she

played a crucial part in unleashing. It is not accidental that the metaphors used by Laurel involve modern colonial patriotism and European medieval romance. The contradictions of his Philippine reality is shown here in these symbols.

42 Vicente Rafael, 'Nationalism, Imagery and the Filipino Intelligentsia,' p. 600.

43 *People Power,* p. 54.

44 Everyone who participated had funny stories to tell afterwards. In spite of the overall dramatic tone of hegemonic accounts of the revolt, there is no hiding the humour most people found in it. Even in a text like *People Power* with a strong sacred bias (explicitly 'dedicated to Mary, the Mother of God') contains many funny, even ridiculous, anecdotes, jokes and humorous insights.

45 But not the war that continues to be waged against US imperialism and Philippine cacique democracy. This war has been continuously waged on different terrains not excluding, of course, that of the sign. It is important to stress that the battle fought on EDSA could not have been possible without the material conditions secured by a long-standing struggle against the Marcos dictatorship.

46 Sylvia Mayuga, *People Power,* p. 49 (emphasis mine). It is instructive to note that the negative definition 'not oak' reveals the origins of the color yellow as the color of protest. Yellow ribbons were tied around all the trees on the street where the Aquinos lived, awaiting Ninoy's return, a gesture inspired by the American song, 'Tie a Yellow Ribbon 'Round the Old Oak Tree'. This is a demonstration of the power of appropriation, an example of an artifact of subordination turned into an act of resistance and affirmation.

47 'With the assassination of Benigno Aquino, there was an upsurge in women's political activity. An all women's protest demonstration against the Marcos regime was held; a new militant women's organization — WOMB (Women for the Ouster of Marcos and Boycott) — was established; and coalitions and congresses of women's organizations began to form. The most significant of these coalitions was the militant General Assembly Binding Women for Reforms, Integrity, Equality, Leadership and Action — GABRIELA — founded in March 1984' (*Philippines Reader,* pp. 308–9).

48 One man recalls: 'Our wives were always for her. They feel that since Marcos has become synonymous to corruption and abuse of power, they wanted Marcos out. "Why not give Cory a chance? We believe she is really sincere," they would assiduously tell everyone.' Another man remembers that as soon as Cardinal Sin made an appeal on Radio Veritas for the support of the Filipino people, his wife heeded without hesitation: '"Let's

go," my wife said immediately. She is responsive to issues like these, more so if they are raised by a prince of the Church. I was much slower in responding to the idea because it was midnight, and ours was to be a strictly two-man journey to a new conflict. My wife also did not consider that the issue was between two armed groups. Rubber shoes, flashlights, and a Spanish fan did not really add up to adequate protection.' But it was precisely this spontaneous, almost reckless action on the part of his wife that constituted 'people power'.

49 Teresa C. Pardo, *People Power*, p. 110 (emphasis mine). Also, June Keithley's account, *People Power*, p. 192.

50 Dolores de Manuel, *People Power*, p. 204 (emphasis mine). De Manuel is a teacher. It is interesting to note that teachers, who are mostly female, were integral to the historical developments, not only because of their high visibility as electoral proctors and counters, but also because of their moral authority as mother figures. Rizal's adoring portrait of his own mother as his first teacher has been well inscribed in the national consciousness through the educational system.

51 Sister Gemma A. Silverio (Mother Superior of the Missionary Sisters of the Sacred Heart), *The Turning Point*, p. 81.

52 Benedict Anderson, *Imagined Communities: Reflections On The Origin And Spread Of Nationalism* (London; New York: Verso, 1991), p. 140.

53 Deleuze and Guattari, *Anti-Oedipus*, p. 183. 'The desiring sexual relationships of man and woman (or of man and man, or woman and woman) are the index of social relationships between people. Love and sexuality are the exponents or the indicators, this time unconscious, of the libidinal investments of the social field' (Ibid., pp. 352–3).

54 Food was an important element in the conversion-courtship process, in the securing of love. Offering food is an indispensable social and religious ritual, a symbol and means of unity. It also signifies the fulfillment of needs and desires, a fulfillment that is erotically founded and sublimated in the discourses of love and faith.

55 As Colonel Joseph Espina vividly recalls: 'the ladies came over, pretty girls and the nuns, offering us food ... And then the girls started embracing us, hugging all of us, and kissing us. You should have seen that girl, hugging me, kissing me — oh, my God — I wouldn't know what other country would have something like that' (*The Turning Point*, p. 118).

56 'On Narcissism', p. 101.

57 'On Narcissism', p. 88. Freud adds that the reason narcissistic women are found to be fascinating by men is because 'another person's narcissism has a great attraction for those who have renounced part of their own narcissism and are in search of object-love' (p. 89).

58 Slavoj Žižek, *The Sublime Object of Ideology* (London and New York: Verso, 1989), p. 180.

59 Žižek, *The Sublime Object of Ideology*, p. 65.

60 Sister Gemma A. Silvero, *The Turning Point*, p. 83.

61 One who was inside the camp with all the defecting generals and colonels recalls: 'Enrile said: "This morning, on my way to the inauguration, I heard the people shouting: 'We love our soldiers!' I never heard that before in my life. In all my years with the military, I never heart that — people shouting: 'We love our soldiers!' We have to be worthy of that. Our allegiance is to the people." Beside me was Flotz Aquino, who is a general. Flotz turned to me, and his eyes were wet. As we started out of the room, he said: "It gets you, right here!" And with his closed fist, he struck his chest, just over the heart.' (*People Power*, p. 237).

   And from a soldier himself: 'I was not prepared for what I was seeing: thousands of people were crowding EDSA and were cheering us. We could hardly pass. It was the first time in my life that I have seen the people accepting the soldiers. We had been alienated from them for a long time. Most of us were so moved that we could hardly control our feelings. Not a few guys had misty eyes' (Colonel Tirso Gador, *The Turning Point*, p. 112).

62 Colonel Tirso Gador, *The Turning Point*, p. 114.

63 *The Turning Point*, p. 177.

64 See Caroline Hau on the historical provenance of the nationalist othering of the Chinese. Caroline S. Hau, 'Who Will Save Us From the "Law"?': The Criminal State and the Illegal Alien in Post–1986 Philippines" in Vicente L. Rafael, ed. *Figures of Criminality in Indonesia, the Philippines, and Colonial Vietnam* (Ithaca, NY: Southeast Asia Program Publications, 1999). Rather than being the object of the desire of America in its imperialist fantasy, determined by this Other's social production the Philippines acted now as the desiring subject whose identity was not determined by its historical ego ideal — the international (which in the Free World fantasy is the First World, and more specifically, the US) — but instead by a new ego ideal, the Filipino nation.

65 *The Turning Point*, 149 (emphasis mine).

66 Michael Pinches writes about the experience of the urban poor as a state of communitas: 'their accounts did not stress reasons so much as the occasion itself — the huge crowd, the feeling of enjoyment and pride, and, above all, the spirit of camaraderie. Although support for Aquino, the desire to remove Marcos, and the call of the Catholic Church were important, what mattered most were these feelings.' 'The Working Class Experience of Shame, Inequality, and People Power in Tatalon, Manila'

in *From Marcos to Aquino: Local Perspectives on Political Transition in the Philippines*, ed. Benedict J. Kerkvliet and Resil B. Mojares, p. 185.

67 Lacuesta, Amado L. Jr., in *People Power,* p. 238.

68 Cory here means the whole political apparatus she had built around her, which consisted of an elite opposition (to Marcos).

69 This was the reason that the role of US imperialism with which Marcos was complicit was elided from the national consciousness operating at the time and that consequently, the revolt was not a revolution (for the metonymic operation served to displace the enemy, the source of antagonism which the people's efforts were devoted to expelling — in other words, the people got rid of Marcos, but not the conditions that made his dictatorship possible).

70 *People Power,* p. 245 (emphasis mine).

71 Some read the major intersection at EDSA — *Epifanio de los Santos Avenue* or Epiphany of the Saints Avenue — to symbolize the cross of Christ, as evident in the poem 'Some Rite of Passage' by Ophelia Alcantara-Dimalanta, in which people power is portrayed as 'one prodigious/ ocean of energy whose countless/ tributaries rush with one/ and as one seething force/ into some magnetic core/ forming a cross.' *Versus: Philippine Protest Poetry, 1983–1986*, ed. Alfredo Navarro Salanga and Esther M. Pacheco (Quezon City, Metro Manila: Ateneo de Manila University Press, 1986), p. 115.

72 The post-election statement issued from the Catholic Bishops' Conference of the Philippines exerted much influence in uniting, shaping and lending authority to the growing resistance to Marcos, which the Church had unofficially been sanctioning. 'We must come together and discern what appropriate actions to take that will be according to the mind of Christ. In a creative, imaginative way, under the guidance of Christ's Spirit, let us pray together, reason together, decide together, act together, always to the end that the truth prevail, that the will of the people be fully respected.' *Philippines Reader*, p. 351.

73 *The Turning Point*, p. 153 (emphasis mine).

74 Herminio S. Beltran, Jr. 'The Prize' in *Versus*, p. 105.

75 Amado L. Lacuesta, Jr., *People Power*, p. 125.

76 Concepcion Q. Sonon, *People Power*, p. 232.

77 As one observer put it: 'The revolution is actually depending on a commercial telephone line, a civilian broadcaster and a commercial radio station to establish critical contact with its meagre forces, all within earshot of anyone with a cheap transistor radio.' Lacuesta, *People Power*, p. 190.

78 Even the act of listening, however, was already an act of complicity with the subversive forces, a participatory act: 'I stayed up two nights running, glued to Radio Veritas, with the crazy idea that somehow just listening

would keep the tank columns or the helicopters away' (Kaa Byington, *People Power*, p. 248). Cf. *A Dying Colonialism* in which Fanon discusses the role of the radio in the consolidation of the nationalist forces in the Algerian revolution: 'Having a radio seriously meant *going* to war … Listening in on the Revolution, the Algerian existed with it, made it exist.' Frantz Fanon, *A Dying Colonialism*, trans. Haakon Chevalier, intro., Adolfo Gilly (New York: Grove Press, 1967), p. 93.

79 James B. Reuter, S. J., *People Power*, p. 237.

80 In fact, the main point of criticism against Cory after she had assumed state power was that, as President, she was 'not man enough'. Her failings are constructed as resulting from her weakness, which is, not surprisingly, underpinned by the concept of her femininity. Indeed, most of the petty attacks she has received for her 'unpresidential behaviour' are almost blatantly sexist, for the quality of being presidential is conceived in masculinist terms.

81 One cannot underestimate the effects of this transference. For early in her term, Cory had already begun to rely very heavily on the military. Many of her first acts were in fact acts rewarding the military in one form or another, fortifying both their symbolic and actual power. This transference also accounts for Cory's hesitancy in endangering her own position by pitting herself against a military that had never entirely accepted its new commander in chief, mainly because of the way she had constructed herself against the strongman Marcos — her bearing revolutionary desires meant, for one thing, sympathy for the leftists and communists. It is thus not surprising that Cory quickly became a veritable hostage, and later accomplice, of her own army.

82 When Cory began to assume patriarchal authority as the new Law of the land, the new King, she fell back into the same dynamics of masculine-feminine relations that was prevailing before. This does not reduce the significance of her feat in assuming this position, for after all, the reversal of meanings of categories is crucial to the corruption of their present meanings. Women playing men will not in itself alter what women are and are expected to be, but it can be a step in stretching the imagination within which men and women, masculine and feminine are defined. While Cory was strait-jacketed into acting 'man enough' for her job as President, she did not entirely succumb to the masculine construction of power, authority and humanity (as the bearer of civilization). In fact, there were instances when she tried to redefine those terms. Once, she chided her former defense minister, Enrile, telling him, 'Be a man. Or better yet, be a woman.'

83 *People Power*, p. 251.

84 Ricardo M. De Ungria, 'Epithalium 22–25 February 1986.'

85 De Ungria, 'Epithalium 22–25 February 1986'.

86 Julia Kristeva, *In the Beginning was Love: Psychoanalysis and Faith*, trans. Arthur Goldhammer (New York: Columbia University Press, 1987), p. 24.

87 Many accounts evinced the foreign audience to whom they were addressed, defining the nature of the Filipino character in the attempt to explain the behaviour of people during the events.

88 Patricio Abinales, 'Coalition politics in the Philippines,' *Current History* 100, no. 645 (April 2001): 154–161.

89 This authority was particularly crucial during the spate of military coups that plagued the Aquino administration. Diminishing 'people power', the Aquino administration had to rely on US military intervention to maintain itself in power.

90 Gemino Abad has, for example, written a series of parables of the events leading to the revolt in *Poems and Parables* (Quezon City: Kalikasan Press, 1988). The historical actors have been reduced to archetypal characters bearing names like the King, the Queen, the Minister of War, the General, the Prince of the Church, the widow and the People. It is important to note in this kind of portrayal that only a handful of characters are acknowledged as the makers of history — history once again is the story of kings and queens and armies, and the People are the subjects of their rulers' actions (reduced once again to being 'masses'). In addition, in this account, only the widow's name is not capitalized, and her role as depicted in the parable of the revolt, 'Parable of the People' is confined to one line: 'And a widow stood among them and rejoiced over the miracle of conversion' (p. 84).

91 Quoted in Frantz Fanon, *The Wretched of the Earth*, pref. Jean-Paul Sartre, trans. Constance Farrington (New York: Grove Press, 1965).

CHAPTER 6

1 Eddie Infante, *Inside Philippine Movies 1970–1990: Essays for Students of Philippine Cinema* (Quezon City: Ateneo de Manila University Press, 1991) p. 57.

2 Joel David, *The National Pastime: Contemporary Philippine Cinema* (Metro Manila: Anvil, 1990), pp. 13–4.

3 Virgilio S. Almario, 'Cinderella Superstar: The Life and Legend of Nora Aunor', in *Readings in Philippine Cinema*, ed. Rafael Ma. Guerrero (Manila: Experimental Cinema of the Philippines, 1983), p. 135.

4 At the time of the film's release, Nora Aunor had a television variety show

called 'Superstar', the theme music of which was the title song to the Andrew Lloyd Weber musical 'Jesus Christ, Superstar'. The show stayed on the air for about ten more years.

5   Benilda S. Santos, 'Idol, Bestiary and Revolutionary: Images and Social Roles of the Filipino Woman in Film (1976–1986)' in *Reading Popular Culture*, ed. Soledad Reyes (Quezon City: Office of Research and Publications, Ateneo de Manila University, 1991), p. 216.

6   Santos, 'Idol, Bestiary and Revolutionary,' pp. 215–6.

7   Emmanuel A. Reyes identifies the Catholic equation of suffering and virtue as a primary mythological theme of women's melodrama. 'The World on Her Shoulders: Women in Melodrama' in his *Notes on Philippine Cinema* (Manila: De La Salle University Press, 1989), pp. 43–50. Rafael Ma. Guerrero similarly links the myth of female *masochismo* to Catholicism. As he writes, 'Women in Tagalog movies endure much, because — as Heine said of God — it is their job.' 'Tagalog Movies: A New Understanding' in *Readings in Philippine Cinema*, ed. and intro. Rafael Ma. Guerrero (Manila: Experimental Cinema of the Philippines, 1983), pp. 113–4.

8   Almario, 'Cinderella Superstar,' p. 142.

9   Guerrero, 'Tagalog Movies,' p. 114.

10   Nora wanted to make 'serious' films and created NV productions for this purpose. As she put it, 'I must do this to help my fans. I can't just sing for them all my life. They are also growing up. They have helped me, and I must pay them back by giving them all I can. I have a greater responsibility as a producer ... It's hard to make only 'quality' pictures. I don't have the money. But I'd like the moviegoer to benefit even from a commercial film. Like *Tisoy*. And I would like NV to be able to produce at least one good picture every year. With that, I shall be happy. After all, there are other sensible producers around, aren't there?' (quoted in Almario, 'Cinderella Superstar,' pp. 142–3). Though not produced by NV productions, *Himala* was one of the 'quality' pictures made by 'other sensible producers' that Nora endorsed. It was also one for which she was an active creative consultant.

11   Nora Aunor's following might be seen as a form of 'class' and 'gender' inasmuch as a great many of her fans worked as domestic labour and, more importantly, inasmuch as Nora Aunor's identificatory trait was her personification of the *atsay* [maid], a figure embodying the combined racializing and sexualizing devaluations of menial labour and poor women. This is not to say that all of Nora Aunor's fans fit this dominant profile. Although analyses of Nora Aunor as a media-cultural phenomenon often allude to the role of 'race' in the constitution of this following in the casual,

nonserious way they mention Nora's 'darkness', they almost completely disregard the role of 'sexuality' in this constitution. This disregard is tied to the repressive work of studio publicity machines, which worked to prevent the leakage of Nora's 'lesbian' desires and relations. Michael Salientes, trans. Jessica Zafra, 'Idol Conversation: An Interview with a Movie Icon Turns into Group Therapy,' *Folio* 5 (1998): 69–73, 120–5.

12   Domestic labour is a new form of sociality from the point of view of social mobilization as well as scholarly inquiry. It is invoked by divergent Philippine nationalisms (see E. San Juan, Jr, *Allegories of Resistance: The Philippines at the Threshold of the Twenty-First Century* [Quezon City: University of the Philippines Press, 1994] and Vicente L. Rafael, '"Your Grief Is Our Gossip"' in *White Love and Other Essays in Filipino History* [Durham, NC, and London: Duke University Press], pp. 204–28.) as well as by transnational feminisms in the negotiation of social power, and it serves as the subject of anthropological and sociological research in the analysis of power (see, e.g., Nicole Constable, *Maid to Order in Hong Kong: Stories of Filipina Workers* [Ithaca, NY, and London: Cornell University Press, 1997] and Rhacel Parreñas, *Servants of Globalization: Women, Migration and Domestic Work* [Stanford, Calif.: Stanford University Press, 2001]).

13   Mary Ann Doane, 'The Economy of Desire: The Commodity Form in/of the Cinema,' *Quarterly Review of Film and Video* 11.1 (1989): 23–33. See also Laura Mulvey, *Fetishism and Curiosity* (Bloomington: Indiana University Press, 1996). Mulvey's chapter on Ousmane Sembene's *Xala* is an example of film analyses that view third world film through an allegorical framework, by way of excusing themselves from knowing the cultural particulars of its production. These analyses are able to depict the dominant psychosocial logic at work in societies under the sway of capitalism (here colonial capitalism), a logic that is endemic to the film apparatus itself to the extent that cinema effects and expresses the subjective structures of capitalist relations (the economy of desire). However, these analyses are unable to recognize the practices that come under and create the sway of another logic, one that has no necessary, autonomous, coherent existence apart from capitalism, but is tangential to it.

14   The female star is, in Richard Dyer's analysis, 'both labor and the thing that labor produces' (quoted in Laura Mulvey, 'Some Thoughts on Theories of Fetishism in the Context of Contemporary Culture,' *October* 65 (1993): 15). The 'star image' is hence seen as 'congealed labor', the product that, since it is produced for the phallic order of capital, can only be the means by which female spectators consume their own objectification.

15 Hence, Anne Friedberg argues that the fascination with a film star is really a fascination 'with an entire system of signifiers and a code — the commercialized erotic system'. 'A Denial of Difference: Theories of Cinematic Identification' in *Psychoanalysis and Cinema*, ed. E. Ann Kaplan (London: Routledge, 1990, p. 43.

16 This latter approach, exemplified in the intersectional analyses of multicultural feminist criticism, addresses both the implicit universalism of the former approach's focus on 'female subjects' and the complex multiplicity of stratifying systems (gender, race, sexuality, class and nation) constituting the oppression of women of colour, third world and fourth world women as well as gays and lesbians, both white and of colour. For a discussion of the historical context and political possibilities of multicultural feminism, see Ella Shohat, ed., *Talking Visions: Multicultural Feminism in a Transnational Age* (Cambridge, Mass.: MIT Press, 1998). A key text of 'intersectional analysis' is Kimberle Crenshaw, 'Demarginalizing the Intersection of Race and Sex' in *Feminist Legal Theory*, ed. D. Kelly Weisberg (Philadelphia: Temple University Press, 1993), pp. 383–95. On the one hand, I am making an oblique critique of what I see as the hypostasization of 'intersectionality' in some varieties of postcolonial and US third world feminisms engaged in 'cartographic' work. In such work, analytical categories — 'modalities' or 'axes of power' of class, gender, 'race', sexuality, nationalism — have begun to assume the character of substantive 'areas' and 'forces' in observable 'relationships' with each other. See for example, Avtar Brah, *Cartographies of Diaspora: Contesting Identities* (London and New York: Routledge, 1996). On the other, I see the limits of 'intersectional' analysis, which arose as an important theoretical means of addressing the experiences of women of colour within the juridical framework of US civil society, for understanding social processes outside of or before and beyond this framework.

17 See Jonathan L. Beller, 'The Spectatorship of the Proletariat,' *boundary 2* 22 (3) (1995): 171–228; 'Identity Through Death / The Nature of Capital: The Media-Environment for Natural Born Killers,' *Post-Identity* 1 (2) (1998): 55–67 and Guy Debord, *Society of the Spectacle* (New York: Zone Books, 1994).

18 Almario, 'Cinderella Superstar,' p. 139.

19 Nora Aunor joined the rally held on the twenty-fifth anniversary of the declaration of martial law (21 September 1997) as a protest against the Charter Change proposed to extend the presidential term of Fidel Ramos. Having apologized in the newspaper for her past support of Marcos, Nora sang two nationalist songs during this rally, thereby aligning herself with the people whom she was seen to have abandoned. (Monico Atienza,

personal communication, 30 September 1997). Also, just recently, she joined the 'People Power 2' movement that ousted Joseph Estrada from the office of the president.

20　See, for example, the account provided in a psychoanalytic-anthropological investigation of another faith healer (significantly given the pseudonym Nora Cabral) in Ronald H. Davidson and Richard Day, *Symbol and Realization: A Contribution to the Study of Magic and Healing* (Berkeley: Center for South and Southeast Asia Studies, University of California, 1974), p. 82.

21　Ishmael Bernal's own interest in and sympathetic rendering of such women who are not women might be explored in the context of his own sexual politics. Bernal's inclusion of *bakla* ('queen') 'admirers' in the panning shots of Elsa's fans (rather than patients) renders the gender-crossing appeal of Nora/Elsa's sexuality (evidenced by the fact that Nora's following also consisted of *bakla* fans). The very presence of healthy fans beside ill and ailing supplicants demonstrates Nora Aunor's exceeding of her filmic character as well as Elsa's exceeding of her bodily healing function, and it demonstrates the way in which Nora/Elsa's spiritual and spectacular power surpasses the material demands that give rise to her as their symptomatic answer. It also shows, however, the slippage between women, homosexuals, masses and the ill made by constructions of Nora's following as hysterical — that is, as the pathological displacement of their wants and of their being-in-want (we might say, their lack) onto her spectacular image.

22　Pilo's and Narding's frustration at Chayong — Pilo for her refusal to submit to his desires and Narding for her giving Elsa rather than him her savings — are finally inflicted on both Chayong and Elsa when two drug-crazed men from the city rape the two women. This rape is not the violation of some prior sexual integrity and therefore an act of moral degradation but rather the violation of their claimed sovereignty in sex and love. It is, in other words, the instrument of Elsa's and Chayong's disempowerment by threatened masculinist forces. The men's belief in 'not God, but the dollar' leads them to repudiate the women's resistant faith. Identifying with capital, men become one of the instruments for the debilitation of the feminist potential of women's love and worship.

23　P. L. Kintanar, 'Supernora,' *Focus* 8 (March 1980): 18–9.

24　In her language instruction manual, Teresita V. Ramos defines the grammatical structure of this cultural agency as follows: 'In causative sentences, the causative *actor* is the one who initiates the action, the *non-causative actor* is the one who does or performs the action, and the *object* is that which is acted upon. There are, therefore, two actors in a causative sentence: the *actor (initiator)* of the action and the *actor (agent)* caused to perform the action.' Ramos goes on further to suggest an activity that puts this grammatical structure into practice and in doing so underscores an actual social 'function-situation' for this structure: 'Imagine life in Manila where hired help is very common in most households: *katulong, tsuper, labandera, kusinera, yaya* for the baby, etc. Tell us what things you will have those helpers do and what things you'll be doing yourself around the house.' *Conversational Tagalog: A Functional-Situational Approach* (Honolulu: University of Hawaii Press, 1985), pp. 267–70.

25 Quoted in Slavoj Žižek, *The Sublime Object of Ideology* (London and New York: Verso, 1989), p. 32.

26 What is completely absent from any and all critical writing about Nora Aunor is a serious and sustained consideration of the significance of her singing voice to her phenomenal power. While my own analysis does not dwell on this topic, it does suggest that these dimensions that exceed the spectacularity of her image significantly shape Nora's power. As it was in fact principally Nora's vocal talent that launched her into stardom, it could be said that it was a historical instance of the (mute) instrument assuming voice. See Gayatri Chakravorty Spivak, *In Other Worlds: Essays in Cultural Politics*, (New York: Methuen, 1987).

27 Nora/Cory functions as a 'vector of subjectivization rather than a passively representative image'. (Felix Guattari, *Chaosmosis: An Ethico-Aesthetic Paradigm*, trans. Paul Bains and Julian Pefanis (Bloomington and Indianapolis: Indiana University Press, 1995).

28 While the saint mediates between two worlds, only in one of which people move, the *babaylan* is a mediator between two kinds of worlds, both of which people are a part. F. Landa Jocano, 'Ang Mga Babaylang at Katalonan sa Kinagisnang Sikolohiya' in *Ulat ng Unang Pambansang Kumperensya sa Sikolohiyang Pilipino*, ed. Lilia F. Antonio, Esther S. Reyes, Rogelia E. Pe, Nilda R. Almonte (Lunsod Quezon: Pambansang Samahan sa Sikolohiyang Pilipino, 1976), p. 159. Unlike the saint, the *babaylan* lives in the world. In fact, according to Salazar, who traces a continuous line of filiation from the *babaylans* to present day faith healers, the latter have adopted the saints as their beneficent sponsors in the place of the tutelary *anitos*. See Zeus A. Salazar, ed., 'Ethnic Psychology and History: The Study of Faith Healing in the Philippines' in *The Ethnic Dimension: Papers on Philippine Culture, History and Psychology* (Cologne: Counseling Center for Filipinos, Caritas Association for the City of Cologne, 1983), p. 39.

29 Raul Pertierra, *Philippine Localities and Global Perspectives: Essays on Society and Culture* (Manila: Ateneo de Manila University Press, 1995), p. 118.

30 Ibid.

31 See Reynaldo Clemena Ileto, *Pasyon and Revolution: Popular Movements in the Philippines, 1840–1910* (Quezon City: Ateneo de Manila University Press, 1979).

32 In this view, which tends to be held in cultural studies ethnographic works focusing on 'power' relations, 'culture' assumes the role that the 'body' takes in some mainstream feminist analyses of eating disorders and other symptoms of female oppression — that is, as a displaced, symbolic site of struggle. The 'meaning' of these practices as struggle or resistance is hence read through the interpretative framework derived from the mapping of a dominant logic (effectively, the epistemological framework of the dominant). See, e.g., Constable's analysis of 'the everyday forms of resistance expressed by Filipina domestic workers'. (*Maid to Order in Hong Kong*). For a related critique of Constable, see Yasushi Uchiyamada, 'Maid to Order in Hong Kong: Stories of Filipina Workers,' *Journal of the Royal Anthropological Institute* 5 (4) (1999): 642. Aihwa Ong's work, in particular her attention to the role of 'structures of feeling' of workers in everyday struggles, seems to me to argue importantly against this reverse functionalism; see Aihwa Ong, 'Gender and Labor Politics of Postmodernity,' in *The Politics of Culture in the Shadow of Capital*, ed. Lisa Lowe and David Lloyd (Durham, N.C. and London: Duke University Press, 1993), pp. 61–97. However, religion and other cultural systems still take on a 'superstructural' (as well as 'superstitious') function to the extent that they serve as resources of symbolic instruments for articulating oppression and resistance. See, e.g., Aihwa Ong, *Spirits of Resistance and Capitalist Discipline: Factory Women in Malaysia* (New York: SUNY Press, 1987).

33 Enrique Dussel, *Ethics and Community*, trans. Robert R. Barr (Maryknoll, NY: Orbis Books, 1988), p. 199; Cf. Maria Milagros Lopez, 'Post-Work Selves,' in *The Postmodernism Debate in Latin America*, ed. John Beverley, Jose Oviedo, and Michael Aronna (Durham, N.C., and London: Duke University Press, 1995), pp. 165–91.

34 The objective knowledge produced by this view (the framework of ideological critique as socioeconomic analysis) would be predicated on 'the form of the thought previous and external to thought itself — in short: the symbolic order' (Žižek, *The Sublime Object of Ideology*, pp. 16–9). I would add, the symbolic order of Western modernity.

35 Thus the view of the idolatry of Nora/Elsa's following dissimulates, by displacing onto the 'backward' masses, the idolatry of modern society (the idolatry of money, transparency, enlightenment, progress — instruments and positions of universality necessary for capital exchange and for the sphere of secular, intellectual discourse that rests on it). Hysteria is the

code for the displacement of relations of domination onto objects, the objects being in this case the masses as well as the image of Nora/Elsa. Like the fatal shot that preserves Elsa as an immaculate image (idealizing her by depriving her of any active human relation to the people), the objective, enlightened and secularist critiques of the ritualistic activities surrounding Nora/Elsa are the means of making 'religion' a reified and reifying order, an order co-logical with the logic of commodity-fetishism. Such a view conflates Christianity with capitalism, whether it makes the former an instrument of the latter or the latter the consequence of the former, and denies what Samir Amin calls 'the plasticity of religions' (*Eurocentrism* [New York: Monthly Review Press, 1989], pp. 84–5).

36 Viewing is yoked to consumption through introjective identification (Anne Friedberg, 'A Denial of Difference: Theories of Cinematic Identification' in *Psychoanalysis and Cinema*, ed. E. Ann Kaplan [London: Routledge, 1990], p. 44).

37 The analytical imposition of the dominant rubric of representation, which is endemic to consumerist societies (or spheres of advanced late capitalism), can be considered an example of theoretical imperialism. As William Pietz writes, 'the production of theoretical discourse is always an attempt at once to make intelligible and to make complete (in a functional sense) some already institutionalized social reality. Theory always arises as a supplement not to the logic of a text but to a particular social practice' ('Fetishism and Materialism: The Limits of Theory in Marx' in *Fetishism as Cultural Discourse*, ed. Emily Apter and William Pietz [Ithaca, NY, and London: Cornell University Press, 1993], p. 128). My attempt to supplement a particular social practice (the 'following' of Nora Aunor) is a contribution to the projects of Third World, US third world or women of colour and multicultural feminisms.

38 Gyan Prakash, 'Who's Afraid of Postcoloniality?' *Social Text* 14 (4) (1996): 199.

39 Here the work of international and third world feminist scholars, particularly on the feminization of labour and the role of third world women in multinational production, has been very important in identifying new multinational apparatuses of capture. See Maria Mies, *Patriarchy and Accumulation on a World Scale: Women in the International Division of Labour* (London and Atlantic Highlands, NJ: Zed, 1986; Gita Sen, *Development, Crises and Alternative Visions: Third World Women's Perspectives* (New York: Monthly Review Press, 1987); June Nash and Maria Patricia Fernandez-Kelly, eds., *Women, Men and the International Division of Labor* (New York: SUNY Press, 1983); Liza Largoza Maza, 'Globalisation = Displacement, Commodification and Modern Day Slavery

of Women,' *Asian Women Workers Newsletter* 16 (2) (1997): 1–6; and Delia Aguilar, *Toward a Nationalist Feminism: Essays* (Quezon City: Giraffe Books, 1998).

40   Quoted in F. Landa Jocano, 'Culture Shock: The Case of Filipina Domestic Helpers in Singapore and Hong Kong,' *Solidarity*, no. 143–4 (July-December 1994): 62.

41   Jocano, 'Ang Mga Babaylang,' p. 151. My translation modifies that of Dionisio M. Miranda, *Pagkamakabuhay: On the Side of Life* (Manila: Logos, 1994), pp. 66–7.

42   Salazar describes present-day practices of faith healing as the transmission of 'energy' into the body for the reintegration of the soul, which is conceived as 'a magnetic field or bioplasm' ('Ethnic Psychology and History,' p. 37).

43   Bienvenido Lumbera, 'The Tagalog Film and the Logic of Irony,' in *Revaluation: Essays on Philippine Literature, Cinema and Popular Culture* (Manila: University of Santo Tomas Publishing House, 1997), p. 188.

44   Bienvenido Lumbera, 'Problems in Philippine Film History,' in *Revaluation: Essays on Philippine Literature, Cinema and Popular Culture* (Manila: University of Santo Tomas Publishing House, 1997), p. 181. It could also be pointed out that this increased 'neocolonial' influence was connected to the onset of political 'decontrol' (the liberalization of government economic controls) with the election of Diosdado Macapagal in 1961. It is not surprising that the previous era of import-substitution (1949–1961) was also known as the 'golden age' for elite nationalists. For a discussion of these transformations and contradictions within the different eras, see Lim, 'Our Economic Crisis.'

45   Ibid.

46   Agustin Sotto, 'Notes on the Filipino Action Film,' *East-West Film Journal* 1 (2): 1–14. A revision of Sotto's article depicts the action heroes as Christ figures who restore the lost values of an institutionally corrupt and unjust world. See Sotto, 'Christ Figures in a Troubled Land.' Manuscript.

47   Nicanor G. Tiongson, 'The Filipino Film Industry,' *East-West Film Journal*, 6 (2) (1992): 45. Unlike *sampalataya*, 'faith' here is fidelity to a no particular, transcendent truth.

48   Naomi Schor, 'Fetishism and Its Ironies,' in *Fetishism as Cultural Discourse*, ed. Emily Apter and William Pietz (Ithaca, NY, and London: Cornell University Press, 1993), pp. 97–8.

49   This was an actual historical event that took place in 1967.

50   Teresa De Lauretis, *The Practice of Love: Lesbian Sexuality and Perverse Desire* (Bloomington and Indianapolis: Indiana University Press, 1994), p. 275.

51 The tragic ending accounts for readings of this film as a performance of the ideology of female martyrdom alongside opposed readings of it as a demonstration of this ideology. For example, Cristina Szanton-Blanc, ['Collision of cultures: Historical Reformulations of Gender in the Lowland Vsiayas, Philippines' in *Power and Difference: Gender in Island Southeast Asia*, ed. Jane Moning-Atkinson and Shelly Errington, (Stanford, Calif.: Stanford University Press, 1990): 345–83] reads the film as paradigmatic instance of the general ideological portrayal of Filipina women by the mass media during the 1970s and 1980s while Wimal Dissanayake reads it as a critique of patriarchal ideology ('Cinema, Nation, and Culture in Southeast Asia: Enframing a Relationship,' *East-West Film Journal* 6 (2) (1992): 1–22.). The fact that the film can be seen as both repetition and representation attests to the ambiguity (rather than ambivalence) that I am trying to argue offers and contains the elements of an unrecognized political movement. This movement cannot be recognized because Nora Aunor is not recognized beyond her representational role. For Szanton-Blanc and Dissanayake, that representational role is contained in the ideological meaning of the film, while for local critics, who all at least recognize Nora Aunor and her star power, that representational role is thought of solely in identificatory relations with 'the masses'.

52 Julian E. Dacanay Jr., 'On Investigating Whether Ricky Lee's *Himala* Was Copied from a Cuban Movie or Not,' *Who* (Jan. 26, 1983): 24–6. Ricky Lee's relationship to 'Los Dias del Agua,' (colour film produced by Miguel Mendoza and directed by Manuel Octavio Gomez, Havana, 1971) the Cuban film in question, which he did indeed see but claims not to have 'replicated,' can be seen to enact the complex issues involved in creative 'following' (see discussion above). It might be said that Ricky Lee 'identified' the situation in the Philippines with that of the Cuban film, infusing and 'localizing' the latter with native mythical elements (faith healers, which Lee claims was the spurring interest in the script and the topic of his research in writing it). But, once again, even this generous notion of 'identification' is predicated on the privileging of consumption as the category with which to understand the dominant social relations of the Philippines, as periphery, to the international film community (while Cuba is also peripheral, as its product passes through international film festivals, it comes to signify metropolitan production).

53 Claude Lefort, 'The Image of the Body and Totalitarianism', in *The Political Forms of Modern Society: Bureaucracy, Democracy, Totalitarianism*, ed. John B. Thompson (Cambridge: Polity Press, 1986), p. 297.

54 William Pietz, 'Fetishism and Materialism: The Limits of Theory in Marx',

in *Fetishism as Cultural Discourse,* ed. Emily Apter and William Pietz (Ithaca, NY, and London: Cornell University Press, 1993), p. 149.

55 Elsa's practice, as I mentioned earlier, initially consists primarily of 'magnetic healing'. When Mrs Alba begins to exploit this practice by bottling and selling the holy water Elsa uses, Elsa's powers begin to fail and a cholera epidemic breaks out, effectively wiping out that power and the faith that constituted it. We might see Mrs Alba's efforts as attempts of elite classes to profit from the idol–image they believe Nora to be. This is clearly what is work in present 'designer' uses of Nora kitsch from the 1960s and 1970s. It is the bourgeois entrepreneurs who can be said to be the purveyors of the fetish.

56 Lefort, 'The Image of the Body and Totalitarianism,' p. 300.

57 See Neferti X. M. Tadiar, 'History as Psychology,' *Pilipinas: Journal of the Philippine Studies Group of the Association for Asian Studies*, no. 32 (Spring 1999): 1–22. I have learned much in this regard from third world, postcolonial and multicultural feminist critiques of nationalism. In the Philippines, the critique is practiced by feminist activist groups, such as the short-lived MAKIBAKA (Free Movement of Women) and the current coalitional organization, GABRIELA. In other contexts, see Marie-Aimee Helie-Lucas, 'Women, Nationalism and Religion in the Algerian Liberation Struggle' in *Opening the Gates: A Century of Arab Feminist Writing*, ed. Margot Badran and Miriam Cooke (Bloomington: Indiana University Press, 1990), pp. 105–15 and Geraldine Heng, '"A Great Way to Fly": Nationalism, the State, and the Varieties of Third World Feminism' in *Feminist Genealogies, Colonial Legacies, Democratic Futures*, ed. M. Jacqui Alexander and Chandra Talpade Mohanty (New York and London: Routledge, 1997), pp. 30–45. Also, see the recent collection Caren Kaplan, Norma Alarcon, and Minoo Moallem, eds., *Between Woman and Nation: Nationalisms, Transnational Feminisms, and the State* (Durham, NC: Duke University Press, 1999).

58 Alice Guillermo, *The Covert Presence and Other Essays on Politics and Culture* (Manila: Kalikasan Press, 1989), pp. 81–3.

59 In the diasporic communicative space of *Tinig Filipino*, a magazine written for and by Filipina domestic workers in Asia, Europe and the Middle East, 'They are the superstars ...' (Linda Layosa, editor of *Tinig Filipino*) (quoted in Rhacel Parreñas, *Servants of Globalization: Women, Migration and Domestic Work* [Stanford, Calif.: Stanford University Press, 2001]). Clearly, the individualist cast of this subjective faith is what contains its heretical potential. At the same time, it is the condition of possibility of the heresy of Filipinas leaving home. It is what allows and results from the demise of a national community anchored in the spectacularity of the state and

its figures of power. Both Marcos and Nora are such figures of power who functioned as at once fellow members of a community and as superlative members who could be appealed to and approached for dispensations of power (apart from being representatives of power/the people).

60   The character of this relation as involvement also pertains to the relation between 'culture' and production. We can conceive this involvement in a way that distinguishes this theoreticopolitical approach from a Weberian approach (in which culture determines the mode of production) through the notion of *pakikisangkot* (involvement), whereby culture refers to the socially-organized subjective-experiential dimension of labour expended in production. 'The key thing is how to get taken up in the motion of a big wave, a column of rising air, to "get into something" instead of being the origin of an effort' (Gilles Deleuze, *Negotiations, 1972–1990*, trans. Martin Joughin [New York: Columbia University Press, 1995]). I find this an apt description of Nora Aunor's role in history as well as the role of 'culture' in production.

61   Maurice Merleau-Ponty, *The Prose of the World* (Evanston, IL: Northwestern University Press, 1973), p. 190.

62   The work of Chicana feminisms has been exemplary in forging a similar movement toward faithful knowledges. See Carla Trujillo, ed., *Living Chicana Theory* (Berkeley, Calif.: Third Woman Press, 1998), especially Trujillo's chapter, 'La Virgen de Guadalupe and Her Reconstruction in Chicana Lesbian Desire', for an account of comparative heretical claims. Gloria Anzaldúa's writing about and from *mestizaje* is a significant instance in the US context of such claims forming the theoretical basis of cultural criticism (*Borderlands/La Frontera: The New Mestiza* [San Francisco: Spinsters/Aunt Lute, 1987]). Rather than holding on to the objective of critique to arrive at truth, knowledge moving toward faith heeds the subjective potential of a heretical claim to shape truth.

CONCLUSION

1   Donna J. Haraway, *Modest_Witness@Second_Milliennium.FemaleMan ©_Meets_OncoMouse™* (New York and London: Routledge, 1996), p. 133.

2   Haraway, *Modest_Witness@Second_Milliennium*, p. 135.

3   William Pietz, 'Fetishism and Materialism: The Limits of Theory in Marx,' in *Fetishism as Cultural Discourse*, ed. Emily Apter and William Pietz (Ithaca and London: Cornell University Press, 1993), p. 147. 'The human truth of capital is that, as a means that has become an end, it is a socially constructed, culturally real power-object: it is the instrumentalized power

of command over concrete humans in the form of control over their labour activity through investment decisions. Capital is a form of rule, of social government. It is this political truth that the chiasmic personification-reification structure of capitalist fetishism conceals' (p. 147).

4   'Diffraction is about heterogeneous history, not about originals. Unlike reflections, diffractions do not displace the same elsewhere, in more or less distorted form, thereby giving rise to industries of metaphysics. Rather, diffraction can be a metaphor for another kind of critical consciousness at the end of this rather painful Christian millennium, one committed to making a difference and not to repeating the Sacred Image of the Same' (Haraway, *Modest_Witness@Second_Milliennium*, p. 273).

5   'Scientific fetishists place error in the admittedly irreducibly tropic zones of "culture," where primitives, perverts and other laypeople live, and not in the fetishists' constitutional inability to recognize the trope that denies its own status as figure. In my view, contingency, finitude and difference — but not "error" — inhere in irremediably tropic, secular liveliness' (Haraway, *Modest_Witness@Second_Milliennium*, p. 137).

6   As I've tried to demonstrate in this book, the realist theories of political science and economics, as much as the realist representations of the government and the mass media, partake of and participate in the regimes of desiring-practices that I have been calling fantasy-production. See especially Chapters 2 and 3. I give a fuller critique of the theoretical project of providing adequate representation of logics of domination in the last chapter.

7   Muto Ichiyo, 'For An Alliance of Hope' in *Global Visions: Beyond The New World Order*, ed. Jeremy Brecher, John Brown Childs, and Jill Cutler (Boston: South End Press, 1993).

8   Muto Ichiyo, 'For An Alliance of Hope,' p. 162.

9   Muto Ichiyo, 'Alliance of Hope and Challenges of Global Democracy,' in *Trajectories: Inter-Asia Cultural Studies*, ed. Kuan-Hsing Chen with Hsiu-Ling Kuo, Hans Hang, and Hsu Ming-Chu (London and New York: Routledge, 1998), p. 252.

10   Haraway, *Modest_Witness@Second_Milliennium*, p. 170.

11   'Following an ethical and methodological principle for science studies that I adopted many years ago, I will critically analyze, or "deconstruct," only that which I love and only that in which I am deeply implicated. This commitment is part of a project to excavate something like a technoscientific unconscious, the processes of formation of the technoscientific subject, and the reproduction of this subject's structure of pleasure and anxiety' (Haraway, *Modest_Witness@Second_Milliennium*, p. 151). Haraway also clarifies that the production of difference is neither

a matter of mere 'multiplicity' (or, we might say, pluralist diversity) nor mere 'opposition' (or, resistance) — 'neither "multiplicity" nor "contestation" for their own sake are the point in feminist science studies. Joining analysts to subjects and objects of analysis, questions of power, resources, skills, suffering, hopes, meanings, and lives are always at stake' (p. 188). Naomi Schor calls for 'a feminist irony that would divorce the uncertainty of the ironist from the oscillations of the fetishist'. 'Fetishism and Its Ironies,' in *Bad Objects: Essays Popular and Unpopular* (Durham and London: Duke University Press, 1995), p. 106.

12 Etienne Balibar, 'The Non-Contemporaneity of Althusser,' in *The Althusserian Legacy*, ed. E. Ann Kaplan and Michael Sprinkler (London and New York: Verso, 1993), p. 7.

13 Muto Ichiyo, 'Alliances of Hope and Challenges of Global Democracy,' p. 249.

14 Angela Davis expresses the necessity of this freeing in her call for rethinking society without prisons: 'A radical strategy to abolish jails and prisons as the normal way of dealing with the social problems of late capitalism is not a strategy for abstract abolition. It is designed to force a rethinking of the increasingly repressive role of the state during this era of late capitalism and to carve out a space of resistance.' Quoted in Avery Gordon, p. 157.

15 Ngugi Wa Thiong'o, *Penpoints, Gunpoints, and Dreams: Towards A Critical Theory Of The Arts And The State In Africa* (Oxford and New York: Oxford University Press, 1998), p. 130.

16 Dimitris Papadopoulos, 'World 2. On the Significance and Impossibility of Articulation'. Manuscript, p. 16.

17 'Culture Against War: Philippines on the Axis of Empire' was held on April 6, 2002 at the University of California at Santa Cruz. Some of the organizations that participated in the congress included: Filipino Coalition for Global Justice, Not War, Filipinos for Affirmative Action, Stanford Community for Peace and Justice, Asian and Pacific Islander Coalition Against War, American Muslims for Global Peace and Justice, Committee for Human Rights in the Philippines, All Peoples' Coalition Against the War and the Filipino Workers Association.

18 There are no miracles! It is we who make miracles!

Index